The Role of State Parties to the Rome Statute in the Interpretation of the Statute

International Criminal Law Series

VOLUME 20

The titles published in this series are listed at *brill.com/icls*

The Role of State Parties to the Rome Statute in the Interpretation of the Statute

An Evaluation of Past Practice and Future Prospects

By

Caroline Vicheti Shilaho

BRILL | NIJHOFF

LEIDEN | BOSTON

The Library of Congress Cataloging-in-Publication Data is available online at https://catalog.loc.gov
LC record available at https://lccn.loc.gov/2025038491

Typeface for the Latin, Greek, and Cyrillic scripts: "Brill". See and download: brill.com/brill-typeface.

ISSN 2213-2724
ISBN 978-90-04-72552-2 (hardback)
ISBN 978-90-04-72551-5 (e-book)
DOI 10.1163/9789004725515

This book is printed on acid-free paper and produced in a sustainable manner.

Contents

Acknowledgments

I am deeply grateful to the Almighty for enabling me to complete this book.

My immense gratitude to my thesis Supervisor, on which this book is based, Judge of the International Court of Justice Dire Tladi, for his superb intellectual guidance.

To my beloved children, Collins and Danni, thank you for being my reason for aiming to be a better person. Your understanding and sacrifice when I had to spend hours researching and writing is deeply appreciated.

To Dr Podho Maurice, thank you for understanding my extended hours of research.

Thank you to Dr Evelyn Asaala for the consistent encouragement and acting as a sounding board for my ideas. Dr Ken Obura, thank you.

A special thank you to the Brill staff and team for the professional contribution towards the publication of this book.

I remain grateful to many others who assisted in one way or another.

Acronyms and Abbreviations

AU	African Union
ASEAN	The Association of South East Asian Nations
ASP	Assembly of State Parties
BIT	Business Investment Treaties
CETA	EU-Canada Comprehensive and Economic Trade Agreement
CICC	Coalition for the International Criminal Court
CJEU	Court of Justice of the European Union
CRC	Convention on the Rights of the Child
DRC	Democratic Republic of Congo
ECHR	European Convention on Human Rights
ECTHR	European Court on Human Rights
FIDH	International Federation of Human Rights
FTA	Free Trade Agreement
IACHR	Inter-American Court of Human Rights
IBA	International Bar Association
ICC	International Criminal Court
ICCPR	International Convention on Civil and Political Rights
ICJ	International Court of Justice
ICSID	International Centre for Settlement of Investment Disputes
ICTR	International Criminal Tribunal for Rwanda
ICTY	International Criminal Tribunal for the former Yugoslavia
ILC	International Law Commission
IMO	International Maritime Organization
IOM	Independent Oversight Mechanism
ISDS	Investor State Dispute Settlement
IWC	International Whaling Commission
NAFTA	North American Free Trade Agreement
PCIJ	Permanent Court of International Justice
PTC	Pre-Trial Chamber
RPE	Rules of Procedure and Evidence
SGG	Study Group on Governance
STL	Special Tribunal of Lebanon
UNCTAD	UN Conference on Trade and Development
UNGA	UN General Assembly Resolution
VCLT	Vienna Convention on the Law of Treaties
WTO	World Trade Organization

Foreword

In this book, *The Role of State Parties to the Rome Statute in the Interpretation of the Statute: An Evaluation of Past Practice and Future Prospects,* Caroline Shilaho tackles an important question for international criminal law and public international law in general, namely the role of States in interpreting treaties such as the Rome Statute. She tackles the problem in a mature and systematic way. Yet, at the same time, Caroline is aware that the problem, while a doctrinal in nature, sits at the heart of a tension in international criminal law between two values: expansive interpretation in the pursuit of progressiveness and restrictive interpretation in promotion of the will of the States.

When Caroline first reached out to me about a possible PhD project on interpretation of the Rome Statute, she wore her heart on her sleeve. She was concerned about what she saw as an abuse of the Rome Statute, with States undermining the coherence and progressiveness of the Rome Statute by interfering with the function of the Court. But advocacy (often) makes for poor scholarship, and it wasn't long before Caroline realised that to do justice to her project – even to do justice to the moral imperative that drove her – required the suppression of her emotions, and, instead, demanded that she conducts a dispassionate and objective assessment of the state of the law. This book is the result of that journey.

The means of interpretation – ordinary meaning, context, object and purpose, parties' agreement as to interpretation (reflected in subsequent agreement and subsequent practice), other rules of international law and supplementary means of interpretation – all exist to mediate between competing interests and, in the process, find the objectively correct meaning of a treaty. The competing interests in question include the need to be true to intentions of the parties and the imperative of developing international law. For a proper interpretation, these means of interpretation, or at least the primary means reflected in Article 31 of the Vienna Convention, have to be thrown into the metaphoric crucible in order to find the objectively correct interpretation.

When a treaty provides for a mechanism with the authority to interpret that treaty, as is the case with International Criminal Court established by the Rome Statute – that mechanism performs a dual role. The Court, for example, is, at once, an interpreter, which is to say, it is dutybound to apply the rules of interpretation and thus, balance the means of interpretation at its disposal. At the same time, as an entity endowed with the authority by the Rome Statute to interpret its terms, it serves itself as a tool of interpretation (although not one of the means of interpretations explicitly provided for in the Vienna

Convention), since its interpretation is to be taken into account by other interpreters, i.e. which is to say, it cannot be ignored. Its interpretation is thus authoritative. As the International Court of Justice has said in the *Diallo* case, in the context of human rights mechanisms established to interpret human rights treaties, it, meaning the ICJ, "ascribe[s] great weight to the interpretation adopted by this independent body that was established specifically to supervise the application of that treaty."

In this second role, that of the Court as a tool of interpretation, the Court operates *in a similar, though not the same way* to the means of interpretation in Article 31(3) of the Vienna Convention, including subsequent agreements and subsequent practice. Of course, unlike subsequent agreements and subsequent practice, decisions of Courts, and other treaty-established bodies, cannot be called authentic interpretation. To recall the words of the ICJ in Diallo, the ICJ "is in no way obliged, in the exercise of its judicial functions, to model its own interpretation of the Covenant on that of" a body established to a treaty. Nonetheless, the interpretation of the Court cannot be ignored by either parties or other interpreters.

The question at the heart of Caroline's book concerns the relationship between, on the one hand, the interpretation of States Party to the Rome Statute, the so-called authentic interpretation embodied in subsequent agreements and subsequent practice, and, on the other hand, the authoritative interpretation of a Court established precisely to interpret the Rome Statute. Which interpretation ought to take priority, particularly when there is a conflict. In the context of the normative tension I spoke of at the beginning, it should be accepted that the Court, the body established under the treaty to interpret the Rome Statute, will almost always adopt an expansive interpretation, while the States Party to the Statute, will almost always adopt a restrictive interpretation.

I would like to commend Caroline for taking on this project, and for bringing it to fruition in a mature and coherent way. I recommend this book to anyone interested in the law on interpretation, the International Criminal Court and the intersection between public international law and international criminal law.

Dire Tladi
Judge of the International Court of Justice

CHAPTER 1

Background and Introduction

Much has been written about the role of the International Criminal Court (ICC) and States Parties to the Rome Statute of the International Criminal Court (States Parties), individually and collectively, within the framework of the Rome Statute of the International Criminal Court (Rome Statute). However, there is very little discussion regarding the role of States Parties in interpreting the Rome Statute in light of the ICC's mandate to interpret the Statute. The role of States Parties acting individually or collectively, through subsequent agreements and subsequent practice, on the Statute's interpretation and the impact this has had or may have on the ICC's mandate to interpret the Rome Statute remains unexplored. This gap is particularly pronounced given the statutory role of the ICC in the interpretation of the Statute. Article 119 (1) of the Rome Statute specifies that "any dispute concerning the judicial functions of the Court shall be settled by the decision of the Court."

Consequently, there is the potential for conflict between the function of the ICC in interpreting the treaty and the role of the Assembly of States Parties to the Statute (ASP) based on international customary rules of interpretation under the Vienna Convention on the Law of Treaties (VCLT).[1] This potential remains largely unexplored and is seemingly exacerbated when the ASP adopts resolutions or amendments that touch on ongoing cases (*sub judice*) or decided cases by the ICC. As an example of possible tension, then ICC Prosecutor Fatou Bensouda, in her statement to the ASP, stated that

> The integrity of the Court's proceedings continues to be challenged. Matters that are either *sub judice* or have already been adjudicated must not be undermined by virtue of discussions and decisions of States Parties [...] Discussions and decisions of the States Parties must respect the separation of powers.[2]

1 UN Vienna Convention on the Law of Treaties, 23 May 1969, UN Treaty Series, Vol 1155.

2 Fatou Bensouda, 'Statement by the ICC Prosecutor at the opening of the 14th Session of the Assembly of States Parties to the Rome Statute of the International Criminal Court' (*International Criminal Court*, 18 November 2015) <http://www.icc-cpi.int/fr/news/statement-icc-prosecutor-opening-14th-session-assembly-states-parties-rome-statute> accessed 19 October 2022.

In contrast, it has been stated that "the interpretation of the Rome Statute is primarily the task for the States since it was the States who adopted the Rome Statute."[3] This approach implies that the ASP can deliberate on ongoing or decided cases as the owners of the Statute.

It is this question on the role of the States Parties in the Rome Statute's interpretation and the possible challenges to the ICC's role that this book focuses on analyzing. The book, therefore, has two primary purposes. First is to interrogate the extent to which States Parties, whether collectively or individually, have a role in interpreting the Rome Statute. Secondly, based on any possible ensuing tension between States Parties and the ICC in their interpretive roles, the book recommends possible ways in which this tension could best be eased.

In order to situate the role of States Parties in interpreting the Statute, it is essential first to examine the VCLT rules of interpretation espoused in Articles 31 and 32 with specific attention to Article 31 (3) of the VCLT. Article 31 (1) of the VCLT requires that a treaty be interpreted "in good faith in accordance with the ordinary meaning to be given to the terms of the treaty in their context and in the light of its object and purpose." On the other hand, Article 31 (3), which is central to the study, provides that there shall be taken into account, together with the context:

(a) Any subsequent agreement between the parties regarding the interpretation of the treaty or the application of its provisions.
(b) Any subsequent practice in the application of the treaty which establishes the agreement of the parties regarding its interpretation.

Further elaborating on Article 31(3) of the VCLT and the significance of the States parties' agreements and practice, the International Law Commission (ILC) provides that the "common will of the parties, which underlies the treaty, possesses a specific authority regarding the identification of the meaning of the treaty, even after the conclusion of the treaty."[4]

The book proceeds from the premise that Article 31(3) of the VCLT lays the legal foundation for the continued participation of States parties in interpreting their treaties, whether there is an existing court or not. In this regard, the VCLT interpretation rules are considered relevant to the Rome Statute's interpretation on the basis that Articles 31 and 32 are accepted as customary inter-

3 Report of the Bureau on the Independent Oversight Mechanism, ICC-ASP/9/31, November 19, 2010 para 53.

4 ILC, 'Draft Conclusions on Subsequent Agreements and Subsequent Practice in Relation to the Interpretation of Treaties, Seventieth Session, (A/73/10) 2018' (ILC) Conclusion 3 Commentary 3.

national law on interpretation.[5] As customary international law, all States, irrespective of having ratified the VCLT, are subject to the treaty interpretation rules under the VCLT.[6]

It is, therefore, within the context of Article 31(3) of the VCLT on subsequent agreements and subsequent practice of State parties that the current study specifically interrogates the role of States Parties to the Statute, especially given the existence of the permanent ICC mandated to interpret the Rome Statute. To determine whether the States Parties have a legal basis for playing a role in the Rome Statute's interpretation besides the ICC, the book examines whether the VCLT interpretation rules apply to the Statute's interpretation. The discussion also covers the Rome Statute's own rules on interpretation and whether these exclude or work alongside the VCLT rules.

Based on the second purpose of the book, the study seeks to interrogate the presumption that in the process of the ICC exercising its judicial interpretive role and the States Parties having an implicit role in the Rome Statute's interpretation, the lack of clear boundaries in the roles has led and may potentially lead to some tension or overlap. In this respect, the book investigates two instances where the ASP's resolutions and amendments have been adopted when there are ongoing cases related to the same issue in Court. The book explores whether the timing of these amendments and resolutions created an overlap in the States Parties and the ICC's role in the interpretation of the Rome Statute.

The book recognizes other possible examples of overlap such as where a section of ASP members expressly opposed and refused to implement the ICC's decisions to arrest and surrender then Sudan President *Omar Al Bashir* to the Court.[7] Similarly, Mongolia, an ASP member, declined to arrest Vladimir Putin, the Russian President, when he visited Mongolian territory on 4th September 2024 despite the Court's request for the arrest and surrender of Putin

5 Richard Gardiner, *Treaty Interpretation 2015* (2nd edn, Oxford University Press 2015) 162.

6 Chang-fa Lo, *Treaty Interpretation Under the Vienna Convention on the Law of Treaties: A New Round of Codification* (Springer Singapore 2017) 36.

7 *Decision on the Prosecution's Application for a Warrant of Arrest against Omar Hassan Ahmad Al Bashir, ICC-02/05-01/09 (PTC 1) 4 March 2009; ICC, Decision on the Non-compliance of the Republic of Chad with the Cooperation Requests Issued by the Court Regarding the Arrest and Surrender of Omar Hassan Ahmad Al-Bashir, The Prosecutor V Omar H Al Bashir, ICC-02/05-01/09-15 (PTC 11), 26 March 2013.; ICC Decision under article 87(7) of the Rome Statute on the non-compliance by Jordan with the request by the Court for the arrest and surrender of Omar Al-Bashir, ICC-02/05-01/09-309 (PTC 11), 11 December 2017; AU Assembly, Decisions, Declarations, Resolution and Motions, 32nd Ordinary Session of the Assembly, Assembly/AU/Dec738(XXXII), 10–11 February 2019.*

for crimes of humanity.[8] A similar position arose with respect to the ICC arrest warrant against the Israel Prime Minister Benjamin Netanyahu, for crimes against humanity and war crimes issued in 2024.[9] The Pretrial Chamber of the ICC required Hungary, a State party, to make submissions regarding its failure to comply with a request by the Court to arrest Netanyahu who was in Hungary from 3rd to 6th April 2025.[10] The dilemma for the ASP members in arresting either Putin or Netanyahu may be exacerbated by Sudan, Russia and Israel respectively, not being State parties to the Rome Statute, yet the issue of the immunity of heads of State remains inconclusively settled by the ICJ and ICC.

In this regard, a section of ASP members even sought alternative interpretation from the ASP[11] and the International Court of Justice (ICJ)[12] on the same issues despite the ICC's handling of the cases. The *Omar Al Bashir, Mongolia* and *Hungary* cases are acknowledged but have been excluded from the detailed scope of this book on the basis that only a section of ASP members was involved and not the collective ASP. They do not, therefore, raise the same conceptual challenges that the study seeks to explore based on Article 31(3) of the VCLT.

Based on the lack of clear demarcation in the roles and probable consequential tension, the book aims to identify possible methods and tools to balance the ASP and the ICC's interpretive roles and ease the tension. The necessity arises because Article 112, which outlines the ASP's powers, and Article 119

8 *Finding under Article 87(7) of the Rome Statute on the Non-compliance by Mongolia with the request by the Court to Cooperate in the Arrest and Surrender of Vladimir Vladimirovich Putin and Referral to the Assembly of States Parties,* ICC-01/22-90 *(Pre-Trial Chambers* II*) 24 October 2024* (ICC) 17.

9 *Decision on Israel's challenge to the jurisdiction of the Court pursuant to Article 19(2) of the Rome Statute,* ICC-01/18-374 *(*PTC 1*) 21 November 2024.*

10 *Situation in the State of Palestine, Invitation to Hungary to provide Submissions for the purposes of Proceedings under Article 87(7) of the Rome Statute,* ICC-01/18-421 *(*PTC 1*) 16 April 2025* (ICC).; ICC-01/18-433, *Transmission of Hungary's submission in response to Pre-Trial Chamber I's "Invitation to Hungary to provide submissions for the purposes of proceedings under article 87(7) of the Rome Statute", 16 April 2025,* ICC-01/18-421*, 23 May 2025.*

11 ICC-ASP/14/35, Fourteenth session, Request by South Africa for the inclusion of a supplementary item in the agenda titled 'Application and Implementation of Article 97 and Article 98 of the Rome Statute, 27 October 2015, Annex 1 paras 13 and 14.

12 AU Assembly, Decisions, Declarations and Resolution, 30th Ordinary Session, Assembly/AU/Dec.672(XXX) Jan 28–29 2018 Page 2, Para 5(i) (ii); AU Assembly, Decisions, Declarations, Resolution and Motions, 32nd Ordinary Session, Assembly/AU/Dec.738 (XXXII), 10–11 Feb 2019 paras 3 and 5; Priya Pillai, 'The African Union, the International Criminal Court, and the International Court of Justice: At the Fault Lines of International Accountability (ASIL)' (2018) 22 Issue 10.

of the Statute, which gives the ICC its interpretive powers, do not provide a forum to address existing or potential disputes between the Court and the ASP.[13]

1 General Overview of the Book

The role of States Parties in the interpretation of the Rome Statute remains largely unclear. This book, therefore, analyzes the role of States Parties through their subsequent agreements and practice on the Statute's interpretation and how these impact the ICC's express interpretive role. The book seeks to interrogate the specific extent to which the States Parties participate in the Rome Statute's interpretation despite an existing ICC explicitly endowed with the mandate to interpret. In this regard, balancing the roles of the States Parties and the ICC and avoiding overlap and conflict between the two entities' interpretation of the Statute is considered a significant objective of this study.

In interrogating these objectives, the study first delves into the literature on the role of the VCLT interpretation rules and, specifically, the place that subsequent agreements and subsequent practice of States parties generally hold. This analysis is significant since it lays the foundation of how the ICC positions the subsequent agreements and practice of States Parties through their resolutions and amendments in the Rome Statute's interpretation. While there is considerable literature on subsequent agreements and practice of States parties, it lacks uniformity on whether the subsequent agreements and practice are binding on the court's interpretation or not.

On the one hand, the ILC, some scholars, and court decisions find that subsequent agreements and subsequent practice are not necessarily conclusive or binding.[14] This position denotes that even where the court or tribunal takes subsequent agreements and practice of parties into account, they are not

13 Kritika Sharma, 'The Curious Case of Rule 165 of the Rules of Procedure and Evidence: The Effect of Control Exercised by the Assembly of States Parties over the International Criminal Court' (2020) 20 (2) International Criminal Law Review 285, 316.

14 ILC (n 4) Conclusion 3 para 4.; *Interpretation of the Air Transport Services Agreement between the USA and Italy, 17 July 1965* (RIAA Vol XVI) 107 para 12; Shai Dothan, 'The Three Traditional Approaches to Treaty Interpretation: A Current Application to the European Court of Human Rights' (2019) 42 Fordham International Law Journal 767 para 2; Eirik Bjorge, 'Time Present and Time Past: The Intention of the Parties and the Evolutionary Interpretation of Treaties.' in Abi-Saab Georges et al (ed), *Evolutionary Interpretation and International Law* (Hart Publishing 2019); *Interpretation of the Air Transport Services Agreement between the USA and Italy, 17 July 1965* (RIAA Vol XVI)

treated as decisive or conclusive in the treaty's interpretation. From this perspective, subsequent agreements operate as discretionary elements in interpretation and are not necessarily applied in the final decision outcome.

On the other hand, some scholars and court decisions find that the subsequent agreements and practice are legally binding on the court since they are evidence of the meaning the States parties intended to give the treaty provisions, which the interpreter "must" respect.[15] For instance, Akande avers that the "fact that the masters of the treaty have, through subsequent agreement or practice, offered an 'authentic interpretation' of the treaty cannot be any more legally binding than any utterance included in the treaty."[16] Some courts and tribunals have similarly found the subsequent agreements and practice decisive in the treaty interpretation.[17]

This book goes into greater detail and specificity in discussing the role of the States Parties subsequent agreements and practice in the interpretation of the Rome Statute.

1.1 *The Application of the VCLT Interpretation Rules to the Rome Statute's Interpretation*

The book aims first to interrogate whether the VCLT interpretation rules apply to the Statute or if it has its own rules of interpretation. The significance of this analysis is that if the VCLT rules apply to the Rome Statute's interpretation, then the ICC has the legal basis to incorporate subsequent agreements and practice of States Parties to the Statute's interpretation based on Article 31(3) of the VCLT.

107 para 12; *RSM Production Corporation v. Grenada, ICSID Case No. ARB/05/14, Award (13 March 2009)* para 383.

15 Tarcisio Gazzini, 'Subsequent Agreements and Subsequent Practice', *Interpretation of International Investment Treaties* (Hart Publishing 2016) 188; Mark E Villiger, *Commentary on the 1969 Vienna Convention on the Law of Treaties* (Brill Nijhoff 2009) 429 para 16.; Mark E Villiger, 'The Rules on Interpretation: Misgivings, Misunderstandings, Miscarriage? The 'Crucible 'Intended by the International Law Commission' in Cannizzaro Enzo (ed), *The Law of Treaties Beyond the Vienna Convention* (Oxford Scholarly Authorities on International law 2011) 105, 110.; Oliver Dörr, 'Article 31, General Rule of Interpretation, 2018' in Oliver Dörr and Kirsten Schmalenbach (eds), *Vienna Convention on the Law of Treaties: A Commentary* (Springer 2018) 570 para 19.

16 Dapo Akande and Antonios Tzankopoulos, 'Treaty Law and ICC Jurisdiction over the Crime of Aggression' (2018) 29 No. 3 EJIL 948.

17 *Islamic Republic of Iran vs The United States of America, Interlocutory Award No. ITL 83 B1-FT (Counterclaim) Iran-US Claims Tribunal 9th September 2004, 2004 WL 22010 709* para 134.

In analyzing whether the VCLT rules apply to the Rome Statute, court decisions and scholarly work are examined. It seems generally agreed that the Rome Statute does not provide explicit guidance on the rules guiding its interpretation.[18] Some varied suggestions have consequently arisen. Some scholars suggest that based on its customary international nature, the VCLT rules of interpretation apply to all international treaties, including the Rome Statute.[19]

On the other hand, a few scholars have maintained that the Rome Statute has its own rules of interpretation contained in Articles 21(3) and 22 of the Statute.[20] Article 21(3) provides that the application and interpretation of law must be consistent with internationally recognized human rights and should be without any adverse distinction based on gender and age, among other grounds. Article 22(2) stipulates that the definition of a crime shall be strictly construed and shall not be extended by analogy. It requires that any ambiguity be exercised in favor of the accused. Yet, in other instances, the ICC has provided for the application of both Article 21(3) of the Rome Statute and the VCLT interpretation rules.[21]

The decisions and scholarly work provide a valuable basis for the study to interrogate whether Articles 21(3) and 22 of the Statute form independent interpretation rules excluding the VCLT rules or work together towards the Statute's interpretation. However, the work does not focus in particular detail on the specific role and extent of the States Parties in the Rome Statute's interpretation through their subsequent agreements and practice which is the gap this study fills.

1.2 *The Overlap in the Interpretive Roles of the States Parties and the ICC*

In analyzing whether the interpretive roles of States Parties and the ICC regarding the Rome Statute may overlap, this book focuses on two main examples.

18 William A Schabas, *An Introduction to the International Criminal Court 2020* (6th edn, Cambridge University Press 2020) 213.

19 William A Schabas, *An Introduction to the International Criminal Court 2020* (6th edn, Cambridge University Press 2020) 213.; Valérie V Suhr, *Rainbow Jurisdiction at the International Criminal Court: Protection of Sexual and Gender Minorities Under the Rome Statute* (Springer Nature 2021) 57.

20 Michail Vagias, *The Territorial Jurisdiction of the International Criminal Court* (Cambridge University Press 2014) 64–65; Valérie V Suhr, *Rainbow Jurisdiction at the International Criminal Court: Protection of Sexual and Gender Minorities Under the Rome Statute* (Springer Nature 2021) 54–55.

21 *Decision on Joinder of the cases against Germaine Katanga and Mathieu Ngudjolo Chui*, ICC 01/04-01/07-257 (ICC PTC I) para 7; Gerhard Hafner and Christina Binder, 'The Interpretation of Article 21 (3) ICC Statute 1 Opinion Reviewed' (2006) 9 Austrian Review of International and European Law Online 210.

In examining the possible overlap in roles, the book discusses two instances involving the Kenyan cases of William Ruto and Joshua Sang, where the ASP amendments[22] and reaffirmation[23] are assessed to determine whether they amounted to subsequent agreements or practice of States Parties. The book analyzes their impact on the Rome Statute's interpretation depending on whether they were construed as subsequent agreements or subsequent practice by the ICC.

The scholarly literature provides relevant reference points, but it does not analyze the States Parties' role in interpreting the Rome Statute through their subsequent agreements and practice and the possible overlap or potential tension that may arise from the shared interpretive roles.

This book fills this gap by specifically interrogating the challenges posed by the State parties' interpretive role when an established ICC exists and suggests the possible solutions.

2 Statement of the Problem

Issues of interpretation have been the cause of tension concerning the ICC.[24] The Rome Statute under Article 119 (1) gives the mandate of interpreting the Statute to the judicial arm of the ICC. The ASP is not given an express mandate to interpret the Rome Statute. It, however, has powers "to resolve disputes between two or more States Parties relating to the interpretation or application of the Statute after three months of failed negotiations between the parties."[25] This provision implicitly creates the space for the ASP to interpret the Statute.

The ASP also has a definite law-making power in the form of its mandate to adopt amendments to the Rome Statute, the Rules of Procedure and Evidence (RPE), the Elements of Crime (Elements), and through the adoption of reso-

---

22 *Reasons for the Decision on Excusal from Presence at Trial under Rule 134 quater, The Prosecutor v William Samoei Ruto and Joshua Arap Sang, ICC-01/09-01/11-1186 (TrC V[A] 18 Feb 2014* para 56.

23 ASP Official Records ICC-ASP/14/20 (14th session)18–26 November 2015, Vol 1 p 12–13 para 61; ICC-ASP/12/Res.7, 27 November 2013; *Public redacted version of the "Ruto Defence appeal against the 'Decision on Prosecution Request for Admission of Prior Recorded Testimony', ICC-01/09-01/11-1981-Conf. 5 October 2015.*

24 Rome Statute of the International Criminal Court (Rome Statute) 2187 UNTS 90, entered into Force 1 July 2002.

25 Article 119 (2) of the Rome Statute.

lutions.[26] In certain instances, these amendments or resolutions may be construed as subsequent agreements and practice based on Article 31(3) of the VCLT. The ASP has amended the RPE or adopted resolutions based on requests of one or several States Parties on issues being handled by the ICC in ongoing or previously decided cases. This practice by the ASP creates some conflict, especially where the resolutions or amendments appear to be aimed at influencing the outcome of ongoing ICC cases.[27] The timing of the ASP amendments may appear to interfere with the ICC's interpretive function and create tension between the ASP collectively or its members and the Court.

There is, therefore, no clear distinction between the roles of the ICC and the ASP concerning when each institution can interpret the Rome Statute. On the one hand, under international law, parties to a treaty are considered to be the "authentic interpreters"[28] of the treaty through subsequent agreement or practice. On the other hand, where a treaty gives a court the mandate to interpret a treaty, the court's interpretation should be authoritative. The book aims to identify possible tools and methods for alleviating any (potential) tension that may arise from the authority of both States Parties and the ICC to interpret the Rome Statute.

3 The Objectives of the Book

The study aims to assess the role, if any, of States Parties, acting individually or collectively, in the interpretation of the Rome Statute in the light of the fact that the Statute has bestowed the role of its interpretation to the ICC. It seeks to determine the extent to which any such role might cause tension and, if so, how such tension might be eased.

4 Chapter Overview

This book contains six chapters. Chapter 1 has presented the background, the introduction, and the general overview of the study. It also contains the statement of the problem and the study objectives.

26 Article 121, 122 and 51 (2) of the Rome Statute.

27 Hannah Woolaver and Emma Palmer, 'Challenges to the Independence of the International Criminal Court from the Assembly of States Parties' (2017) 15 JICJ 646 para 4.

28 ILC (n 4) Conclusion 3 paras 1, 2.

The role of States parties in the interpretation of their treaty after its conclusion has a foundational basis in the VCLT interpretation rules in Articles 31 and specifically 31(3) and 32. Chapter 2, therefore, examines the VCLT rules of interpretation contained in Article 31(1) on the ordinary meaning, the context, and the object and purpose. It then discusses Article 31(3) in-depth, which situates States parties in treaty interpretation through their subsequent agreements and practice. Article 32 on supplementary interpretation means is also briefly discussed. The position of the subsequent agreements and practice in treaty interpretation is analyzed to determine whether courts and tribunals are mandatorily bound by the subsequent agreements and practice of State parties in interpretation or whether they are a supplementary and discretionary interpretation means.

Chapter 3 focuses on the rules of interpretation guiding interpretation under the Rome Statute. The application of the VCLT to the Statute's interpretation is discussed, with several ICC decisions applying the VCLT rules and scholarly material also examined. The discussion on the VCLT's applicability to the Rome Statute lays the basis for determining whether the ASP's resolutions and amendments should be construed as subsequent agreements and practice and consequently incorporated into the Statute's interpretation by the ICC. Articles 21(3) and 22 under the Rome Statute are also examined as internal rules of interpretation, and whether they are independent interpretive rules separate from the VCLT or work within and alongside the VCLT interpretive rules.

Chapter 4 addresses the specific roles of the States Parties and the ICC in interpreting the Rome Statute. It first lays out the general role of States parties internationally in interpreting their treaties. It then narrows down to the specific roles played by the ASP and the ICC in the Statute's interpretation.

Chapter 5 addresses the coherence of States parties' resolutions and amendments as subsequent agreements and practice vis-avi the ICC's jurisprudence in interpreting the Rome Statute. It discusses two specific instances in which the ASP's resolutions and amendments were adopted when a related case was ongoing in Court. The implications of the timing of the resolution on the ICC's interpretation are examined.

Chapter 6 contains a summary of the study's findings, conclusions drawn from the findings, and recommendations for further action.

CHAPTER 2

Interpretation under the Vienna Convention on the Law of Treaties (VCLT)

1 Introduction

The role of States Parties to the Rome Statute of the International Criminal Court (States Parties) in the interpretation of the Rome Statute of the International Criminal Court (Rome Statute) is linked to the Vienna Convention on the Law on Treaties (VCLT) interpretation rules in Article 31(3). Articles 31 to 32 of the VCLT help to situate subsequent agreements and subsequent practice of States Parties and their role in interpreting the Rome Statute within the general legal framework of the interpretation of treaties.

The chapter, therefore, begins by examining the VCLT rules of interpretation, focusing primarily on Articles 31 and 32 of the VCLT as accepted customary international law. An examination of the "general rule" of interpretation and whether it is based only on Article 31(1) or the whole of Article 31 of the VCLT follows. The specific elements of interpretation under Article 31(1) of the VCLT including the ordinary meaning, context, object and purpose are then analyzed, followed by the definitive aspects of subsequent agreements and subsequent practice based on Article 31(3) (a) and (b). An examination of the supplementary means of interpretation under Article 32 with an emphasis on subsequent agreements and practice as supplementary means of interpretation comes after. Given its centrality to the study, a detailed analytical discussion of subsequent agreements and subsequent practice and their legal effect on treaty interpretation follows.

2 The Vienna Convention Rules of Interpretation as Customary International Law

Articles 31, 32, and 33 of the VCLT are generally accepted by international courts, tribunals, and scholars as reflecting the codified customary international law of treaty interpretation.[1] Article 31(1) of the VCLT provides that "a

1 *Kasikili/Sedudu Island (Botswana/Namibia), Judgment, ICJ Rep 1999* (ICJ) 1059 para 18 (Kasikili/Sedudu); *Pulp Mills on the River Uruguay (Argentina v Uruguay)* (ICJ) 46 para 65; Chang-

 | DOI:10.1163/9789004725515_003

treaty shall be interpreted in good faith in accordance with the ordinary meaning to be given to the terms of the treaty in their context and in the light of its object and purpose." Article 31(2) defines what the context entails but is not a primary focus of this study. Article 31(3)(a) states that "there shall be taken into account, together with the context, any subsequent agreement between the parties regarding the interpretation of the treaty or the application of its provisions."

Further to be taken into account is any subsequent practice in the treaty's application that establishes the parties' agreement regarding its interpretation (Article 31[3]b). Article 31 (4) gives special meaning to the treaty provisions where the parties propose so. In addition, Article 32 contains the supplementary means of interpretation, while Article 33 deals with treaties authenticated in more than one language. Articles 31 (1), 31(3)(a), and (b) and 32 will form the main focus of the study, with Articles 31(3)(c) and 31 (4) only referred to in passing.

Articles 31–33 are generally accepted as customary international law on interpretation, although not all international courts, tribunals, and scholars acknowledge that all three articles constitute customary interpretation rules.[2] The customary law status is relevant to the interpretation of the Rome Statute on the basis that treated only as an international treaty, the VCLT Articles 31–33 are binding only on the parties to the VCLT.[3] However, taken as customary international law, all States are legally obligated to adhere to customary international law rules as a matter of law and are, therefore, subject to the treaty interpretation rules under the VCLT.[4] This position is based on the definition of customary international law as a "binding set of international norms arising from general and consistent State practice and has been followed by States as a binding legal obligation (accepted as law or *opinio juris*)."[5] This approach implies that the States Parties and the Rome Statute would also be subject to the VCLT interpretation rules as customary law since the Statute is an international treaty.[6]

---

fa Lo, *Treaty Interpretation Under the Vienna Convention on the Law of Treaties: A New Round of Codification* (Springer Singapore 2017) 36; Oliver Dörr, 'Article 31, General Rule of Interpretation, 2018' in Oliver Dörr and Kirsten Schmalenbach (eds), *Vienna Convention on the Law of Treaties: A Commentary* (Springer 2018) 560 para 2.

2 Richard Gardiner, *Treaty Interpretation 2015* (2nd edn, Oxford University Press 2015) 162.

3 Ulf Linderfalk, *On the Interpretation of Treaties: The Modern International Law as Expressed in the 1969 Vienna Convention on the Law of Treaties* (Springer Netherlands 2007) 7 para 1.

4 Chang-fa Lo (n 1) 36.

5 Ibid., 34,36.

6 William A Schabas, *An Introduction to the International Criminal Court 2020* (6th edn, Cambridge University Press 2020) 213.

Notably, though, while Articles 31 and 32 are referred to by most courts, tribunals, and scholars as reflecting international customary law, not all similarly recognize Article 33. For instance, the ILC has explicitly acknowledged Articles 31 and 32 of the VCLT as reflecting customary international law on interpretation.[7] The ILC has, however, avoided express recognition of Article 33 as reflective of customary law.[8] The international courts that have affirmed Articles 31–33 of the VCLT as customary law on interpretation include the ICJ, which has not explicitly distinguished between the rules in Articles 31 to 33 as binding customary law.[9] For example, the ICJ, in *Qatar vs UAE*, among other cases, has held that "it is well established that Articles 31 and 32 of the Vienna Convention reflect rules of customary international law."[10]

Similarly, in the case of *Immunities and Criminal Proceedings* (*Equatorial Guinea v France*), the ICJ, in its decision, referred to "customary international law, as reflected in Articles 31 and 32 of the Vienna Convention on the Law of Treaties."[11] The ICJ took a similar position in the *Maritime Dispute case* (*Peru and Chile*), where it referred to "the customary international law of treaty interpretation, as reflected in Articles 31 and 32 of the Vienna Convention on the Law of Treaties."[12] The ICJ has reiterated the same position in several other cases.[13]

The World Trade Organization (WTO) Appellate Body in the *US-Carbon Steel* report also held that "it is well settled in WTO case law that the principles codified in Articles 31 and 32 of the Vienna Convention on the Law of Treaties

7 ILC, 'Draft Conclusions on Subsequent Agreements and Subsequent Practice in Relation to the Interpretation of Treaties, Seventieth Session, (A/73/10) 2018' (ILC) Conclusion 2 Commentary 2 (ILC 2018).

8 Ibid. Conclusion 2 Commentary 5.

9 Dörr (n 1) 562 para 1.

10 *Application of the International Convention on the Elimination of All Forms of Racial Discrimination* (*Qatar v United Arab Emirates*), *Preliminary Objections, Judgment, ICJ Reports 2021* 95 para 75.

11 *Immunities and Criminal Proceedings* (*Equitorial Guinea v France*), *Preliminary Objections, Judgment, ICJ Reports 2018 p 320 para 91.*

12 *Case concerning Maritime Dispute* (*Peru and Chile*) *ICJ Reports*, 27 Jan 2014 para 57.

13 *Case concerning Oil Platforms* (*Islamic Republic of Iran versus United States of America* 2003 (ICJ) 161 para 41 (article 31(3)C recognized); *Dispute Regarding Navigational and Related Rights* (*Costa Rica v. Nicaragua*), *Judgment* (*13 July 2009*), *ICJ Reports 2009*, 237 para 47; Kasikili/Sedudu (n 1)1059 para 18; *Territorial Dispute* (*Libyan Arab Jamahiriya/ Chad*), Judgment (*3 Feb 1994*) *ICJ Reports, 1994* at 21–22, para 41; *Arbitral Award of 31 July 1989* (*Guinea-Bissau v Senegal*), *1991 ICJ* (*Nov 12*) para 48.

(the Vienna Convention) are such customary rules."[14] The WTO, other regional courts, and tribunals have taken a similar position in several other cases.[15] However, the ICJ in *Nicaragua vs Colombia* (*Preliminary objections*) and multiple other cases has also held that "it is well established that Articles 31 to 33 of the Convention reflect rules of customary international law."[16]

A look at the cited cases and the scholarly approaches seem to indicate that most international courts, tribunals, and scholars predominantly recognize Articles 31 and 32 as customary law on interpretation, with fewer expressly acknowledging Article 33. Therefore, some scholars have suggested that the customary nature of Article 33 is not yet clearly established.[17]

Based on their customary status, the VCLT interpretation rules also apply to treaties outside the VCLT limits,[18] including treaties concluded before the VCLT came into force[19] and treaties between non-party States to the VCLT.[20] With respect to the current study, the implication is that the ICC and other

---

14 *Appellate Body Report, WTO, United States – Countervailing Duties on Certain Corrosion-Resistant Carbon Steel Flat Products from Germany, WT/DS213/AB/R, WT/DS213/AB/R/Corr1* (*adopted 19 Dec 2002*) para 61; See also *United States-Standards for Reformulated and Conventional Gasoline, WTO Appellate Body Report, WT/DS2/AB/R* (*adopted 20 May 1996*) 17.

15 ECtHR Golder v United Kingdom App No 4451/70, Ser A 18, para 29 (1975); See also *The Rhine Chlorides Arbitration concerning the Auditing of Accounts* (*The Netherlands/France*), *PCA, Arbitral Award, 12 March 2004* 59,60; *Jany C-268/99* [*2001*] *ECR I-8615* para 35; *US-Final Countervailing Duty Determination with Respect to Certain Softwood Lumber from Canada IV, WTO Appellate Body Report, WT/DS25/AB/R, AB-2003–6, 19 January 2004* para 59.

16 *Alleged Violations of Sovereign Rights and Maritime Spaces in the Caribbean Sea* (*Nicaragua v Colombia*), *Preliminary Objections, Judgment, ICJ Reports 2016* p 19 para 35; *Application of the International Convention for the Suppression of the Financing of Terrorism and of the International Convention on the Elimination of All Forms of Racial Discrimination* (*Ukraine v Russian Federation*), *Preliminary Objections, Judgment, ICJ Reports 2019* (*II*), p 598 para 106; *Question of the Delimitation of the Continental Shelf between Nicaragua and Colombia beyond 200 Nautical Miles from the Nicaraguan Coast* (*Nicaragua v. Colombia*), *Preliminary Objections, Judgment, ICJ Reports 2016* p 116 para 33.

17 Barton Legum and Anna Crevon-Tarassova, 'VCLT Article 33: Interpretation of Treaties Authenticated in Two or More Languages' [2021] SSRN Scholarly Paper 5.

18 Dörr (n 1) 563 para 7.

19 Kasikili/Sedudu (n 1) 1045 para 20 (The ICJ interpreted an 1890 treaty using the VCLT); *Pulp Mills on the River Uruguay* (*Argentina v Uruguay*) *2010* (ICJ) 14 para 65 (a 1975 Statute of Uruguay was interpreted using the VCLT); *Maritime Dispute* (*Peru v Chile*) [*2014*] *ICJ Rep* at 3 para 57 (treaty of 1952).

20 Chang-fa Lo (n 1) 35 para 3; Kasikili/Sedudu (n 1) 1059 para 18; *Dispute regarding Navigational and Related rights* (*Costa Rica v Nicaragua*), *Judgment of 13 July 2009* (ICJ) 237 para 47.

interpretive institutions, such as the States Parties, can apply the VCLT interpretation rules.

Significantly, the VCLT interpretation rules are recognized as forming a "single framework of interpretation,"[21] with the rules considered the "starting point" of interpretation.[22] Article 31 is, in this respect, titled "the general rule of interpretation."

2.1 *The "General Rule" of Interpretation under Article 31 of the VCLT*

While Articles 31 to 32 of the VCLT are recognized as customary international law on interpretation, it is Article 31 that bears the title of the "general rule of interpretation."[23] Despite its title, there are varied opinions by international courts, tribunals, and scholars on whether it is Article 31 as a whole that constitutes the general rule or whether only Article 31(1) forms the general rule of interpretation. In other instances, the general rule is restricted even further to not just Article 31(1) but specifically to the ordinary meaning of terms with the other means under Article 31 treated as discretionary.[24] Whether the whole of Article 31 constitutes the general rule or only Article 31(1) is relevant because it plays a role in determining the weight given to subsequent agreements and practice of States Parties, a significant aspect of this study.

For those who subscribe to the approach that Article 31 as a whole constitutes the general rule, it means that Article 31(1), which provides for interpretation based on good faith in accordance with the ordinary meaning to be given to the treaty terms in their context and in the light of its object and purpose forms part of the rule. Similarly, Article 31(3)(a) and (b) and (c), which provides for "subsequent agreements," "subsequent practice" by States parties, and relevant international law rules being "taken into account" during interpretation, also form part of the general rule. In line with this approach, the ILC stipulates that the title "general rule and means of interpretation" in Article 31 of the VCLT signifies that Article 31 as a "whole" is the general rule of interpretation.[25]

In the same vein, the ILC has described subsequent agreements and subsequent practice as authentic means of interpretation "in the application of

21 Gardiner (n 2) 6.

22 Linderfalk (n 3) 7 para 2; Chang-fa Lo (n 1) 36.

23 Dörr (n 1) 561 para 5; *ECtHR Hassan v United Kingdom* (GC) *App No 29750/09, ECHR 2014-VI* (2014) Application no. 29750/09 para 100 (ECtHR Hassan v United Kingdom); ILC 2018 (n 7) Conclusion 2 Commentary 1.

24 Mark E Villiger, *Commentary on the 1969 Vienna Convention on the Law of Treaties* (Brill 2009) 436 para 32.

25 ILC 2018 (n 7) Conclusion 2 Commentary 2.

the general rule of treaty interpretation reflected in Article 31."[26] This provision equally recognizes the whole of Article 31 as the general rule. Similarly, Gardiner asserts that the singular word "general rule" in the title of Article 31 was adopted carefully to emphasize that "the whole of the article was to be applicable," implying that the relevant elements in a specific case "must" be applied together and not separately.[27] Villiger also points out that there is a singular reference to all means under Article 31.[28]

French takes a similar stance, emphasizing that "it is Article 31 in its entirety that is entitled the 'general rule of interpretation' and not just the foundational rule in Article 31(1), as is sometimes presumed."[29] Equally, the ECtHR in the *Hassan v UK* case referred to the entire Article 31 as "Article 31 of the Vienna Convention, which contains the 'general rule of interpretation.'"[30] Additionally, the words "shall be taken into account, together with the context," used in reference to Article 31(3)(a) and (b) have been construed as making Articles 31(3) (a) and (b) an "integral part of the general rule of interpretation."[31] Arato and Moloo support a similar position, positing that other than Article 31(1), subsequent practice and subsequent agreements in Articles 31(3) (a) and (b) also form part of the general rule.[32]

Gardiner adds that the ILC has highlighted the importance of subsequent agreements and practice in interpretation, therefore acting as a "necessary antidote to the occasional misunderstanding which suggests that the first part of the general rule is the main rule to which the rest is somehow subsidiary."[33] Nevertheless, Gardiner and Villiger concede that Article 31(1) has been cited more than the other means of treaty interpretation, which may give the false impression that only Article 31(1) constitutes the general rule while the other elements under Article 31 are discretionary.[34]

---

26 Ibid. Conclusion 3.

27 Gardiner (n 2) 161–162, 201; Duncan French, 'Treaty Interpretation and the Incorporation of Extraneous Legal Rules' (2006) 55 ICLQ 301.

28 Mark E Villiger (n 24) 435 para 29; French (n 27) 301.

29 French (n 27) 301.

30 ECtHR Hassan v United Kingdom (n 23) para 100.

31 ILC 2018 (n 7) Conclusion 2 Commentary 7; 'Yearbook of the ILC 1966 Volume II' 220 para 8 (ILC 1966 Vol II).

32 Julian Arato, 'Subsequent Practice and Evolutive Interpretation: Techniques of Treaty Interpretation over Time and Their Diverse Consequences' (2010) 9 The Law & Practice of International Courts and Tribunals 458; Rahim Moloo, 'When Actions Speak Louder than Words: The Relevance of Subsequent Party Conduct to Treaty Interpretation' (2013) 31 Berkeley Journal of International Law 39, 40.

33 Gardiner (n 2) 227.

34 Mark E Villiger (n 24) 436 para 32; Gardiner (n 2) 162,222.

One implied effect of the title "general rule" is that the means of interpretation under the rule "must" be applied in interpretation, unlike the "supplementary" means under Article 32, which are discretionary.[35] Another suggested effect of the entire Article 31 being the "general rule" is that the interpretation means under Article 31 are all seen as equal and, consequently, applied in "the same single process" of interpretation.[36] However, based on the different approaches regarding what constitutes the general rule, international courts and scholars have varied views about the equality or otherwise of the various elements of interpretation under Article 31.[37]

For instance, the ILC provides that the entire Article 31 is referred to as the "general rule" in the singular form to show that the application of the interpretation means in the article would be a "single combined" interpretation with all the various elements "thrown into the crucible" to give an interpretation.[38] The ILC emphasizes that Article 31 does not provide for any hierarchy or superiority, and having Article 31 (1) in a separate paragraph does not suggest priority over other interpretation means within Article 31.[39] It is additionally observed that the reference to the whole of Article 31 as the general rule signifies that the ILC "rejected the primacy of Article 31(1), opting to suggest, even if implicitly, that Article 31(3) had a value on its own, which value was equivalent to that of Article 31(1)."[40] Consequently, the deliberate singular reference

35 J G Merrills, 'Two Approaches to Treaty Interpretation' (1971) 4 The Australian Year Book of International Law Online 56 para 2 <https://brill.com/view/journals/auso/4/1/article-p55.xml> accessed 16 February 2021; Georg Nolte, 'First Report on Subsequent Agreements and Subsequent Practice in Relation to Treaty Interpretation ILC Sixty-Fifth Session (A/CN.4/660) 2013' para 8.

36 Mark E Villiger (n 24) 435 para 29.

37 Shai Dothan, 'The Three Traditional Approaches to Treaty Interpretation: A Current Application to the European Court of Human Rights' (2019) 42 Fordham International Law Journal 766 para 1.

38 ILC 2018 (n 7) Conclusion 2 Commentary 13; ILC 1966 Vol II (n 31) 220 para 8; Anja Seibert-Fohr, 'The Effect of Subsequent Practice on the European Convention on Human Rights: Considerations from a General International Law Perspective', *The European Convention on Human Rights and General International Law* (Oxford University Press 2018).

39 ILC 2018 (n 7) Conclusion 2 Commentary 6 and 12; Mark E Villiger (n 24) 435–436 para 29.

40 Dire Tladi, 'Is the International Law Commission Elevating Subsequent Agreements and Subsequent Practice?' (*EJIL: Talk!*, 30 August 2018) <https://www.ejiltalk.org/is-the-international-law-commission-elevating-subsequent-agreements-and-subsequent-practice/> accessed 19 April 2020; See also G Nolte 'Treaties and their practice 'Collected Courses of the Hague Academy of International law (2018) 336;Dörr (n 1) 594 para 74; ILC 1966 Vol II (n 31) 95 para 6; Donald H Regan, 'Sources of International Trade Law: Understanding What the Vienna Convention Says about Identifying and Using 'Sources for Treaty Inter-

to the "general rule" of interpretation is construed as implying that all the interpretation means under Article 31 have equal value and will be considered a "single, closely integrated rule."[41] French adds that the whole of Article 31 constitutes "mandatory" aspects of the "general rule," which are all on the same level, with no option to ignore Article 31(3).[42]

In the same respect, it was held in the case of *Rhine Chloride* that

> Article 31 of the VCLT should be viewed as forming an integral whole, the constituent elements of which cannot be separated … All the elements of the general rule of interpretation provide the basis for establishing the common will and intention of the parties by objective and rational means.[43]

Several international courts and tribunals have similarly held that all the elements in Article 31 depend on each other and should be considered holistically rather than separately.[44] It is noted that the elements do not follow any hierarchical order but rather a pragmatic approach with the ordinary meaning as the natural starting point since they cannot all be applied simultaneously.[45]

---

pretation' in S Besson and J d'Aspremont (ed), *The Oxford Handbook of the Sources of International Law* (Oxford University Press, USA 2018) 1054; Malgosia Fitzmaurice, 'Subsequent Agreement and Subsequent Practice: Some Reflections on the International Law Commission's Draft Conclusions' (2020) 22 International Community Law Review 14, 17.

41 Allain Pellet, 'Canons of Interpretation under the Vienna Convention in (Eds) Joseph Klingler, Yuri Parkhomenko, Constantinos Salonidi, Between the Lines of the Vienna Convention? Canons and Other Principles of Interpretation in Public International Law' *European Journal of International Law*, vol 30 (2019) 5 ; ILC 1966 Vol II (n 31) 95 para 6; Mark E Villiger (n 24) 435 para 29; Dörr (n 1) 580 para 38, 594 para 74; Stefan Kadelbach, 'International Law Commission and Role of Subsequent Practice as a Means of Interpretation under Articles 31 and 32 VCLT' (*QIL QDI*, 2018) 16.

42 French (n 27) 301.

43 *Case concerning the auditing of accounts between the Kingdom of the Netherlands and the French Republic pursuant to the additional Protocol of 25 September 1991 to the Convention on the Protection of the Rhine against Pollution by Chlorides of 3 December 1976 arbitral award of 12 March 2004* para 62.

44 *Judgment pursuant to article 74 of the Statute, The Prosecutor v Germain Katanga, ICC-01/04-01/07-3436-tENG, Trial Chamber II* paras 44–45 (Judgment pursuant to Article 74 Katanga); *WTO Appellate Body, China–Publications and Audiovisual Products WT/DS363/AB/R* para 399; *European Communities-Customs Classification of Frozen Boneless Chicken Cuts, WTO Appellate Body Report, WT/DS269/AB/R, WT/DS286/AB/R, 12 September 2005* para 176.

45 'Yearbook of the ILC 1966 Volume I Part II' Mustafa Yasseen, 197 paras 48 and 220 para 9; Mark E Villiger (n 24) 436 para 30.

In contrast, Kadelbach and Fabri observe that it is only Article 31(1) of the VCLT that constitutes the general rule, even referring to "the general rule of Article 31(1) of the VCLT" and "the general rule set up by Article 31(1)"[46] respectively. Similarly, Dorr interprets the general rule as referring to only Article 31(1) of the VCLT.[47] Dorr observes that the singular use of the word "general rule" refers to one single rule found in Article 31(1) and should be interpreted as one combined operation.[48] In Dorr's and Regan's opinion, subsequent agreements and subsequent practice under Article 31(3)(a) and (b) should consequently be incorporated into the "general rule contained in Article 31 (1)."[49] Fabri similarly states that the subsequent paragraphs in Article 31 "only complete" and "complement" the general rule found in Article 31(1).[50]

Other divergent views observe that considering all the elements in a single combined application does not give all the elements equal weight.[51] In this regard, it is pointed out that, in practice, different courts and tribunals prioritize different elements under Article 31.[52] An example is the ICJ, which has held in various judgments that "interpretation must be based above all upon the text of the treaty,"[53] seemingly prioritizing the ordinary means. However, in the *Nuclear Weapons Advisory Opinion* and the *Kasikili/Sedudu* Island cases, the ICJ referred to Article 31(1) and subsequent practice under Article 31(3)(b) as part of the interpretation process.[54]

---

46 Hélène Ruiz Fabri, 'Subsequent Practice, Domestic Separation of Powers, and Concerns of Legitimacy', *Treaties and Subsequent Practice* (Oxford University Press 2013) 161; Stefan Kadelbach, 'International Law Commission and Role of Subsequent Practice as a Means of Interpretation under Articles 31 and 32 VCLT' Questions of International Law-QIL, Milão, 2018;46.

47 Dörr (n 1) 579 para 37.

48 Ibid., 561 para 5.

49 Donald H Regan (n 40)1052; Dörr (n 1) 561 para 5.

50 Hélène Ruiz Fabri, 'Subsequent Practice, Domestic Separation of Powers, and Concerns of Legitimacy', *Treaties and subsequent Practice* (Oxford University Press 2013) 160.

51 Dire Tladi, 'Is the International Law Commission Elevating Subsequent Agreements and Subsequent Practice?' (*EJIL: Talk!*, 30 August 2018) <https://www.ejiltalk.org/is-the-international-law-commission-elevating-subsequent-agreements-and-subsequent-practice/> accessed 19 April 2020.

52 Mark E Villiger (n 24) 436 para 32.

53 *Territorial Dispute (Libya v Chad), Judgment, ICJ Reports 1994* 22 para 41; *Legality of Use of force (Serbia and Montenegro v Belgium) Preliminary objections, Judgment, ICJ Reports 2004* (ICJ) 318 para 100; *Maritime Delimitation and Territorial Questions (Qatar v Bahrain) (Jurisdiction and Admissibility) case ICJ rep 1995 18,* para 33; *Oil Platforms (Iran/US) (Preliminary Objections) Case* ICJ reports 1996 812 para 23.

54 Kasikili/Sedudu (n 1)1059–1060; *Legality of the Use by a State of Nuclear Weapons in Armed Conflict, Advisory Opinion, 1996 ICJ (July 8)* para 75.

Significantly, the ILC seemingly contradicts itself, where, on the one hand, it promotes a unified approach to the general rule, lacking a hierarchy of the interpretation means under Article 31.[55] On the other hand, it provides for "only taking into account" subsequent agreements and practice[56] instead of the seeming obligatory application of Article 31(1) elements. The approach to the "general rule" impacts the current study, which predominantly focuses on subsequent agreements and practice of States parties under Article 31(3)(a) and (3)(b) respectively, and whether they consequently form primary and obligatory means of interpretation under the general rule or subsidiary means. This evaluation helps to determine the weight of the States Parties subsequent agreements and practice in the Rome Statute's interpretation.

Based on the general rule, the individual elements under Article 31 of the VCLT, except for Articles 31(2) and 31(3)(C), are discussed next. The elements under Article 31(1) are, however, analyzed only briefly since the primary focus of the study is on Article 31(3)(a) and (b) elements, which are discussed more broadly.

2.1.1 Ordinary Meaning of the Terms

The first element of the general rule of interpretation requires that an ordinary meaning "be given" to the "terms of the treaty."[57] The "terms" to which the meaning is to be given are deemed to refer to the words and phrases written down in the treaty.[58] The ordinary meaning is considered the meaning which is "regular, normal or customary" or "familiar, everyday, unexceptional."[59] However, where the ordinary meaning does not apply to all treaty terms, Article 31(4) of the VCLT provides that a special meaning be given to the terms if the parties wish it to be so. The ordinary meaning is considered the most likely reflection of what the parties intended.[60] Consequently, determining the ordinary meaning is regarded as the commencement stage of the interpretation process.[61] Applied to the Rome Statute, the text's ordinary meaning becomes the starting point of its interpretation.[62]

Despite being the first element under the general rule, it is asserted that the ordinary meaning of the terms should not be treated as a separate element

---

55 ILC 2018 (n 7) Conclusion 2 Commentary 6.
56 Ibid. Conclusion 3 Commentary 4.
57 Dörr (n 1) 580 para 39.
58 Gardiner (n 2) 183; Dörr (n 1) 580 para 39.
59 Gardiner (n 2) 183–184; Linderfalk (n 3) 63 para 3.
60 Anthony Aust, *Handbook of International Law* (Cambridge University Press 2010) 84.
61 Mark E Villiger (n 24) 426 para 9.
62 Valérie V Suhr, *Rainbow Jurisdiction at the International Criminal Court: Protection of Sexual and Gender Minorities Under the Rome Statute* (Springer Nature 2021) 58.

when applied to treaty interpretation.[63] Instead, it is contended that the ordinary meaning should be arrived at based on the context and other elements under the general rule, with the ordinary meaning formed at first impression being only a provisional beginning point.[64] Consequently, it is averred that the ordinary meaning may only be conclusive when the context and the treaty's object and purpose, together with the elements in Article 31(3), confirm the meaning and do not contradict that conclusion.[65] From this perspective, being the starting point does not make the ordinary meaning superior or have priority over the other elements under the general rule.[66] In contrast however, a different approach finds that other interpretation elements under the general rule become inapplicable where the ordinary meaning is clear and unambiguous.[67]

Notably, while establishing the ordinary meaning, the text is generally accepted as the starting point of analysis. In that regard, the general rule in Article 31 (1) is deemed to be based on the textual approach, with the text construed as the authentic expression of the parties' intentions.[68] The textual approach requires the text's clear meaning to be established as a starting point for each interpretation.[69] In this case, the interpreter needs to consider the text of the whole treaty, including the title, the preamble and annexes, any protocols, and any external material under Article 31(2) and (3).[70] Under this approach, the treaty's text is given "pride of place" compared to the other elements in interpretation.[71] Waldock noted that "the signed text is, with very few exceptions, the only and the most recent expression of the common will

63 Gardiner (n 2) 181.

64 Ibid., 181,222.

65 Tarcisio Gazzini, 'Ordinary Meaning of the Terms of the Treaty', *Interpretation of International Investment Treaties* (Oxford Hart Publishing 2016) 67; Ibid., 185; *South West Africa Cases (Ethiopia v South Africa; Liberia v South Africa), Preliminary Objections, Judgment of 21 December 1962, ICJ Rep 1962* (ICJ) 336.

66 Ibid., 181.

67 *Arbitral Award of 31 July 1989 (Guinea-Bissau v Senegal), Judgment ICJ Rep 1991* para 48 endorsing observations made in *Competence of the General Assembly for the Admission of a State to the United Nations, Advisory Opinion, ICJ Rep 1950* at 8.

68 Dörr (n 1) 579–580 para 37; ILC 1966 Vol II (n 31) 220 para 11.

69 ILC 1966 Vol II (n 31) 220 para 11; House *of Lords- In re B* (FC) *(Appellant)* (2002) *Regina v Special Adjudicator (Respondent) ex parte Hoxha* (FC) *(Appellant)* [2005] *UKHL 19* Lord Hope para 8.

70 Dörr (n 1) 582 para 44.

71 Eirik Bjorge, 'Time Present and Time Past: The Intention of the Parties and the Evolutionary Interpretation of Treaties' in Abi-Saab Georges et al (ed), *Evolutionary Interpretation and International Law* (Hart Publishing 2019) 45.

of the parties."[72] Reuter adds that "the primacy of the text, especially in international law, is the cardinal rule for any interpretation."[73] Several courts and tribunals have reached similar findings with the ICJ in *Territorial Dispute (Libyan Arab Jamahiriya/Chad)* and in the *Maritime Delimitation and Territorial Questions (Qatar v. Bahrain)* cases, holding that "interpretation must be based above all upon the text of the treaty."[74]

Gardiner nevertheless points out that there is a misconception that the general rule is only based on the treaty's text, yet the text is only the beginning point since there are other elements.[75] This view aligns with the ILC's position that all elements under Article 31 of the VCLT play a role in the interpretation process in a "single combined" operation despite the text being the starting point.[76] Under this approach, none of the elements, including the treaty's text, is superior to the other interpretation elements.[77]

In this respect and as stated earlier, the importance of subsequent agreements and practice of States parties in interpretation is hinged on whether there is any hierarchy in Article 31 elements. If the ordinary meaning and the text are construed as hierarchically superior, as reiterated by several scholars and courts above, this impliedly gives subsequent agreements and practice a less significant and non-obligatory role in treaty interpretation. If this is taken as the correct position, then the ICC would not need to treat the ASP's subsequent agreements and practice as obligatory in the Rome Statute's interpretation where the text is clear. Some scholars have argued that Article 22 of the Rome Statute, which requires the ICC to conform to the strict construction of crimes without extension by analogy, gives primacy to the text based on Article 31(1) of the VCLT.[78] In this context, the ordinary meaning would be considered dominant in the Rome Statute's interpretation compared to the ASP's subsequent agreement or practice.

---

72 ILC 1966 Vol II (n 31) 220.

73 Paul Reuter, *Introduction to the Law of Treaties* (Routledge 1995) para 142.

74 *Maritime Delimitation and Territorial Questions between Qatar and Bahrain, Jurisdiction and Admissibility, Judgment, ICJ Reports 1991* (ICJ) para 48; *United States – Import Prohibition of Certain Shrimp and Shrimp Products WTO Report of Appellate Board AB-1998-4, WT/DS58/AB/R, 12 October 1998* para 114 (WTO US Import Prohibition of Certain Shrimp); *Re B* (FC) (2002), *R v Special Adjudicator ex parte Hoxha* [2005] *UKHL 19, at* paras 8–9.

75 Gardiner (n 2) 227.

76 ILC 2018 (n 7) Conclusion 2 para 5.

77 Ian M Sinclair, *The Vienna Convention on the Law of Treaties* (2nd ed, Manchester University Press 1984) 130; ILC 2018 (n 7) Conclusion 2 Commentary 6 and 12.

78 Leena Grover, *Interpreting Crimes in the Rome Statute of the International Criminal Court* (Cambridge University Press 2014) 378–379.

If, however, the contrast is true, as argued by other scholars, that there is no hierarchy, then the ordinary meaning and the subsequent agreements and practice should be treated as being on the same level and consequently as obligatory in the Rome Statute's interpretation. This position would make it difficult for the ICC to ignore States Parties subsequent agreements and practice in the Rome Statute's interpretation.

2.1.2 Context

Under Article 31(1) of the VCLT, a treaty shall be interpreted in good faith in accordance with the ordinary meaning to be given to its terms in their context. The context element is based on the fact that words do not apply in seclusion since their meaning is gathered from the context in which they are used.[79] Additionally, treaty terms are not segregated while being drafted, and their meaning can only be determined by considering the whole treaty's text.[80] The context is seen as ensuring consistency between the treaty terms and the "surrounding circumstances."[81] It is argued that there is interpretative significance in the position of words in a sentence or, amidst other words, and the connection of words to the whole treaty.[82] Some scholars have argued that, on this basis, words lack primacy over context because words lack "independent significance" without the context.[83] Under this perspective, the interpreter "must" consider the context and not only when the interpretation of the text is unclear or ambiguous.[84]

Gardiner infers that the context has a two-pronged role in treaty interpretation. Under the first role, the context assists in preventing the "over-literal" approach to interpretation.[85] Under this perspective, the context may involve reading words in their surrounding circumstances, or where a word forms part of a phrase, the whole phrase becomes the context to be considered.[86]

79 *Constitution of the Maritime Safety Committee of the Inter-Governmental Maritime Consultative Organization, Advisory Opinion of 8 June 1960 ICJ Reports 1960* 158; ILC 1966 Vol II (n 31) 221 para 12.

80 Mark E Villiger (n 24) 427 para 10; Dörr (n 1) 582 para 43.

81 Mark E Villiger (n 24) 427.

82 Dörr (n 1) 582 para 44.

83 Donald H Regan (n 40) 1052.

84 *Asian Agricultural Products Ltd AAPL v Sri Lanka, ICSID ARB/87/3 Final Award 27 June 1990* para 40 Rule C.

85 Gardiner (n 2) 197.

86 Ibid; See *Land, Island and Maritime Frontier Dispute (El Salvador/Honduras: Nicaragua intervening v Honduras, Judgment ICJ GL No. 75 (1992) ICJ Reports* 351.

The second use of context in treaty interpretation is confirming the ordinary meaning where one clear meaning emerges or identifying the ordinary meaning where two or more possible meanings emerge.[87] The context may, therefore, be used as a supplementary means to establish the text's clear meaning where the ordinary meaning is ambiguous.[88]

Article 31(2) of the VCLT defines the context as including the text, which incorporates the preamble and the annexes, among others.[89] Significantly, the context under Article 31(2) also includes any agreement made between all the parties or some of the parties and accepted by others in connection with the treaty's conclusion. Therefore, Article 31(2) shares the aspect of agreement between all parties with subsequent agreements under Article 31(3) of the VCLT. As the ILC points out, however, the difference is that the parties reach agreements under Article 31(2) at the time of the treaty conclusion, while those under Article 31(3) are reached after the treaty conclusion.[90]

2.1.3 The Object and Purpose of Treaties

Article 31(1) of the VCLT requires that the ordinary meaning of a term of the treaty shall be determined "in light of the treaty's object and purpose." Gazinni observes that the word "shall" conveys a mandatory requirement to examine the object and purpose, following the analysis of the ordinary meaning of the terms.[91] Some scholars note that while the "object and purpose" under Article 31(1) of the VCLT is referred to in the "singular," a treaty may occasionally have more than one object and purpose.[92] In addition, treaties may sometimes have different and conflicting objects and purposes.[93] In the instances where the treaty appears to have more than one object, it is recommended that the interpreter must consider all the relevant objects and purposes in a neutral, unbiased manner.[94] Additionally, reference should be made to the treaty as a whole and not to specific treaty provisions to determine the object and purpose with certainty.[95]

---

87 Ibid., 198.

88 Linderfalk (n 3) 102 para 2.

89 See also Gardiner (n 2) 197.

90 ILC 2018 (n 7) Conclusion 4 Commentary 3.

91 Tarcisio Gazzini, 'Object and Purpose', *Interpretation of International Investment Treaties* (Oxford Hart Publishing 2016) 159.

92 Mark E Villiger (n 24) 427 para 11; Tarcisio Gazzini, 'Object and Purpose'(n 91) 160.

93 Sinclair (n 77) 130; Dörr (n 1) 585 para 54; WTO US Import Prohibition of Certain Shrimp (n 74) para 17.

94 Tarcisio Gazzini, 'Object and Purpose' (n 91) 161.

95 Gardiner (n 2) 210; Dörr (n 1) 585 para 55.

The treaty's object and purpose may be determined from the different elements, including the title, the preamble, the preparatory work, and the overall treaty.[96] Some treaties have provisions indicating the object and purpose in their substantive articles.[97] An example is Article 1 of the UN Charter, which states the purposes of the UN[98]. The Rome Statute also states its objects and purpose, including ending impunity for the perpetrators of the most serious international crimes.[99] The ICC has occasionally referred to the object and purpose in interpreting the Statute.[100]

One of the primary roles of the object and purpose in interpretation is clarifying the ordinary meaning, especially when the text is ambiguous or where confirmation of the meaning of the treaty text is required.[101] From this perspective, the *US–Iran Claims Tribunal* held that the treaty's object and purpose can only be used "to clarify the text, not to provide independent sources of meaning that contradict the clear text."[102] In contrast, Gazzini avers that even where the text has only one clear, possible interpretation, the literal interpretation must still be confirmed against the object and purpose.[103] In this respect, when seeking the ordinary meaning, the first interpretational conclusion reached is analyzed and either confirmed or changed based on the treaty's object and purpose.[104] The basis is that the treaty terms under Article 31(1) should be interpreted to advance the treaty's object and purpose.[105] Notably, the object and purpose may also assist in deciding between different possible interpretations to determine which one best reflects the parties' intentions.[106]

---

96 Gardiner (n 2) 213.

97 Ibid.

98 United Nations *Charter of the United Nations*, 24 October 1945, 1 UNTS XVI.

99 Suhr (n 62) 62.

100 *Judgement on the Prosecutor's Application for Extraordinary Review of Pre-Trial Chamber I's 31 March 2006 Decision Denying Leave to Appeal* (*DRC*) *ICC-01/04-168* (*AC*) *13 July 2006* para 33(Judgment on the Application for Extraordinary Review).

101 Gardiner (n 2) 211; WTO US Import Prohibition of Certain Shrimp (n 74) para 114.

102 *United States Claims Tribunal Federal Reserve Bank of New York v The Islamic Republic of Iran Bank Markazi* (*Decision No DEC 130-A28-FT*), *Case A 28 of 2000* (Iran US Claims Tribunal Rep.5 (USCT) para 58; See also WTO US Import Prohibition of Certain Shrimp (n 74) para 114; Ibid., 211 para 2; Mark E Villiger (n 24) 427 para 14; Tarcisio Gazzini, 'Object and Purpose' (n 91) 180.

103 Tarcisio Gazzini, 'Object and Purpose' (n 91) 174.

104 Sinclair (n 77) 130; *Oil Platforms* (*Islamic Republic of Iran v USA*), *Preliminary Objection, Judgment, ICJ Reports 1996* 815 para 31; Gardiner (n 2) 216–217; Tarcisio Gazzini, 'Object and Purpose' (n 91) 175; See also *Colombian-Peruvian asylum case, Judgment 20 November 1950, ICJ Reports 1950*, 282.

105 Dörr (n 1) 584 para 52.

106 Tarcisio Gazzini, 'Object and Purpose' (n 91) 174, 175.

Further, the object and purpose may guide the interpreter in rectifying an error or inaccuracy in the treaty's text.[107]

Significantly, all the elements of interpretation under Article 31(1) discussed above must be carried out in good faith. Article 31 (1) of the VCLT gives the principle of "good faith" a prominent position by placing it at the opening of the general rule of interpretation, although it is not an independent element in interpretation.[108] Under the good faith perspective, the parties to a treaty are expected to act "honestly, fairly and reasonably and to refrain from taking unfair advantage" of the other parties or situation.[109]

The next section focuses on Article 31(3) on subsequent agreements and subsequent practice of States parties, which is central to the study.

2.2 *Subsequent Agreements and Subsequent Practice under Article 31(3) (a) and (b) of the VCLT*

2.2.1 Relationship between Subsequent Agreements and Subsequent Practice

Subsequent agreements are provided for under Article 31(3)(a) of the VCLT, while subsequent practice is covered under Article 31(3)(b). Article 31(3)(a) provides that there shall be taken into account, together with the context, any subsequent agreement between the parties regarding the interpretation of the treaty or the application of its provisions. On subsequent practice, Article 31(3)(b) states that there shall be taken into account, together with the context, any subsequent practice in the application of the treaty, which establishes the agreement of the parties regarding its interpretation. Subsequent agreements and practice are consequently seen as giving States parties who are the treaty "masters," the foundation to continue playing a role in determining the treaty's meaning.[110] On this basis, a legal foundation may be built for the States Parties to the Rome Statute to continue participating in the Statute's interpretation.

Notably, in analyzing the subsequent agreements and subsequent practice under Article 31(3) of the VCLT, the "agreement" and "practice" sometimes coincide in certain areas, making it difficult to distinguish them.[111] It has

107 Ibid. 174.

108 Gardiner (n 2) 168.

109 Anthony D'Amato, 'Good Faith,' in: Encyclopedia of Public International Law (1992), 599–601.

110 ILC 2018 (n 7) Conclusion 5 Commentary 10; Georg Nolte, 'Treaties and Their Practice: Symptoms of Their Rise or Decline', *Treaties and their Practice* (Brill Nijhoff 2019) 17.

111 ILC 2018 (n 7) Conclusion 4 Commentary 11; Conclusion 1 among others.

been noted that even international courts and tribunals are reluctant to distinguish between subsequent agreements and practice authoritatively.[112] In other instances, "subsequent practice" has been used generally to include both subsequent agreements under Article 31(3)(a) and subsequent practice under Article 31(3)(b) of the VCLT.[113] Therefore, certain aspects may coincide and intersect when discussing subsequent agreements and practice.

2.2.2 Common Features of Subsequent Agreements and Subsequent Practice under Article 31(3)(a) and 31(3)(b) of the VCLT

Both subsequent agreements and subsequent practice under Article 31(3)(a) and (b) of the VCLT are hinged on States parties agreement.[114] Conventionally, agreement means mutual assent, common purpose, or opinion.[115] The ILC has used the term "agreement" to denote the "common understanding" of the parties.[116] In this context, the term "party" borrows from Article 2(1)(g) of the VCLT, where a party is defined as a State that has consented to be bound by the treaty and for which the treaty is in force. The agreement under Article 31 (3)(a) is based on the "agreement between the parties" while under Article 31 (3)(b) it is based on "practice [...] which establishes the agreement of the parties."[117] The ILC stipulates that identifying subsequent agreements or subsequent practice under Article 31(3) consists of determining whether the parties, either through agreement or practice, "have taken a position" regarding the treaty interpretation.[118] The parties' agreement has, therefore, been described as "the normative heart" of both subsequent agreements and subsequent practice.[119] The State parties agreement manifests the consent principle, which forms the foundation of the law of treaties and States sovereign equality.[120]

Significantly, an agreement under both Article 31(3)(a) and 31(3)(b) of the VCLT is "subsequent" to a treaty. The implication is that the agreement was

112 Katharina Berner, *Subsequent Agreements and Subsequent Practice in Domestic Courts* (Springer 2017) 101; ILC 2018 (n 7) Conclusion 4 Commentary 7.

113 ILC 2018 (n 7) Conclusion 4 Commentary 11.

114 Gardiner (n 2) 230.

115 Black law dictionary.

116 ILC 1966 Vol II (n 31) 221–222 para 15.

117 Rahim Moloo, 'When Actions Speak Louder than Words: The Relevance of Subsequent Party Conduct to Treaty Interpretation' (2013) 31 Berkeley Journal of International Law 57.

118 ILC 2018 (n 7) Conclusion 6 para 1.

119 Berner (n 112) 101 para 1.

120 Ian Brownlie and James Crawford, *Brownlie's Principles of Public International Law* (OUP Oxford 2012) 449.

reached after the treaty's conclusion or when the treaty text "has been established as definitive."[121] Since they are reached after the treaty conclusion, subsequent agreements and subsequent practice under Article 31 (3)(a) and (b) of the VCLT are considered essential for determining the current consensual meaning of a treaty.[122] In this context, subsequent agreements and practice recognize the parties' current will instead of their intention at the time of the treaty conclusion, allowing parties to adapt to changing circumstances.[123] Consequently, subsequent agreements and subsequent practice are considered extrinsic to the treaty under interpretation.[124]

It has therefore been observed that subsequent agreements and subsequent practice are two connected notions and "for all practical purposes have the same relevance to the interpretative process."[125] In support, Gardiner states that subsequent practice and subsequent agreements serve the same role in treaty interpretation.[126]

Subsequent agreements and practice may intersect, for instance, where parties reach an informally recorded agreement executed through practice, with the practice giving it the same status as a formal agreement.[127] In defining agreement under Article 31(3)(a) and 31(3)(b), the Arbitral Tribunal in the case of *HICEE v Slovak Republic* held that

> Both refer to processes that amount to a form of agreement between the treaty parties. In sub-paragraph (a), the agreement is *ex hypothesi* conscious and express; in sub-paragraph (b), it arises by implication from the parties' action. A further common feature is that the agreement in

121 ILC 2018 (n 7) Conclusion 4 commentary 2; Linderfalk (n 3) 164.: Article 10 of the VCLT.

122 Dörr (n 1) 561 para 4; Anja Seibert-Fohr, 'The Effect of Subsequent Practice on the European Convention on Human Rights: Considerations from a General International Law Perspective,' *The European Convention on Human Rights and General International Law* (Oxford University Press 2018).

123 Stefan Kadelbach, 'Domestic Constitutional Concerns with Respect to the Use of Subsequent Agreements and Practice at the International Level in Georg Nolte, Treaties and Subsequent Practice' (Oxford University Press 2013) 145 para 1; Luigi Crema, 'Subsequent Agreements and Subsequent Practice within and Outside the Vienna Convention' 17 <https://papers.ssrn.com/abstract=2247544> accessed 27 January 2021.

124 Leena Grover, *Interpreting Crimes in the Rome Statute of the International Criminal Court* (Cambridge University Press 2014) 346.

125 Tarcisio Gazzini, 'Subsequent Agreements and Subsequent Practice, Interpretation of International Investment Treaties' [2016] Oxford Hart Publishing, 201.

126 Gardiner (n 2) 231.

127 Ibid., 232.

> both cases is 'subsequent,' which must, in this context, mean that it supervenes after the conclusion of the treaty itself.[128]

Significantly, subsequent agreements under Articles 31(3)(a) and subsequent practice under Article 31(3)(b) are deemed to represent an "authentic" interpretation on the basis that all parties agree to the interpretation of the treaty terms by means which are external to the treaty.[129] However, the ILC also distinguishes the two. The ILC states that a subsequent agreement "has the effect of constituting an authentic means of interpretation of the treaty, whereas a 'subsequent practice' only has this effect if its different elements, taken together, show 'the common understanding of the parties as to the meaning of the terms.'"[130]

There are, therefore, areas where the agreements under Articles 31(3)(a) and 31(3)(b) are merged or intersect while they differ in other minor areas.

2.2.3 Subsequent Agreements under Article 31(3)(a) of the VCLT

As mentioned, Article 31(3)(a) of the VCLT provides for the taking into account, together with the context, "any subsequent agreement between the parties regarding the interpretation of the treaty or the application of its provisions." Grounding itself on Article 31(3)(a) of the VCLT, the ILC defines a subsequent agreement under Article 31(3)(a) as "an agreement between the parties, reached after the conclusion of a treaty, regarding the interpretation of the treaty or the application of its provisions."[131] As used in Article 31(3)(a), the term agreement focuses on whether parties have reached a consensus regarding the interpretation of the treaty provisions.[132] Gardiner further points out that subsequent agreements may cover specific issues which have arisen between the parties.[133]

The consensus of all treaty parties is vital if the agreement is to be deemed a "subsequent agreement" under Article 31(3)(a) of the VCLT.[134] Therefore, the ILC reiterates that the agreement under Article 31(3)(a) includes "a common act or undertaking between all the parties" or varied "individual acts" demonstrating the parties' common understanding regarding the treaty interpreta-

128 *Hicee V Slovak Republic, PCA Case NO 2009–11, Partial Award* para 134.
129 Mark E Villiger (n 24) 429 para 16.
130 ILC 1966 Vol II (n 31) 222 para 15: ILC 2018 (n 7) Conclusion 4 Commentary 9.
131 ILC 2018 (n 7) Conclusion 4(1).
132 Gardiner (n 2) 244.
133 Ibid., 231.
134 Dörr (n 1) 594 para 74; Mary E O'Connell, Christian J Tams and Dire Tladi, *Self-Defense against Non-State Actors* (Cambridge University Press 2019) 126.

tion.[135] The description of a common act by the ILC appears to put little distinction between subsequent agreements and practice, which also constitutes acts or conduct. However, the consent to a subsequent agreement may sometimes be indirect.[136] Nonetheless, the joint approval or consensus by States parties is deemed to give a declaration or agreement a "high probative value."[137] As an example of a common act, it is observed that the ASP reached a subsequent agreement under Article 31(3)(a) that defined the "Elements of Crimes" under Articles 6–8 of the Rome Statute in a document that was not a treaty.[138]

In the *Convention for the Regulation of Whaling* case, the ICJ emphasized the aspect of consensus. It held that the International Whaling Commission's (IWC) recommendations, "which take the form of resolutions are not binding. However, when adopted by consensus or a unanimous vote, they may be relevant for the interpretation of the Convention or its Schedule."[139] The *Whaling* decision reiterated that where a resolution related to the treaty interpretation is adopted by consensus, it is to be considered an authentic interpretation of the treaty.[140] Additionally, in the *Territorial Dispute* (*Libya v Chad*) case, the ICJ found that an Anglo-French Convention of 1919, which was concluded to interpret an 1899 declaration between the two States, "constituted the correct and binding interpretation of the earlier declaration" since the parties reached a consensus about the treaty.[141]

The ILC has also emphasized consensus, stating that a decision of the Conference of States Parties based on a unanimous vote in which all parties participate constitutes a subsequent agreement under Article 31(3)(a) if it relates to the treaty interpretation.[142] The ILC nevertheless adds that consensus alone is insufficient unless there is also agreement on the substance. In this regard,

---

135 ILC 2018 (n 7) Conclusion 4 Commentary 10; *United States-Measures Concerning the Importation, Marketing Products, and Sale of Tuna and Tuna Products, WTO Appellate Body Report, WT/DS381/AB and WT/DS381/AB/R, adopted 13 June,* para 371.

136 Dörr (n 1) 595 para 76.

137 D M Mcrae, 'The Legal Effect of Interpretative Declarations' [1979] British Yearbook of International Law 169.

138 The Elements of Crimes, ICC-ASP/1/3, Part II-B, Official Records of the Assembly of States Parties to the Rome Statute of the International Criminal Court, First Session, New York, (Sept. 3–10, 2002); Moloo (n 32) 62; Grover (n 78) 365.

139 *ICJ Whaling in the Antarctic (Australia v Japan: New Zealand intervening): Judgment of 31 March 2014* (ICJ) Paras 46 and 83.

140 Dapo Akande and Antonios Tzanakopoulos, 'Treaty Law and ICC Jurisdiction over the Crime of Aggression' (2018) 29 EJIL 945.

141 *ICJ Territorial Dispute (Libya v Chad)* [*1994*] *ICJ Rep 6*, para 60.

142 ILC 2018 (n 7) Conclusion 11 Commentary 28.

the ILC provides that a resolution by a Conference of States Parties constitutes a subsequent agreement or subsequent practice "where there is agreement in substance on the interpretation of the treaty [...] 'including adoption by consensus."[143] The ILC provision has been interpreted to mean that adoption by consensus is necessary but inadequate to warrant a decision or resolution falling under Article 31(3)(a) or (b) of the VCLT unless there is also agreement on the substance.[144]

Using the ILC approach on Conference of States Parties, Akande posits that the Kampala resolution[145] adopted by consensus by the ASP adding the crime of aggression to the ICC's jurisdiction is a subsequent agreement.[146] Akande bases this on the fact that no State Party to the Rome Statute expressed disagreement with the interpretation offered since its adoption, therefore representing agreement in substance.[147] Grover adds that the "Seven interpretive Understandings" accompanying the Kampala Resolution constitute a subsequent agreement under Article 31(3)(a) of the VCLT, having been adopted by consensus at the ASP Review Conference.[148] Consequently, the lack of consensus demonstrated through divergent positions by State parties may lead to the conclusion that there is no agreement relating to the treaty interpretation.[149]

2.2.3.1 *The Form Taken by Agreements*

Regarding the form that agreements should take, it is observed that it is the existence of an agreement between the parties that matters, regardless of what form the agreement takes.[150] In specific reference to the Conference of States Parties, the ILC has reiterated that it is the substance of the agreement by the Conference that is important and not the form or procedure used to arrive at a decision.[151] The study considers the ASP as falling under the Confer-

---

143 Ibid. Conclusion 11 para 3.

144 Akande and Tzanakopoulos (n 140) 946; ILC 2018 (n 7) Conclusion 11 Commentary 30.

145 Kampala Amendments on the Crime of Aggression (Kampala Amendments), Resolution RC/Res. 6, 11 June 2010, reprinted in S Barriga and C Kreß (eds), The Travaux Préparatoires of the Crime of Aggression (2012), at 101–107, available at https://asp.icc-cpi.int/iccdocs/asp_docs/Resolutions/RC-Res.6-ENG.pdf.

146 Akande and Tzanakopoulos (n 140) 947.

147 Ibid.

148 Grover (n 78) 368.

149 Georg Nolte, 'Jurisprudence of the ICJ and Arbitral Tribunals of Ad Hoc Jurisdiction Relating to Subsequent Agreements and Subsequent Practice: Introductory Report for the ILC Study Group on Treaties over Time', *Treaties and Subsequent Practice* (Oxford University Press 2013) 190; ILC 2018 (n 7) Conclusion 10 Commentary 3.

150 Moloo (n 32) 57; ILC 2018 (n 7) Conclusion 6 para 2.

151 ILC 2018 (n 7) Conclusion 11 Commentary 28.

ence of States Parties. Additionally, since Article 31(3)(a) of the VCLT does not require "subsequent agreements" to take any particular form, the agreement can be informal as long as it illustrates the parties' common intention to reach an agreed interpretation.[152]

The ILC has reiterated that a subsequent agreement or practice under Article 31(3) of the VCLT may take different forms.[153] There are consequently no specific requirements on which form an agreement should take.[154] The WTO Appellate Body reinforced this position in the *Measures Affecting the Production and Sale of Clove Cigarettes* (*USA*) case, holding that Article 31(3)(a) of the VCLT does not provide for the form which a subsequent agreement should take.[155] The WTO body emphasized that Article 31(3)(a) of the VCLT referred to the "substance rather than form."[156]

This aspect has been reiterated by the ILC, citing the *IMO Sub-Division for Legal Affairs*, that no specific form is required for subsequent agreements under Article 31(3)(a). The decision specified that "provided the intention is clear, the interpretation could take various forms, including a resolution adopted at a meeting of the parties, or even a decision recorded in the summary records of a meeting of the parties."[157] Subsequent agreements may also consist of instruments expressing the parties' agreement, including adopted interpretative declarations or recommendations through "consensus or unanimous vote."[158]

In addition, since neither the VCLT in Article 31(3)(a) nor the ILC require a written agreement, the agreement may either be oral or written.[159] The lack of formality also extends to the language used in subsequent agreements since legally binding language is not a requirement.[160] In this regard, the tribunal in

152 Gardiner (n 2) 245; Dörr (n 1) 594 para 75.

153 ILC 2018 (n 7) Conclusion 6 para 2.

154 Ibid. Conclusion 10 Commentary 7.

155 *United States – Measures Affecting the Production and Sale of Clove Cigarettes, WTO, Appellate Body Report adopted on 4 April 2012, WT/DS406/AB/R* para 267.

156 Ibid.

157 ILC 2018 (n 7) Conclusion 11 Commentary 12; The IMO Sub-Division of Legal Affairs, document LC 33/J/6, para 3.

158 ILC, 'Guide to Practice on Reservations to Treaties, Report of the ILC on the Work of Its Sixty-Third Session, 2011, Vol II, A/66/10' 35 para 4.7.3 (ILC Guide to Practice on Reservations); *ICJ Whaling in the Antarctic* (*Australia v Japan: New Zealand intervening*)*: Judgment of 31 March 2014* para 46; Tarcisio Gazzini, 'Subsequent Agreements and Subsequent Practice', *Interpretation of International Investment Treaties* (Hart Publishing 2016) 192 para 1.

159 Berner (n 112) 106.

160 Dörr (n 1) 594 para 75.

the *European Molecular Biology Laboratory Arbitration case* (*EMBL vs. Germany*) referred to informal agreements, including letters exchanged between the parties and some guidelines reached, to determine that these constituted subsequent agreements under Article 31(3)(a) of the VCLT.[161]

In the same vein, a subsequent agreement does not have to be part of the treaty nor be in treaty form, but it must clearly show the parties' consensus about an agreed interpretation.[162] The Arbitral Tribunal in the case of *Methanex vs USA*, while citing the *Kasikili/Sedudu* case, held that subsequent agreements under Article 31(3)(a) did not need to fulfill formal requirements similar to those of a treaty since this would result in the agreement "serving no practical purpose."[163] Similarly, the ILC states that if the parties in a bilateral treaty "agree on an interpretation, that interpretation prevails and itself takes on the nature of a treaty regardless of its form."[164]

In a divergent opinion, Moloo suggests that some formality is required under Article 31(3)(a) of the VCLT to distinguish agreements covered by Article 31(3)(a) and those under 31(3)(b).[165] Moloo argues that when parties record their agreement in writing, this falls under Article 31(3)(a).[166] He consequently suggests that subsequent agreements should hold more interpretative weight than subsequent practice on the basis that subsequent agreements under Article 31(3)(a) require a higher and stricter evidentiary threshold to establish party agreement compared to subsequent practice under Article 31(3)(b).[167] Related to this view, some scholars have suggested that when the subsequent agreement is less formal, it is more likely to be treated as subsequent practice.[168] However, the ILC and the VCLT have not indicated any hierarchy between subsequent agreements and practice.

---

161 *European Molecular Biology Laboratory Arbitration case* (*EMBL Vs Germany*) *Award of 29 June 1990 105 ILR* 54–56.

162 Gardiner (n 2) 245,247; Anthony Aust, Handbook *of International Law* (2nd edn, Cambridge University Press 2010) 85 para 3.

163 *International Arbitration under Chapter 11 of the North American Free Trade Agreement and the UNCITRAL Arbitration rules, Methanex vs USA* (*Merits*)*, Award of 3rd August 2005 44 ILM* part 11 Chapter B 8–10 para 20.

164 ILC Guide to Practice on Reservations (n 158) Guideline 1.6. 3 Commentary para 2 Addendum to report.

165 Moloo (n 32) 58.

166 Ibid., 59; See also North American Free Trade Agreement, USA-Canada-Mexico, Dec. 17 1992, Article 1131, 2001(2)(b) (the parties wrote down their common understanding of the meaning of Article 1105 of NAFTA recognized as a subsequent agreement under Article 31(3) (a).

167 Ibid., 58.

168 Dörr (n 1) 594 para 75.

2.2.4 Subsequent Practice under Article 31(3)(b) of the VCLT

Under Article 31(3)(b) of the VCLT, there shall be taken into account, together with the context, "any subsequent practice in the application of the treaty, which establishes the agreement of the parties regarding its interpretation." The ILC, in elaboration, states that a subsequent practice under Article 31(3)(b) involves conduct in the treaty's application after the treaty's conclusion, which establishes the parties' agreement regarding the treaty's interpretation.[169] In summary, Article 31(3)(b) requires that for subsequent practice to be applicable in treaty interpretation, it has to meet four requirements, including that the act or omission must be considered as a "practice," which practice must relate to the treaty application.[170] Further, the practice must be "subsequent," and it must establish the parties agreement regarding its interpretation.[171] Consequently, a practice that does not entail the application of the treaty and does not show the agreement of all the parties on interpreting a treaty term does not fall under subsequent practice in Article 31(3)(b) of the VCLT.[172]

Subsequent practice is construed as the demonstrated evidence of the parties' intention to give a particular interpretation to a treaty provision.[173] Subsequent practice is also taken as the treaty's "common-sense, practical interpretation," keeping current and future occurrences into account.[174] Article 31(3)(b) uses the phrase "any subsequent practice in the application of the treaty." Application in this context comprises "conduct by which the rights under a treaty are exercised, or its obligations are complied with, in full or in part."[175]

Despite using the word "practice," the VCLT has not defined the type of practice relevant for purposes of Article 31(3)(b).[176] On the other hand, Dorr defines practice as "any external behavior of a subject of international law…

169 ILC 2018 (n 7) Conclusion 4 para 2.

170 Linderfalk (n 3) 165; ILC 2018 (n 7) Conclusion 6 Commentary 3 and 4.

171 Ibid; ILC 2018 (n 7) Conclusion 6 Commentary 3 and 4.

172 Y Dinstein, 'Interaction between Customary International Law and Treaties' (2006) 322 Recueil des Cours de l'Academie de Droit International 408 cited in Grover, Interpreting crimes 387; Richard K Gardiner, *Treaty Interpretation 2008* (Oxford University Press 2008) 226.

173 Julian Arato, 'Subsequent Practice and Evolutive Interpretation: Techniques of Treaty Interpretation over Time and Their Diverse Consequences (September 29, 2010), Law & Practice of International Courts and Tribunals, Vol. 9, No. 3, 2010' 461.

174 Gerald P McGinley, 'Practice as a Guide to Treaty Interpretation' [1985] The Fletcher Forum 227 para 4 <https://dl.tufts.edu/pdfviewer/cz30q377g/3j333c56k> accessed 25 December 2020.

175 ILC 2018 (n 7) Conclusion 6 Commentary 3.

176 Gerald P McGinley, 'Practice as a Guide to Treaty Interpretation' (1985) 9 Fletcher Forum 214.

insofar as it is potentially revealing of what the party accepts as the meaning of a particular treaty provision."[177] Subsequent practice, therefore, includes all relevant conduct by the treaty parties that aids in identifying an agreement of the treaty parties' regarding the treaty interpretation.[178] Notably, the conduct may consist of positive actions or omissions, including relevant silence of the State parties, which contribute to establishing an agreement.[179]

Arato points out that subsequent practice may additionally show evidence of the parties' intention to interpret and reinterpret the treaty.[180] Reinterpretation may include strengthening or declining a previous interpretation by giving a new interpretation that varies or contradicts the earlier meaning.[181] Besides interpretation and reinterpretation, the subsequent practice may also determine the limits of applying a treaty.[182]

Requiring that practice should be towards the treaty application is construed to mean that the treaty under interpretation and the one to which the practice relates must be the same.[183] Additionally, conduct by treaty parties should be based on a treaty obligation, otherwise, it will not be deemed as being in the treaty's application or as related to its interpretation.[184] Judge Holtzmann reiterated this in his dissenting opinion in the *Iran-US Tribunal Claims* case, holding that

> Subsequent conduct by a State party is a proper basis for interpreting a treaty only if it appears that the conduct was motivated by the treaty [...] in the absence of any indication that conduct was motivated by the treaty, it is incorrect to use that conduct in interpreting the treaty.[185]

177 Dörr (n 1) 597 para 79.

178 ILC 2018 (n 7) Conclusion 4 Commentary 11.

179 Ibid. Conclusion 4 Commentary 17; Dörr (n 1) 597 para 79; *Case concerning Military and Paramilitary Activities in and against Nicaragua (Nicaragua v. United States of America), Jurisdiction and Admissibility, Judgment, ICJ Reports 1984* at 410 para 39; *Case concerning the Temple of Preah Vihear (Cambodia v Thailand), Merits, Judgment of 15 June 1962, ICJ Reports 1962* at 23.

180 Julian Arato, 'Subsequent Practice and Evolutive Interpretation: Techniques of Treaty Interpretation over Time and Their Diverse Consequences' (2010) 9 No. 3 The Law & Practice of International Courts and Tribunals 461.

181 Ibid.

182 Dörr (n 1) 598 para 82.

183 Berner (n 112) 128.

184 ILC 2018 (n 7) Conclusion 6 Commentary 7.

185 *Islamic Republic of Iran and United States of America, Iran-United States Claims Tribunal Reports, Partial Award No. 382-B1-FT (1988)* Separate Opinion of Judge Holtzmann, Concurring in Part, Dissenting in Part, para 22.

In identifying what constitutes subsequent practice, the type of practice is examined next. This analysis will assist in construing what ASP actions or States Parties conduct can be considered subsequent practice for purposes of the Rome Statute's interpretation.

2.2.4.1 *Forms of Practice*

As stated earlier, the VCLT does not define the type of conduct making up subsequent practice. However, examples of State practice construed as relevant to interpretation may include "diplomatic and other official correspondence; press releases, [...] votes on resolutions in international organizations, written submissions to international courts or tribunals; decisions by domestic courts, drafts of Statutes, reports and parliamentary material" among others.[186] Other practice may include relying on treaty provisions to justify a State's choice of action,[187] the adoption of legislation,[188] enforcement grounded on a treaty,[189] and failing to act based on treaty provisions.[190] Though uncommon, a State's argument in a legal dispute[191] has also been deemed as subsequent practice. Additional forms of conduct recognized include the exchange of letters and *notes verbales*.[192] The list is, therefore, non-exhaustive.[193]

Besides the positive action, it has been recognized that subsequent practice may take an inactive form.[194] Reiterating this point, the ILC avers that the silence of one or more parties can constitute acceptance of the subsequent practice when the circumstances call for some reaction.[195] However, silence or inaction has raised varied and sometimes conflicting interpretations in proving agreement.[196]

---

186 Dörr (n 1) 597 para 79; In the matter of an UNCITRAL Arbitration, Decision on Jurisdiction between National Grid v Argentina 20 June 2006 para 85 (on diplomatic notes).

187 The Chamizal Case (Mexico/United States), Award by the International Boundary Commission, 15 June 1911, 11 RIAA 309, 328.

188 *Maritime Dispute (Peru v Chile), ICJ Reports,* Judgment of 27 January 2014, para 119.

189 Ibid. para 126.

190 Linderfalk (n 3) 165; ILC, Seventieth session, Draft Conclusions on identification of Customary International law, 2018 Conclusion 10 para 3 and Commentary 8.

191 ILC 2018 (n 7) Conclusion 4 Commentary 18.

192 Gruslin v Malaysia, ICSID ARB/99/3, Award 27 November 2000 para 23.4.

193 Irina Buga, *Modification of Treaties by Subsequent Practice* (1st edition, OUP Oxford 2018) 25.

194 ILC 2018 (n 7) Conclusion 4 Commentary 4.

195 Ibid. Conclusion 10 para 2 Commentary 14.

196 See *Dispute between Argentina and Chile concerning the Beagle Channel, RIAA, 18 February 1977, Volume XXI* 187 para 169 (a); *Assange (Appellant) v The Swedish Prosecution Authority (Respondent), Judgment, Easter Term* (2012) *UKSC 22 On appeal from* (2011)

Nonetheless, what is considered necessary is not the form of practice but the existence of the parties' agreement regarding the treaty's interpretation as required by Article 31(3)(b) of the VCLT.[197]

As an example of subsequent practice by States Parties to the Rome Statute, the Appeal's Chamber in the *Tadic* case found that the adoption of the Statute by States which were present at the Rome Diplomatic Conference and the further affirmation by the Committee of the UN General Assembly constituted State practice.[198] Therefore, the practice to be considered under Article 31(3)(b) depends on the treaty's subject matter.[199]

2.2.4.2 *The Place of Subsequent Practice in Interpretation*

Subsequent practice has been used in interpretation by several international courts and tribunals. For instance, the ICJ in the *Kasikili/Sedudu Island* case acknowledged that "when called upon to interpret the provisions of a treaty, the court has itself frequently examined the subsequent practice of the parties in the application of that treaty."[200] The ICJ in the *Kasikili/Sedudu Island* case further referred to the parties' subsequent practice, holding that

> Those events cannot, therefore, constitute "subsequent practice in the application of the treaty (of 1890) which establishes the agreement of the parties regarding its interpretation" (1969 Vienna Convention on the Law of Treaties, Art 31 para 3(b).[201]

EWHC Admin 2849 118, para 131; *Dispute regarding Navigational and Related Rights* (*Costa Rica v Nicaragua*), *Separate Opinion of Judge Skotnikov 13th July 2009* (ICJ) 285 para 10; *Appellate Body Report WTO, European Communities – Customs Classification of Frozen Boneless Chicken Cuts, WT/DS269/AB/R, WT/DS286/AB/R, WT/DS269/AB/R/Corr.1, WT/DS286/AB/R/Corr.1* (*adopted 12 Sept 2005*) para 272 (where silence was construed to establish agreement). In contrast, silence as establishing agreement was rejected in *Question of the Delimitation of the Continental Shelf between Nicaragua and Colombia beyond 200 Nautical Miles from the Nicaraguan Coast* (*Nicaragua v Colombia*), *Preliminary Objections, Judgment, ICJ Reports 2016* Rep 100 para 44; *Chile - Price Band System and Safeguard Measures Relating to Certain Agricultural Products, WTO Panel Report WT/DS207/R, 3 May 2002* para 7.78–7.79.

197 Buga (n 193) 25.

198 *The Prosecutor v Dusko Tadic Case No ICTY-94-1-A, Appeals Chamber Judgement, 15 July 1999* para 223.

199 Dörr (n 1) 597 para 79.

200 Kasikili/Sedudu (n 1) 1076 para 50.

201 Ibid., 1087 para 63.

Equally, Hudson, who, even though referring mainly to the UN organs vis-avi the role of the ICJ, gave prominence to subsequent State practice averring that

> No great international instrument is ever completely self-explanatory, and meaning needs to be given to its provisions, not so much by the rulings of judges on the bench as by the experience of those who have the responsibility of making the instrument work.[202]

While the role of subsequent practice in treaty interpretation is acknowledged, it also has limitations since it is challenging to evaluate the practice of many States in a multilateral treaty and determine how to deal with the varied practice.[203] It is especially challenging because the State practice is usually confidential and may not be documented or publicized.[204] It is pointed out that subsequent practice in interpretation is therefore subjective and inconsistent, with some judges giving importance to State parties conduct while others ignore the same conduct. [205]

2.2.4.3 *Whose Practice?*

Notably, the ILC specifically discusses the authors of subsequent agreements and practice under the title of subsequent practice.[206] Nevertheless, the same "authors" also apply to subsequent agreements under Article 31(3)(a). This position is in tandem with the view that subsequent practice is sometimes used generally to include both subsequent agreements and practice under Article 31(3)(a) and 3(b)of the VCLT.[207]

The main emphasis, as phrased under Article 31(3)(a) and (b) of the VCLT and elaborated by the ILC, is that the agreements and practice in question have to be that of the treaty parties.[208] The ILC has emphasized that subse-

---

202 Manley O Hudson, 'The Twenty-Sixth Year of the World Court' (1948) 42 American Journal of International Law 16.

203 Sean D Murphy, 'The Relevance of Subsequent Agreement and Subsequent Practice for the Interpretation of Treaties' in Georg Nolte (ed), *Treaties and Subsequent Practice*, vol 82 (Oxford University Press 2013) 12; ILC 2018 (n 7) Conclusion 10 Commentary 18.

204 Buga (n 193) 27.

205 A Mark Weisburd, 'The International Court of Justice and the Concept of State Practice' (2009) 31 U Pa J Int'l L 348; *LaGrand (Germany v United States of America) ICJ Rep, 27 June 2001* 550; Gerald P McGinley, 'Practice as a Guide to Treaty Interpretation' (1985) 9 Fletcher Forum 219.

206 ILC 2018 (n 7) Conclusion 5.

207 Ibid. Conclusion 4 Commentary 11.

208 Ibid. Conclusion 4 paras 1, 2 and 3.

quent practice under Articles 31 and 32 constitutes State parties conduct in the treaty application, whether in the exercise of its executive, legislative, judicial, or other functions.[209] The *Iran-US Claims Tribunal*, similar to the ILC, has reiterated that subsequent practice "must be a practice of the parties to the treaty."[210] In this regard, the tribunal rejected the conduct of United States (US) banks that were not government entities and whose practice could not be attributed to the US government.[211] The role of State parties as the main creators of subsequent practice is a recognition that parties are the masters of the treaty who are ultimately responsible for its application.[212]

In line with the centrality of State parties, the ILC has recognized explicitly that decisions of a Conference of States Parties constitute subsequent agreements and practice under Article 31(3) or supplementary means under Article 32 of the VCLT.[213] The ILC defines a Conference of States Parties as a meeting of parties to a treaty to review or implement the treaty.[214] On this basis, the study concludes that the ASP, which constitutes representatives of all States Parties that have ratified the Rome Statute,[215] forms an example of a Conference of States Parties. Under Articles 112 and 51 of the Rome Statute, the ASP has the mandate to review or amend the Rome Statute and the Rules and ensure the implementation of the Statute. Some scholars have contended that the Conferences of Parties to any Convention are the "ultimate authority as to its interpretation."[216] Nevertheless, the decisions of a Conference of States Parties, while embodying subsequent agreements or practice, are not considered by the ILC as necessarily legally binding, but they can be a source of authoritative treaty interpretation.[217]

The book mainly revolves around the ASP decisions, resolutions, and amendments and whether they constitute subsequent agreements and practice.

---

209 Ibid. Conclusion 5 para 1.

210 Iran-United States Claims Tribunal, *United States of America et al. v. Islamic Republic of Iran et al.*, Award No. 108-A-16/582/591-FT, *Iran-United States Claims Tribunal Reports*, Vol. 5 (1984) para 38.

211 Ibid. para 39.

212 ILC 2018 (n 7) Conclusion 5, Commentary 10.

213 Ibid. Conclusion 11 para 2.

214 Ibid. Conclusion 11(1).

215 'Assembly of States Parties' (*International Criminal Court*) <https://www.icc-cpi.int/asp> accessed 13 February 2023.

216 ILC 2018 (n 7) Conclusion 5 Commentary 22; Report of the Conference of the Parties to the Basel Convention on the Control of Transboundary Movements of Hazardous Wastes and Their Disposal on its tenth meeting (Cartagena, Colombia, 17–21 October 2011), UNEP/CHW.10/28 para 65.

217 Ibid. Conclusion 5 Commentary 14.

The legal effect of the Conference of States Parties decisions on treaty interpretation within the ILC context is therefore significant since this directly affects the place and weight of ASP decisions and resolutions if construed as subsequent agreements and practice by the ICC. With the study having taken the position that the ASP falls under the Conference of States Parties, Akande reiterates that an ASP resolution is a statement of the parties to the Rome Statute.[218] Akande asserts that an ASP resolution that expressly seeks to give meaning to the Rome Statute provisions and their application in specific circumstances becomes the practice of the States Parties regarding the interpretation of the Statute.[219]

Based on State parties being the primary producers of subsequent agreements and practice, non-state actors and other players can only aid in assessing subsequent conduct if their actions are attributable to the State party.[220] In this regard, it is noted that Article 31(3)(b) of the VCLT contemplates the practice of States but not of international organizations.[221] It is consequently averred that unless the treaty expressly provides otherwise, the role of non-state actors is only indirectly relevant to subsequent practice.[222] In this respect, other conduct, including for non-state actors, does not constitute subsequent practice under Articles 31 and 32, but it may be relevant only to "assess" the parties' subsequent practice.[223] To this extent, it is suggested that relevant agreements or practice is not confined to that of States[224], but it has to be attributable to State parties.

For instance, while the ILC has recognized States parties as the primary creators of subsequent agreements and practice, it also mentions that pronouncements by expert treaty bodies "may give rise to, or refer to" a subsequent agreement or subsequent practice by parties under Article 31(3) or subsequent practice under Article 32.[225] From this perspective, while the conduct

---

218 Akande and Tzanakopoulos (n 140) 944.

219 Ibid.

220 Georg Nolte, 'Treaties and Their Practice: Symptoms of Their Rise or Decline', *Treaties and their Practice* (Brill Nijhoff 2019) 194–195; ILC 2018 (n 7) Conclusion 5 Commentary 10 and Conclusion 6 Commentary 22.

221 Gardiner, *Treaty Interpretation 2008* (n 172) 246.

222 Luigi Crema, 'Subsequent Agreements and Subsequent Practice within and Outside the Vienna Convention in Treaties and Subsequent Practice.' in Georg Nolte (ed) (Oxford University Press 2013) 26.

223 ILC 2018 (n 7) Conclusion 5 para 3.

224 Buga (n 193) 35.

225 ILC 2018 (n 7) Conclusion 13 para 3.

of non-state actors or international organizations may reflect or initiate the parties subsequent practice, it should not be treated as being similar to the practice by the treaty parties.[226] In this respect, resolutions of plenary bodies of international organizations may constitute subsequent agreements or subsequent practice under Article 31(3)(a) and (b) of the VCLT, where they can be attributed to States.[227] Based on this approach, the ICJ in the *Whaling in the Antarctic* case considered the effect of resolutions of the International Whaling Commission (IWC), a plenary body, on interpreting the Whaling Convention.[228]

Similarly, pronouncements and judicial decisions of international courts and tribunals are deemed only indirectly relevant for identifying subsequent agreements and subsequent practice where they "reflect, give rise to, or refer" to subsequent agreements and practice of the parties themselves.[229] However, scholars appear to differ on the place of judicial decisions. From one perspective, the judiciary, through its decisions, laws, and speeches such as that of the ICTY, ICTR, and ICC, are deemed sources and not creators of subsequent practice.[230] Nevertheless, with respect to the ICC, some authors argue that since States Parties empowered judges to interpret the crimes in the Rome Statute, their decisions are a subsequent practice where the States Parties agreement can be established.[231] Grover also refers to Article 21(2) of the Rome Statute, which allows the ICC to refer to its previous decisions, to argue that the Statute treats the ICC's jurisprudence as subsequent practice, which the judges may but are not obliged to take into account.[232]

However, the study focuses primarily on ASP resolutions and amendments under the Conference of State Parties, States Parties conduct, and court decisions, not on other international organizations or non-State actors.

---

226 Ibid. Conclusion 5 Commentary 12.

227 Akande and Tzanakopoulos (n 140) 945.

228 Whaling in the Antarctic (Australia v. Japan: New Zealand intervening), Judgment, 31 March 2014, ICJ Reports (2014) 226; International Convention for the Regulation of Whaling 1946, 161 UNTS 72.

229 ILC 2018 (n 7) Conclusion 3 Commentary 11.

230 Grover (n 78) 387; Gardiner (n 2) 258; Georg Nolte, 'Second Report, Jurisprudence under Special Regimes Relating to Subsequent Agreements and Subsequent Practice' in Nolte G (ed), *Treaties and Subsequent Practice* (Oxford University Press, 2013) 210.

231 Grover (n 78) 388; Gardiner (n 2) 258; International Law Association, Committee on International Human Rights Law and Practice, 'Final Report on the Impact of the Findings of the United Nations Human Rights Treaty Bodies', Berlin Conference (2004) 6–7..

232 Grover (n 78) 388.

2.2.4.4 *The Practice of All or Some Parties?*

On the number of parties required to participate in the practice, the ILC provides that "the number of parties that must actively engage in subsequent practice in order to establish an agreement under Article 31, paragraph 3 (b), may vary."[233] It follows from the provision that the ILC does not require all parties to engage in a particular practice, but the nonparticipants should also have accepted the practice as relating to the treaty interpretation.[234] In this regard, it is noted that the ILC dropped the word 'all' parties, contained in an earlier draft, to remove the notion that the practice had to be actively performed by all the parties.[235] Notably, there must be strong evidence that the parties who did not participate have consented to that practice as being applicable to the treaty interpretation.[236]

Using this approach, Akande contended that the New York resolution adopted by the ASP by consensus, attributing the ICC jurisdiction for the aggression crime under the Rome Statute, did not necessarily represent subsequent practice establishing the agreement of all the parties under Article 31 (3)(b) of the VCLT.[237] Akande contended that not all parties were present, and some of those absent subsequently differed with some provisions adopted.[238] The need for acceptance by all parties was reiterated in the partly dissenting opinion of Judges Spano, Nicolaou, Bianku, and Kalaydjieva in the case of *Hassan vs UK*, where the judges held that

> Article 31(3)(b) of the Vienna Convention must be understood to cover only subsequent practice *common to all parties*, as well as requiring that the practice be concordant, common and consistent.[239]

Similarly, the WTO Appellate Body reiterated that the conduct of only one of the parties "may be relevant" but has "limited value than the practice of all parties."[240]

---

233 ILC 2018 (n 7) Conclusion 10 para 2 Commentary 14.

234 ILC 1966 Vol II (n 31) 222 para 15; *European Communities-Customs Classification of Frozen Boneless Chicken Cuts, WTO Appellate Body Report, WT/DS269/AB/R, WT/DS286/AB/R, 12 September 2005* para 259; Dörr (n 1) 599 para 84.

235 ILC 1966 Vol II (n 31) Commentary to Article 27, 222, para 15; Ibid.

236 Ibid., 601 para 87.

237 Akande and Tzanakopoulos (n 140) 946.

238 Ibid.

239 ECtHR Hassan case Vs United Kingdom (n 23) Partly Dissenting Opinion of Judge Spano, Joined by Judges Nicolaou, Bianku and Kalaydjieva, 16 September 2014 para 13.

240 *European Communities-Customs Classification of Certain Computer Equipment WTO Appellate Body Report WT/DS62/AB/R WT/DS67/AB/R WT/DS68/AB/R, 5 June 1998* para 93.

Nonetheless, the evidence of State practice is considered difficult to find since it remains unpublished by most States.[241] It has consequently been contended that proof that international courts and tribunals treat subsequent practice as a vital element of treaty interpretation is limited and uncommon.[242]

2.2.4.5 *Agreement under Article 31(3)(B) of the VCLT*

What an agreement under Article 31(3)(b) of the VCLT entails has not been well defined.[243] As noted earlier, Article 31(3)(b) provides for the taking into account, together with the context, any subsequent practice in the application of the treaty, which establishes the agreement of the parties regarding its interpretation. The VCLT does not give a particular form on how an agreement should be manifested.[244] Consequently, acceptance may be construed from a party's reaction, silence, or lack of reaction to the practice, as held in the *Chicken Cuts* case by the WTO Appellate Body.[245] The consent may include "acquiescence, informal approval, and the will to comply," which can be established from accepting the decisions taken.[246]

Additionally, no objection should have been raised.[247] In line with this, the ICJ in the *Whaling in the Antarctic (Australia v Japan)* case held that where agreement is expressed through the adoption of instruments by treaty organs, the adoption should be through consensus or unanimous vote with all States parties supporting it.[248] Akande consequently notes that the implication of the ICJ decision in the *Whaling* case was that where relevant resolutions are

241 'Yearbook of the ILC, 1964 Vol I, 11 May-24 July 1964' 275 para 2.

242 Sean D Murphy (n 203) 4, 5.

243 Dörr (n 1) 602 para 88.

244 *Case Concerning a dispute between Argentina and Chile Concerning the Beagle Channel, UNRIAA, vol XXI, Part II 18 February 1977* at 187 para 169(a).

245 *Appellate Body Report WTO, European Communities – Customs Classification of Frozen Boneless Chicken Cuts, WT/DS269/AB/R, WT/DS286/AB/R, WT/DS269/AB/R/Corr1, WT/DS286/AB/R/Corr1 (adopted 12 Sept 2005)* 106 para 272; Akande and Tzanakopoulos (n 140) 949.

246 Stefan Kadelbach, *Domestic Constitutional Concerns with respect to the use of Subsequent agreements and Practice at the International level, in Georg Nolte, Treaties and Subsequent Practice, Oxford University Press 2013* 152 para 4.

247 ILC 1966 Vol II (n 31) 225 para 15; *Dispute between Argentina and Chile concerning the Beagle Channel, RIAA, 18 February 1977, Volume XXI* paras 168–169; Mark E Villiger (n 24) 431 para 22.

248 *ICJ Whaling in the Antarctic (Australia v Japan: New Zealand intervening): Judgment of 31 March 2014* (ICJ) para 46, 83.

adopted with the consent of all States parties, they may be considered by the court in interpretation under Article 31(3)(a) or (b) of the VCLT.[249]

In the same vein, it has been stated that proof of agreement can be determined from "the consistent and concordant practice of the parties."[250] It is generally agreed that State parties consistent and frequent practice carries more weight in interpretation.[251] Consistency in practice is said to be established through "a sequence of facts or acts" and is not based on an "isolated fact or act or several individual applications."[252] Notably, even where the conduct is common and consistent, it only becomes relevant under Article 31(3)(b) of the VCLT if the parties consider their conduct to fall within the treaty application and in accomplishing the treaty requirements.[253]

In contrast, some courts and scholars argue that neither the VCLT nor the ILC stipulate that there has to be consistency in the practice but were focused on whether the practice by the parties demonstrated a "common understanding."[254] The study aligns with the argument that one persuasive way of proving agreement in conduct would be through the consistency of practice among treaty parties. Consequently, where the practice is by one or more States but fails to establish agreement by all treaty parties, it may instead apply as a supplementary means of interpretation under Article 32 of the VCLT.[255]

2.3 *Supplementary Means of Interpretation under Article 32 of the VCLT*

2.3.1 General

Article 32 of the VCLT provides for supplementary means of interpretation, stating that "recourse may be had to supplementary means of interpretation, including the preparatory work of the treaty and the circumstances of its conclusion." Article 32 further states that the resort would be "to confirm the meaning resulting from the application of Article 31, or to determine the meaning when the interpretation according to Article 31(a) leaves the mean-

249 Akande and Tzanakopoulos (n 140) 945.

250 Gardiner, Treaty Interpretation 2008 (n 172) xxix; Sinclair (n 77) 137 para 6; *Japan Taxes on Alcoholic Beverages, WTO Appellate Body WT/DS8/AB/R; WT/DS10/AB/R; WT/DS11/AB/R, AB-1996–2, 4 October 1996* 12–13..

251 'Yearbook of the ILC 1964, Vol II, A/CN.4/SER.A/1964/ADD.1' 59 para 24; Seibert-Fohr (n 38).

252 Sinclair (n 77) 137 para 6.

253 Dörr (n 1) 598 para 81.

254 Gardiner (n 2) 256; Linderfalk (n 3) 166; ILC 1966 Vol II (n 31) 222 para 15; Robert Kolb cited in Georg Nolte, *Treaties and Subsequent Practice* (OUP Oxford 2013) 310–311..

255 ILC 2018 (n 7) Commentary to Conclusion 2 para 8; Dörr (n 1) 603 para 90.

ing ambiguous or obscure or (b) leads to a result which is manifestly absurd or unreasonable."

Article 32, similar to Article 31(2) and 31(3), refers to external material introduced into the context of the treaty interpretation, albeit carrying less weight.[256] Based on the text as the authentic expression of the States parties' agreement, the means of interpretation under Article 32 are supplementary and considered as having lower dependability.[257] For instance, Grover discourages the reference to the preparatory material of the Rome Statute, which falls under Article 32, because the existing material constitutes too many pages, some of which are incomplete in certain aspects and are not readily available.[258]

Article 32 is deemed applicable only after the general rule of interpretation in Article 31 has been applied and found inadequate and not before.[259] However, the language in Article 32 of the VCLT and the ILC provisions do not make it obligatory for the interpreter to resort to supplementary means to confirm the interpretation reached based on Article 31.[260] Notably, the ILC has acknowledged that the Article 32 list is not exhaustive of all supplementary interpretation means.[261]

It is consequently noted that the lack of an exhaustive list of supplementary means under Article 32 and the failure to provide a criterion for identifying the means leaves a broad discretion to the interpreter to ascertain what is relevant and applicable.[262] In this respect, subsequent agreements and practice have not been mentioned under Article 32 as supplementary interpretation means. However, the ILC has indicated that where the subsequent agreements and practice do not meet the conditions under Article 31(3)(a) and (b) of the VCLT, they may fall under Article 32 of the VCLT as supplementary means.[263]

256 Ibid., 617 para 1; Gardiner (n 2) 348.

257 Mark E Villiger (n 24) 447 para 11; Linderfalk (n 3) 153.

258 Grover (n 78) 72.

259 Dörr (n 1) 618 para 4.

260 Tarcisio Gazzini, 'Supplementary Means', *Interpretation of International Investment Treaties* (Oxford Hart Publishing 2016) 245; ILC 1966 Vol II (n 31) 218 para 4.

261 ILC 2018 (n 7) Conclusion 2 Commentary 8.

262 Allain Pellet, 'Canons of Interpretation under the Vienna Convention' in Joseph Klingler, et al (ed), *Between the Lines of the Vienna Convention? Canons and Other Principles of Interpretation in Public International Law* (Kluwer Law International BV 2018) 8; Tarcisio Gazzini, 'Supplementary Means', *Interpretation of International Investment Treaties* (Oxford Hart Publishing 2016) 261.

263 Mark E Villiger (n 24) 432 para 1; Dörr (n 1) 603 para 90.

2.3.2 Subsequent Agreements and Subsequent Practice as Supplementary Means of Interpretation

As noted earlier, Article 32 of the VCLT does not mention subsequent agreements or practice among the supplementary means. Nevertheless, elaborating on Article 32 of the VCLT, the ILC has determined that certain subsequent agreements and practice which do not meet the requirements under Article 31(3)(a) and (b), such as not meeting the agreement of "all" parties, will fall under Article 32 instead.[264] Based on the ILC provisions, where only some and not all treaty parties reach an agreement or establish a practice regarding the treaty interpretation, this would fall under Article 32 of the VCLT as supplementary means.[265] As an example, Akande has argued that based on the divergent views regarding the ASP's New York resolution on the crime of aggression,[266] the Resolution constitutes a supplementary subsequent agreement and practice falling under Article 32 of the VCLT.[267]

Following the same approach, the partly dissenting opinions of Judges Spano, Nicolaou, Bianku, and Kalaydjieva in the *Hassan* vs *UK* case found that

> The Court has been rather cautious in its application of the subsequent practice rule, as Article 31(3)(b) of the Vienna Convention must be understood to cover only subsequent practice common to all Parties, as well as requiring that the practice be concordant, common and consistent. The subsequent practice of States Parties which does not fulfill these criteria may only constitute a supplementary means of interpretation of a treaty.[268]

The ILC states that supplementary practice under Article 32 carries less weight and cannot be considered an "authentic" interpretation similar to the subsequent practice under Article 31(3) (b).[269]

264 ILC 2018 (n 7) Conclusion 3 Commentary 12.

265 ILC 2018 (n 7) Conclusion 4 Commentary 12; Mark E Villiger (n 24) 432 para 1; Dörr (n 1) 603 para 90.

266 New York Resolution, ICC-ASP/16/Res.5, Activation of the jurisdiction of the Court over the Crime of Aggression, 14 December 2017.

267 Akande and Tzanakopoulos (n 140) 949; Nikolas Stürchler, 'The Activation of the Crime of Aggression in Perspective' (*EJIL: Talk!*, 26 January 2018) <https://www.ejiltalk.org/the-activation-of-the-crime-of-aggression-in-perspective/> accessed 20 April 2022.

268 ECtHR Hassan V United Kingdom (n 23) *Partly Dissenting Opinion of Judge Spano, Joined by Judges Nicolaou, Bianku and Kalaydjieva* at 13.

269 ILC 2018 (n 7) Conclusion 3 Commentary 12.

The probative value of subsequent agreements or subsequent practice in interpretation also depends on how clear and precise the agreement or practice is.[270] Consequently, the failure to meet the "clear and precise" requirement means that the practice could be considered supplementary and fall under Article 32 of the VCLT and not 31(3)(b).[271] Seibert also suggests that State practice that is not uniform falls under Article 32.[272] Additionally, some scholars include "subsequent practice," which was not strictly by State parties or which is unrelated to the treaty application as falling under Article 32.[273] The State parties' infrequent conduct or conduct applied once would also fall under Article 32, and not under Article 31(3)(b).[274]

Several effects are proposed for the supplementary agreements and practice as indicated under Article 32. It has been pointed out that the subsequent practice under Article 32 will be primarily used to confirm the meaning resulting from the application of Article 31.[275] The WTO Appellate Body reiterated this position in *China-Measures Affecting Trading Rights and Distribution Services for Certain Publications and Audiovisual Entertainment Products*, where recourse was made to supplementary practice to confirm the initial meaning of "sound recording" distribution services' arrived at by applying Article 31.[276] Similarly, in the *Kasikili/Sedudu* case, the ICJ reviewed a report by a technical expert contracted by one party,[277] holding that the conduct did not amount to subsequent practice under Article 31(3)(b) but could support deductions reached by the court through other interpretation means.[278] Impliedly, the conduct was construed as falling under supplementary means in Article 32 of the VCLT despite the court not explicitly stating so.[279]

Other uses of subsequent practice under Article 32 include clarifying the treaty's meaning, similar to subsequent practice under Article 31(3)(b).[280] Subsequent practice under Article 32 may also be used to resolve possible con-

270 Ibid. Conclusion 9 para 1.
271 Dörr (n 1) 597 para 79.
272 Seibert-Fohr (n 38).
273 Oliver Dörr and Kirsten Schmalenbach (eds), *Vienna Convention on the Law of Treaties: A Commentary* (Springer-Verlag 2012) 581.
274 ILC 2018 (n 7) Conclusion 4 Commentary 33.
275 Ibid. Conclusion 7 Commentary 15.
276 *WTO Appellate Body Report, China-Measures Affecting Trading Rights and Distribution Services for Certain Publications and Audiovisual Entertainment Products, AB-2009-3 (WT/DS363/AB/R), adopted 19 January 2010* para 403.
277 Kasikili/Sedudu (n 1) 1078 para 55.
278 Ibid., 1096 para 80.
279 Moloo (n 32) 77; Georg Nolte (n 149) 188.
280 ILC 2018 (n 7) Conclusion 7 para 2.

flicts where the "object and purpose" of the whole treaty appears to contradict purposes specifically provided for in the rules.[281] For example, in the *Kasikili/ Sedudu* case, the ICJ considered one party's practice, to reconcile the main object and purpose of the parties, which was to achieve free navigation of the river and the specific objective of limiting their boundaries.[282]

Given that the list of supplementary subsequent agreements and practice is inexhaustive, other areas worth considering may include State party interventions in court and arbitral proceedings. The ICJ Statute in Article 63, for example, allows States parties with an interest in a treaty's construction, the right to express their interpretation to the court before the ICJ reaches a decision on the matter.[283] Interventions arguably raise the question of whether a court or tribunal should treat them as subsequent agreements or supplementary agreements especially where a substantial number of States parties make interventions providing a uniform preferred interpretation. For instance, in the *Allegations of Genocide under the Convention on the Prevention and Punishment of the Crime of Genocide* (*Ukraine v Russia*) case, an unprecedented thirty-three (33) State parties to the 1948 Genocide Convention made interventions in ICJ proceedings expressing their preferred interpretation regarding certain provisions of the Convention.[284]

The Ukraine v Russia intervention would not meet the threshold as a subsequent agreement under Article 31(3)(a) of the VCLT due to the lack of a collective agreed interpretation by all State parties. This book however, suggests that such interventions should be considered by the courts or tribunals as supplementary agreements under Article 32 of the VCLT. The study further proposes that where all or almost all the State parties to a Convention present a uniform preferred interpretation of a treaty while intervening in proceedings, the court should treat such interpretation as subsequent agreements under Article 31(3)(a) of the VCLT.

281 Ibid. Conclusion 7 Commentary 16.

282 Kasikili/Sedudu (n 1) at 1074 para 45, 1096 para 80.

283 Article 63 of the ICJ Statute; See similar provisions in Article 37 of the Revised General Act for the Pacific Settlement of International Disputes New York, 28 April 1949; Article 32 of the Statute of the International Tribunal for the Law of the Sea.

284 Latvia, Lithuania, New Zealand, the United Kingdom of Great Britain and Northern Ireland (UK), Germany, the United States of America, Sweden, Romania, France, Poland, Italy, Denmark, Ireland, Finland, Estonia, Spain, Australia, Portugal, Austria, Luxembourg, Greece, Croatia, Czech Republic, Bulgaria, Malta, Norway, Belgium, Canada, Netherlands, Slovenia, Cyprus and the Principality of Liechtenstein in *ICJ Allegations of Genocide under the Convention on the Prevention and Punishment of the Crime of Genocide (Ukraine v. Russian Federation: 32 States Intervening) Preliminary objections, ICJ GL 182, 2 February 2024* para 14.

Alvarez concludes that a decision reached about a provision based on subsequent agreements under Article 32 cannot override one based on subsequent agreements under Article 31(3) of the VCLT.[285] As Berner has observed, the legal effect of Article 32 is that while subsequent agreements and practice under Article 31(3)(b) have to be "taken into account," the interpreter has the discretion to apply or reject supplementary means under Article 32 including subsequent agreements and practice.[286]

2.4 *The Legal Effect of Subsequent Agreements and Practice on Treaty Interpretation*

2.4.1 Overview of the Legal Effect

As noted earlier, the discussion of the legal effect of subsequent agreements and practice on treaty interpretation directly impacts the current study. Whether subsequent agreements and practice are construed as binding and conclusive in interpretation or non-binding and discretionary affects how the ICC treats the ASP's resolutions and amendments while interpreting the Rome Statute.

In discussing the legal effects of subsequent agreements and practice, the earlier position that there is little difference between subsequent agreements and practice, which establish the parties' agreement[287] is reiterated. In this regard, Nolte averred that the ILC did not intend the disparity between Article 31(3)(a) and (b) "to denote a difference concerning their possible substantive effects."[288] This view aligns with the ILC's that any difference between subsequent agreements and subsequent practice does not affect their authentic character.[289] In this regard, subsequent agreements and practice, together with other interpretation means, may assist in clarifying the treaty's meaning, leading to the "narrowing, widening, or otherwise determining the range of possible interpretations."[290] Additionally, the VCLT and the ILC granted subsequent practice equal status with subsequent agreements based on Article 31 (3)(a) and (b), requiring that both "shall be taken into account."[291] Therefore,

---

285 Dr Alberto A Jimenez, 'The International Law Gaze: Subsequent Agreements and Subsequent Practice in the Interpretation of International Treaties' 4.

286 Art 32 of the VCLT; Berner (n 112) 137.

287 Sean D Murphy (n 242) 4; Dörr (n 1) 593 para 72.

288 Georg Nolte (n 149) 173.

289 ILC 2018 (n 7) Conclusion 3 Commentary 10.

290 Ibid. Conclusion 7 para 1.

291 Gerald P McGinley, 'Practice as a Guide to Treaty Interpretation' (1985) 9 Fletcher Forum 211, 220–221; Tarcisio Gazzini, 'Authentic (or Authoritative) Interpretation of Investment Treaties by the Treaty Parties' (*EJIL: Talk!*, 17 August 2020) 189 <https://www.ejiltalk.org/

the discussion of the legal effects will deal with both the subsequent agreements and subsequent practice.

By subsequent agreements and practice being referred to as authentic means of interpretation, which "shall be taken into account," the question becomes whether they must mandatorily be considered in treaty interpretation or whether they are discretionary means.

2.4.2 "Taking into Account" Subsequent Agreements and Subsequent Practice

The phrase under Article 31(3)(a) and (b) of the VCLT that the interpreter "shall take into account" the subsequent agreements and subsequent practice has raised varied opinions among scholars, international courts, and tribunals regarding its meaning. Some views consider the interpretation agreed on by the parties as "decisive and binding" since the parties are the masters of their treaty.[292] Others have argued that a subsequent agreement or practice is non-binding and serves more of a confirmatory position, forming only one of several factors the interpreter should consider in applying Article 31 of the VCLT.[293] In effect, "taking into account" as used in Article 31(3)(a) and (b) of the VCLT is construed, on the one hand, as the obligatory consideration of subsequent agreements and practice in interpretation. On the other hand, the phrase is seen to denote the discretionary consideration of subsequent agreements and practice. Yet other scholars aver that the phrase "shall take into account" is vague and lacks precision, consequently failing to specify the role of subsequent agreements and practice in the interpretative process.[294]

Proponents of the mandatory consideration argue that subsequent agreements and practice are obligatory interpretation elements that are not inferior to the other elements under the general rule and, hence, must be considered in interpretation.[295] In seeming support for this argument, the ILC used the word "obligatory" regarding Article 31(3), stating, "but these three elements are all of an obligatory character and by their very nature could not be considered to be norms of interpretation in any way inferior to those which precede them."[296]

---

authentic-or-authoritative-interpretation-of-investment-treaties-by-the-treaty-parties/> accessed 21 August 2020.

292 Mark E Villiger (n 24) 429 para 16.

293 Jean-Marc Sorel & Vale'rie B Eveno, 'Article 31, General Rule of Interpretation' in Olivier Corten; Pierre Klein (ed), *The Vienna Conventions on the Law of Treaties: A Commentary* (Oxford University Press 2011) 826, 828.

294 Tarcisio Gazzini, 'Subsequent Agreements and Subsequent Practice' (n 125) 187 para 3.

295 Gardiner (n 2) 224, 288.

296 ILC 1966 Vol II (n 31) 220 para 9; ILC 2018 (n 7) Conclusion 2 Commentary 12.

Further, the ILC has stipulated that an agreement relating to the interpretation of a "provision reached after the treaty's conclusion represents an authentic interpretation by the parties which 'must' be read into the treaty for purposes of its interpretation."[297] Gardiner and Gazinni point out that using the words "authentic interpretation" by the parties, which "must be read" into the treaty, connotes a mandatory consideration of subsequent agreements and practice in interpretation.[298] The stated ILC provision has also been cited with approval by the ICJ in the *Kasikili/ Sedudu* case[299] and the Investment tribunal in the *Methanex v United States* case to emphasize the obligation to incorporate subsequent agreements and practice during interpretation.[300]

The ILC's reference to subsequent agreements and practice as "authentic" means of interpretation has been equated to "authoritative interpretation," which is superior to all other meanings, especially when agreed on in a bilateral treaty.[301] This approach would denote that subsequent agreements and practice must be considered during interpretation. Akande, however, acknowledges that while the VCLT requires that subsequent agreements or practice that qualify under Article 31(3) shall be "taken into account," it does not stipulate the substantive role they hold in interpretation.[302] Akande nevertheless warns that subsequent agreements and practice have high probative value, and it would be unsafe for the interpreter to ignore them.[303] In the same vein, Gardiner asserts that "a clear agreement of the parties on what their treaty means will usually be the strongest element in the crucible of interpretation."[304] Impliedly, the interpreter should not only consider the subsequent agreements and practice but should apply the outcome in the decision.

Further support of the obligatory consideration of subsequent agreements and practice is hinged on the proposal that the interpreter includes subsequent agreements in the "crucible" of all interpretative elements from the start of the interpretative process alongside the text and all other ele-

297 ILC 2018 (n 7) Conclusion 3; ILC 1966 Vol II (n 31) 221 para 14; Akande and Tzanakopoulos (n 140) 947.

298 Gardiner (n 2) 228; Tarcisio Gazzini, 'Subsequent Agreements and Subsequent Practice' (n 125) 186,189; ILC 1966 Vol II (n 31) 221 para 14.

299 Kasikili/Sedudu (n 1) para 49.

300 *Methanex Corporation v United States of America, UNCITRAL, Award Part II 2005* para 19.

301 Gardiner (n 2) 225.

302 Akande and Tzanakopoulos (n 140) 947.

303 Ibid., 948.

304 Gardiner (n 2) 224.

ments.[305] Significantly, the ILC has also used the words "take into account" concerning the whole of Article 31, stating that "the application of the primary means of interpretation according to Article 31, all of which are to be taken into account in the process of interpretation."[306] The ILC appears to construe "taking into account" in this context as the mandatory consideration of all interpretation means under Article 31, including subsequent agreements and practice. Similarly, the ILC has also referred to "the 'mandatory character' of taking into account" the interpretation means in Article 31, as opposed to the discretionary elements under Article 32.[307]

Describing subsequent agreements and practice as "objective evidence" of the parties understanding "which possesses considerable authority as a means of interpretation" and as "taking precedence" also suggests that the subsequent agreements and practice carry considerable weight during interpretation.[308] Additionally, the ILC stipulation that subsequent agreements and practice should be taken into account as "part of the treaty" since they are on the same level as the context strengthens the argument for the obligatory consideration of subsequent agreements and practice.[309]

In the same vein, Akande asserts that an interpreter "must" consider any subsequent agreements under Article 31(2) and any subsequent agreement or practice under Article 31(3) as part of the context during interpretation.[310] Similarly, Sir Fitzmaurice emphasized in the *Expenses* case that "practice must be a very relevant factor." By using the word "must," Fitzmaurice and Akande appear to construe the consideration of subsequent agreements and practice as mandatory in the interpretation and the outcome.

Following a similar approach, French has equated the phrase "taking into account" with the "obligation to consider."[311] French consequently argues that the interpreter lacks the discretion in choosing whether to use subsequent agreements and practice in interpretation since "article 31(2) and (3) are not discretionary add-ons, but prescriptive and mandatory aspects of the general rule."[312] He acknowledges that not all means under Article 31 will apply in all

305 Tarcisio Gazzini, 'Subsequent Agreements and Subsequent Practice' (n 125) 188 para 4.
306 ILC 2018 (n 7) Conclusion 2 Commentary 3.
307 Ibid. Conclusion 2 Commentary 8.
308 Gardiner (n 2) 34,414–415; Linderfalk (n 3) 153.
309 ILC 1966 Vol II (n 31) 95 para 3; Tarcisio Gazzini, 'Subsequent Agreements and Subsequent Practice' (n 125) 188 para 3.
310 Akande and Tzanakopoulos (n 140) 947.
311 French (n 27) 301.
312 Ibid.

instances, but they "must" be used when relevant.[313] Using the same approach, Grover asserts that the ICC judges have an obligation to consider the subsequent practice of the States Parties to the Statute when interpreting crimes in the Rome Statute based on Article 31(3)(b) of the VCLT.[314]

In the same vein, the ICSID, in the case of *Azpetrol vs Azerbaijan*, held that "the subsequent practice of the parties can be of utmost importance" in the treaty interpretation. Similarly, the *Iran United States Claims* Tribunal categorically stated that "far from playing a secondary role in the interpretation of treaties, the subsequent practice of the parties constitutes an important element in the interpretation of treaties."[315] Therefore, all these scholars and the courts give the subsequent agreements and practice an essential and obligatory role in interpretation.

It has, however, been pointed out that "taking into account" does not necessarily equate to the court applying the subsequent agreements and practice in the interpretation outcome. Reiterating this perspective, Tladi contends that there is an "absolute obligation" to apply Article 31(1), which contains the ordinary meaning of the terms in their context, taking the treaty's object and purpose into consideration.[316] Tladi, however, argues that this "absolute obligation" does not apply to Article 31(3), which "only" requires the interpreter "to take into account" subsequent agreements and subsequent practice.[317] Tladi, therefore, distinguishes between "taking into account" under Article 31(3)(a) and (b) and "application" under Article 31(1), asserting that one can choose to take an element into account but not apply it.[318] He, therefore, emphasizes that while applying the elements under 31(1) is mandatory, it is only obligatory for subsequent agreements and practice to be taken into account but not applied.[319]

This position appears to be validated by the wording in the ILC provision that "subsequent agreements and subsequent practice shall, after all, 'only be

313 Ibid.

314 Grover (n 78) 387.

315 *Islamic Republic of Iran vs The United States of America, Interlocutory Award No. ITL 83-B1 -FT (Counterclaim) Iran-US Claims Tribunal 9th September 2004, 2004 WL 22010709* para 111 (Iran vs USA Interlocutory Award 2004).

316 Tladi (n 40).

317 Dire Tladi, 'Interpretation of Treaties in an International Law-Friendly Framework: The Case of South Africa' in Helmut Philipp and Georg Nolte (eds), *The Interpretation of International Law by Domestic Courts: Uniformity, Diversity, Convergence* (Oxford University Press 2016) 145 footnote 48.

318 Tladi (n 40) Response to M Bradley.

319 Ibid.

taken into account' in the interpretation of a treaty."[320] The ILC further emphasizes that

> Whereas some courts have assumed that subsequent agreements and practice by the parties under the treaty may produce certain binding effects, others have rightly emphasized that Article 31 paragraph 3, only requires that subsequent agreements and subsequent practice "be taken into account."[321]

The phrase "only be taken into account," repeated in the draft conclusions, seems to lend credence to the argument that applying subsequent agreements and practice in interpretation is not obligatory.[322] It also seemingly construes "taking into account" as a less weighty alternative compared to "mandatory." In the same vein, Grover avers that judges of the ICC are obligated to take subsequent practice into account, although they can refuse to apply the interpretation emanating from the practice by giving good reasons for the rejection.[323]

Using a similar approach, Crawford construes "taking into account" with only "having regard to." Crawford points out that "agreements" by State parties are not considered conclusive, but rather, the requirement is to "only have regard" to the subsequent agreements.[324] Crawford concludes that the phrase "only having regard" to subsequent agreements suggests that it is not mandatory to consider or apply subsequent agreements and practice in interpretation.[325] Crema similarly construes "taking into account" to mean that it is not mandatory to consider subsequent practice because it carries less weight in treaty clarification.[326] Following the same thinking, in the *Canadian Case of Coblentz* vs. *Canada*, the Canadian Court of Appeal held that the words "shall be taken into account" found in Article 31(3) reduce the interpretative weight to be given to documents falling under Article 31(3) compared to those under Article 31(2).[327]

---

320 ILC 2018 (n 7) Conclusion 3 Commentary 4.
321 Ibid. Conclusion 3 Commentary 8.
322 Ibid. Conclusion 4 Commentary 6.
323 Grover (n 78) 388.
324 James Crawford, 'A Consensualist Interpretation of Article 31 (3) of the Vienna Convention on the Law of Treaties' in Georg Nolte (ed), *Treaties and Subsequent Practice*, vol 29 (Oxford University Press 2013) 31.
325 Ibid. 31–32.
326 Luigi Crema (n 222) 24–25.
327 *Coblentz v Canada (1997) 1 FC 368 (1996) Can LII 4091 (Federal Court of Appeal)* paras 10–18.

In a contrary view, Gardiner concedes that, at first glance, the VCLT seems to give more weight to agreements under Article 31(2), which are part of the context compared to subsequent agreements that are "only to be taken into account."[328] Gardiner nevertheless points out that closer scrutiny reveals that the whole of Article 31 is considered as the "general rule," and all elements are considered together and their weight determined without considering hierarchy.[329] Gardiner reiterates that as part of the general rule, subsequent parties' agreements in Article 31(3) are not inferior to the elements in Article 31(1).[330] In this context, Article 31(3) is treated as part of the general rule under Article 31, and seemingly, all the elements in Article 31 need to be obligatorily considered and applied in the interpretation outcome.

Notably, even the ILC lacks a uniform position by referring to the "mandatory character" of taking into account the elements in the whole of Article 31,[331] which includes subsequent agreements and practice on the one hand. On the other hand, as stated, it refers to the discretionary nature of subsequent agreements and practice. Determining the meaning of "taking into account" consequently appears to directly affect whether subsequent agreements and practice are treated as binding or have a conclusive legal effect on the treaty interpretation.

2.4.2.1 *Subsequent Agreements as Binding and Conclusive in Interpretation*

The ILC attempted to distinguish between subsequent agreements and practice which have a legally binding and conclusive legal effect on the treaty interpretation on the one hand and those which are not.[332] In this context, the binding nature seemingly leaves no room for the interpreter to avoid including subsequent agreements and practice in its interpretation and applying that interpretive outcome in its decision. Gardiner and Gazinni construe being "binding" to mean that the interpreter "must" (mandatorily) consider the meaning to be established from subsequent agreements and practice during interpretation.[333]

---

328 Gardiner (n 2) 230.
329 Ibid.
330 Ibid., 288.
331 ILC 2018 (n 7) Conclusion 2 Commentary 8.
332 'Comments from the United States on the ILC's Draft Conclusions on Subsequent Agreements and Subsequent Practice in Relation to the Interpretation of Treaties As Adopted by the Commission in 2016 on First Reading' 2; ILC 2018 (n 7) Conclusion 3 Commentary 4–7.
333 Gardiner (n 2) 224; Tarcisio Gazzini, 'Subsequent Agreements and Subsequent Practice' (n 125) 188, 189.

Gazinni emphasizes that since subsequent agreements reveal what meaning the State parties intended to give the treaty provisions and the purpose of treaty interpretation is to determine the State parties intent, then the interpreter "must" respect the agreement as legally binding in interpretation.[334] In effect, Gazinni asserts that subsequent agreements cannot just be taken into account, but being legally binding, the interpreter "must" adopt the interpretation gathered from assessing the treaty's text and the subsequent agreements.[335] From this perspective, it is not enough for the interpreter to consider the subsequent agreements or practice but must incorporate the interpretation emanating from the subsequent agreements into the decision.

Grover appears to attribute a binding effect to subsequent agreements and practice where State parties unanimously reach them. For example, as noted earlier, Grover argues that the "Seven Interpretive Understandings" accompanying the ASP's Kampala Resolution constitute a subsequent agreement under Article 31(3)(a) of the VCLT, having been adopted by consensus.[336] Grover contends that, consequently, the ICC "must" consider the "Understandings" when relevant since they reflect the States Parties authentic or common understanding of the interpretation issues.[337] In the same vein, Weisburd and Berner argue that the phrasing of Article 31(3)(b) leaves no room for the interpreter to choose whether to consider subsequent practice but makes its application in treaty interpretation mandatory.[338]

Moloo consequently asserts that a tribunal should find it difficult to fail to adopt an agreement jointly reached by the State parties.[339] Similarly, Gazinni posits that when treaty parties "officially, consistently, and persistently express identical positions on the interpretation of the very same treaty," the interpreter lacks a legitimate reason to fail to take the parties' interpretation under Article 31(3)(b) into account.[340] The language used by Gazinni, Weisburd, and Moloo appears to find that a court must apply the subsequent agreement and practice of treaty parties in the final decision even though the scholars do not expressly use the word "binding."

334 Tarcisio Gazzini, 'Subsequent Agreements and Subsequent Practice' (n 125) 188.

335 Ibid., 189.

336 Grover (n 78) 368.

337 Ibid.

338 A Mark Weisburd, 'The International Court of Justice and the Concept of State Practice' (2009) 31 U Pa J Int'l L 341; Katharina Berner, *Subsequent Agreements and Subsequent Practice in Domestic Courts* (Springer 2017) 137–138.

339 Moloo (n 32) 39, 75.

340 Tarcisio Gazzini, 'Subsequent Agreements and Subsequent Practice' (n 125) 205.

However, the distinction between binding and nonbinding subsequent agreements and practice appears to lack clarity, a position also acknowledged by Rapporteur Waldock and varied court decisions.[341] The ILC states that subsequent agreements and practice are not necessarily binding or conclusive.[342] However, it also provides that the parties to a treaty may reach a binding agreement regarding the treaty interpretation if they wish to.[343]

On the other hand, Villiger observes that subsequent agreements and practice under Article 31(3) (a) and (b) of the VCLT represent the authentic interpretation that is "not only particularly reliable, it is also endowed with binding force."[344] Similarly, in the *Territorial Dispute* (*Libya v Chad*) case, the ICJ found that an Anglo-French Convention of 1919 concluded to interpret an 1899 declaration "constituted the correct and binding interpretation of the earlier declaration."[345] Reiterating this approach, Sir Humphrey Waldock averred that "subsequent practice, when it is consistent and embraces all of the parties, would appear to be decisive of the meaning to be attached to the treaty, at any rate when it indicates that the parties consider the interpretation to be binding upon them."[346]

In some instances, the treaty parties explicitly stipulate in the treaty that the subsequent agreements and practice are binding on the tribunal or the court. As an example, the ILC recognized Article 1131(2) of the North American Free Trade Agreement (NAFTA), which states that "an interpretation by the (intergovernmental) Commission of a provision of this agreement shall be binding on a tribunal established under this section"[347] as a binding subsequent agreement. The binding effect of the agreement under NAFTA was, in this case, expressly provided for by the treaty parties in the treaty. In the same vein, the United Nations Commission on International Trade Law (UNCITRAL) tribunal sought to distinguish between the binding nature of subsequent agreements grounded on a specific provision contained in the NAFTA FTC treaty

341 ILC 2018 (n 7) Conclusion 3 Commentary 5 and 8.
342 Ibid. Conclusion 3 para 4.
343 Ibid. Conclusion 3 Commentary 5.
344 Mark E Villiger (n 24) 429 para 16; Dörr (n 1) 570 para 19; Mark E Villiger, 'The Rules on Interpretation: Misgivings, Misunderstandings, Miscarriage? The 'Crucible 'Intended by the International Law Commission' in Cannizzaro Enzo (ed), *The Law of Treaties Beyond the Vienna Convention* (Oxford Scholarly Authorities on International law 2011) 105, 110.
345 *Territorial Dispute* (*Libya v Chad*), *Judgment, ICJ Reports 1994* para 60.
346 ILC 2018 (n 7) Conclusion 3 Commentary 5; Waldock, 'Third Report on the Law of Treaties', 2 ILC Yearbook (1964) 60 para 25.
347 ILC 2018 (n 7) Conclusion 3 Commentary 6.

Article 1131(2) and, on the other hand, non-binding subsequent agreements not mentioned in any particular treaty provision. According to the tribunal,

> Under the general rule on interpretation set out in the Vienna Convention, a NAFTA tribunal would only need to 'take into account' the subsequent agreement. However, by virtue of NAFTA Article 1131(2), acts of authentic interpretation by the States parties to the Agreement, like the Notes just referred to, are binding and conclusive.[348]

In a related approach, the ICJ refused to apply subsequent practice where the treaty did not expressly provide for its application in the *Land, Island, and Maritime Frontier Dispute* case.[349] The ICJ held that while the VCLT and customary law provided for the "taking into account" of practice in interpretation, "none of these considerations … can prevail over the absence from the text of any specific reference to delimitation."[350] Other scholars who support the notion that subsequent agreements are not binding on interpreters unless their inclusion is expressly laid down in the treaty have also made similar observations.[351] Notably, the study is not persuaded by the approach that subsequent agreements and practice must be provided for explicitly in the treaty for them to apply. In the same regard, most international courts and tribunals rarely require the explicit mention of subsequent practice in the treaty before it can be applied in interpretation.[352]

In this respect, Gazinni differs with the UNCITRAL tribunal's approach, arguing that the interpreter "must" respect States parties' agreements whether the relevant treaty contains any provision on that or not since subsequent agreements are legally binding regardless.[353] Akande, commenting on the Rome Statute, is more categorical, stating that where "the masters of the

348 *William Ralph Clayton, William Richard Clayton, Douglas Clayton, Daniel Clayton and Bilcon of Delaware Inc v Government of Canada, UNCITRAL, PCA Case No 2009–04, Jurisdiction and Liability, 17 March 2015* para 430 (William Ralph Clayton UNCITRAL); See Art 17(2) of the BIT between the United Kingdom and Mexico which provides that an interpretation by the parties is binding on any tribunal.

349 *Land, Island and Maritime Frontier Dispute (El Salvador v Honduras, Nicaragua intervening), ICJ Rep 1992* 586 para 380.

350 Ibid.

351 Catharine Titi, 'The Timing of Treaty Party Interpretations' (*EJIL: Talk!* 18 August 2020) <https://www.ejiltalk.org/the-timing-of-treaty-party-interpretations/> accessed 18 August 2020.

352 Georg Nolte (n 149) 179.

353 Tarcisio Gazzini, 'Subsequent Agreements and Subsequent Practice' (n 125); William Ralph Clayton UNCITRAL (n 348) para 430.

treaty" give an "authentic interpretation" of the treaty through their subsequent agreements or practice, it "cannot be any more legally binding than any utterance included in the treaty."[354]

Further reiterating the decisive nature of subsequent agreements and practice of State parties, Gazinni posits that where the parties adopt an "authoritative interpretation" that makes sense, resorting to other interpretation means becomes unnecessary.[355] Gazinni further emphasizes that an interpreter is most likely to affirm the authentic interpretation arrived at through the parties' subsequent agreement.[356] Gazinni adds that where there are two or more probable interpretations, the interpreter "must" choose the one formally agreed upon by the parties.[357]

In the same vein, Linderfalk, while discussing "subsequent agreements," emphatically states that an authentic interpretation "always takes precedence" over an interpretation arrived at through applying other VCLT interpretation rules.[358] This approach also seemingly finds subsequent agreements and practice conclusive in interpretation. Similarly, in the *Expenses* case, Sir Fitzmaurice stated that the treaty parties "interpretation is good presumptive (and may in certain cases be virtually conclusive) evidence" of the correct legal interpretation.[359] Similarly, Arato, Linderfalk, and Gazinni point out that the meaning derived from State parties agreements and practice, being the parties' authentic interpretation, takes priority and can override the text and the other interpretation means.[360] Gardiner even adds that there are scarcely any circumstances when other interpretation elements take precedence over the parties' joint interpretation.[361] This approach is grounded on the argument that subsequent agreements and practice provide the "best and the most reliable" evidence to establish the State parties intentions and understanding of the treaty.[362]

---

354 Akande and Tzanakopoulos (n 140) 948.

355 Tarcisio Gazzini, 'Ordinary Meaning of the Terms of the Treaty', *Interpretation of International Investment Treaties* (Oxford Hart Publishing 2016) 65 footnote 3.

356 Tarcisio Gazzini, 'Subsequent Agreements and Subsequent Practice' (n 125) 188.

357 Ibid.

358 Linderfalk (n 3) 153.

359 *Certain Expenses of the UN (Article 17(2) of the Charter) Advisory Opinion of 20 July 1962* (ICJ) Separate Opinion Sir Fitzmaurice at 201.

360 Arato (n 32) 458; Dörr (n 1) 561 para 4; Tarcisio Gazzini, 'Subsequent Agreements and Subsequent Practice' (n 125) 188 para 5.

361 Gardiner (n 2) 226.

362 Donald H Regan (n 40) 1057; Linderfalk (n 3) 170; Gardiner (n 2) 236; ILC 1966 Volume II (n 31) 55 para 12(v).

Further, the stated lack of hierarchy among the means under Article 31 can be construed to mean that subsequent agreements and practice give authoritative meaning and have equal weight, similar to all the other elements, including the text.[363] Based on this approach, subsequent agreements and practice play a primary role in the interpretation, not a subordinate role. Several other scholars consider interpretation from subsequent agreements and practice conclusive, not just confirmatory. In this regard, the Arbitral tribunal in the *Eritrea/Ethiopia Boundary Commission* case and the *Iran United States Claims* tribunal have used subsequent agreements and practice as decisive in interpretation.[364] The *Iran-US Claims* Tribunal held that

> The effect of subsequent conduct may be so clear in relation to matters that appear to be the subject of a given treaty that the application of an otherwise pertinent treaty provision may be varied or may even cease to control the situation, regardless of its original meaning.[365]

The *Iran United States Claims* Tribunal further held that "the subsequent practice of the parties clearly supports interpreting Article 11, paragraph 2 of the Claims Settlement Declaration [...]. The Tribunal considers this factor to be decisive."[366] Nevertheless, not all courts, tribunals, or scholars consider the subsequent agreements and practice conclusive or binding in interpretation.

2.4.2.2 *Subsequent Agreements and Practice as Playing Only a Confirmatory or Clarifying Role*

In contrast, some scholars, courts, and tribunals find subsequent agreements and practice to be lower in the hierarchy than the other means of interpretation under Article 31(1) of the VCLT, hence not mandatory or binding in treaty interpretation. For instance, the ILC has stipulated that subsequent agreements and subsequent practice are not necessarily conclusive or binding.[367] With specific regard to resolutions by a Conference of States Parties, which this study attributes the ASP to be, the ILC recognizes that an interpreter "must" give appropriate weight to the resolutions reached by the Conference of States

363 Donald H Regan (n 40) 1054; Arato (n 32) 458; ILC 2018 (n 7) Conclusion 2 Commentary 6.

364 Iran vs USA, Interlocutory Award 2004 (n 315) paras 133, 134; *Decision regarding Delimitation of the Border between Eritrea and Ethiopia, Vol XXV, Reports of International Arbitral Awards* 110–111 para 3.8.

365 Iran vs USA, Interlocutory Award 2004 (n 315) para 113.

366 Ibid. para 134.

367 ILC 2018 (n 7) Conclusion 3 (4) and Conclusion 7 commentary 1.

Parties as subsequent agreement or practice but adds that the said resolutions are not necessarily legally binding.[368]

From this perspective, while taking subsequent agreement or practice into account is obligatory, it does not require that the interpreter must apply the agreement or practice in its decision. If the ICC took this approach, the resolutions by the ASP under the Conference of States Parties cannot be deemed binding on the Court in the Rome Statute's interpretation. The latter ILC provision appears to conflict with the prior ILC stipulation, giving an obligatory character to subsequent agreements and practice and terming them as part of the treaty.[369] As stated earlier, the ILC appears to lack a consistent position regarding the weight and decisive nature of subsequent agreements and practice in interpretation.[370]

Aligning with the ILC's position that subsequent agreements and practice are neither necessarily binding nor mandatory, Jimenez asserts that treaty interpretation cannot be based solely on subsequent agreements and subsequent practice, nor do they hold any superior status in interpretation.[371] Nolte similarly posits that the ILC did not propose any superior status for subsequent agreements and practice in interpretation.[372] In the same vein, Cohen, commenting on subsequent practice, asserts that

> Treaty parties deliberately decided not to keep their agreement informal, therefore, the formalities involved in negotiating and ratifying treaties [...] 'cannot simply be replaced by an interpretation given to some activity on the ground.[373]

In the same respect, it has been emphasized that judges must begin with determining the ordinary meaning, and they lack the discretion to resort to other interpretation means, such as the subsequent agreements and practice, unless the treaty text is unclear.[374] The ICJ reiterated this position in

368 Ibid. Conclusion 11 Commentary 38.
369 ILC 1966 Vol II (n 31) 220 para 9.
370 Akande and Tzanakopoulos (n 140) 947.
371 Alberto Alvarez-Jimenez, 'The International Law Gaze: Subsequent Agreements and Subsequent Practice in the Interpretation of International Treaties' (2019) 2 New Zealand Law Journal 2.
372 Georg Nolte (n 149) 172.
373 Marcelo Gustavo Kohen, 'Keeping Subsequent Agreements and Practice in Their Right Limits', *Nolte G (ed) Treaties and Subsequent practice* (Oxford University Press 2013) 34.
374 Shai Dothan, 'The Three Traditional Approaches to Treaty Interpretation: A Current Application to the European Court of Human Rights' (2019) 42 Fordham International

the *Guinea-Bissau v Senegal* Arbitral award[375] while endorsing observations made in the *Competence of the General Assembly for the Admission of a State to the UN* case that "if the relevant words in their natural and ordinary meaning make sense in their context, that is an end of the matter."[376] The ICJ added that it is only where the words "in their natural and ordinary meaning are ambiguous or lead to an unreasonable result, then, and then only, must the court resort to other methods of interpretation."[377] Following similar reasoning, the Arbitral tribunal in the *Interpretation of the Air Transport Services Agreement* (*USA and Italy*) refused to consider subsequent practice, holding that it was only applicable "if the literal interpretation does not lead to clear and unequivocal results."[378]

In his dissenting opinion, J Monaco went further to refer to subsequent practice as a "subsidiary element in interpretation" only justifiably used when the ordinary meaning was unclear.[379] The ICSID tribunal in *RSM v Grenada* also found that subsequent practice was subordinate to the textual meaning holding that

> Even though the International Law Commission, in its Final Draft Articles (suggested that the "process of interpretation is a unity and that the provisions of the article [now Article 31] form a single, closely integrated rule," nevertheless [....] Article 31, when read in conjunction with Articles 32 and 33 of the Vienna Convention reveals an interpretive structure in which subsequent practice and the other two methods of treaty interpretation, subjective and teleological, are supplementary in nature. They are to be used to assist in the interpretation when the textual method is insufficient.[380]

Law Journal 767 para 2; Eirik Bjorge, 'Time Present and Time Past: The Intention of the Parties and the Evolutionary Interpretation of Treaties.'" in Abi-Saab Georges et al (ed), *Evolutionary Interpretation and International Law* (Hart Publishing 2019).

375 *Arbitral Award of 31 July 1989* (*Guinea-Bissau v Senegal*), *Judgment ICJ Rep 1991* para 48.

376 *Competence of the General Assembly for the Admission of a State to the United Nations, Advisory Opinion, ICJ Rep 1950* para 8 (Competence of the General Assembly 1950).

377 Competence of the General Assembly 1950 (n 376) para 8; See also *Interpretation of the Air Transport Services Agreement between the USA and Italy, 17 July 1965* (RIAA Vol XVI) 107 para 12 (Air Transport Services USA and Italy); *RSM Production Corporation v Grenada, ICSID Case No. ARB/05/14, Award* (*13 March 2009*) para 383 (RSM v Grenada 2009).

378 Air Transport Services USA and Italy (n 377) 107 para 12.

379 *Interpretation of the Air Transport Services Agreement of 6 February 1948* (*Italy v USA*), *16 RIAA 75*, (1965) (Monaco J dissenting) 107 para 12; See also Beagle Channel Arbitration (Arg v Chile), 21 [RIAA] 1977 para 169.

380 RSM v Grenada 2009 (n 377) para 383.

The ILC has also pointed out that international courts and tribunals usually begin by determining the treaty's ordinary meaning, with subsequent agreements and practice only considered later to confirm or modify the ordinary meaning arrived at.[381] Similarly, Sorel and Eveno assert that a rational approach requires that subsequent agreements and practice be considered only when the other interpretation means in Article 31(1) have failed to produce a clear result.[382] In this respect, subsequent agreements and practice are applied to confirm the correct interpretation when different possible ordinary meanings arise.[383] Different courts and tribunals have reached similar decisions.[384] This approach gives the treaty text primacy in interpretation, not the parties' subsequent agreements and practice.[385]

Based on the above perspective, some scholars posit that subsequent agreements and practice are not primary elements of interpretation but merely confirm the meaning arrived at under Article 31(1).[386] Reiterating the confirmatory position, Murphy contends that the confirmation of the ordinary meaning is the most critical role subsequent practice plays in interpreting the treaty and is bound to be the position for a long time.[387] Murphy reiterates that while its role in interpretation is growing, subsequent practice is less controversial when used to confirm the ordinary meaning and not as a free-standing element of interpretation.[388] Sorel and Eveno similarly aver that subsequent agreements and practice "seem more in the order of confirmation

381 ILC 2018 (n 7) Conclusion 7 Commentary 3; Stefan Kadelbach, 'International Law Commission and Role of Subsequent Practice as a Means of Interpretation under Articles 31 and 32 VCLT' Questions of International Law-QIL, Milão, 2018;46.

382 Jean-Marc Sorel & Vale'rie B Eveno (n 293) 826.

383 Mark E Villiger (n 24) 111; *Legality of the Use by a State of Nuclear Weapons in Armed Conflict, Advisory Opinion, ICJ Reports, 1996* 248 para 55; ILC 2018 (n 7) Conclusion 7 commentary 2.

384 Air Transport Services USA and Italy (n 377) 107–108; RSM v Grenada 2009 (n 377) para 383; *Competence of the ILO in regard to International Regulation of the Conditions of Labour of Persons Employed in Agriculture, Advisory Opinion, 12 August 1922, (PCIJ)* 55; *Certain Expenses of the UN (Article 17(2) of the Charter) Advisory Opinion of 20 July 1962* (ICJ) Judge Pender's Separate Opinion 189,194.

385 Eirik Bjorge, 'Time Present and Time Past: The Intention of the Parties and the Evolutionary Interpretation of Treaties' in Abi-Saab Georges et al (ed), *Evolutionary Interpretation and International Law* (Hart Publishing 2019) 45.

386 Gerald P McGinley, 'Practice as a Guide to Treaty Interpretation' (1985) 9 Fletcher Forum 211, 220.

387 Sean D Murphy (n 242) 5.

388 Ibid., 7.

rather than assertion."[389] In this regard, the ICJ, in the *Kasikili/Sedudu* case, used subsequent practice to confirm the ordinary meaning holding that

> The Court finds that these facts, while not constituting subsequent practice by the parties in the interpretation of the 1890 Treaty, nevertheless support the conclusions which it has reached by interpreting Article III, para. 2 of the 1890 Treaty in accordance with the ordinary meaning to be given to its terms.[390]

Several other decisions have reiterated that subsequent practice can only be applied to confirm the ordinary meaning or meaning arrived at through other elements under Article 31(1).[391]

Besides confirming the textual interpretation, subsequent agreements and practice are considered applicable in confirming the treaty's object and purpose.[392] For instance, the ICJ used subsequent practice to clarify the treaty's object and purpose in *Oil Platforms (Iran vs USA)*,[393] *Denmark vs Norway*,[394]and the *Whaling in the Antarctic* cases.[395] The object and purpose of the treaty to be confirmed through subsequent practice may include the parties' evolutionary or "emergent purpose."[396] Additionally, Seibert avers that subsequent practice should only confirm the interpretation which does not

389 Jean-Marc Sorel & Vale´rie B Eveno (n 293) 826.

390 Kasikili/Sedudu (n 1) 1059.

391 *Case Concerning Sovereignty over Palau Ligitan and Palau Sipidan (Indonesia/Malaysia) Judgment of 17 December 2002* (ICJ) 665 para 80; *Territorial Dispute (Libya v Chad), Judgment, ICJ Reports 1994* paras 66–71; *Competence of the ILO, Series B No 2, 1922* (PCIJ) 39; *Military and Paramilitary Activities in and against Nicaragua (Nicaragua vs USA) Jurisdiction and Admissibility), Judgment, ICJ Reports 1984* 411 para 42; *Loizidou v Turkey, 40/1993/435/514, Council of Europe: European Court of Human Rights, 23 February 1995* para 79.

392 Paul Reuter, *Introduction to the Law of Treaties* (Routledge 1995) 24; Eirik Bjorge, 'Time Present and Time Past: The Intention of the Parties and the Evolutionary Interpretation of Treaties' in Georges Abi-Saab, and Clément Marquet (eds), *Evolutionary interpretation and international law* (Bloomsbury Publishing 2019) 44–45.

393 *Oil Platforms (Iran vs USA) (preliminary objections) ICJ Reports 1996* 803 paras 29–30.

394 *Case concerning Maritime Delimitation in the area between Greenland and Jan Mayen (Denmark vs Norway) ICJ Reports 1993* at 51 para 27.

395 *ICJ Whaling in the Antarctic (Australia v Japan: New Zealand intervening): Judgment of 31 March 2014* (ICJ) 251 para 56; *Competence of the General Assembly for the Admission of a State to the United Nations, Advisory Opinion, ICJ Rep 1950* dissenting opinion Judge Azevedo at 24 para 5.

396 Sean D Murphy (n 203) 5.

contradict the text, the context, and the treaty's object and purpose.[397] Further, subsequent agreements and practice may also clarify the special meaning based on Article 31(4) of the VCLT if the parties do not wish to rely on the ordinary meaning.[398]

Following a similar approach, Gardiner points out that even the ILC, in its Guide to Practice on Reservations to Treaties, appeared to have doubts about admitting interpretative declarations under Articles 31 and 32 of the VCLT but accepted their role of confirming the treaty's meaning.[399] The implication is that the subsequent agreements and practice are not decisive elements in interpretation but serve more of a confirmatory or clarifying role, which would arguably fall under Article 32 of the VCLT and not Article 31(3).

However, differing with the approach that subsequent practice only confirms the unclear ordinary meaning, Judge Dillard, in a separate opinion in the case of *Namibia Advisory Opinion*, held that

> The brief statement above is not intended to convey the impression that a finding of "ambiguity" is a precondition for recourse to subsequent conduct as a legitimate mode of enquiry into meaning.[400]

Nonetheless, it has also been pointed out that only a few decisions by international courts and tribunals, such as the *Namibia Advisory Opinion* case, have referred to State practice without first referring to Article 31(1) of the VCLT.[401] Consequently, it is observed that it is quite infrequent "for adjudicatory bodies to find that subsequent agreement or practice played a 'determinative role for the outcome of a decision."[402] The study agrees with the position that most courts and tribunals rarely apply subsequent agreements and practice as the decisive element in treaty interpretation. However, the study takes the stance that subsequent agreements and practice are not subordinate or inconclusive elements in all instances. It argues that depending on the nature of each case,

397 Seibert-Fohr (n 38).

398 ILC 2018 (n 7) Conclusion 7 Commentary 3.

399 Addendum to ILC Report, 63rd session (2011) UN general Assembly Official Records, 66th session, Supplement No 10, A/66/10/Add.1 Guideline 4.7.1 commentary para 24.

400 *Legal Consequences for States of the Continued Presence of South Africa in Namibia (South West Africa) notwithstanding Security Council Resolution 276 (1970) Advisory Opinion, ICJ Reports 1971* separate opinion of Judge Dillard 142 footnote 1.

401 Tladi (n 40).

402 Report of the ILC, 63rd session (2011) UN General Assembly Official Records, 66th session, Supplement No 10, A/66/10/Add.1 at 283 para 6; Sinclair (n 77) 136.

they can play a decisive role in some cases, especially where there is party consensus and a supplementary role in others.

The discussions, therefore, show varied views about the place and weight of subsequent agreements and practice in interpretation. Impliedly, it is up to States parties to authoritatively determine whether their subsequent practice and agreements should be construed as binding on the interpreting institution or not. From this perspective, and with no uniform position, the ICC might only determine the weight of the ASP's subsequent agreements and practice based on the circumstances and on a case-by-case basis.

2.5 *Conclusion*

The chapter has focused predominantly on the rules of interpretation under Articles 31 to 32 of the VCLT, which have been accepted as recognized customary international law on interpretation. The focus on the VCLT interpretation rules was to situate the continued States parties' role in their treaty interpretation after the treaty's conclusion. The interpretation rules under the VCLT Article 31 and, more specifically, Article 31(3)(a) and (31(3)(b) were seen to give the State parties the grounding for such continued participation through their subsequent agreements and subsequent practice. Based on the conclusion that the VCLT interpretation rules are recognized as customary law, the rules were found to lay the legal foundation for the continued participation of States Parties to the Rome Statute in the Statute's interpretation.

However, it was evident that while States parties may participate in treaty interpretation, the place and weight of the subsequent agreements and practice in the interpretation is inconsistent. It emerged that taken as part of the general rule in Article 31, subsequent agreements and practice play a primary and more decisive role in interpretation. However, where only Article 31(1) elements including the ordinary meaning, the context, and the object and purpose are construed as the general rule, the subsequent agreements and practice under Article 31(3) of the VCLT appear to have a subordinate and less decisive role in interpretation.

The analysis showed that the VCLT, the ILC, and the different courts and tribunals lack a uniform position on the place and weight of subsequent agreements and practice in treaty interpretation. While some scholars, courts, and tribunal decisions construe subsequent agreements and practice as central and binding in interpretation, others consider them lower in hierarchy and, therefore, non-binding and discretionary in treaty interpretation. Individual courts and tribunals consequently decide whether to consider subsequent agreements or practice at all and whether or not to treat them as central to the interpretation.

However, most decisions analyzed reveal that it is only in a few instances that subsequent agreements and practice are used as the decisive element in interpretation decisions. Impliedly, therefore, the ICC's use of subsequent agreements and practice of the States Parties to the Rome Statute in interpretation may follow the same inconsistent path with the decision left to individual judges on a case-by-case basis.

CHAPTER 3

Rules of Interpretation under the Rome Statute

1 Introduction

Having established the customary nature of the Vienna Convention on the Law of Treaties (VCLT) interpretation rules, this Chapter examines whether the rules apply to the Rome Statute of the International Criminal Court (Rome Statute). It further analyzes whether the Statute has its own rules of interpretation that displace the VCLT or work together with the VCLT interpretation rules. Whether the VCLT interpretation rules apply to the Rome Statute is significant to the study. If the Rome Statute has its own interpretation rules that exclude the VCLT rules, then the role of the Assembly of States Parties to the Statute (ASP) and that of the States Parties to the Statute (States Parties) in interpretation through their subsequent agreements and practice lacks a legal basis. However, if the VCLT rules are applicable, the International Criminal Court (ICC) has the legal basis for considering the States Parties subsequent agreements and practice in the Rome Statute's interpretation.

The Chapter, therefore, begins by examining whether the Rome Statute provides its own interpretative rules to be followed by the ICC. In this regard, a brief examination of the "applicable" law as hierarchically provided for under Article 21 of the Statute is assessed. These include the Rome Statute, the elements of crimes (Elements), and the Rules of Procedure (RPE), among others. To evaluate whether the "applicable" law as provided under Article 21 constitutes interpretation rules, a general examination of the terms "application" and "interpretation" is done.

The discussion regarding whether the VCLT interpretation rules apply to the Rome Statute's interpretation follows next. In this respect, how the interpretation elements under Articles 31(1) and 31(3) of the VCLT have been applied in the Rome Statute's interpretation collectively and individually is examined. These elements include the ordinary meaning in their context in light of the object and purpose and the subsequent agreements and practice of States parties.

Beyond the VCLT interpretation rules, Article 21(3) of the Rome Statute, which urges consistency with human rights in interpreting and applying the Statute, and Article 22, which provides for the *nullum crimen* or legality principle, are analyzed. The analysis is to determine whether Articles 21(3) and 22 form interpretation rules for the Rome Statute and, if so, whether they dis-

 | DOI:10.1163/9789004725515_004

place the VCLT rules or are, in fact, dependent on the VCLT interpretation rules. The Chapter concludes with an analysis of whether the VCLT provisions align with, conflict with, or are limited by both the legality principle under Article 22 and the human rights provision under Article 21(3) of the Rome Statute.

2 Reference to Interpretation under the Rome Statute

The question regarding what interpretation rules apply to the Rome Statute attracts varied views. Some scholars maintain that the Rome Statute gives very little guidance on the rules that the ICC should follow while interpreting the Statute.[1] Heikkila posits that the Statute generally fails to discuss its interpretation.[2] From this perspective, the Rome Statute does not recognize any primary interpretation rules binding the judges during the Statute's interpretation.[3] Other scholars argue that while the Statute does not expressly address interpretation, it gives some guidelines to the ICC regarding its interpretation.[4] In effect, there appears to be a general consensus that the Rome Statute does not expressly stipulate the interpretation rules applicable.

Some suggestions have, however, been given regarding the interpretation of the Rome Statute. For instance, based on the lack of explicit interpretive rules, Schabas concludes that since the Rome Statute is an international treaty, the VCLT interpretation rules apply to its interpretation.[5] On the other hand, a few scholars, such as Viebig, argue that the legal sources under Article 21 are not just applicable law but primarily serve as interpretation rules.[6] Yet other scholars posit that beyond the VCLT interpretation rules applying to the Rome Statute's interpretation, the Statute provides its own

1 William A Schabas, *An Introduction to the International Criminal Court 2020* (6th edn, Cambridge University Press 2020) 213.
2 M Heikkila, 'Article 21' in Mark Klamberg (ed), *Commentary on the law of the International Criminal Court editor* (Torkel Opsahl Academic Publisher 2017) 243.
3 Leena Grover, *Interpreting Crimes in the Rome Statute of the International Criminal Court* (Cambridge University Press 2014) 102; Leena Grover, 'A Call to Arms: Fundamental Dilemmas Confronting the Interpretation of Crimes in the Rome Statute of the International Criminal Court' (2010) 21 Issue 3 EJIL 583.
4 Heikkila (n 2) 243–244.
5 Schabas (n 1) 213.
6 Petra Viebig, 'Legal Sources and Legal Methodology Under the ICC Statute' in Petra Viebig (ed), *Illicitly Obtained Evidence at the International Criminal Court* (TMC Asser Press 2016) 27.

interpretation rules primarily found in Articles 21(3) and 22 of the Statute.[7] Article 21(3) requires that the application and interpretation of the Rome Statute should be consistent with human rights.

Article 22, on the other hand, stipulates that there should be strict construction of words and no resort to analogy. Based on the above different views, the following section looks briefly at the "applicable" law under Article 21 and whether, as few scholars argue, it constitutes interpretation rules. The discussion on whether the VCLT interpretation rules apply to the interpretation of the Rome Statute follows.

2.1 *"Applicable Law" under Article 21 of the Rome Statute*

Article 21 of the Rome Statute is titled "applicable law." The "applicable law" in Article 21 has been construed as enumerating the legal sources the ICC can refer to.[8] Notably, Article 21 hierarchically lists the applicable law to be used during the ICC's adjudication of cases. The hierarchy can be deduced from Article 21's description of what sources of law apply in the "first place" and the "second place," establishing three hierarchical levels.[9] Under Article 21(1)(a), the ICC "shall apply" in the "first place" the Rome Statute, the Elements and the RPE. The Statute is, therefore, considered to be on top of the hierarchy or superior to the other sources.[10]

---

7 Michail Vagias, *The Territorial Jurisdiction of the International Criminal Court* (Cambridge University Press 2014) 64; Valérie V Suhr, *Rainbow Jurisdiction at the International Criminal Court: Protection of Sexual and Gender Minorities Under the Rome Statute* (Springer Nature 2021) 54–55.

8 Schabas (n 1) 203; Schabas states that 'Article 21 of the Rome Statute titled "Applicable law", sets out the legal sources upon which the International Criminal Court may draw.'; J Verhoeven, 'Article 21 of the Rome Statute and the Ambiguities of Applicable Law' (2002) 33 NYIL 8.

9 William A Schabas, *An Introduction to the International Criminal Court, 2017* (5th edn, Cambridge University Press 2017) 190–191.

10 Joseph Powderly, 'The Rome Statute and the Attempted Corseting of the Interpretative Judicial Function: Reflections on Sources of Law and Interpretative Technique' in Carsten Stahn (ed), *The Law and Practice of the International Criminal Court* (Oxford University Press 2015) 463; Gerhard Hafner and Christina Binder, 'The Interpretation of Article 21 (3) ICC Statute 1 Opinion Reviewed' (2006) 9 Austrian Review of International and European Law Online 161, 163; *Decision on the Prosecution's Application for a Warrant of Arrest against Omar Hassan Ahmad Al Bashir, ICC-02/05-01/09 (PTC 1) 4 March 2009* para 126 (Decision on Bashir Arrest Warrant); *Judgment on the Prosecutor's Application for Extraordinary Review of Pre-Trial Chamber I's 31 March 2006 Decision Denying Leave to Appeal (DRC) ICC-01/04-168 (AC) 13 July 2006* para 23 (Judgment on the Application for Extraordinary Review).

Article 21(1)(b) states that "in the second place" and where appropriate, the ICC shall refer to applicable treaties and the principles and rules of international law, including the established principles of the international law of armed conflict. Significantly, applicable treaties and international law should only be referred to as a source of law "where appropriate" and when the primary sources in Article 21(1)(a) have been referred to first and failed to resolve the issue.[11]

The meaning of "applicable treaties and the principles and rules of international law" under Article 21(1)(b) has not been well defined either by the ICC or the Rome Statute, leading to varied interpretations.[12] However, there appears to be a broad consensus that Article 21(1)(b) includes customary international law despite the failure to mention it expressly under the article.[13] In this regard, a few scholars construe the VCLT as part of the customary law falling under Article 21(1)(b) of the Rome Statute.[14] Other scholars link Article 21(1)(b) of the Statute to Article 31(3)(C) of the VCLT, which requires judges to take into account any relevant rules of international law applicable between the parties.[15] Based on Article 21(1)(b), the ICC has referred to external instruments such as the Additional Protocols to the Geneva Conventions,[16] the Con-

11 Article 21 (1) (b) and (c) of the Rome Statute; Daniel Sheppard, 'The International Criminal Court and "Internationally Recognized Human Rights": Understanding Article 21(3) of the Rome Statute' (2010) 10 Int CLR 46; Margaret M deGuzman, 'Article 21, Applicable Law in Kai Ambos, Otto Triffterer (Ed)', *The Rome Statute of the International Criminal Court, A Commentary* (3rd edn, Nomos 2016) 935; Judgment on the Application for Extraordinary Review (n 10) para 23.

12 Gilbert Bitti, 'Article 21 and the Hierarchy of Sources of Law before the ICC' in Carsten Stahn (ed), *The Law and Practice of the International Criminal Court* (Oxford University Press 2015) 427.

13 Schabas (n 1) 205–206; deGuzman (n 11) 939 para 24; Alain Pellet, 'Applicable Law' in A Cassese et al. (ed), *The Rome Statute of the ICC: A Commentary*, vol 2 (Oxford University Press 2002) 1072; Gudrun Hochmayr, 'Applicable Law in Practice and Theory Interpreting Article 21 of the ICC Statute' (2014) 12 JICJ 667; Grover, 'A Call to Arms: Fundamental Dilemmas Confronting the Interpretation of Crimes in the Rome Statute of the International Criminal Court' (n 3) 572.

14 Yudan Tan, 'The Identification of Customary Rules in International Criminal Law' (2018) 34 Utrecht Journal of International and European Law; Powderly (n 10) 428–431.

15 Grover, 'A Call to Arms: Fundamental Dilemmas Confronting the Interpretation of Crimes in the Rome Statute of the International Criminal Court' (n 3) 572.

16 The Geneva Conventions of 1949 and their Additional Protocols; Article 8 of the Statute refers to the Geneva Convention; Schabas (n 1) 206; Gudrun Hochmayr, 'Applicable Law in Practice and Theory Interpreting Article 21 of the ICC Statute' (2014) 12 JICJ 665; Article 8(2) of the Statute.

vention on the Rights of the Child, and the African Charter on the Rights and Welfare of the Child,[17] among others.

Next in the hierarchy is Article 21(1)(C), which uses the phrase "failing that," the ICC will apply general principles of law derived by the Court from national laws of legal systems of the world, including, where appropriate, the national laws of States that would normally exercise jurisdiction over the crime. The principles should not contradict the Rome Statute, international law, and internationally recognized norms and standards. The use of the words "failing that" implies that Article 21(1)(C) is only applicable when Articles 21(1)(a) and 21(1)(b) have been referred to first, and the issues remain unresolved.

Article 21(2), which states that the "Court may apply the principles and rules of law as interpreted in its previous decisions," follows. The word "may" implies that the ICC has the discretion to use or not use its precedent, therefore disregarding the doctrine of binding precedent (*stare decisis*) used in some national judicial systems.[18]

In Article 21(3), there is a slight variation in the wording, with the provision stating that "the application and interpretation" of law pursuant to Article 21(3) "must" be consistent with internationally recognized human rights and be without any adverse distinction on gender among other grounds. Notably, the general inclusion of Article 21(3) under the applicable law, its phrasing, and the use of the word "must" have raised varied opinions concerning its place in the Rome Statute's interpretation. Article 21(3) and the diverse related opinions will be examined in detail in the subsequent section.

The applicable law under Article 21 of the Statute is said to be generally modelled on Article 38 of the Statute of the International Court of Justice (ICJ), which lists the sources of law as international conventions, international custom, general principles of law, principles recognized by civilized nations, judicial decisions, and publications by scholars.[19] Sheppard consequently avers that understanding the applicable law in Article 21 of the Rome Statute is comparable to understanding the sources of international law as captured

---

17 *Judgment Pursuant to Article 74 of the Statute, Prosecutor v Thomas Lubanga Dyilo, ICC-01/04-01/06-2842 (TrC 1) 14 March 2012* para 604 (Judgment Pursuant to Article 74 Lubanga).

18 Heikkila (n 2) 249,254.

19 Statute of the International Court of Justice (ICJ Statute), 18 April 1946 (Art 38 of the ICJ Statute); Daniel Sheppard (n 11) 45 para 2; William A Schabas, *An Introduction to the International Criminal Court, 2017* (5th edn, Cambridge University Press 2017) 191; Stephen Bailey, 'Article 21(3) of the Rome Statute: A Plea for Clarity' (2014) 14 Int CLR 520 para 1.

in Article 38 (1) of the Statute of the ICJ.[20] Article 21 is deemed the first international law provision codifying the law to be applied by an international criminal court.[21]

Nevertheless, different views have been raised regarding whether Article 21 constitutes only sources of law or if they are interpretive rules. On the one hand, there is a minority approach that portrays the entire Article 21 of the Rome Statute as constituting interpretive rules.[22] Mimoza et al., for instance, aver that "the general principles of interpretation are set out in Article 21" of the Statute.[23] Other views restrict Article 21 to sources of law only.

On the other hand, other scholars consider only Articles 21(3) and 22(2) of the Rome Statute as constituting interpretation principles for crimes in the Statute.[24] Notably, Article 22 has not been placed under the "applicable law" in the Statute. It stipulates that judges should strictly construct the definitions of crimes in the Rome Statute and refrain from analogy. Article 22 further requires that in case of ambiguity, the interpretation should favor the person being investigated, prosecuted, or convicted. These varied views necessitate a consideration of the relationship between "applicable law" and "interpretation." This analysis will enable a conclusion on whether Article 21, titled "applicable law," constitutes interpretive rules for the Rome Statute or not.

2.1.1 Application versus Interpretation

On the one hand, it has been posited by a minority view that the difference between the interpretation and application of international norms is "difficult," or "even impossible," to determine.[25] Pound, for instance, states that

---

20 Ibid., 45.

21 Alessandro Bufalini, 'The Principle of Legality and the Role of Customary International Law in the Interpretation of the ICC Statute' (2015) 14 Law & Practice of International Courts & Tribunals 233, 238; deGuzman (n 11) 935.

22 Petra Viebig, 'Legal Sources and Legal Methodology Under the ICC Statute' in Petra Viebig (ed), *Illicitly Obtained Evidence at the International Criminal Court* (TMC Asser Press 2016) 27; Powderly (n 14) 447; Mimoza Sadushaj and others, 'Interpretation and Application of Article 98 of the Rome Statute' (2017) Vol. 6 No. 1 (2017) Academic Journal of Interdisciplinary Studies 144.

23 Sadushaj and others (n 22) 144.

24 Suhr (n 7) 54–55; Michail Vagias (n 7) 64 para 3; Grover, *Interpreting Crimes in the Rome Statute of the International Criminal Court* (n 3) 5 and 102; Grover, 'A Call to Arms: Fundamental Dilemmas Confronting the Interpretation of Crimes in the Rome Statute of the International Criminal Court' (n 3) 549.

25 Anastasios Gourgourinis, 'The Distinction between Interpretation and Application of Norms in International Adjudication' (2011) 2 Journal of International Dispute Settlement 31; Andrew D Mitchell and David Heaton, 'The Inherent Jurisdiction of WTO Tri-

interpretation apart from a judicial application is impracticable, and it is "futile" trying to distinguish between interpreting and applying the law.[26] In the same vein, Sir Berman posited that in international law:

> There is a virtually inseparable link between interpretation and application; jurisdictional clauses in treaties invariably cover.... "disputes over the interpretation or application of the present treaty" in such a way that the competent tribunal is not required to distinguish the one from the other.[27]

Similarly, McNair has pointed out that the word "interpretation" is broadly used as if it includes "application."[28]

On the other hand, the more common approach views application and interpretation as different concepts that are nevertheless closely related and dependent on each other.[29] Under this approach, application and interpretation are closely interlinked but distinguishable. In this respect, Sur considers interpretation as incorporating all application aspects.[30] In the same vein, Judge Ehrlich, in his dissenting opinion in the PCIJ case of *Factory at Chorzów,* held that

> The words "interpretation and application" do not, by themselves, imply such an affirmative answer. They refer to processes, of which one, interpretation, is that of determining the meaning of a rule, while the other, application, is, in one sense, that of determining the consequences which the rule attaches to the occurrence of a given fact; in another sense, application is the action of bringing about the consequences which, according to a rule, should follow a fact.[31]

---

26 Roscoe Pound, *The Spirit of the Common Law* (Marshall Jones Company 1921) 179.

27 Franklin Berman, 'International Treaties and British Statutes' (2005) 26 Statute Law Review 10.

28 Lord McNair, *The Law of Treaties* (Oxford University Press 1986) 365.

29 Mitchell and Heaton (n 25) 559, 570; ILC, 'Draft Conclusions on Subsequent Agreements and Subsequent Practice in Relation to the Interpretation of Treaties, Seventieth Session, (A/73/10) 2018' (ILC) Conclusion 6 Commentary 3 (ILC 2018).

30 Anastasios Gourgourinis, 'The Distinction between Interpretation and Application of Norms in International Adjudication' (2011) 2 Journal of International Dispute Settlement 32 citing S Sur, L'interpre´tation en droit international public (Librairie ge´ne´rale de droit et de jurisprudence, Paris 1974) 317.

31 *Factory at Chorzów (Jurisdiction)* (1927) PCIJ Series A No 9 (Dissenting Opinion of Judge Ehrlich) p 39; See also a discussion on interpretation and application in Eirik Bjorge, *The*

Also illustrating the different but close connection between "application" and "interpretation," the ILC states that the "application of a treaty almost inevitably involves some element of interpretation."[32] In this regard, the ILC has noted that interpretation is the process through which the meaning of treaty provisions is clarified while application espouses the conduct of exercising rights under a treaty or compliance with treaty obligations.[33]

The difference between application and interpretation has further been demonstrated by the argument that even the VCLT allocates different sections to the "application" and the "interpretation" of treaties.[34] In further distinguishing the two processes, it is noted that most judges usually first determine the meaning of a treaty provision before applying it.[35] Gardiner similarly reiterates that interpretation comes first, followed by application.[36] In contrast to the interpretation-first approach, however, a few scholars suggest that application is the first step before interpretation in determining a dispute.[37] Mcnair, for instance, argues that if the treaty's meaning is clear, no interpretation takes place, and the provision is "applied" but not "interpreted."[38] Gardiner has questioned McNair's approach, arguing that a clear meaning can only be determined after it is subjected to an interpretation.[39]

The decision in *Berschader and Berschader v Russian Federation* case more specifically distinguished between the Russian treaty as a source of law and the VCLT as the interpretive principle where the tribunal held that

> The Tribunal finds that the principal source of law applicable to the question of the Tribunal's jurisdiction must be provisions of the Treaty. Insofar as the terms of the Treaty are unclear or require interpretation or supplementation, the Vienna Convention requires the Tribunal to

---

Evolutionary Interpretation of Treaties (Oxford University Press 2014) 15–17; The Harvard Draft Convention 29 (1935) AJIL Supp 938.

32 ILC 2018 (n 29) Conclusion 6 Commentary 3; Also see Richard Gardiner, *Treaty Interpretation 2015* (2nd edn, Oxford University Press 2015) 238.

33 Ibid. Conclusion 6 Commentary 3.

34 Chang-fa Lo (n 25) 210.

35 *Kasikili/Sedudu Island (Botswana/Namibia), Judgment, ICJ Rep 1999* (ICJ) 1059 para 18. (Kasikili/Sedudu); *ICSID Waste Management, Inc v* United Mexican States, *Case No ARB (AF)/00/3*, Award of 30 April 2004, (2004) p 31 para 88; Pajzs, Czáky, Esterházy (Judgment) PCIJ Series A/B No 68 1936 63.

36 Gardiner (n 32) 28.

37 Chang-fa Lo (n 25) 240–241; McNair (n 28)365.

38 McNair (n 28)365; See also Leena Grover, *Interpreting Crimes in the Rome Statute of the International Criminal Court* (Cambridge University Press 2014) 262.

39 Gardiner (n 32) 29.

> consider "the relevant rules of international law applicable in relations between the parties."[40]

Similarly, the *Kasikili Sedudu* case distinguished between the source of law and "interpretation." In this respect, the ICJ held that

> The law applicable to the present case has its source first of all in the 1890 Treaty [....]. As regards the interpretation of that Treaty, the court notes that neither Botswana nor Namibia are parties to the Vienna Convention on the Law of Treaties of 23 May 1969, but that both of them consider that Article 31 of the Vienna Convention is applicable.'[41]

Therefore, the court clearly distinguished between the 1890 treaty as the source of law and the VCLT as the rules of interpretation. This distinction can also be applied to determine whether Article 21 of the Statute is a source of law or an interpretation rule.

2.1.2 Application and Interpretation in Relation to the Rome Statute

With specific relation to the Rome Statute, the phrasing of some articles in the Statute also appears to distinguish between interpretation and application. For instance, Article 9(1) of the Rome Statute provides that the Elements of Crimes shall assist judges in the "interpretation and application of Articles 6, 7, 8 and 8 bis". As previously mentioned, Article 21(3) of the Statute also states that the article should be "interpreted and applied" consistently with internationally recognized human rights. In this respect, the Appeal Chamber's decision in the *Lubanga Challenge to Jurisdiction* case further illustrated the difference between interpretation and application finding with respect to Article 21(3) that

> Article 21 (3) of the Statute stipulates that the law applicable under the Statute must be *interpreted as well as applied* in accordance with internationally recognized human rights. [....] Its provisions must be *inter-*

40 Vladimir *Berschader and Moise Berschader v Russian Federation,* Arbitration Institute of the Stockholm Chamber of Commerce Case No. 080/2004, 21 April 2006 para 95; *Judgment pursuant to Article 74 of the Statute, The Prosecutor v Germain Katanga,* ICC-01/04-01/07-3436 (*Tr C II*), *7 March 2014* para 37 (Judgment pursuant to Article 74 Katanga).

41 Kasikili/Sedudu (n 35) 1059 para 18.

> *preted and, more importantly, applied* in accordance with internationally recognized human rights.[42]

Similarly, in the Lubanga case, the Trial chamber was clear in distinguishing between the sources and the interpretation rules, holding that "having first identified the sources of law on which it will draw [....] the Chamber will set out the principles and the rules it must take into account in its interpretation of the law."[43]

Based on the analysis of "application" and "interpretation" above, the study assumes the position that the applicable law under Article 21 only refers to sources of law to be drawn upon by the ICC. The sources are distinguished from the interpretation rules applied to the Rome Statute's interpretation. In effect, the sources or applicable law cannot be equated to rules of interpretation. The study consequently does not consider Article 21(1) and 21(2) of the Statute as interpretive rules but only applicable sources of law.

As mentioned earlier, however, some scholars and courts deem Articles 21(3) and 22 as internal interpretive rules for the Rome Statute. The following section considers whether the VCLT rules of interpretation apply to the Statute's interpretation in light of the provisions of Articles 21(3) and 22 of the Statute.

3 The Role of the VCLT Interpretation Rules in the Rome Statute's Interpretation

Whether the VCLT interpretation rules apply to the Rome Statute attracts varied opinions, with several scholars, on the one hand, advocating that the rules apply to the Statute's interpretation.[44] On the other, albeit in the minority, some argue that the VCLT interpretation rules do not apply to the Stat-

---

42 *Judgment on the Appeal of Thomas Lubanga Dyilo against the Decision on the Defence Challenge to the Jurisdiction of the Court pursuant to Article 19 (2) (a) of the Statute of 3 October 2006 ICC-01/04-01/06-772, 14 December 2006* (Appeal's Chamber) para 37; see also *Decision on Joinder of the cases against Germaine Katanga and Mathieu Ngudjolo Chui, ICC 01/04-01/07-257 (PTC 1)10 March 2008* (PTC I) p 7 (Decision on Joinder of cases Katanga and Ngudjolo).

43 Judgment Pursuant to Article 74 Lubanga (n 17) para 37.

44 Leila N Sadat and Jarrod M Jolly, 'Seven Canons of ICC Treaty Interpretation: Making Sense of Article 25's Rorschach Blot' (2014) 27 LJIL 759; Suhr (n 7) 57.

ute.[45] In this regard, a few scholars and decisions suggest that the Rome Statute has its own rules of interpretation constituting Articles 21(3) and 22, with the VCLT applied only as a last resort.[46] Similarly, Hochmayr posits that only when the Rome Statute lacks a related interpretative rule can the VCLT be referred to.[47] These approaches raise the question of whether the VCLT interpretation rules apply to the Statute's interpretation at all and, if they do, whether they form the primary interpretive rules. These questions are significant, especially considering that the Statute is a specialized criminal international treaty.[48]

3.1 *The VCLT Interpretation Rules as Applicable to the Rome Statute's Interpretation*

As previously discussed, Articles 31 and 32 of the VCLT are broadly accepted as customary rules on interpretation for international treaties.[49] Proponents of the VCLT being an integral part of the Rome Statute's interpretation consequently point out that based on its customary international nature, the VCLT interpretation rules apply to all international treaties, including the Statute.[50] In the same vein, in the *Authorization of an Investigation into Kenya's situation* case, the Judge held that

> The chamber wishes to point out that since the Statute is a multilateral treaty, the interpretation of its provisions is governed by the customary

45 Dov Jacobs, 'International Criminal Law' in Jean D'Aspremont and Kammerhofer Jörg (eds), *International Legal Positivism in a Post-Modern World* (Cambridge University Press 2014) 469; Gregor Maučec, 'The International Criminal Court and the Issue of Intersectionality – A Conceptual and Legal Framework for Analysis' (2021) 21 International Criminal Law Review 1, 469.

46 Michail Vagias (n 7) 64 para 3; Grover, *Interpreting Crimes in the Rome Statute of the International Criminal Court* (n 3) 5 and 102; Dov Jacobs, 'The ICC Katanga Judgment: A Commentary (Part 1): Investigation, Interpretation and The Crimes' (*Spreading the Jam*, 10 March 2014) <https://dovjacobs.com/2014/03/10/the-icc-katanga-judgment-a-commentary-part-1-investigation-interpretation-and-the-crimes/> accessed 29 December 2020.

47 Hochmayr (n 13) 667.

48 Sadat and Jolly (n 44) 759.

49 Grover, *Interpreting Crimes in the Rome Statute of the International Criminal Court* (n 3) 28, 29; Kasikili/Sedudu Island (n 35)1059 para 18; *Pulp Mills on the River Uruguay (Argentina v Uruguay)* (ICJ) 46 para 65; *Alleged Violations of Sovereign Rights and Maritime Spaces in the Caribbean Sea (Nicaragua v. Colombia), Preliminary Objections, Judgment, ICJ Reports 2016* para 35; *Maritime Dispute (Peru v. Chile), Judgment, ICJ Reports 2014* at 28 para 57; *Arbitral Award of 31 July 1989 (Guinea-Bissau v Senegal), 1991 ICJ (Nov 12)* para 48.

50 Schabas (n 1) 213; Suhr (n 7) 57.

> rules of treaty interpretation embodied in Articles 31 and 32 of the Vienna Convention on the Law of Treaties.[51]

Reiterating the Rome Statute as a treaty subject to the VCLT rules, the Trial Chamber in the *Lubanga Article 74* case held that "the legal nature of the Statute is that of a treaty, and the interpretative criteria provided for in the Vienna Convention are also applicable to the interpretation of the Statute and the Rules."[52]

Several scholars agree that Article 31, which comprises "the general rule of interpretation," and Article 32 of the VCLT apply to interpreting the Statute's provisions as customary interpretation rules.[53] In multiple other cases, the ICC has reiterated that the VCLT "must" be applied in interpreting the Rome Statute based on the Statute being a multilateral treaty and the VCLT Articles 31 and 32 being accepted customary law on interpretation.[54] Sadat and Jolly, therefore, aver that there is considerable validation for using the VCLT interpretation rules in the Statute's interpretation.[55] Grover also avers that the VCLT interpretation rules apply to the Rome Statute's interpretation unless strong evidence is produced by States Parties explicitly excluding the VCLT provisions.[56]

---

51 *Decision Pursuant to Article 15 of the Rome Statute on the Authorization of an Investigation into the Situation in the Republic of Kenya*, ICC-01/09 19 (ICC, 11) para 19 (Decision pursuant to Article 15 Investigations Kenya); Judgment pursuant to Article 74 Lubanga (n 17) para 601; *Decision on the Prosecutor's Application for Warrants of Arrest, Article 58 against Thomas Lubanga Dyilo and Mr Bosco Ntaganda, ICC-01/04-02/06-20-Anx2* 69 (ICC PTC 1) para 43.

52 Judgment Pursuant to Article 74, Lubanga (n 17) pg 6.

53 Schabas (n 1) 213; Michael Kourabas, 'A Vienna Convention Interpretation of the Interests of Justice Provision of the Rome Statute, the Legality of Domestic Amnesty Agreements, and the Situation in Northern Uganda: A Great Qualitative Step Forward, or a Normative Retreat' (2007) 14 U C Davis Journal of International Law & Policy 69; Petra Viebig, 'Legal Sources and Legal Methodology Under the ICC Statute' in Petra Viebig (ed), *Illicitly Obtained Evidence at the International Criminal Court* (TMC Asser Press 2016) 16; Suhr (n 7) 54–55; Grover, *Interpreting Crimes in the Rome Statute of the International Criminal Court* (n 3) 29.

54 Decision Pursuant to Article 15 Investigations Kenya (n 51) para 19; Judgment Pursuant to Article 74 Lubanga (n 17) para 601; *Decision on the Prosecutor's Application for Warrants of Arrest, Article 58 against Thomas Lubanga Dyilo and Bosco Ntaganda, ICC-01/04-01/07* 69 (ICC PTC 1) para 43.

55 Sadat and Jolly (n 44) 762.

56 Grover, *Interpreting Crimes in the Rome Statute of the International Criminal Court* (n 3) 28.

It has been suggested that the VCLT was formally incorporated into the Rome Statute's interpretation by the Appeal Chamber's decision in the *Extraordinary Review* case,[57] referred to as the "authentic guide" to the Statute's interpretation.[58] In the case, the Appeal's Chamber referred to all Article 31(1) elements, including the ordinary meaning, the context, and the object and purpose in its interpretation, holding as follows:

> The principal rule of interpretation is set out in Article 31(1)..... The rule governing the interpretation of a section of the law is its wording read in context and in light of its object and purpose. The context of a given legislative provision is defined by the particular sub-section of the law read as a whole in conjunction with the section of an enactment in its entirety. Its object may be gathered from the Chapter of the law in which the particular section is included and its purposes from the wider aims of the law as may be gathered from its preamble and general tenor of the treaty.[59]

The above extract from the Appeal Chamber's decision was first referred to as "the authentic guide to the interpretation of the Statute" by a different bench of the Appeal's Chamber in the *Lubanga Admissibility* Appeal case.[60] The ICC has subsequently cited the guide in several cases, including the *Pierre Bemba Adjournment* case.[61]

While reiterating the central role of the VCLT interpretation rules in the Rome Statute's interpretation, the *amici curiae* in the *State of Palestine* case

57 Judgment on the Application for Extraordinary Review (n 10) para 33.

58 Michail Vagias (n 7) 61–62.

59 Judgment on the Application for Extraordinary Review (n 10) para 33.

60 *Decision on the admissibility of the Appeal by Thomas Lubanga Dyilo against the decision of PTC I entitled "Decison Sur La Confirmation des charges' of 29/1/2007, ICC-01/04-01/06 OA8, 13 June 2007* (ICC, Appeal's Chamber) para 8. (Decision on the admissibility of the Appeal "Decison Sur La Confirmation des charges" Lubanga).

61 *ICC Decision Adjourning the Hearing pursuant to Article 61(7)(c)(ii) of the Rome Statute, Prosecutor v Jean Pierre Bemba Gombo, ICC-01/05-01/08* (PTC III) 3 March 2009 para 31; *[Redacted]* (*ICC-RoR216-01/14*), *Decision concerning the 'Application to the Presidency Pursuant to Regulation 216 of the Regulations of the Registry for Judicial Review of the Registrar's Decision Notified on 7 February 2014', 28 February 2014* para 23 (Decision concerning the Application to the Presidency); *Judgment on the Appeals of the Prosecutor and the Defense against Trial Chamber I's Decision on Victims' Participation of 18 January 2008, The Prosecutor v Thomas Lubanga Dyilo, ICC-01/04-01/06-1432* (ICC, AC) para 56.

challenged the Prosecutor's submission that the VCLT was inapplicable in defining whether Palestine was a State. They submitted that

> Rather remarkably, the Prosecutor's Submission does not agree that the Court should apply the normal rules of treaty interpretation under Article 31 of the Vienna Convention on the Law of Treaties [...] the fact that the issue is in a very few cases controversial hardly seems to justify jettisoning the long-accepted Vienna Convention rules for interpreting the terms of the treaty.[62]

Further advocating for the use of the VCLT interpretation rules in the Rome Statute's interpretation, some scholars aver that the VCLT interpretation rules provide a more explicit and detailed interpretive framework for the Statute, making it logical for the judges to rely on the rules.[63] Sadat and Jolly similarly aver that the ICC should apply Articles 31(1) and 32 of the VCLT while interpreting the Statute.[64] Sheppard is more categorical, asserting that the Statute is a treaty and "must be interpreted" based on the VCLT.[65]

The Appeal's Chamber has further emphasized that the "interpretation of treaties and the Rome Statute is no exception, is governed by the VCLT, specifically ... Articles 31 and 32".[66] The embrace of the VCLT as the primary guiding interpretative principle to the Rome Statute was demonstrated further in the *Lubanga* case,[67] where all the participants agreed that the Rome Statute's main interpretation rule was Article 31(1) of the VCLT. Similarly, the Appeal's Chamber in the *Lubanga's Victims' Participation* decision held that "the interpretation of the Statute is governed by the general principle of interpretation of treaties as set out in Article 31(1) of the Vienna Convention."[68]

---

62 Submission Pursuant to Rule 103 (Todd F Buchwald and Steven J Rap, Situation in the State of Palestine, ICC-01/18 (PTC 1) 16 March 2020 at pg 26–27.

63 Hochmayr (n 13) 761; Grover, *Interpreting Crimes in the Rome Statute of the International Criminal Court* (n 3) 350–351; Sadat and Jolly (n 44) 761.

64 Sadat and Jolly (n 44) 764; See also Dire Tladi, 'Cooperation, Immunities, and Article 98 of the Rome Statute: The ICC, Interpretation, and Conflicting Norms: Africa and the International Criminal Court' (2012) 106 ASIL Proceedings 308.

65 Sheppard (n 11) 54–55.

66 Judgment on the Application for Extraordinary Review (n 10) para 33.

67 Decision on the admissibility of the Appeal "Décision sur la confirmation des charges" Lubanga (n 60) para 8.

68 *Judgment on the appeals of The Prosecutor and The Defence against Trial Chamber I's Decision on Victims' Participation of 18 January 2008, ICC-01/04-01/06 11 July 2008* paras 55, 56.

Additionally, in the *Palestine Jurisdiction* case, the Pre-trial Chamber (PTC) determined the jurisdiction question based on Article 19(3) of the Rome Statute using the ordinary meaning, the context, in light of the object and purpose, which are elements under Article 31(1) of the VCLT.[69] However, it did not explicitly mention the VCLT. Similarly, Judge Eboe-Osuji, in his concurring opinion in the *Jordan Appeal* case, referred to all elements of Article 31(1) of the VCLT, and in addition, the preamble and annexes in line with Article 31(2) of the VCLT.[70]

In several other decisions, the ICC has asserted that the general principles of interpretation under Article 31(1) of the VCLT "must" be applied during the Statute's interpretation.[71] As an example, the ICC held in the *Lubanga Final System of Disclosure* case that in determining the statutory framework provided for in the Statute, the RPE, and the ICC regulations, the "judge *must* look at the general principles of interpretation as set out in Article 31(1) of the Vienna Convention on the Law of Treaties."[72] Additionally, the Trial Chamber, in the case of the *Katanga Application under Article 74*, held regarding the VCLT interpretation rules that

---

69 *Decision on the 'Prosecution request pursuant to Article 19(3) for a ruling on the Court's territorial jurisdiction in Palestine*, (*PTC 1*) *ICC-01/18, 5 February 2021* 68–83.

70 *Judgment in the Jordan Referral re Al-Bashir Appeal, Joint Concurring Opinion of Judges Eboe-Osuji, Morrison, Hofmański and Bossa ICC-02/05-01/09-397-Anx1* (*AC*) *06 May 2019* paras 390–393.

71 Decision on Joinder of the cases Katanga and Ngudjolo (n 42) p 7; *Corrigendum: Decision Establishing General Principles Governing Applications to Restrict Disclosure pursuant to Rule 81* (*2*) *and* (*4*) *of the Rules of Procedure and Evidence ICC-01/04-01/06-108-Corr* (*Pre-Trial Chamber I*), *20 May 2006* para 7(ii); Decision concerning the 'Application to the Presidency' (n 61) para 23; *Judgment on the Appeal of Germain Katanga against the Decision of Pre-Trial Chamber I Entitled "Decision on the Defence Request Concerning Languages" ICC- 01/04-01/07-522, 27 May 2008* paras 38,39; *Decision Adjourning the Hearing pursuant to Article 61(7)(C)(ii) of the Rome Statute, The Prosecutor v Jean-Pierre Bemba Gombo, ICC-01/05-01/08-388*(*PTC III*) *3 March 2009* paras 21, 30, 31 (Decision adjourning Bemba's hearing); *Prosecutor v. Lubanga Dyilo, Decision on the Final System of Disclosure and the Establishment of a Timetable, ICC-01/04–01/06* (*PTC 1*) *15 May 2006, Annex I,* para 1 (Decision on the Final System of Disclosure and the Establishment of a Timetable Lubanga);*Judgment on the Appeals of the Prosecutor and the Defense against Trial Chamber I's Decision on Victims' Participation of 18 January 2008, The Prosecutor v Thomas Lubanga Dyilo, ICC-01/04-01/06-1432* (ICC, AC) para 54; *Decision on Application for Leave to Appeal by the Defense of Mathieu Ngudjolo Chui against the Decision on Joinder, ICC-01/04-01/07-384* (ICC, PTC 1) para 28; *ICC Final Submissions of the Prosecution following the Appeal Hearing, The Prosecutor v Omar H A Al Bashir, ICC-02/05-01/09-392* (*AC*) *28 September 2018* paras 6, 7.

72 Decision on the Final System of Disclosure and the Establishment of a Timetable Lubanga, *Annex I,* para 1.

> To interpret the relevant provisions of the Statute and the Elements of Crimes, the chamber must draw on the method of interpretation laid down in the Vienna Convention on the Law of Treaties ("the Vienna Convention"), specifically articles 31 and 32. The chambers of the Court have unanimously and systematically based their interpretation of the Statute on the principles established by the Vienna Convention.[73]

Significantly, the decision acknowledged the ICC's frequent and unanimous use of the VCLT interpretation rules in interpreting the Statute.

The Chambers in the *Katanga Application* case also proceeded to reiterate that

> Nonetheless, the ultimate meaning which the chamber will apply must always be underpinned by the above-mentioned method of interpretation, which means that it must construe, in good faith, the terms used in accordance with their ordinary meaning, considered in their context and in the light of the purpose and object of the Statute.[74]

The word "must" could imply that the VCLT should be obligatorily applied to the Rome Statute's interpretation. The VCLT's primary role in the Statute's interpretation was further reinforced by Judge Eboe-Esuji, who, while interpreting Article 7(2) of the Statute in the *Ruto and Sang* case, referred to the VCLT's Article 31 as "the cardinal principle of treaty interpretation."[75] Similarly, the Appeal's Chamber has referred to Article 31(1) of the VCLT as the Rome Statute's "principal rule of interpretation."[76]

It is notable from the ICC decisions and scholarly input that the VCLT interpretation rules are recognized as the primary interpretation rules applicable to the Rome Statute's interpretation. However, it is equally significant that the ICC decisions and the scholarly writing focus mainly on Article 31(1) elements of the VCLT in the Statute's interpretation and rarely on Article 31(3), which deals with subsequent agreements and practice of States parties. One implication of the skewed application is that subsequent agreements and practice are not treated as central elements in the Rome Statute's interpretation. On the

73 Judgment pursuant to Article 74 Katanga (n 40) para 43.

74 Ibid. para 47.

75 *Decision on Defence Applications for Judgments of Acquittal, The Prosecutor v William Samoei Ruto and Joshua Arap Sang, (TrC V A), ICC-01/09-01/11, 5 April 2016* para 303.

76 Judgment on the Application for Extraordinary Review (n 10) para 33; see also Decision concerning the 'Application to the Presidency' (n 61) para 23.

other hand, it may be that the need for their application has not arisen often. Nonetheless, a different approach does not consider the VCLT rules as the primary interpretive rules in the Statute's interpretation.

3.2 *The VCLT Interpretation Rules as Non-primary in the Rome Statute's Interpretation*

Grover posits that the VCLT interpretation rules apply to the Rome Statute's interpretation, but they may be inadequate to interpret the crimes in the Statute unless applied alongside the Statute's internal rules.[77] In a similar approach, Schaack refers to the VCLT Articles 31 to 33 as "a generic, 'off the rack' approach to treaty interpretation," which fails to specifically provide for criminal treaties.[78] Sadat and Jolly also contend that relying only on the VCLT interpretation rules is unsuitable, especially while dealing with the Statute's substantive law, because of the limitations imposed by Article 22 of the Rome Statute on legality.[79]

From these perspectives, it is contended that due to the nature of the Statute, the "traditional interpretative methodologies (including a straightforward application of the Vienna Convention) do not fit neatly with the unique characteristics of the Rome Statute."[80] In this case, the unique characteristics entail the Rome Statute being an international treaty but, additionally, legislation incorporating a criminal code.[81] In the same vein, Akande acknowledges that the starting point of interpretation should be the Statute's text based on Article 31(1) of the VCLT but adds that since the Statute is also a criminal law instrument, other interpretation rules besides the VCLT apply.[82] From this perspective, it is contended that the Rome Statute's distinct legal nature as a criminal law statute requires other rules, such as the legality principle and human rights, to apply besides the VCLT.[83]

77 Grover, *Interpreting Crimes in the Rome Statute of the International Criminal Court* (n 3) 88.

78 Beth Van Schaack, 'Crimen Sine Lege: Judicial Lawmaking at the Intersection of Law and Morals' (2008) 97 Georgetown Law Journal 119, 149.

79 Sadat and Jolly (n 44) 762–763; Grover, *Interpreting Crimes in the Rome Statute of the International Criminal Court* (n 3) 44.

80 Sadat and Jolly (n 44) 759.

81 Ibid.

82 Dapo Akande, 'Treaty Interpretation, the VCLT and the ICC Statute: A Response to Kevin Jon Heller & Dov Jacobs' <https://www.ejiltalk.org/treaty-interpretation-the-vclt-and-the-icc-statute-a-response-to-kevin-jon-heller-dov-jacobs/> accessed 29 December 2020.

83 Ibid; Sadat and Jolly (n 44) 762–763; Suhr (n 7) 54–55; Michail Vagias (n 7) 73 para 2.

In a related approach, it is suggested that the ICC may only apply the VCLT interpretation rules where a lacuna is established in the Statute, and the legality interpretation is impossible. For instance, in the case of *Mathieu Ngudjolo*, the Court held that

> Since no provision expressly regulating the issue of joint or separate pre-trial proceedings of a case appears in the Statute or in the Rules, [...] and there is the existence of a legislative lacuna in the regulation of a procedural matter, the strict literal interpretation of the relevant provisions required by the principle of legality is not possible. The chamber, acting under Article 21(1)(a) of the Statute, must apply the interpretative criteria provided for in the Vienna Convention.[84]

One reading of the extract from the decision is that the VCLT rules can apply but not as the primary rule unless the strict interpretation under Article 22 cannot first resolve the issue. Similarly, the Appeal's Chamber in the *Katanga and Ngudjolo Joinder* case held that if

> The words in their natural and ordinary meaning are ambiguous or lead to an unreasonable result, then, and then only, must the Court, by resort to other methods of interpretation, seek to ascertain what the parties really did mean when they used these words. Consequently, in the unlikely event that the Vienna Convention were to be found to be applicable, then it would be appropriate, pursuant to article 32 of the Vienna Convention, to refer to the *travaux préparatoires* of the ICC Statute.[85]

Impliedly, the VCLT interpretation rules are unlikely to be applied where the wording has no lacuna or ambiguity. The decision, however, seemingly fails to acknowledge that determining the ambiguity of the ordinary words requires reference to the VCLT rules. Similarly, in the case of the *Bashir Warrant of Arrest Application*, the PTC appeared to suggest that the VCLT is applied only when there is a lacuna in the written law of the Rome Statute. The PTC held that

84 *Decision on Application for Leave to Appeal by the Defense of Mathieu Ngudjolo Chui against the Decision on Joinder, ICC-01/04-01/07-384* (ICC, PTC 1) para 5, 6.

85 *Appeal Against the Decision on Joinder rendered on 10 March 2008 by the Pre- Trial Chamber in the Germain Katanga and Mathieu Ngudjolo Cases, Prosecutor v. Germain Katanga and Mathieu Ngudjolo, ICC-01/04-01/07(AC) 21 April 2008* para 37.

> According to article 21(1)(a) of the Statute, the Court must apply "in the first place" the Statute, the Elements, and the Rules ... Those other sources of law provided for in paragraphs (1)(b) and (1)(c) of Article 21 of the Statute can only be applied when the following two conditions are met: (i) there is a lacuna in the written law contained in the Statute, the Elements, and the Rules; and (ii) such lacuna cannot be filled by the application of the criteria provided for in articles 31 and 32 of the VCLT and Article 21 (3) of the Statute.[86]

However, some scholars disagreed with the PTC's decision in the *Al Bashir* case above. Grover, for instance, disagrees with the decision that seemingly asserts that the VCLT comes into play only if there is a continued gap after the Statute and the Elements have been applied in accordance with Article 21(1)(a).[87] Grover's position implies that the VCLT should be applied in the first instance and not as a secondary means.[88] Additionally, Cryer and Powderly faulted the decision, arguing that determining the existence of a lacuna in the Rome Statute cannot happen in a vacuum and depends on the Statute's interpretation applying Article 31 of the VCLT.[89] This book adopts Cryer's and Powderly's perspectives on the basis that ambiguity cannot be determined without first resorting to the VCLT interpretation rules in Article 31.

A rare approach considers that the VCLT falls under the "applicable treaties" in Article 21(1)(b) of the Rome Statute.[90] In this regard, Hochmayr avers that the VCLT interpretive rules fall under "applicable treaties" and as part of customary international law, they emanate from "principles and rules of international law" provided for under Article 21(1)(b) of the Statute.[91] Based on this approach, Hochmayr argues that the VCLT can only apply to the Statute "in the second place" under Article 21(1)(b).[92] This approach appears to treat the VCLT rules not as interpretive rules but as sources of law similar to those in

86 Decision on Bashir Arrest Warrant (n 10) paras 44, 126.

87 *Decision on Confirmation of Charges, Prosecutor v Germain Katanga and Mathieu Ngudjolo, ICC-01/04-01/07-717 (PTC 1) 30 September 2008* para 508; Grover, *Interpreting Crimes in the Rome Statute of the International Criminal Court* (n 3) 364, 365 para 1.

88 Ibid., 365 para 1; Martti Koskenniemi and Päivi Leino, 'Fragmentation of International Law? Postmodern Anxieties' (2002) 15 LJIL 228–232.

89 Robert Cryer, 'Royalism and the King: Article 21 of the Rome Statute and the Politics of Sources' (2009) 12 New Criminal Law Review: An International and Interdisciplinary Journal 397–398; Powderly (n 10) 473–474.

90 Schabas (n 1) 205; Hochmayr (n 13) 667; deGuzman (n 11) 938–939.

91 Hochmayr (n 13) 667.

92 Ibid.

Article 21 of the Statute. Following a similar approach, Davidson refers to the VCLT as an "additional source of law" to be used by judges to interpret the crimes in the Statute.[93] In contrast, Sadat and Jolly aver that the Rome Statute's interpretation as an internal court document should be treated differently from the VCLT interpretation.[94] The book aligns with the position that the VCLT interpretation rules interpret sources of law, and the two are distinguishable.

Another approach to the VCLT rules applying in a secondary position is based on considering the Rome Statute as a document for an independent international organization.[95] Based on this perspective, two positions emerge. The first approach contends that as an international organization, the interpretation rules explicitly provided for in a constituent instrument should be prioritized over the general rules of the VCLT.[96] In this context, the VCLT interpretation rules would seemingly apply only on a secondary basis. The second approach assumes that the Statute provisions should be interpreted using the interpretation rules from both the VCLT and the Rome Statute.[97] Under this approach, the ICC combines the different interpretation means found both in the VCLT and the Rome Statute, depending on the case.[98] In this respect, Vagias proposes a two-pronged approach. Vagias posits that when dealing with rules that relate to the ICC as an organization, an object and purpose interpretation based on the VCLT should be applied, while provisions containing substantive criminal rules should be interpreted based on the legality rule under Article 22 of the Statute.[99] This approach implies that the VCLT interpretive rules are not the primary rule in the Statute's interpretation in each circumstance.

In a rare and contrasting approach, a few scholars, however, find the VCLT inapplicable to the Statute's interpretation since it has its own internal inter-

93 Caroline Davidson, 'How to Read International Criminal Law: Strict Construction and the Rome Statute of the International Criminal Court' (2017) 91 St. John's Law Review, 38 para 2.

94 Sadat and Jolly (n 44) 760.

95 'The ICC at a Glance ICC-PIOS-FS-01-007/19_Eng' <www.icc-cpi.int>; Article 2 of the Statute.

96 Art 5(3) of the VCLT uses the phrase 'without prejudice to the rules of the organizations'; Henry Schermers, 'Interpretation of the Constituent Instruments', in R J Dupuy (ed.), *A Handbook on International Organizations* (2nd edn Dordrecht Martinus Nijhoff, 1998) 406; Heikkila (n 2) 241.

97 Michail Vagias (n 7) 73 para 2.

98 Judgment on the Prosecutor's Application for Extraordinary Review (n 10) paras 33–41.

99 Michail Vagias (n 7) 73–74.

pretive rules. Using this approach, Jacobs contends that the Rome Statute has express and specific provisions on interpretation grounded on the legality principle, and the VCLT interpretation rules, therefore, should not apply to the Statute.[100] Jacobs argues that international criminal courts should only use interpretation rules consistent with the legality principle; consequently, Articles 31 and 32 of the VCLT should be excluded as a means of interpreting international criminal statutes, including the Rome Statute.[101]

However, other scholars and several court decisions differ with Jacob's view, stating instead that the general rules of interpretation under the VCLT also apply to international criminal law.[102] Additionally, other international criminal tribunals, such as the ICTY,[103] the ICTR,[104] and the Special Tribunal of Lebanon (STL),[105] have recognized the applicability of Articles 31–33 of the VCLT in interpreting international criminal law statutes.

Having established the general use of the VCLT in the Rome Statute's interpretation by the ICC and scholars, the following section considers the reference to the specific elements of interpretation under Articles 31 and 32 of the VCLT in interpreting the Statute.

3.2.1 The Collective Use of Article 31 Elements of the VCLT in Interpreting the Rome Statute

As previously indicated, the ICC has repeatedly relied on the provisions of Articles 31 and 32 of the VCLT as the primary source of interpretative princi-

---

100 Dov Jacobs, 'International Criminal Law' in Jean D'Aspremont and Kammerhofer Jörg (eds), *International Legal Positivism in a Post-Modern World* (Cambridge University Press 2014) 469; Gregor Maučec, 'The International Criminal Court and the Issue of Intersectionality – A Conceptual and Legal Framework for Analysis' (2021) 21 International Criminal Law Review 1, 469.

101 Dov Jacobs, 'Positivism and International Criminal Law: The Principle of Legality as a Rule of Conflict of Theories' (2012) SSRN Scholarly Paper ID 2046311 36 <https://papers.ssrn.com/abstract=2046311> accessed 10 February 2022.

102 Gerhard Werle and Florian Jeßberger, *Principles of International Criminal Law* (Oxford University Press 2020) para 191.

103 *Prosecutor v Dusko Tadic a/k/a 'Dule', Decision on the Defence Motion for Interlocutory Appeal on Jurisdiction, ICTY (IT-94-1) 2 October 1995* paras 71–80; *Prosecutor v Zejnil Delalij Judgment, ICTY-96-21-T, 16 November 1998* para 1161.

104 *Prosecutor Theoneste Bagosora and 28 Others, Decision on the Admissibility of the Prosecutor's Appeal from the Decision of a Confirming Judge Dismissing an Indictment against Theoneste Bagosora and 28 Others, ICTR 98-37-A, 8 June 1998* paras 28–29.

105 *Interlocutory Decision on the Applicable Law: Terrorism, Conspiracy, Homicide, Perpetration, Cumulative Charging, STL-11-Ol/1 16 February 2011* para 26.

ples governing the Rome Statute's interpretation.[106] In this respect, the ICC has alternately applied all the elements in Article 31(1) or 32 of the VCLT in the Statute's interpretation while applying only individual elements in other instances.

In several cases, the ICC has referred to all or most of the elements under Article 31(1) of the VCLT while interpreting the Statute. For example, in the *Palestine Jurisdiction* case, the Pre-trial chamber referred to the ordinary meaning, the context, the object and purpose, and even the drafting history of Article 19(3) in determining the issue of jurisdiction.[107] Similarly, in his concurring but separate decision, Judge Mindua held that

> To interpret the "interests of justice" as contained in the Statute, I am going to use the interpretative tools suggested by Articles 31 to 33 of the Vienna Convention on the Law of Treaties as the general rules of treaty interpretation under customary international law. Hence, I will consider the text and context of the relevant provisions of the Statute in connection with its object and purpose. In so doing, I will take into account, in good faith, the ordinary meaning of every word. If this exercise is not entirely satisfactory, I am not going to hesitate to recourse to supplementary tools of interpretation, such as the preparatory works (*travaux préparatoires*) of the Statute.[108]

Additionally, the PTC in the *Lubanga Dyilo Warrant of Arrest* case also referred to the three elements under Article 31(1) of the VCLT, which are the ordinary meaning, the context, and the object and purpose to determine that the ICC lacked discretion in finding a case inadmissible when the requirements on the "gravity" of the case had not been met.[109] Similarly, Judge Eboe-Osuji, while

106 Judgment on the Application for Extraordinary Review (n 10) paras 5,33,39; Decision on Bashir Arrest Warrant (n 10) para 44; Decision adjourning Bemba's hearing (n 71) para 361).

107 *Decision on the 'Prosecution request pursuant to Article 19(3) for a ruling on the Court's territorial jurisdiction in Palestine,* (*PTC I*) *ICC-01/18, 5 February 2021* 68–72,76 (Decision on Territorial jurisdiction in Palestine).

108 *Concurring and Separate Opinion of Judge Antoine Kesia-MBE Mindua, Decision Pursuant to Article 15 of the Rome Statute on the Authorisation of an Investigation into the Situation in the Islamic Republic of Afghanistan, ICC-02/17-33-Anx-Corr* (*PTC II*) *31 May 2019* para 29.

109 *Prosecutor v Thomas Lubanga Dyilo, ICC-01/04-01/06, Under Seal Decision on the Prosecutor's Application for a Warrant of Arrest, Article 58* (*Annexed to Decision Concerning Pre-Trial Chamber I's Decision on 10 February 2006 and the Incorporation of Documents into Record of the Case Against Mr Thomas Lubanga Dyilo* (*PTC I*), *24 February 2006*) paras 42–44.

interpreting Article 7(2) of the Statute, referred to the wording, the context, the object and purpose of the Statute based on Article 31 of the VCLT, which he designated as "the cardinal principle of treaty interpretation."[110] The Appeal's Chamber in the *Jordan Appeal* also referred to the Statute's context, object and purpose without expressly mentioning the VCLT.[111] More expressly, Judge Eboe-Osuji, in a concurring decision in the said *Jordan Appeal* case, applied the VCLT Article 31(1) elements and 31(2) in the decision to harmonize Articles 27 and 98 of the Rome Statute.[112] The *Regulations of the Registry Judicial Review* case made a similar reference to the three elements under Article 31(1) of the VCLT.[113]

The Appeal's Chamber also used the contextual interpretation of Rule 85, the object and purpose of the Rome Statute, and the ordinary meaning based on the VCLT Article 31(1) to determine the participation of victims in leading evidence against the accused's guilt or innocence.[114] Additionally, in the *Lubanga Trial* judgment, the majority cited the Appeal chamber's decision with approval, noting that the Rome Statute should be interpreted in conformity with Article 31(1) of the VCLT.[115] Judge Hans Kaul, in his dissenting opinion, while defining "organizational policy," interpreted Article 7(2) of the Statute based on the VCLT's Article 31(1), dividing the subheadings under the "ordinary meaning" "contextual interpretation" and the "object and purpose."[116]

110 *Decision on Defence Applications for Judgments of Acquittal, The Prosecutor v William Samoei Ruto and Joshua Arap Sang, (TrC V A), ICC-01/09-01/11, 5 April 2016* paras 303, 304.

111 *ICC Judgment in the Jordan Referral re Al-Bashir Appeal, The Prosecutor v Omar H Ahmad Al Bashir, ICC-02/05-01/09-397 (AC) 6 May 2019* para 121.

112 *Judgment in the Jordan Referral re Al-Bashir Appeal, Joint Concurring Opinion of Judges Eboe-Osuji, Morrison, Hofmański and Bossa ICC-02/05-01/09-397-Anx1 (AC) 06 May 2019* paras 390–393.

113 Decision concerning Application to the Presidency (n 61) paras 23 and 36.

114 *Judgment on the appeals of The Prosecutor and The Defence against Trial Chamber I's Decision on Victims' Participation of 18 January 2008*, ICC-01/04-01/06, 11 July 2008 paras 57 and 58; See also *Judgment on the appeal of the Prosecutor against the decision of Trial Chamber I entitled 'Decision on the consequences of non-disclosure of Exculpatory materials covered by Article 54(3)(e) agreements and the application to Stay the prosecution of the accused, together with certain other issues raised at the Status Conference on 10 June 2008', ICC-01/04-01/06-1486, 21 October 2008* paras 40, 41.

115 Decision concerning the Application to the Presidency (n 61) Para 36; Judgment on the Application for Extraordinary Review (n 10) para 33.

116 *Decision Pursuant to Article 15 of the Rome Statute on the Authorization of an Investigation into the Situation in the Republic of Kenya, ICC-01/09 (PTC II), 31 March 2010* Dissenting Opinion of Judge Hans-Peter Kaul paras 33, 45, 54–56.

Several scholars have also reiterated the use of Article 31(1) elements as vital to the Rome Statute's interpretation.[117] Alex Davidson, for instance, considers the use of the VCLT's "general rule" of Article 31(1) as obligatory, emphasizing that the ICC "must" consider the ordinary meaning of the text, its context, which includes preambles and annexes, and the object and purpose of the provision.[118]

Additionally, based on the ordinary meaning under Article 31(1), the ICC has, in several cases, emphasized the textual interpretation of the Statute's provisions.[119] In the same vein, the ICC has made specific reference to the object and purpose of the Rome Statute provisions in the *Katanga and Ngudjolo Admissibility* case and several other cases to clarify provisions that were too generally worded or ambiguous.[120]

---

117 Michael Kourabas, 'A Vienna Convention Interpretation of the Interests of Justice Provision of the Rome Statute, the Legality of Domestic Amnesty Agreements, and the Situation in Northern Uganda: A Great Qualitative Step Forward, or a Normative Retreat' (2007) 14 U C Davis Journal of International Law & Policy 69; Gilbert Bitti (n 12) 434; Grover, 'A Call to Arms: Fundamental Dilemmas Confronting the Interpretation of Crimes in the Rome Statute of the International Criminal Court' (n 3) 572; Sadat and Jolly (n 44) 764,766; Meagan S Wong, 'The Activation of the International Criminal Court's Jurisdiction over the Crime of Aggression: International Institutional Law and Dispute Settlement Perspectives' (2020) 22 International Community Law Review 197, 221.

118 Alex Davidson, 'Human Rights Protection before the International Criminal Court: Assessing the Scope and Application of Article 21(3) of the Rome Statute' (2016) 18 International Community Law Review 83.

119 Decision on Territorial jurisdiction in Palestine (n 107) para 69; *Prosecutor v Dominic Ongwen Defense Request for the Chamber to Issue an Immediate Ruling Confirming the Burden and Standard of Proof Applicable to Articles 31(a) and (d) of the Rome Statute ICC-02/04-01/15* (ICC, Trial Chamber IX) para 13; Judgment on the Prosecutor's Application for Extraordinary Review (n 10) paras 38,39; Judgment Pursuant to Article 74 Lubanga (n 17) Separate decision of Judge Fulford para 13; *Decision on Application for Leave to Appeal by the Defence of Mathieu Ngudjolo Chui against the Decision on Joinder, ICC-01/04-01/07-384, 9 April 2008* para 5 (ICC, PTC 1) 6, 7;*Judgement on the appeal of the Prosecutor against the decision of Trial Chamber I entitled "Decision on the consequences of non-disclosure of exculpatory materials covered by Article 54(3)(e) agreements and the Application to Stay the Prosecution of the accused, together with Certain other issues raised at the Status, Conference on 10 June 2008 the Appeal of the Prosecutor, Prosecutor v. Thomas Dyilo, ICC-01/04-01/06-1486, 21 Oct 2008* Separate opinion of Judge Georghios Pikis para 37.

120 *Reasons for the Oral Decision on the Motion Challenging the Admissibility of the Case (Art 19 of the Statute), The Prosecutor v Germain Katanga and Mathieu Ngudjolo Chui ICC-01/04-01/07 (TC II) 16 June 2009* paras 35-36;*Judgment on the Appeal of Mr Germain Katanga against the Oral Decision of Trial Chamber II of 12 June 2009 on the Admissibility of the Case, Prosecutor v Germain Katanga and Ngudjolo Chui, ICC-01/04-01/07 OA 8 (AC) 25 September 2009* para 79; *The Prosecutor v Thomas Lubanga Dyilo, Decision on the confirma-*

The contextual interpretation based on Article 31(1) of the VCLT has also been referred to by scholars and the ICC in the Rome Statute's interpretation, albeit less frequently than the textual interpretation. For instance, the judges in the *Gbagbo* case read Article 12(3) of the Rome Statute in the context of Rule 44(2) and Article 13 of the Statute to determine that States Parties had the competence to accept the Court's jurisdiction over future crimes.[121] The ICC has referred to the context based on Article 31(1) of the VCLT to interpret the Statute in multiple other cases.[122] Schabas also refers to the VCLT Article 31(1) to conclude that the Rome Statute's preamble, the Statute's Final Act, and the Elements constitute the context.[123]

3.2.2 Subsequent Agreements and Practice under the VCLT and the Rome Statute

In order to analyze whether States Parties have a role in the Rome Statute's interpretation, an examination of subsequent agreements and practice of States Parties as grounded on Article 31(3) of the VCLT and their impact on the Statute's interpretation, if any, is vital. Notably, there are diverse opinions regarding what constitutes "subsequent agreements and practice" of States Parties in relation to the interpretation of the Rome Statute. In this regard, Nolte has noted that subsequent agreements and subsequent practice have a less significant role in interpreting crimes in the Statute due to the difficulty of

---

tion of charges, ICC-01/04-01/06-803, *29 January 2007* (PTC 1) paras 278, 281; Judgment Pursuant to Article 74 Lubanga (n 17) separate and dissenting opinion of Judge Benito paras 6-8,13; Judgment pursuant to Article 74 Katanga, (n 40) para 55; Decision Adjourning Bemba's Hearing (n 71) para 36.

121 *Judgment on the appeal of Laurent Koudou Gbagbo against the decision of Pre-Trial Chamber I on jurisdiction and stay of the proceedings*, ICC-02/11-01/11-321, *12 December 2012* para 83; Michail Vagias (n 7) 62 para 3.

122 Decision on the Territorial jurisdiction in Palestine (n 107) paras 71–73; *Decision on the appeals of William Samoei Ruto and Joshua Arap Sang against the decision of Pre-Trial Chamber II of 23 January 2012 entitled 'Decision on the Confirmation of Charges Pursuant to Article 61(7)(a) and (b) of the Rome Statute' (Appeals Chamber)*, ICC-01/09-01/11-414, *24 May 2012* (ICC) paras 25, 27; *The Prosecutor v. Germain Katanga and Mathieu Ngudjolo Chui, Reasons for the Oral Decision on the Motion Challenging the Admissibility of the Case (Art. 19 of the Statute)* ICC-01/04-01/07, *16 June 2009* para 33; Decision Adjourning Bemba's hearing (n 71) para 35.

123 Schabas (n 1) 213; Grover, *Interpreting Crimes in the Rome Statute of the International Criminal Court* (n 3) 363; Petra Viebig, 'Legal Sources and Legal Methodology Under the ICC Statute' in Petra Viebig (ed), *Illicitly Obtained Evidence at the International Criminal Court* (TMC Asser Press 2016) 16–17.

proving agreement among States Parties about a particular practice and how to interpret it.[124]

Nevertheless, there has been some reference to subsequent practice and subsequent agreements by the ICC and scholars, albeit quite rarely. For instance, the ASP resolutions adopting the RPE and the Elements have been construed as subsequent agreements of the States Parties.[125] The Elements have been referred to as "subsequent agreements" based on Article 31(3)(a) of the VCLT since they were adopted by consensus in 2000 by the ASP.[126] Consequently, it is averred that based on Article 31(3) of the VCLT, where the Elements are relevant, they "must" be considered in interpretation.[127] Cryer, however, appears to differ, stating that the Elements are neither authentic subsequent practice nor "binding" agreements in the Rome Statute's interpretation.[128]

The Trial Chamber made specific reference to subsequent agreements and practice in the *Ruto and Sang Excusal from Presence* case, which related to the ASP's amendments to the RPE 134 *bis*, *ter*, and *quater*, allowing an accused to be excused from attending parts of the trial.[129] The Trial Chamber held that "Rules 134 *ter* and 134 *quater* of the Rules are part of the Resolution adopted by the ASP, and as such can be regarded as a 'subsequent agreement' about the scope and application of Article 63(1) of the Statute under Article 31(3)(a) of Vienna Convention."[130] At the time of writing this book, this case remains the only one where the ICC has explicitly referred to the subsequent agreement of States Parties and used it decisively in the interpretation of the Rome Statute.

124 Grover, *Interpreting Crimes in the Rome Statute of the International Criminal Court* (n 3) 391–392.

125 Schabas (n 1) 213; Grover, *Interpreting Crimes in the Rome Statute of the International Criminal Court* (n 3) 363.

126 Grover, *Interpreting Crimes in the Rome Statute of the International Criminal Court* (n 3) 363; Suhr (n 7) 61; Article 9(3) of the Rome Statute.

127 Grover, *Interpreting Crimes in the Rome Statute of the International Criminal Court* (n 3) 365; Suhr (n 7) 61; Decision on Bashir Arrest Warrant (n 10) para 126.

128 Cryer (n 89) 398.

129 *Decision on Ruto's Excusal Request for Excusal from Continuous Presence at Trial, The Prosecutor v William Samoei Ruto and Joshua Arap Sang, ICC-01/09-01/11-777, 18 June 2013, Trial Chamber V (A* (Decision on Ruto's excusal request).

130 *Reasons for the Decision on Excusal from Presence at Trial under Rule 134 quater, The Prosecutor v William Samoei Ruto and Joshua Arap Sang, ICC-01/09-01/11-1186* (*TrC V[A] 18 Feb 2014* para 56 (Reasons for the Decision on Ruto's Excusal).

In the same vein, most scholars widely accept that the ASP resolutions adopted at the Kampala Review Conference[131] and the attached Seven interpretive declarations (Understandings)[132] constitute "subsequent agreements" regarding the interpretation and application of the crime of aggression under the Rome Statute.[133] Based on Article 31(3)(a) of the VCLT and the ILC provisions,[134] the Kampala resolutions are seen as constituting subsequent agreements because they were adopted by consensus, and no States Parties objected.[135]

Additionally, the New York Resolution[136] on activating the ICC's jurisdiction on the crime of aggression has been referred to by some scholars as a "subsequent agreement" and "subsequent practice" within the meaning of Article 31(3) of the VCLT, having been adopted through the ASP's consensus.[137] Nevertheless, some scholars dispute that the New York resolution represent subsequent agreements or subsequent practice under Article 31(3) of the VCLT due to objections raised subsequently by some ASP members to some of the propositions after the ASP's adoption.[138]

131 Kampala Amendments on the Crime of Aggression (Kampala Amendments), Resolution RC/Res.6, 11 June 2010 para 1, available at <https://asp.icc-cpi.int/iccdocs/asp_docs/Resolutions/RC-Res.6-ENG. Pdf>.

132 Ibid.

133 Schabas (n 1) 213; Grover, *Interpreting Crimes in the Rome Statute of the International Criminal Court* (n 3) 368, 378; Dapo Akande and Antonios Tzanakopoulos, 'Treaty Law and ICC Jurisdiction over the Crime of Aggression' (2018) 29 EJIL 952–954.

134 ILC 2018 (n 29) Conclusion 4(1).

135 Akande and Tzanakopoulos (n 133) 952; Darin Clearwater, 'When (and How) Will the Crime of Aggression Amendments Enter into Force? Interpreting the Rome Statute by Recognizing Participation in the Adoption of the Crime of Aggression Resolutions as "Subsequent Practice" under the VCLT' (2018) 16 JICJ 53.

136 RC/Res.6, Adopted at the 13th plenary meeting, on 11 June 2010, by consensus; ICC-ASP /16/ Res.5, Adopted at the 13th plenary meeting, on 14 December 2017, by consensus titled 'Activation of the jurisdiction of the Court over the Crime of Aggression.

137 Clearwater (n 135) 33; Grover, *Interpreting Crimes in the Rome Statute of the International Criminal Court* (n 3) 368, 378; Meagan S Wong, 'The Activation of the International Criminal Court's Jurisdiction over the Crime of Aggression: International Institutional Law and Dispute Settlement Perspectives' (2020) 22 International Community Law Review 201.

138 Akande and Tzanakopoulos (n 133) 946–947; Nikolas Stürchler, 'The Activation of the Crime of Aggression in Perspective' (*EJIL: Talk!*, 26 January 2018) <https://www.ejiltalk.org/the-activation-of-the-crime-of-aggression-in-perspective/> accessed 20 April 2022; ILC 2018 (n 29) Conclusion 11(3); Kevin Jon Heller, 'The Uncertain Legal Status of the Aggression Understandings' (2011) SSRN Scholarly Paper ID 1883351 9 <https://papers.ssrn.com/abstract=1883351> accessed 20 April 2022.

As can be gathered from the ICC's decisions and scholarly writings, the explicit reference to subsequent agreements and practice regarding the Rome Statute's interpretation is quite limited. On the one hand, this scanty reference may speak to the ICC not treating subsequent agreements and practice of States Parties as central to the Rome Statute's interpretation. In this case, it may be a basis for calling on the ICC to apply the subsequent agreements and practice more frequently. On the other hand, it may imply that States Parties have not generated enough subsequent agreements and practice for the ICC to rely on.

However, as earlier mentioned, besides the VCLT interpretation rules applying to the Rome Statute's interpretation, some scholars and court decisions have deemed Articles 21(3) and 22 to constitute interpretation rules for the Statute. Their place in the Rome Statute's interpretation and the connection with the VCLT interpretation rules are discussed next.

4 Article 21(3) and 22 of the Rome Statute as Interpretive Rules

4.1 *Articles 21(3) and 22 Overview*

It has been posited that beyond the VCLT interpretation rules applying to the Rome Statute's interpretation, the Statute also provides its own interpretation rules primarily found in Articles 21(3) and 22.[139] Grover refers to Articles 21(3) and 22 as "interpretive imperatives."[140] Other scholars have similarly found that Articles 21(3) and 22(2) constitute interpretation principles.[141]

4.2 *Consistency with Human Rights under Article 21 (3) of the Rome Statute*

Article 21(3) requires that the application and interpretation of law must be consistent with internationally recognized human rights and be without any adverse distinction founded on grounds such as gender, among others. Article 21(3) is said to illustrate the vital role the Rome Statute's drafters attached to protecting human rights for the accused, the victims, and witnesses.[142]

139 Michail Vagias (n 7) 64.

140 Grover, *Interpreting Crimes in the Rome Statute of the International Criminal Court* (n 3) 29.

141 Suhr (n 7) 54–55; Michail Vagias (n 7) 64 para 3.

142 Grover, 'A Call to Arms: Fundamental Dilemmas Confronting the Interpretation of Crimes in the Rome Statute of the International Criminal Court' (n 3) 558–563.

Notably, the ICC jurisprudence has neither expressly defined the phrase "internationally recognized human rights," espoused in Article 21(3), nor given its boundaries.[143] Consequently, several related issues remain unresolved, including the precise meaning of "internationally recognized human rights."[144] Additionally, its explicit content[145] and how to incorporate human rights in the Rome Statute's interpretation remain unsettled.[146] Further, there is no consensus regarding which applicable law is subject to Article 21(3).[147] Also debatable is whether Article 21(3) holds primacy over the other applicable law under Article 21.[148] The Appeal's Chamber has also not conclusively given a distinct hierarchy regarding the human rights approach to interpretation.[149] This lack of clarity raises the question of the place of human rights in the Rome Statute's interpretation, especially in light of the VCLT rules. Scholars and the ICC have consequently taken varied approaches to explaining Article 21(3).

Some scholars state that the Article 21(3) permits judges to refer to various external rules and jurisprudence while interpreting the Rome Statute.[150] On this basis, the ICC has referred to international instruments such as the International Convention on Civil and Political Rights (ICCPR)[151] and the CRC while interpreting the Statute provisions.[152] The ICC has also frequently referred to regional instruments such as the European Convention on Human Rights (ECHR), the jurisprudence of the European Court of Human Rights

143 Stian Øby Johansen, *The Human Rights Accountability Mechanisms of International Organizations* (Cambridge University Press 2020) 241; Lorenzo Gradon et al 'General Framework of International Criminal Procedure' in Guran Sluiter et al (eds), International Criminal Procedure; Principles and Rules (OUP) 2013, 92–94.

144 Rebecca Young, 'Internationally Recognized Human Rights' before the International Criminal Court' (2011) 60 The International and Comparative Law Quarterly 189; Pellet (n 13) 1080.

145 Grover, *Interpreting Crimes in the Rome Statute of the International Criminal Court* (n 3) 118; Hafner and Binder (n 10) 161, 183; Gilbert Bitti (n 12) 434.

146 Hochmayr (n 13) 679; Pellet (n 13) 1080.

147 J Verhoeven, 'Article 21 of the Rome Statute and the Ambiguities of Applicable Law' (2002) 33 NYIL 14.

148 Grover, 'A Call to Arms: Fundamental Dilemmas Confronting the Interpretation of Crimes in the Rome Statute of the International Criminal Court' (n 3) 543, 560.

149 Michail Vagias (n 7) 66 para 2.

150 Grover, *Interpreting Crimes in the Rome Statute of the International Criminal Court* (n 3) 559; Powderly (n 10) 486; Gilbert Bitti (n 12) 434.

151 Judgment on the Application for Extraordinary Review (n 10) para 38.

152 Judgment Pursuant to Article 74 Lubanga (n 17) para 604; Decision on the Final System of Disclosure and the Establishment of a Timetable Lubanga (n 71) Annex 1 para 3.

(ECtHR),[153] and the Inter-American Court of Human Rights (IACHR).[154] The ICC has even occasionally cited some soft law human rights instruments.[155] It has, however, been noted that the ICC has failed to clarify the criteria used to select the human rights it refers to in the Rome Statute's interpretation.[156]

4.2.1 Whether Article 21(3) Is a Rule of Interpretation or a Source of Law

In relation to the Rome Statute's interpretation, some scholars construe Article 21(3) as a rule of interpretation, while others consider it only as a source of law. Notably, unlike the other provisions in Article 21(1) and (2) of the Statute, which only require application, the phrase "interpreted and applied" is used with regards to Article 21(3). Some scholars, like Bitti, recognize Article 21(3) not as an interpretative principle but as a source of law for the Court. [157] In this regard, Bitti states that a "distinction must be made between the rules of interpretation of treaties as set forth in the Vienna Convention on the Law of Treaties and the material source of law, such as the one stipulated in Article 21 paragraph 3."[158]

Hafner and Binder similarly refer to Article 21(3) as a source of law.[159] Based on Article 21(3) as a source of law, some scholars have deemed it as creating an international "super-legality" hierarchy with human rights having a superior status over the applicable law under Article 21 of the Rome Statute.[160] From

153 *Judgment on the Appeal of Mr. Thomas Lubanga Dyilo against the Decision on the Defence Challenge to the Jurisdiction of the Court pursuant to article 19 (2) (a) of the Statute of 3 October 2006, ICC-01/04-01/06, 14 December 2006* para 38; Gilbert Bitti (n 12) 434; Sheppard (n 11) 52–53.

154 Gilbert Bitti (n 12) 434; Sheppard (n 11) 52–53.

155 The Court cited the Standard Minimum Rules for the Treatment of Prisoners and the United Nations Body of Principles for the Protection of All Persons under Any Form of Detention or Imprisonment in *Prosecutor v. Germain Katanga and Mathieu Ngudjolo Chui, Decision on 'Mr Mathieu Ngudjolo's Complaint Under Regulation 221(1) of the Regulations of the Registry Against the Registrar's Decision of 18 November 2008', ICC-RoR21702/08-8, The Presidency, 10 March 2009*, paras 27, 28.

156 Sheppard (n 11) 43, 49.

157 Gilbert Bitti (n 12) 437.

158 Gilbert Bitti, 'Article 21 Of the Statute of the International Criminal Court and the Treatment of Sources of Law in the Jurisprudence of the ICC' in Carsten Stahn (ed), *The Emerging Practice of the International Criminal Court* (Brill Nijhoff 2009) 303.

159 Hafner and Binder (n 10) 174.

160 Pellet (n 13) 1081; Grover, *Interpreting Crimes in the Rome Statute of the International Criminal Court* (n 3) 113; Gilbert Bitti (n 12) 436; Judgment Pursuant to Article 74 Lubanga (n 17) para 602; Situation in the DRC, ICC-01/04-01/06-772, (AC) 14 December 2006, para

this perspective, the ICC and all its organs are required to conform to the primacy requirements of Article 21(3).[161]

Schabas compares Article 21(3) to a constitutional provision since it governs the application and interpretation of all the Rome Statute's provisions and all the sources of applicable law.[162] Article 21(3) is consequently considered one of the most critical provisions in the Statute[163] since it sets the standard against which the ICC tests all applicable law.[164] In contrast, the Trial and the Appeal Chambers have, in some cases, cautioned against the ICC "acting as a court of human rights" since "it was never conceived as such."[165]

Significantly, in several instances, the difference between Article 21(3) as a source of applicable law and as an interpretation rule has appeared unclear. In this respect, it has been noted that even the ICC has, in certain instances, failed to distinguish between Article 21(3) as an interpretive rule and a source

36; Mahnoush H Arsanjani, 'The Rome Statute of the International Criminal Court' (1999) 93 AJIL 22, 28–29.

161 Alex Davidson, 'Human Rights Protection before the International Criminal Court: Assessing the Scope and Application of Article 21 (3) of the Rome Statute' (2016) 18 International Community Law Review 79; *Decision on an Amicus Curiae application and on the "Requête tendant à obtenir présentations des témoins DRC-D02-P-0350, DRC-D02-P-0236, DRC-D02-P-0228 aux autorités néerlandaises aux fins d'asile" (articles 68 and 93(7) of the Statute), The Prosecutor v Germain Katanga and Mathieu Ngudjolo Chui ICC-01/04-01/07, 9 June 2011* para 77 (Decision on Amicus Curiae application Katanga and Ngudjolo).

162 William Schabas, *The International Criminal Court; A Commentary on the Rome Statute 2010* (2nd edn, Oxford University Press 2010) 530;Grover, *Interpreting Crimes in the Rome Statute of the International Criminal Court* (n 3) 114; Alex Davidson, 'Human Rights Protection before the International Criminal Court: Assessing the Scope and Application of Article 21 (3) of the Rome Statute' (2016) 18 International Community Law Review 84 para 3; Young (n 144) 193; Barboza, Julio, "International Criminal Law (Volume 278)", in *Collected Courses of the Hague Academy of International Law* Consulted online on 11 May 2021 <http://dx.doi.org/10.1163/1875-8096_pplrdc_A9789041113962_01> First published online: 1999; deGuzman (n 11) 947 para 48.

163 deGuzman (n 11) 948 para 51.

164 Mahnoush H Arsanjani, 'The Rome Statute of the International Criminal Court' (1999) 93 AJIL 22, 29.

165 *Decision on the Application for the Interim release of Detained Witnesses DRC-D02-P-0236, DRC-D02-P-0228 and DRC-D02-P-AS0350, Prosecutor vs Germain Katanga (TRC 11) 1 October 2013* para 27;*Judgment on the appeal of Mr Abdullah Al-Senussi against the decision of Pre-Trial Chamber I of 11 October 2013 entitled "Decision on the admissibility of the case against Abdullah Al-Senussi", Prosecutor v. Saif Al-Islam Gaddafi and Abdullah Al-Senussi (AC) ICC-01/11-01/11-565, 24 July 2014* para 219.

of law.[166] For example, the Appeal's Chamber, in overturning the Trial Chamber's decision in the case of *Notice of appeal by Witnesses*[167] held that

> Article 21(3) [...] creates a sort of "international super legality" of internationally recognized human rights norms to the extent that, in keeping with such rights, an international criminal judge may be led deliberately to breach all the sources of law applicable to the Court, including the Court's own Statute.[168]

In this case, it is unclear whether Article 21(3) was being referred to as a source or as an interpretation rule. A similar position arose where the Appeal's Chamber reiterated the central role played by Article 21(3) in the Statute's interpretation in the *Lubanga Challenge to the Court's Jurisdictio*n case, where it held

> Article 21 (3) of the Statute stipulates that the law applicable under the Statute must be interpreted as well as applied in accordance with internationally recognized human rights. Human rights underpin the Statute; every aspect of it, including the exercise of the jurisdiction of the Court. Its provisions must be interpreted and, more importantly, applied in accordance with internationally recognized human rights.[169]

Notably, Young has interpreted the above Appeal Chamber's decision as a recognition that Article 21(3) is a rule of interpretation.[170]

---

166 Young (n 144) 200,201.

167 *Prosecutor vs Germain Katanga ICC-01/04-01/07-3411-Corr-tENG Corrigendum to the Brief in support of the "Notice of appeal by Witnesses DRC-D02-P-0236, DRC-D02- P-0228 and DRC-D02-P0350 against the Décision relative à la demande de mise en liberté des témoins détenus DRC-D02-P-0236, DRC-D02-P-0228 et DRC-D02-P-0350 issued by Trial Chamber II on 1 October 2013 (ICC-01/04-01/07-3405)" (ICC-01/04-01/07-3408)* para 15.

168 Ibid.

169 *Judgment on the Appeal of Thomas Lubanga Dyilo against the Decision on the Defence Challenge to the Jurisdiction of the Court pursuant to Article 19(2)(a) of the Statute of 3 October 2006 ICC-01/04-01/06-772(AC) 14 December 2006* para 37; See also *Decision Establishing General Principles Governing Applications to Restrict Disclosure pursuant to Rule 81(2) and (4) of the Rules of Procedure and Evidence, Prosecutor v Thomas Lubanga Dyilo, ICC-01/04-01/06, 19 May 2006* para 7; *Decision on Joinder of cases Katanga and Ngudjolo* (n 42) pg 7; *Judgment on the appeal of Mr. Thomas Lubanga Dyilo against the decision of Pre-Trial Chamber I entitled 'Décision sur la demande de mise en liberté provisoire de Thomas Lubanga Dyilo', Prosecutor v. Lubanga Dyilo, Separate opinion of Judge Pikis ICC-O1/04-ol/06-824, 13 February 2007*, para 16.

170 Young (n 144) 387.

Reiterating the seeming mandatory consideration of Article 21(3), the Appeal's Chamber in the *Extraordinary Review Application*, held that "like every other article of the Statute, Article 82 *must* be interpreted and applied in accordance with internationally recognized human rights, as declared in Article 21(3) of the Statute."[171] The word "must" in defining Article 21(3) is seen to impose an obligation on the ICC to apply international human rights without exception.[172]

The above decisions can be looked at in two ways. On the one hand, the decisions can be argued to consider Article 21(3) only as a superior source of law. In this respect, the decisions appear to indicate that Article 21(3) can override all other applicable sources of law, including the Rome Statute.[173] Additionally, the ICC can refuse to apply "internal" law provisions constituting the Statute, the Elements, and the RPE where they fail to conform to internationally recognized human rights.[174] In contrast, the above decisions have also been considered as evidence that the Appeal's Chamber construes Article 21(3) as an "overriding rule of interpretation" applicable to all other Statute provisions.[175]

There is, however, also express recognition of Article 21(3) as a rule of interpretation for the Rome Statute. For example, the Pre-Trial Chamber in *Katanga's Proprio Motu* case acknowledged that the chambers have "repeatedly stated" that:

> The chamber, in determining the contours of the statutory framework provided for in the Statute, the Rules, and the Regulations, must, *in addition to applying the general principle of interpretation set out in Article 21(3) of the Statute*, give due regard to the general principles of interpretation as set out in Article 31(1) of the Vienna Convention on the Law of Treaties.[176]

171 Judgment on the Application for Extraordinary Review (n 10) para 38.

172 Georghios M Pikis, *The Rome Statute for the International Criminal Court: Analysis of the Statute, the Rules of Procedure and Evidence, the Regulations of the Court and Supplementary Instruments* (Brill Nijhoff 2010) 81, 89.

173 Grover, *Interpreting Crimes in the Rome Statute of the International Criminal Court* (n 3) 113; Gilbert Bitti (n 12) 436.

174 William Schabas, *The International Criminal Court; A Commentary on the Rome Statute* (2nd edn, Oxford University Press 2010) 209; Grover, *Interpreting Crimes in the Rome Statute of the International Criminal Court* (n 3) 113; Powderly (n 10) 485; Sheppard (n 11) 62.

175 Young (n 144) 201.

176 *Decision on the Powers of the Pre-Trial Chamber to Review Proprio Motu the Pretrial Detention of Germain Katanga, ICC-01/04-01/07-330* (*PTC 1*) *19 March 2008* pg 6.

This specific extract has also been cited in the *Katanga and Ngudjolo Joinder of Cases* and repeated in several other cases explicitly referring to Article 21(3) as a "general principle of interpretation" of the Rome Statute in addition to Article 31(1) of the VCLT interpretive rules.[177] The decision extract has been construed as reinforcing Article 21(3) as an interpretation rule alongside the VCLT interpretation rules.[178] Notably, the Pre-Trial Chamber seemingly framed Article 21(3) as a mandatory interpretation rule alongside the VCLT rules during the Statute's interpretation by using the word "must." The Pre-Trial Chamber similarly referred to Article 21(3) as a "general rule of interpretation" in the *Lubanga Witness Proofing* case.[179]

Further reiterating the article as an interpretive principle, Article 21 (3) has been defined as an "overarching" interpretative provision.[180] Similarly, Vagias points to Articles 21(3) and 22 of the Rome Statute as rules of interpretation provided by the Statute itself.[181] Vagias adds that Article 21(3) has primacy over all other means of treaty interpretation.[182] In the same vein, Young uses a stronger description, referring to Article 21(3) as "an overriding general rule of interpretation, rather than a source of substantive applicable law."[183] Young specifically asserts that unlike Article 21(1) and 21(2) of the Statute which are applicable sources of law, Article 21(3) is a general rule of interpretation.[184] Sheppard also posits that, at a minimum, Article 21(3) serves as an interpretation rule.[185] Sheppard, however, also considers Article 21(3) not just as an interpretive principle but as a source of law.[186]

177 *Decision on Joinder of cases Katanga and Ngudjolo* (n 42) p 7; *Decision on the Set of Procedural Rights Attached to Procedural Status of Victim at the Pre-Trial Stage of the Case, The Prosecutor v Germain Katanga and Mathieu Ngudjolo Chui, ICC-01/04-01/07 (PTC 1) 13 May 2008* para 78; *Prosecutor v Thomas Lubanga Dyilo, Decision Establishing General Principles Governing Applications to Restrict Disclosure pursuant to Rule 81(2) and (4) of the Rules of Procedure and Evidence ICC-01/04-01/06* para 7(i); *Decision on the Practices of Witness Familiarization and Witness Proofing, Prosecutor v Thomas Lubanga Dyilo, ICC-01/04–01/06 (PTC 1) 8 November 2006* para 10 (Decision on Witness Proofing Lubanga).

178 Sheppard (n 11) 58.

179 Decision on Witness Proofing, Lubanga (n 177) para 10.

180 Young (n 144) 192–193.

181 Michail Vagias (n 7) 64.

182 Ibid. 64–65.

183 Young (n 144) 193.

184 Ibid.

185 Sheppard (n 11) 58.

186 Ibid., 60.

In what can further be construed as using Article 21(3) as an interpretive principle, the ICC has used the article to exercise increased powers and formulate remedies not expressly stipulated in the Rome Statute or the RPE.[187] As an example, the Trial Chamber held that transferring witnesses back to the Democratic Republic of Congo (DRC) would be a violation of their human rights to apply for asylum based on Article 21(3), a decision which went against Article 93(7)(b) of the Rome Statute which required immediate return of such witnesses after testifying.[188] The chamber, therefore, disregarded a Rome Statute provision that did not conform to human rights and offered a remedy that the Statute or the rules did not provide for.[189] Bitti, however, terms the ICC's mandate to disregard a Statute provision that contradicts internationally recognized human rights as a "controversial interpretation of Article 21(3)."[190]

Other remedies introduced by the ICC based on Article 21(3) include the right to privacy in criminal proceedings,[191] with the Trial Chamber reiterating that it was "duty-bound to respect this right pursuant to Article 21(3) of the Statute."[192] Further, the Appeal's Chamber, based on Article 21(3), has provided a new remedy to "stay proceedings," especially in "abuse of process" cases where the accused's fair trial rights are violated, despite the remedy not being provided for in the Rome Statute or RPE.[193] Similarly, Bitti points out that based on Article 21(3), the ICC can refuse to exercise its jurisdiction

187 Gilbert Bitti (n 12) 437; Stephen Bailey, 'Article 21(3) of the Rome Statute: A Plea for Clarity' (2014) 14 Int CLR 536.

188 Decision on Amicus Curiae application Katanga and Ngudjolo (n 161) para 73; Gilbert Bitti (n 12) 438.

189 William A Schabas, *An Introduction to the International Criminal Court, 2017* (5th edn, Cambridge University Press 2017) 532.

190 Gilbert Bitti (n 12) 440.

191 *Decision on Prosecution requests to Impose restrictions on Mr Ntaganda's Contacts, Prosecutor v Ntaganda ICC-01/04-02/06 18 August 2015* para 42; *Decision on Prosecution's Request Relating to Three Forensic Reports, Prosecutor v Katanga and Ngudjolo Chui, ICC-01/04-01/07 (TC II) 25 March 2009* para 5.

192 *Decision on Kilolo Defence Motion for Inadmissibility of Material, Prosecutor v Bemba, Kilolo et al, ICC-01/05-01/13 (TC VIII) 16 September 2015* para 16.

193 *Judgment on the Appeal of Mr Thomas Lubanga Dyilo against the Decision on the Defence Challenge to the Jurisdiction of the Court Pursuant to Art 19(2)(a) of the Statute of 3 October 2006, Prosecutor v Lubanga Dyilo, ICC-01/04-01/06-772 (AC) 14 December 2006* para 37; *Judgment on the Appeal of the Prosecutor against the Decision of Trial Chamber I entitled 'Decision on the Consequences of Non-Disclosure of Exculpatory Materials Covered by Article 54(3)(e) Agreements and the Application to Stay the Prosecution of the Accused, Together with Certain Other Issues Raised at the Status Conference on 10 June 2008', Prosecutor v Lubanga Dyilo, ICC-01/04-01/06-1486 (AC) 21 October 2008* paras 77–83.

where the accused's cardinal human rights have been abused, even when the Statute and RPE only provide for compensation in such instances.[194]

Besides using Article 21(3) to introduce new remedies, the ICC has referred to the article to define ambiguous words or words whose meaning is not given in the Rome Statute. It is argued that Article 21(3) was used as an interpretive tool in this context. As an example, while applying Article 21(3), the Appeal's Chamber referred to the UN General Assembly Resolutions (UNGA) and to the jurisprudence of the IACHR and ECtHR to interpret the word "harm" and the due compensation, which was neither defined in the Rome Statute or the rules.[195]

Additionally, and seemingly using Article 21(3) as an interpretive rule, the Appeal's Chamber has found that Article 21(3) mandates the judges "to undertake an evolutive interpretation of the statutory provisions."[196] This approach allows the ICC to interpret the Rome Statute in line with the constantly evolving nature of human rights rather than adhering only to the prevailing values at the time of the Statute's adoption. The dynamic approach may, however, open up a conflict with the strict construction rule under Article 22(2) of the Statute, which discourages analogy. From this basis, it can be argued that the evolutionary effect to interpretation to this extent makes Article 21(3) an interpretive principle.

From the different references by the ICC to Article 21(3), it is notable that there is no consistency regarding its use. The ICC's practice has alternately used Article 21(3) as a rule of interpretation on the one hand, while on the other, it is used as a source of law with the ability to override certain Rome Statute provisions.[197]

---

194 Gilbert Bitti (n 12) 438.

195 *Decision on the Final System of Disclosure and the Establishment of a Timetable Lubanga (n 71)* Annex 1 para 2–3; *Situation in the Democratic Republic of Congo, Decision on the Applications for Participation in the Proceedings of VPRS 1, VPRS 2,VPRS 3, VPRS 4, VPRS 5 and VPRS 6) (PTC 1), ICC-01/04-101, 17 January 2006* 80–81; See also *Prosecutor vs Ahmad Harun and Ali Kushayb, Decision on the Prosecution Application under Article 58(7) of the Statute (27 April 2007) ICC-02/05-01/07-1-Corr* para 28.

196 *Corrigendum to the Brief in support of the "Notice of appeal by Witnesses DRC-D02-P-0236, DRC-D02- P-0228 and DRC-D02-P0350 against the Décision relative à la demande de mise en liberté des témoins détenus DRC-D02-P-0236, DRC-D02-P-0228 et DRC-D02-P-0350 issued by Trial Chamber II on 1 October 2013 (ICC-01/04-01/07-3405)" (ICC-01/04-01/07-3408)*, Prosecutor *vs Germain Katanga, ICC-01/04-01/07-3411-Corr,* 9 October 2013 para 8.

197 Amit Kumar, 'Is Article 21 of the Rome Statute Aiming for Legality or Hierarchy? A Dilemma' [2020] Vol 20 ISIL Year Book of International Humanitarian and Refugee Law 56, 77; Young (n 144) 201.

Based on Article 21(3) and the VCLT interpretation rules having been acknowledged as interpretation rules by some decisions, the interplay between the two regarding the Rome Statute's interpretation becomes relevant.

4.2.2 Relationship of Article 21(3) with the VCLT Rules of Interpretation

Demonstrating the interconnection between the VCLT interpretation rules and Article 21(3) of the Rome Statute, Sheppard asserts that the rational commencement point should be that Article 21(3) "must" be interpreted "in good faith in accordance with the ordinary meaning to be given to the terms of the treaty in their context and in the light of its object and purpose" based on Article 31(1) of the VCLT.[198] In essence, Sheppard proposes that Article 21(3) should be interpreted using the VCLT interpretation rules. In this case, Article 21(3) is not regarded as an interpretive rule but as being subject to the VCLT rules.

Similarly, while Young has referred to Article 21(3) as an "overriding" interpretation rule, she reaches this conclusion by first referring to Article 31(1) of the VCLT to determine the plain meaning of the phrasing for Article 21(3).[199] Young further refers to the context of Article 21(3) within the whole Rome Statute, the object and purpose of the Statute, and the preamble, all based on the VCLT Article 31(1).[200] She further refers to the *travaux préparatoires* based on Article 32[201] to determine the meaning of the phrase "internationally recognized human rights." Hafner and Binder similarly start by referring to the elements in Article 31(1) of the VCLT to interpret the meaning of "internationally recognized human rights" as phrased in Article 21(3) of the Statute.[202] Even Vagias, who considers Article 21(3) to be a rule of interpretation, has acknowledged that to establish the ICC's jurisdiction, Article 21(3), together with the VCLT rules in Article 31(1) and the preparatory works of the Rome Statute should be referred to.[203]

This approach is also noted from the various ICC decisions discussed above, which emphasize that reference should be made to both Article 21(3) as a "general rule of interpretation" in addition to the general rule in Article 31(1) of the VCLT. [204] The study suggests that in these instances, Article 21(3) is seen

198 Sheppard (n 11) 54.
199 Young (n 144) 192.
200 Ibid., 193.
201 Ibid. 196–198.
202 Hafner and Binder (n 10) 178.
203 Michail Vagias (n 7) 78.
204 *Decision on the Set of Procedural Rights Attached to Procedural Status of Victim at the Pre-Trial Stage of the Case, The Prosecutor v. Germain Katanga and Mathieu Ngudjolo Chui,*

not as an independent interpretive rule but one that must work in tandem with the VCLT to give it meaning and effectiveness.

Besides the link to Article 31(1) of the VCLT, Article 21(3) of the Rome Statute has also been linked to Article 31(3)(C) of the VCLT. In determining the ordinary meaning of "Internationally recognized human rights," it has been suggested that Article 31(3)(C), which provides that "any relevant rules of international law applicable in the relations between the parties," should be considered.[205] In this context, Article 21(3), based on Article 31(3)(c), would allow the ICC to refer to applicable external law, including other international instruments and international judicial and quasi-judicial decisions.[206] Some scholars contend that Article 21(3) only applies where several interpretations are possible, and based on Article 31(3)(C) of the VCLT, the ICC has to select the interpretation that conforms to international human rights.[207]

Taking a contrary position from those advocating for Article 21(3)'s central role, Vagias has pointed out that in certain instances, Article 21(3) has been treated as a secondary means of interpretation compared to the "authentic guide" based on the VCLT Article 31(1) elements.[208] In this context, when the meaning of a provision can be established by reference to the VCLT rules, examining the issue under Article 21(3) is considered unnecessary.[209] For example, the majority of judges in the *Lubanga Appeal* found it unnecessary to consider the human rights aspect in the proposed separate opinion of Judge Pikis because the text had already been considered.[210]

Similarly, Suhr recommends that the human rights interpretation should only be used to expand the crime definition to support or confirm the interpretation arrived at based on the VCLT rules.[211] It is also averred that where a

---

ICC-01/04-01/07 (PTC I) 13 May 2008 para 78; *Prosecutor v Thomas Lubanga Dyilo, Decision Establishing General Principles Governing Applications to Restrict Disclosure pursuant to Rule 81 (2) and (4) of the Rules of Procedure and Evidence* ICC-01/04-01/06 para 7(i); *Decision on Joinder of cases Katanga and Ngudjolo* (n 42) p 7; Decision on Witness Proofing, Lubanga (n 177) para 10.

205 Hafner and Binder (n 10) 178; Young (n 144) 194, 195.

206 Young (n 144) 194, 195.

207 Hafner and Binder (n 10) 171, 178; Pellet (n 13) 1080; J Verhoeven (n 147); Ibid., 15; deGuzman (n 11) 947.

208 Michail Vagias (n 7) 66.

209 *Judgment on the appeal of Mr Thomas Lubanga Dyilo against the decision of Pre-Trial Chamber I entitled 'Décision sur la demande de mise en liberté provisoire de Thomas Lubanga Dyilo' ICC-01/04-01/06-824 (AC) 12 February 2007* para 107.

210 Ibid.

211 Suhr (n 7) 91.

human rights interpretation must be used, it must not contradict the wording of the Rome Statute.[212] Likewise, Verhoeven asserts that prioritizing human rights over the general rules of interpretation, which enjoy an international status, would go against the general State practice.[213] In this context, the VCLT interpretation rules are construed as the principal rules guiding the Rome Statute's interpretation, with Article 21(3) playing a supplementary role.

The lack of clarity concerning Article 21(3) may reinforce Vagias' view that the Appeal's Chamber has failed to expressly state which interpretation means between human rights, the VCLT, and others, take priority in resolving particular issues under the Rome Statute.[214] However, it is notable from the above analysis that the ICC rarely, if ever, uses Article 21(3) alone as the decisive factor in the Statute's interpretation.[215] The book takes the position that even in instances when it is deemed an interpretative rule, Article 21(3) cannot stand independently as a substantive interpretation rule without the VCLT interpretive rules. It can only work within or in addition to the VCLT rules, which would be used to interpret the wording of Article 21(3).

4.3 *The Legality Principle* (nullum crimen sine lege) *under Article 22 and Its Impact on the Rome Statute's Interpretation*

4.3.1 Legality Provisions under the Statute

Article 22 of the Rome Statute is titled *"Nullum crimen sine lege."* Article 22(1) provides that a person shall not be criminally responsible under the Statute unless the conduct in question constitutes, at the time it takes place, a crime within the jurisdiction of the ICC. Article 22(2) stipulates that the definition of a crime shall be strictly construed and shall not be extended by analogy. Article 22(2) further states that in case of ambiguity, the definition shall be interpreted in favor of the person being investigated, prosecuted, or convicted. Article 22 (2) of the Rome Statute is deemed to protect the States Parties' interests by ensuring that judges interpret the Statute narrowly, protecting the person under investigation whose criminal responsibility would be judged strictly according to the law.[216]

---

212 Ibid; Grover, *Interpreting Crimes in the Rome Statute of the International Criminal Court* (n 3) 116.

213 J Verhoeven (n 147) 15 para 1.

214 Michail Vagias (n 7) 66.

215 Young (n 144) 206; Gilbert Bitti (n 12) 441.

216 Camilla Lind, *Commentary on the Law of the ICC* (FICHL Series 29, 2017) 255.

Some scholars have recognized Article 22 as a principle of interpretation.[217] For instance, Schabas terms Article 22 as the only actual attempt to set down interpretation principles for the Rome Statute.[218] Grover also asserts that the "guiding interpretive principle" for crimes in the Statute is the legality principle under Article 22.[219] Despite being considered an interpretive rule by some, there is also the question of whether it is a substantive interpretive rule independent of the VCLT. The book focuses more specifically on Article 22(2).

4.3.2 The Place of Legality in the Statute's Interpretation and the Interlink with the VCLT Interpretation Rules

Significantly, while the legality principle and the strict construction rule under it are deemed to apply to the Rome Statute's interpretation, it is the place the principle holds in interpretation that remains a matter of varied opinions. For instance, some scholars argue that all methods of interpretation, including the VCLT and Article 21(3) on human rights, "must be compatible" with the legality rule.[220] Such an approach appears to consider the legality rule as overriding even the VCLT interpretation rules.

Other scholars nevertheless contend that Article 22 is of limited application since it only applies to Article 5 crimes and their elements under Articles 6, 7, 8, and 8 *bis* and not to the rest of the Statute.[221] In contrast, another school of thought maintains that although judges should consider the legality principle in interpreting criminal offenses, the strict construction principle lacks a specific position in interpretation.[222] Nevertheless, even where Article 22 is regarded as an interpretive rule, it is debatable whether it stands as an independent and separate interpretive rule away from the VCLT interpretation rules. A consideration of their connection is, therefore, also significant.

Among the scholars who advocate for Article 22(2)'s primary role in interpretation, the legality principle has been described as the "primary or guiding

217 Suhr (n 7) 54–55.

218 William A Schabas, *The International Criminal Court: A Commentary on the Rome Statute* (Second Edition, Oxford University Press 2016) 547 para 2.

219 Grover, *Interpreting Crimes in the Rome Statute of the International Criminal Court* (n 3) 378–379.

220 Suhr (n 7) 67.

221 Talita de Souza Dias, 'The Retroactive Application of the Rome Statute in Cases of Security Council Referrals and Ad Hoc Declarations' (2018) 16 Journal of International Criminal Justice 65; Schabas (n 1) 216; Grover, *Interpreting Crimes in the Rome Statute of the International Criminal Court* (n 3) 378–379.

222 Grover, 'A Call to Arms: Fundamental Dilemmas Confronting the Interpretation of Crimes in the Rome Statute of the International Criminal Court' (n 3) 555–556.

interpretive principle."[223] It has also been termed a "central component"[224] and the "most important aspect of interpretation" for the Rome Statute.[225] Further reiterating its importance, Powderly refers to the legality principle as the "golden rule" of interpreting international criminal instruments.[226] In the same vein, Grover proposes that with no clear interpretive guidelines laid out by the Rome Statute,[227] the legality principle should be the guiding interpretive principle for the Statute, with consistency with internationally recognized human rights forming a secondary interpretive principle.[228] Grover specifically emphasizes that the legality principle should be the main interpretative principle applying to articles 6, 7, 8, and 8 *bis* of the Rome Statute.[229]

Judge Van den Wyngaert appeared to take the same approach in the *Ngudjolo* case, finding that the VCLT interpretation rules can only be used to interpret other parts of the Rome Statute, but not those dealing with the criminal responsibility of persons, which require the principles of strict construction to be applied.[230] In the same vein, the ICC held in the *Katanga* case that the chamber would rely on the general rule in the VCLT in interpreting the Rome Statute provisions, particularly those dealing with definitions of the crimes and the accused's criminal responsibility while adhering to Article 22(2).[231]

While also seemingly advocating for Article 22's central place in the Rome Statute's interpretation, the Pre-Trial Chamber used mandatory language in its judgment in *Prosecutor v. Katanga*, holding that Article 22 (2) "must" be considered when interpreting the Statute.[232] The Pre-Trial Chamber also referred to Article 22(2) in the *Bemba* case, holding that "this interpretation is consistent with the principle of strict construction mirrored in Article 22(2) of the Statute which, as a part of the principle *nullum crimen sine lege*, compels

223 Ibid., 543,558; Grover, *Interpreting Crimes in the Rome Statute of the International Criminal Court* (n 3) 378–379.

224 Powderly (n 10) 490.

225 Suhr (n 7) 68.

226 Powderly (n 10) 490.

227 Grover, 'A Call to Arms: Fundamental Dilemmas Confronting the Interpretation of Crimes in the Rome Statute of the International Criminal Court' (n 3) 583.

228 Grover, *Interpreting Crimes in the Rome Statute of the International Criminal Court* (n 3) 220.

229 Ibid. 378–379.

230 *The Prosecutor v Mathieu Ngudjolo Chui, Judgment pursuant to Article 74 of the Statute Concurring Opinion of Judge Christine Van den Wyngaert*, ICC-01/04-02/12, *18 December 2012* para 18.

231 Judgment pursuant to Article 74 Katanga, (n 40) para 57.

232 *Judgment, The Prosecutor v Germain Katanga: Situation in the DRC*, ICC-01/04-01/07-3436 (ICC, Trial Chamber II) para 50; Decision on Bashir's Arrest Warrant (n 10) para 156.

the Chamber to interpret this provision strictly."[233] Another notable direct reference to the central place of Article 22(2) by the ICC appears in the separate opinion of Judge Van den Wyngaert in the *Ngudjolo* case, where the Judge held that

> I attach the greatest importance to Article 22(2) of the Statute, which obliges the Court to interpret the definition of crimes strictly and prohibits any extension by analogy. There can be little doubt that this fundamental principle applies with equal force in relation to the definition of criminal responsibility. Indeed, I believe that this article overrides the conventional methods of treaty interpretation, as defined in the Vienna Convention on the Law of Treaties, particularly the teleological method. Whereas these methods of interpretation may be entirely adequate for interpreting other parts of the Statute, I consider that for interpreting articles dealing with the criminal responsibility of individuals, the principles of strict construction and in *dubio pro reo* are paramount.[234]

Judge Wyngaert's decision appears to emphasize that the legality principle overrides the VCLT's interpretation rules and, more specifically, the teleological (object and purpose) method in interpreting crimes. Similarly reiterating Article 22's importance, the Pre-Trial Chamber held that its restrictive interpretation of Article 30 aimed "to ensure that any interpretation given to the definition of crimes is in harmony with the rule of strict construction set out in Article 22(2) of the Statute."[235] The Pre-Trial Chamber in the *Katanga Confirmation of Charges* case also appeared to use Article 22 as an interpretational tool by referring to Article 7(l)(k) of the Rome Statute and the principle of *nullum crimen sine lege* under Article 22 of the Statute to define "other inhumane acts."[236]

---

233 *Decision Pursuant to Article 61(7)(a) and (b) of the Rome Statute on the Charges of the Prosecutor Against Jean-Pierre Bemba Gombo, Prosecutor v Jean-Pierre Bemba Gombo, ICC-01/05-01/08 (PTC II) 15 June 2009* para 423 (Decision on charges against Bemba).

234 *Judgment pursuant to Article 74 of the Statute, Concurring Opinion of Judge Christine Van den Wyngaert, Prosecutor v Mathieu Ngudjolo Chui ICC-01/04-02/12 (TR C II) 18 December 2012* para 18; See also *Minority Opinion of Judge Christine Van den Wyngaert, The Prosecutor v Germain Katanga, ICC-01/04-01/07-3436-AnxI, (TRC II) 10 March 2014* para 278; Grover, 'A Call to Arms: Fundamental Dilemmas Confronting the Interpretation of Crimes in the Rome Statute of the International Criminal Court' (n 3) 557 para 2.

235 Decision on Charges Against Bemba (n 233) para 369.

236 *Decision on Confirmation of Charges, Prosecutor v Germain Katanga and Mathieu Ngudjolo, ICC-01/04-01/07-717 (PTC 1) 30 September 2008* para 448; Camilla Lind, *Commentary on the Law of the International Criminal Court* (Mark Klamberg ed, FICHL 2017) 255.

On the other hand, Article 22 is accorded a secondary position by some scholars and judges in the Rome Statute's interpretation. From this perspective, it is observed that Article 22 can only be considered after all other interpretation tools have been applied, and ambiguity remains.[237] Similarly, it is argued that strict construction is only resorted to when the VCLT interpretation rules, including the ordinary meaning of words in their context and in light of their object and purpose, result in more than one interpretive outcome.[238] In the same vein, Davidson points out that an approach strictly based on the Statute alone in line with the legality rule sometimes goes against the States parties' intent.[239] Similarly, and despite arguing that the legality rule forms the primary interpretive rule, Grover acknowledges that international criminal law treaties are not so autonomous that they entirely conflict with the general rules of treaty interpretation.[240]

Following similar thinking, some scholars argue that elevating strict construction over other interpretative means is inappropriate.[241] The PTC in the *Ngudjolo* case followed this approach when it dismissed the defense argument that the interpretation based on strict construction under Article 22 overrode the interpretation arrived at based on the VCLT interpretation rules.[242] Additionally, without explicitly mentioning Article 22(2), Judge Herrera held that "the requirement of strict construction must not reach the point where it would be contrary to the object and purpose of the Statute or to internationally recognized human rights."[243] Judge Herrera's decision implied that the legality rule should not be applied in isolation but should additionally be consistent with the VCLT interpretation rules and human rights under Article 21(3). In the same respect, Schabas posits that the ICC regularly ignores the strict construc-

237 Caroline Davidson (n 93) 91; Bruce Broomhall, 'Article 22, Nullum Crimen Sine Lege' in Otto Triffterer and Kai Ambos (eds), *Commentary on the Rome Statute of the ICC Observers' Notes, Article by Article* (Beck/Hart 2016) 961 para 44; Suhr (n 7) 70.

238 A Ashworth, Principles of Criminal Law, 4th edn (Oxford University Press 2003) at 81; Suhr (n 7) 70.

239 Caroline Davidson (n 93) 76–77.

240 Grover, *Interpreting Crimes in the Rome Statute of the International Criminal Court* (n 3) 29.

241 Grover, 'A Call to Arms: Fundamental Dilemmas Confronting the Interpretation of Crimes in the Rome Statute of the International Criminal Court' (n 3) 555.

242 *Decision on Application for Leave to Appeal by the Defence of Mathieu Ngudjolo Chui against the Decision on Joinder, Prosecutor v Ngudjolo Chui, ICC-01/04-01/07-384* (*PTC 1*) *9 April 2008* pg 7.

243 *Decision on Defence Applications for Judgments of Acquittal, The Prosecutor v William Samoei Ruto and Joshua Arap Sang,* (*TrC V A*), *ICC-01/09-01/11, 5 April 2016* Dissenting Opinion of Judge Herrara Carbuccia para 38.

tion rule in favor of the purpose-based approach provided under the VCLT Article 31(1).[244] Similarly, Grover concedes that the legality rule in Article 22(2) of the Rome Statute cannot be used to impede the ordinary interpretive process based on the VCLT.[245]

In a similar vein, it is observed that several international criminal judges ordinarily begin interpreting criminal statutes by reference to the VCLT interpretation rules, followed by the legality rule, and finally, the international tribunal's criminal law.[246] Several ICC decisions have also taken the approach that Article 22 (2) does not take precedence over Articles 31 and 32 of the VCLT. For instance, the majority of the judges in the *Katanga* case found that the legality rule only becomes applicable after the VCLT has been referred to, holding that Article 22(2)'s guarantee of strict construction

> Is applicable only "in case of ambiguity" and clearly should be relied on only after an unsuccessful attempt at interpretation effected in good faith and in accordance with the General Rule of the Vienna Convention or in accordance with Article 32 of the Convention.[247]

Similarly, it is averred that the legality principle, which requires the strict construction of terms, makes the ordinary meaning of words significant.[248] This approach, therefore, emphasizes the ordinary meaning under the VCLT Article 31(1) in effecting the legality rule. In this respect, Grover adds that in respecting the strict construction principles, the definitions of crimes should be based on the wording as a starting point and should be interpreted in good faith and in light of their purpose as espoused in Article 31(1) of the VCLT.[249] Davidson also reiterates that strict construction emphasizes the text, and examining the Statute's text without having regard to the context of other Statute provisions would render the other Statute provisions meaningless.[250]

---

244 Schabas (n 1) 216; W A Schabas, 'Strict Construction and the Rome Statute' in S Dewulf (ed), *la [CVDW]: Liber Amicorum Chris Van den Wyngaert* (Maklu 2017) 423.

245 Grover, *Interpreting Crimes in the Rome Statute of the International Criminal Court* (n 3) 356.

246 Dov Jacobs (n 100) 466–467; Judgment on the Application for Extraordinary Review (n 10) para 33.

247 Judgment pursuant to Article 74 Katanga (n 40) para 53.

248 Suhr (n 7) 59; Sadat and Jolly (n 44) 759; Judgment pursuant to Article 74 Katanga (n 40) para 52.

249 Grover, *Interpreting Crimes in the Rome Statute of the International Criminal Court* (n 3) 207.

250 Caroline Davidson (n 93) 76.

Grover also emphasizes that the legality principle requires judges to begin with the text of the crime and return to the text again before deciding if the presumed interpretation respects the accused's rights.[251] Other scholars have similarly reiterated that Articles 21 and 22 of the Rome Statute emphasize textual interpretation, in line with Article 31(1) of the VCLT.[252]

Also linking the VCLT and the legality rule, Broomhall argues that while Article 22(2) prohibits analogy, a narrow analogy is nonetheless permissible where the text's ordinary meaning in its context and in light of the object and purpose of the Rome Statute reveals a gap which then leaves room for analogy.[253] From this approach, the VCLT interpretation rules are first applied to determine if the words are ambiguous and, consequently, whether a narrow analogy is necessary. Similarly, Suhr posits that for the ICC to determine that a provision is ambiguous in the first place and resolve it in the accused's favor as required by the legality rule, the interpretation based on the general rules of interpretation under the VCLT would apply first.[254] The legality principle in this context applies only as the last step in the interpretive process.[255] The study identifies with the latter approach. It is noted that ambiguity in the wording exercisable in the accused's favor can only be established by first examining the ordinary meaning in its context and based on the object and purpose as provided for in the VCLT Article 31(1).

Grover consequently argues that the legality rule in Article 22 should not be used to frustrate the interpretive process, and instead, all interpretation elements in Article 31 of the VCLT "must" be considered during the Rome Statute's interpretation to preserve the legality rule. [256] In effect, Grover seemingly sees the strict construction rule as working in conjunction with the VCLT interpretation rules. This approach considers the VCLT applicable even where the legality principle is treated as the primary guide for interpreting crimes by

251 Grover, 'A Call to Arms: Fundamental Dilemmas Confronting the Interpretation of Crimes in the Rome Statute of the International Criminal Court' (n 3) 556.

252 Sadat and Jolly (n 44) 759.

253 Broomhall (n 237) 962 para 44; Grover, *Interpreting Crimes in the Rome Statute of the International Criminal Court* (n 3) 143.

254 Suhr (n 7) 70.

255 Judgment pursuant to Article 74 Katanga (n 40) para 53; Broomhall (n 237) 726; Cryer (n 89) 403.

256 Grover, 'A Call to Arms: Fundamental Dilemmas Confronting the Interpretation of Crimes in the Rome Statute of the International Criminal Court' (n 3) 574; Grover, *Interpreting Crimes in the Rome Statute of the International Criminal Court* (n 3) 202; Gregor Maučec, 'The International Criminal Court and the Issue of Intersectionality – A Conceptual and Legal Framework for Analysis' (2021) 21 International Criminal Law Review 1, 25.

the ICC since the text is prioritized in line with the VCLT's Article 31(1).[257] Akande similarly appears to agree that the VCLT rules and the legality rule should work together, stating that if ambiguity remains even after applying Article 31 of the VCLT and the Rome Statute, it should be resolved in the accused's favor.[258]

Additionally, the case has been made that strict construction aims to ensure that the express or implied intentions of States Parties are adhered to, which intentions can only be determined by applying the VCLT interpretation rules.[259]

Based on the above analysis, the book concludes that the legality rule is not a substantive independent rule of interpretation for the Statute but must work within or together with the VCLT interpretation rules. Nonetheless, the legality rule appears to put some limits on the VCLT-based interpretation of the Rome Statute.

4.3.3 Limitations on the VCLT Interpretive Rules by Article 22 on Legality

While not construed in most instances as the primary interpretive guide to the Rome Statute, the legality rule nevertheless seems to put some limitations on the VCLT interpretive rules. Some scholars, for example, assert that some VCLT features contradict the legality principle under Article 22 of the Statute.[260] In the *Katanga* case, for example, the Trial Chamber reiterated the limitations that the legality rule has on the VCLT, holding that the implementation of the general rule of the VCLT

> Must therefore always be consistent with that provision, which constitutes a clear and explicit restriction on all interpretative activity. The

---

257 Richard K Gardiner, *Treaty Interpretation 2008* (Oxford University Press 2008) 145; Grover, 'A Call to Arms: Fundamental Dilemmas Confronting the Interpretation of Crimes in the Rome Statute of the International Criminal Court' (n 3) 557; Sadat and Jolly (n 44) 759.

258 Dapo Akande, 'Sources of International Criminal Law' in Antonio Cassese (ed), *The Oxford Companion to International Criminal Justice* (Oxford University Press 2009) 45.

259 Grover, *Interpreting Crimes in the Rome Statute of the International Criminal Court* (n 3) 203.

260 Dov Jacobs, 'The ICC Katanga Judgment: A Commentary (Part 1): Investigation, Interpretation and The Crimes' (*Spreading the Jam*, 10 March 2014) <https://dovjacobs.com/2014/03/10/the-icc-katanga-judgment-a-commentary-part-1-investigation-interpretation-and-the-crimes/> accessed 29 December 2020; Dapo Akande, 'Sources of International Criminal Law' (n 258) 45; Leena Grover, 'A Call to Arms: Fundamental Dilemmas Confronting the Interpretation of Crimes in the Rome Statute of the International Criminal Court' (2010) 21 Issue 3 EJIL 559 ; Suhr, (n 7) 91; Sadat and Jolly (n 44) 761.

> bench must therefore respect the two corollaries of the principle of legality, namely the principle of strict construction and the principle of in *dubio pro reo*.[261]

In the same vein, it is observed that while the Rome Statute's preparatory work may sometimes be used in the Statute's interpretation, the principle of legality limits its use by disallowing the use of supplementary means to amend the definitions of crimes in the Statute.[262] In the same respect, Akande points out that the legality principle bars the resort to the *travaux préparatoires* to resolve an ambiguity unfavorably to the suspect or accused.[263]

It has also been pointed out that the Rome Statute's object and purpose of ending impunity and preventing crime contradict the legality principle under Article 22(2).[264] In this respect, Jacobs cites the *Lubanga Appeals* case[265], arguing that the judges applied the object and purpose approach of ending impunity to justify a regulation unfavorable to the accused, contrary to the legality principle.[266]

Suhr, however, argues that an object and purpose interpretation does not conflict with the legality rule as long as the provision's wording is adhered to and there is foreseeability as required by the legality rule.[267] This perspective aligns with Grover's that the best interpretive approach is to give an interpretation that respects the Rome Statute's ordinary meaning, the human rights requirements under Article 21(3), and is also consistent with the legality provision.[268] In effect, Grover strives to give all three "rules" a place in the Stat-

261 Judgment pursuant to Article 74 Katanga (n 40) para 51.

262 Grover, *Interpreting Crimes in the Rome Statute of the International Criminal Court* (n 3) 395 para 2; Gardiner (n 32) 202–203.

263 Dapo Akande, 'Sources of International Criminal Law' (n 258) 45.

264 Judgment pursuant to Article 74 Katanga (n 40) para 54; Sadat and Jolly (n 44) 766; Gerhard Werle and Florian Jeßberger, *Principles of International Criminal Law* (Oxford University Press 2020) para 228; Dov Jacobs, 'Positivism and International Criminal Law: The Principle of Legality as a Rule of Conflict of Theories' [2012] SSRN Electronic Journal <https://papers.ssrn.com/abstract=2046311> accessed 17 January 2021.

265 *Judgment on the appeals of Mr Lubanga Dyilo and the Prosecutor against the Decision of Trial Chamber I of 14 July 2009 entitled 'Decision giving notice to the parties and participants that the legal characterization of the facts may be subject to change in accordance with Regulation 55(2) of the Regulations of the Court', ICC-01/04-01/06, 8 December 2009* para 77.

266 Jacobs (n 264).

267 Suhr (n 7) 63.

268 Grover, *Interpreting Crimes in the Rome Statute of the International Criminal Court* (n 3) 116.

ute's interpretation, which could limit the primacy of the VCLT rules. The legality principle may also restrict the VCLT's application, where the rule is prioritized over the text, object, and purpose.[269]

Jacobs and Akande further point out that subsequent practice in Article 31(3) of the VCLT may conflict with the non-retroactivity requirement under the legality principle.[270] Another possible limitation is that while the legality principle requires that any ambiguity be interpreted in the accused's favour, Article 32 of the VCLT stipulates a resort to the supplementary means of interpretation instead. In order to adhere to the legality rule, the ICC has to exercise any ambiguity in favor of the accused.

A different but rare approach asserts that international criminal courts should only use interpretation rules compatible with the legality principle.[271] Jacobs consequently contends that Articles 31 and 32 of the VCLT and customary law should be excluded as a means of interpreting international criminal statutes, including the Statute.[272] This view seeks to exclude the VCLT entirely from the Rome Statute's interpretation. Jacob's view has, however, been criticized by scholars who find the VCLT applicable to international criminal statutes.[273] The study is also unpersuaded by Jacob's argument and instead aligns with the position that the VCLT applies to the Statute's interpretation.

This book, therefore, argues that the legality rule, just like Article 21(3), is not a substantive interpretive rule independent from the VCLT interpretation rules. The study takes the approach that the VCLT remains the main interpretive rule while the legality principle is not a substantive interpretive rule but provides the parameters within which the Rome Statute's interpretation must be made. Articles 22 and 21(3) consequently function within the VCLT interpretation rules.

4.4 *Conclusion*

Based on the above analysis, this study concluded that the applicable sources of law under Articles 21(1) and 21(2) of the Rome Statute cannot be equated to interpretation rules. Further, based on an analysis of the ICC decisions and scholarly literature, the most persuasive conclusion is that the primary inter-

269 Grover, 'A Call to Arms: Fundamental Dilemmas Confronting the Interpretation of Crimes in the Rome Statute of the International Criminal Court' (n 3) 557 para 2.

270 Dapo Akande, 'Sources of International Criminal Law' (n 258) 45; Dov Jacobs (n 100) 467.

271 Dov Jacobs (n 100) 469.

272 Ibid.

273 Gerhard Werle and Florian Jeßberger, *Principles of International Criminal Law* (Oxford University Press 2020) para 191.

pretive means for the Statute's interpretation is the VCLT rules of interpretation. It was noted that the VCLT rules have been accepted as customary law and apply to international treaties, including the Rome Statute. However, it was also noted that in interpreting the Statute using the VCLT rules, the ICC commonly refers to the elements of interpretation under Article 31(1) of the VCLT with the textual interpretation being the most cited. In contrast, Article 31(3) of the VCLT, which provides for the subsequent agreements and practice of States Parties, has to date been referred to very rarely both by the ICC decisions and scholars in relation to the Rome Statute's interpretation. Indeed, the ICC has applied the subsequent agreements of the ASP decisively in its interpretation of the Statute only once.

In addition to the VCLT rules, Article 21(3) on human rights and the legality principle under Article 22 are also considered interpretive principles for the Rome Statute's interpretation. Nevertheless, the conclusion reached was that Articles 21(3) and 22 of the Statute are not substantive and independent interpretation rules that would function without the VCLT. The two articles function under the umbrella of the VCLT rules and in addition to the VCLT rules. This conclusion is reached on the basis that the textual interpretation and the strict construction emphasized by Article 22 can only be determined by, firstly, referring to the VCLT Article 31(1) elements of ordinary meaning, context, object and purpose. Similarly, as noted from the decisions, determining adherence to Article 21(3) first requires an interpretation of the ordinary meaning of the words in their context based on the VCLT Article 31(1).

Nonetheless, while interlinked, the legality rule appears to limit the interpretation based on the VCLT interpretation rules by requiring that the outcome from the VCLT interpretation rules be compatible with the legality rule. This limit is also imposed by Article 21(3), which requires the interpretation to be consistent with human rights.

CHAPTER 4

The Role of States Parties in the Interpretation of the Rome Statute of the International Criminal Court

1 Introduction

The question regarding which entities have the authority to interpret the Rome Statute of the International Criminal Court (Rome Statute) is central to this study. As its objective, the book seeks to determine whether States Parties to the Statute (States Parties) acting individually or through the Assembly of States Parties (ASP) have any specific interpretive authority regarding the Statute. This interpretive authority, or lack thereof, is juxtaposed against that of the International Criminal Court (ICC) established by the States Parties primarily to interpret the Statute.

Therefore, this chapter begins by placing the topic into context by reviewing the general role, if any, of State parties in interpreting their treaties. The discussion examines whether State parties have the authority to interpret their treaties, especially where an existing body has been delegated to interpret. Adopting the premise that State parties have a role in interpreting their treaties, the discussion then focuses on how they may participate. This analysis hinges on subsequent agreements and practices reached before, during, or after judicial decisions are rendered.

In further analyzing the State parties' role in interpretation, it is considered that there are differing interpretations concerning whether subsequent agreements are binding on the courts and tribunals or not. As one of the ways to determine the role of States parties in interpretation, the book relies on treaty provisions expressly indicating that the parties' subsequent agreements are binding on the courts or tribunals. The resultant implication on the courts' independent authority to interpret is examined. Next follows the examination of the State parties' role in either shaping, correcting, or rejecting decisions by courts and tribunals through their subsequent agreements and practice.

To give the context of the role of States parties versus that of the courts or tribunals, the book examines the delegated authority by States parties to courts and tribunals to interpret their treaties. This discussion also involves analyzing the relevant delegation theories, such as the principal-agent and principal-trustee theories. In the premise that States delegate their interpre-

 | DOI:10.1163/9789004725515_005

tive authority, it becomes necessary to discuss the shared interpretive authority between the States parties and the courts and tribunals. The general mandate of courts and tribunals to interpret treaties is then examined, followed by an analysis of the role of States parties' subsequent agreements when a case is ongoing in the court or tribunal and the consequential impact. This discussion entails canvassing the potential tension that may arise from the shared authority, especially during ongoing cases and forms the chapter's final part.

2 The General Role of States Parties in the Interpretation of Their Treaties

2.1 *General*

Articles 31 to 33 of the VCLT, widely considered as constituting the international customary rules of interpretation,[1] do not designate the persons or bodies to interpret treaties.[2] However, the Harvard Research on International Law, in its commentary on the draft Convention on the Law of Treaties, identified different possible interpreters of treaties, stating that

> In so far as treaties in their international aspect are concerned, they may be authoritatively interpreted by the parties themselves through mutual agreement, either directly and through the ordinary channels of international relations, or indirectly as the result of recourse to good offices, mediation, or conciliation. Or they may be interpreted by an international organ or agency, permanent or ad hoc, to whose decision and interpretation the parties to the dispute agree to submit. In other words, the parties to a treaty may agree to an interpretation of their own making, or they may decide to accept that of some outside person, organ, or authority mutually agreed upon.[3]

---

1 *Kasikili/Sedudu Island (Botswana/Namibia), Judgment, ICJ Rep 1999* (ICJ) 1059 para 18 (Kasikili/Sedudu); *Pulp Mills on the River Uruguay (Argentina v Uruguay) 2010* (ICJ) 46 para 65; Oliver Dörr, 'Article 31, General Rule of Interpretation, 2018' in Oliver Dörr and Kirsten Schmalenbach (eds), *Vienna Convention on the Law of Treaties: A Commentary* (Springer 2018) 560 para 2.

2 J R Weeramantry, *Treaty Interpretation in Investment Arbitration* (Oxford University Press 2012) 31 para 2.39.

3 Harvard Research on International Law, reprinted in 29 AJIL (Supplement) 657 (1935) at 975–976.

It is commonly agreed that the starting point of interpretation lies with the State parties.[4] Indeed, Kolb considers the State parties' interpretation not only as the starting point but also as the endpoint.[5] The interpretation of treaties by States emanates from States having sovereign powers and the fact that treaties are founded on agreements between States.[6] States are the only actors recognized by international law as having original legal personality.[7] From this perspective, all set-up international tribunals and courts, among other actors, only have the competence and powers given to them either expressly or impliedly by States.[8]

Consequently, Kolb contends that under international law, judges lack any mandatory authority since their mandate depends on the consent of the States in dispute.[9] It is averred that interpretation by the States parties protects the parties from obligations they did not intend to have.[10] However, the role of the State parties in interpreting treaties through subsequent agreements and practice as well as the claim by other institutions to interpretive authority, is said to depend on the type of treaty and the different types of international courts and tribunals.[11]

2.2 *The States Parties' Right to Interpret Their Treaties*

State parties are considered to have the mandate to interpret their treaties. Article 31(3) of the VCLT provides the foundation for the participation of State parties in interpreting their treaties. Specifically, Article 31(3)(a) of the VCLT provides that treaty interpretation shall take into account, together with the treaty's context, any subsequent agreement between the parties regarding the interpretation of the treaty or the application of its provisions. Article 31(3)(b) requires the taking into account any subsequent practice in the

---

4 Oliver Morse, 'Schools of Approach to the Interpretation of Treaties' 9 Issue 1 Catholic University Law Review 17, 37.

5 Robert Kolb, *The Law of Treaties* (Edward Elgar Publishing 2016) 129 para 2.

6 Franklin Berman, 'International Treaties and British Statutes' (2005) 26 Statute Law Review 10.

7 Henry G Schermers, Niels M Blokker, *International Institutional Law* (5th edn, Brill 2011) para 1565.

8 *Reparation for Injuries Suffered in the Service of the United Nations, Advisory Opinion of 11 April (1949) ICJ Rep* 179; Schermers and Blokker (n 7) para 1565.

9 Kolb (n 5) 129 para 2.

10 Eleni Methymaki and Antonios Tzanakopoulos, 'Masters of Puppets? Reassertion of Control Through Joint Investment Treaty Interpretation' in Andreas Culick (ed), *Reasserting of Control over the Investment Treaty Regime* (Cambridge University Press 2016) 161–162.

11 Anthea Roberts, 'Subsequent Agreements and Practice: The Battle Over Interpretive Power' [2013] SSRN Scholarly Paper.

application of the treaty, which establishes the parties' agreement regarding its interpretation. Article 31(3) of the VCLT is deemed to recognize the significant and ongoing role that States parties play in interpreting and applying their treaties over time.[12]

Additionally, the ILC provides that subsequent agreements and subsequent practice under Article 31(3)(a) and (b) are objective evidence of the parties' understanding of the treaty's meaning and constitute authentic means of interpretation.[13] The reiteration of State parties as the primary actors in creating subsequent agreements and practice is an acknowledgement that they are the masters of the treaty and are ultimately responsible for its application.[14] One justification of this perspective is that as masters of their treaty, States should continue to have a role in determining the treaty's meaning.[15] In this regard, several scholars argue that even where a separate organ is set up to interpret, only the parties to a treaty can give an authoritative or authentic interpretation of the treaty.[16] The study aligns with the position that subsequent agreements and practice constitute a primary method for States to participate in their treaty interpretation after the treaty's conclusion.

Reiterating the States parties' role in interpretation, Sinclair states that "it follows naturally from the proposition that the parties to a treaty are legally entitled to modify the treaty or indeed to terminate it that they are empowered to interpret it."[17] A similar position had been emphasized by the PCIJ decision in the *Jaworzina* case, where the court held that "the right of giving an authoritative interpretation of a legal rule belongs solely to the person or body who has power to modify or suppress it."[18] Villiger takes the same position, stating that

---

12 Ibid.

13 ILC, 'Draft Conclusions on Subsequent Agreements and Subsequent Practice in Relation to the Interpretation of Treaties, Seventieth Session, (A/73/10) 2018' (ILC) Conclusion 3 (ILC 2018); 'Independent Expert Review of the International Criminal Court and the Rome Statute System Final Report, 30 September 2020' para 948.

14 ILC 2018 (n 13) Conclusion 5, Commentary 10; Georg Nolte, 'Treaties and Their Practice: Symptoms of Their Rise or Decline', *Treaties and their Practice* (Brill Nijhoff 2019) 198.

15 Ibid.; Ibid., 17.

16 Oliver Dörr, 'Article 31, General Rule of Interpretation, 2018' in Oliver Dörr and Kirsten Schmalenbach (eds), *Vienna Convention on the Law of Treaties: A Commentary* (Springer 2018) 570 para 19 ; Ibid., 95,102.; Dire Tladi, 'Presence of the Accused: Right or Duty? The Art of Interpretation in a Tense Political Climate' in Bantekas Ilias Jalloh Charles C (ed), *The International Criminal Court and Africa* (Oxford University Press 2017) 178 para 1.

17 Ian M Sinclair, *The Vienna Convention on the Law of Treaties* (2nd ed, Manchester University Press 1984) 136.

18 *Permanent Court of International Justice, Jaworzina, Advisory Opinion, 1923, PCIJ, Series B, No. 8*, p 37.

"since the parties to the treaty are their own masters ... they may amend, extend or delete a text" by engaging in subsequent practice within the meaning of Article 31(3)(b) of the VCLT whenever they choose.[19] A similar approach is taken by Crawford, among other scholars, who asserts that "international law says that the parties to a treaty own the treaty and can interpret it. One [...] might not question their application of reason as they see fit."[20]

In the same vein, it is contended that as "masters" of their treaties, tribunals cannot question whether States have gone beyond their limitations on their interpretative powers under international law.[21] Methymaki argues that as a consequence of States being masters of their treaties, tribunals cannot claim to be the masters of the treaties.[22] Under this approach, State parties are considered to have the final word regarding interpreting particular treaty provisions in several treaties.[23] This approach was also taken by the tribunal in *Methanex v the United States*, which found that;

> If a legislature, having enacted a statute, feels that the courts implementing it have misconstrued the legislature's intention, it is perfectly proper for the legislature to clarify its intention. In a democratic and representative system in which legislation expresses the will of the people, legislative clarification in this sort of case would appear to be obligatory.[24]

Gardiner also posits that treaty interpretation issues are commonly negotiated or agreed upon between States or through international organizations, with the judicial or arbitral institutions handling only a small number of cases.[25] In

19 Mark E Villiger, *Commentary on the 1969 Vienna Convention on the Law of Treaties* (Brill 2009) 429.

20 James Crawford, 'A Consensualist Interpretation of Article 31(3) of the Vienna Convention on the Law of Treaties' in Georg Nolte (ed), *Treaties and Subsequent Practice*, vol 29 (Oxford University Press 2013) 31.

21 Loris Marotti, 'Masters of Their (Investment) Treaties? States Mutual Treaty Actions between the Law of Treaties and the Integrity of Arbitration' (*Kluwer Arbitration Blog*, 5 March 2022) <http://arbitrationblog.kluwerarbitration.com/2022/03/05/masters-of-their-investment-treaties-states-mutual-treaty-actions-between-the-law-of-treaties-and-the-integrity-of-arbitration/> accessed 29 August 2022.

22 Methymaki and Tzanakopoulos (n 10) 181.

23 Ian Johnstone, 'Treaty Interpretation: The Authority of Interpretive Communities' (1990) 12 Michigan Journal of International law 371, 372, 375.

24 *Methanex V United States, Jurisdiction and Merits* (*NAFTA Ch 11/UNCITRAL Arb Trib 3 Aug 2005* Part IV, Chapter C para 22.

25 Richard Gardiner, *Treaty Interpretation 2015* (2nd edn, Oxford University Press 2015) 124–125.

this regard, the main interpreters of legal texts are considered to be the "parties bound by, or subjected to" legal rules, which Kolb refers to as "self-interpretation."[26] Under the approach, even when judges interpret treaties, they "must" include the parties' interpretive agreements since, as masters of the treaty, the parties are considered free to interpret as they see fit.[27] It is consequently averred that even when courts interpret, States retain the power to override the court's decision through their response to the interpretation through subsequent agreements.[28]

The debate regarding the authority of State parties in interpretation also arose during the drafting of Article 38 of the International Court of Justice (ICJ) Statute's sources of law.[29] Baron Descamps, then President of the Advisory Committee of Jurists to the Council of the League of Nations, argued that "it would be dangerous to allow the judges to apply the law of right and wrong exclusively according to their own personal understanding of it."[30] Deschamps further contended that the State parties had to make it mandatory for judges to adhere to the preferences of the States.[31] Deschamps appeared to give the State parties complete control over the interpretation of their treaties, even with an established court.

In the same vein, the seemingly secondary role of the courts' and tribunals' interpretation was expressed in the *Camuzzi* case, where Argentina argued that the State parties were the most qualified to interpret their treaties and not the arbitral tribunals.[32] Akande similarly reinforces the superior role of State parties in interpretation, averring that as masters of the treaty, State parties, through their subsequent agreement or practice, offer an "authentic interpretation" that is as legally binding as any provision included in the treaty.[33] The tribunal held a similar position in the *ADF Group* case regarding parties' subsequent agreements, holding, "We have the parties themselves, all

26 Kolb (n 5) 129 para 2.

27 Ibid., 131 para 1.

28 Gardiner (n 25) 124; Methymaki and Tzanakopoulos (n 10) 159.

29 Statute of the International Court of Justice, 18th April 1946.

30 League of Nations Advisory Committee of Jurists for the Establishment of a Permanent Court of International Justice, *Procès-verbaux Des Séances Du Comité, 16 Juin-24 Juillet 1920, Avec Annexes* (The Lawbook Exchange, Ltd 2006) 318 (League of Nations).

31 Ibid.

32 *In the Proceedings between Camuzzi International S A (Claimant) and The Argentine Republic (Respondent), Decision on Objection to Jurisdiction, ICSID Case No (ARB/03/2)* para 135.

33 Dapo Akande and Antonios Tzanakopoulos, 'Treaty Law and ICC Jurisdiction over the Crime of Aggression' (2018) 29 EJIL 948.

the parties, speaking to the Tribunal. No more authentic and authoritative source of instruction on what the parties intended to convey in a particular provision of NAFTA is possible."[34] Referring to the *ADF Group* decision, Marotti notes that the tribunal reinforced the inability of judicial powers to constrain the State parties' interpretive powers.[35]

While underlining the significance of States parties' subsequent agreements, some international courts and tribunals have embraced subsequent agreements and practices in interpretation, even where they are inconsistent with the treaty parties' initial intention or wording.[36] Specifically, in the *Dispute Regarding Navigational and Related Rights* case, the ICJ held that "subsequent practice [...] can result in a departure from the original intent on the basis of a tacit agreement between the parties."[37] This approach aligns with Steinberg's that international law allows international judicial bodies to be "highly deferential" to States when interpreting, on the basis that States are only bound to treaties and decisions by their consent.[38]

In the same vein, the UNCITRAL tribunal in the *Canadian Cattlemen* case held that "the authentic interpretation of a treaty remains the exclusive province of the States parties themselves that may construct the treaty either expressly or tacitly through subsequent conduct." Under this approach, ignoring the interpretation by the State parties, which is considered equal to other interpretation elements under Article 31 of the VCLT, would be questionable.[39] This perspective seems to consider the interpretation by courts or tribunals less authoritative than that of States parties.

In the same regard, some International Investment Agreements (IIAs) include explicit provisions on the right of States parties to interpret their trea-

34 *In the matter of an Arbitration under Chapter Eleven of the North American Free Trade Agreement between ADF Group Inc. and USA, ICSID Case No. Arb* (AF/00/1) para 177.

35 Marotti (n 21).

36 For instance, Article 27(3) of the UN Charter, requires nonprocedural votes in the Security Council to be passed by 'an affirmative vote of nine members including the concurring votes of the permanent members.' In practice, the UN members allows a nonprocedural vote to be passed by an affirmative vote of nine members without a veto by any permanent members therefore moving away from the original party intention and text as confirmed in *Legal Consequences for States of the Continued Presence of South Africa in Namibia (South West Africa) notwithstanding Security Council Resolution 276 (1970) Advisory Opinion, ICJ Reports 1971* para 22.

37 *Dispute regarding Navigational and Related rights (Costa Rica v Nicaragua), Judgment of 13 July 2009* (ICJ) para 64.

38 Richard H Steinberg, 'Judicial Lawmaking at the WTO: Discursive, Constitutional, and Political Constraints' (2004) 98 AJIL 247, 258.

39 Mark E Villiger (n 19) 435.

ties through subsequent agreements.[40] Consequently, some scholars observe that State parties have a broad authority to interpret their rights and obligations in treaties through subsequent agreements and practice.[41] The joint interpretive agreements of treaty parties are deemed essential for ensuring that treaties are interpreted in line with the treaty parties' intent and purposes over time.[42]

Indeed, Gardiner emphasizes that the parties' interpretation through subsequent agreements "can trump all other interpretations," thereby invalidating interpretations reached through arbitral awards or judicial judgments.[43] Gardiner reiterates that State parties, through their practice, can interpret the treaty "beyond what a body with the role of independent interpretation can do."[44] The implication is that subsequent agreements by States parties are crucial in that they can overrule judicial interpretations and any limitations on the States parties' interpretive roles. Some scholars may disagree with this argument since some consider the general rules of interpretation under Article 31(1) more obligatory than subsequent agreements and practice.

Further buttressing the State parties' role, Yuwen contends that since States create most international treaties, "States parties are the most important actors in treaty interpretation."[45] Under this approach, the court's role in

---

40 Seung-Woon Lee, 'States' Right to Interpret a Treaty and Whether It Should Be Binding in a Pending Case' (*Kluwer Arbitration Blog*, 3 August 2020) <http://arbitrationblog.kluwerarbitration.com/2020/08/03/states-right-to-interpret-a-treaty-and-whether-it-should-be-binding-in-a-pending-case/> accessed 25 May 2022.

41 Anthea Roberts, 'Power and Persuasion in Investment Treaty Interpretation: The Dual Role of States, Vol 104, Issue 2' [2010] AJIL 185; Georg Nolte, 'ILC Second Report on Subsequent Agreements and Subsequent Practice in Relation to the Interpretation of Treaties 66th Session (26 March 2014)' para 163; Roberts, 'Subsequent Agreements and Practice' (n 11).

42 United Nations Commission on International Trade Law (UNCTAD) Working Group III (Investor-State Dispute Settlement Reform) Thirty-ninth session New York, 30 March–3 April 2020; Possible reform of investor-State dispute settlement (ISDS) Interpretation of investment treaties by treaty Parties, paragraph 46 (UNCTAD WG III); Catharine Titi, 'The Timing of Treaty Party Interpretations A Treaty-Design Perspective on Webinar on Treaty Parties' Involvement and Control Mechanisms in Treaty Interpretation, UNCITRAL WG III' (4 June 2020) 18; Tomoko Ishikawa, 'Keeping Interpretation in Investment Treaty Arbitration "on Track": The Role of State Parties' in Jean E Kalicki and Anna Joubin-Bret (ed), *Reshaping the Investor-State Dispute Settlement System* (Brill Nijhoff 2015) 149.

43 Gardiner (n 25) 124.

44 Ibid. 274–278.

45 Fan Yuwen, 'Revisiting ECtHR Interpretation of the ECHR: Living Up to a Living Instrument' TOAEP FICHL Policy Brief Series No. 65 (2016).

treaty interpretation is displaced by the parties' role.[46] Yuwen concludes that, as an example, the role of the European Court of Human Rights (ECtHR) in interpreting the European Convention on Human Rights (ECHR) is secondary to that of the State parties.[47] On a similar note, Gazinni posits that where the State parties have a unanimous interpretation of specific treaty provisions, the tribunals should align their interpretation with that of the State parties.[48] Where applicable, the State parties may participate in treaty interpretation differently, depending on the timing and level of engagement.

2.2.1 Different Ways in Which States Parties Participate in Their Treaty Interpretation

As masters of their treaties with a presumed mandate to interpret their treaties, there are different ways in which State parties can participate in treaty interpretation through subsequent agreements at different levels. These include States defining ambiguous provisions precisely and reaching agreements to restrict liability.[49] States also participate by clarifying the meaning of treaty provisions through interpretive statements and agreements made after the treaty's conclusion.[50]

Impliedly, State parties can continue to define their rights by either averting or responding to decisions of tribunals.[51] As an example and with specific reference to Investment-State Dispute Settlement (ISDS) tribunals, it has been proposed that when a dispute arises, the State parties can intervene in the ongoing proceedings, and after the dispute conclusion, the parties can respond to the tribunal's interpretation.[52] In this regard, the Statute of the ICJ grants State parties, besides those who are parties in the case, the right to intervene in the proceedings whenever the construction of a Convention is in issue.[53] Article 63 gives State parties to Conventions under the ICJ jurisdiction, the right to express their preferred version of interpretation to the Court

---

46 Berman (n 6) 10.

47 Yuwen (n 45).

48 Tarcisio Gazzini, 'The Role of States in the Interpretation of Investment Treaties', *Interpretation of international investment treaties*, vol 14 (Bloomsbury Publishing 2016) 330; Gus van Harten, *Investment Treaty Arbitration and Public Law* (Oxford University Press 2007) 131–132.

49 Anthea Roberts, 'Recalibrating Interpretive Authority' (Columbia FDI Perspectives 2014) Research Report 113; *E.g* US Model BIT, Art. 5 and Annex B.

50 UNCTAD WG III (n 42) para 23.

51 Crawford (n 20) 33.

52 UNCTAD WG III (n 42) para 23.

53 Article 63 of the Statute of the International Court of Justice

before the Court gives its decision on the matter.[54] Kolb reiterates that Article 63 interventions make it possible for States to influence the court's decision on the main issues even if it is on a restrictive level.[55]

Utilizing Article 63, as previously pointed out, there were, for the first time in the ICJ's history, the largest number of interventions by thirty-three (33) State parties to the 1949 Genocide Convention in the ICJ *Ukraine v Russia* case.[56] The ICJ in its decision in the case made some reference to the submissions by the thirty-three intervening States on the jurisdiction question.[57]

States may also expressly allow amendments and lay out mechanisms through their treaties for the State parties to adopt "authoritative interpretations" of the agreement.[58]

The UNCTAD Working group summarized the different roles that States parties can play in the interpretation of their treaties at various stages, recommending that;

> The drafters need to anticipate future interpretations with farsighted and precise treaty language and clear interpretation guidelines. Once the treaty is concluded, the contracting States can clarify the treaty lan-

---

54 Ton Nu Thanh Binh, 'Article 63 Intervention Before the International Court of Justice: New Developments and the Way Forward' (*Opinio Juris*, 26 July 2024) <https://opiniojuris.org/2024/07/26/article-63-intervention-before-the-international-court-of-justice-new-developments-and-the-way-forward/> accessed 12 April 2025; Alina Miron and Christine Chinkin, 'Commentary of Article 63 of the Statute of the ICJ' in Andreas Zimmermann and others (eds), *The Statute of the International Court of Justice: A Commentary (3rd Edition)* (Oxford University Press 2019) 1773 para 73.

55 Kolb (n 5) 695.

56 Latvia, Lithuania, New Zealand, the United Kingdom of Great Britain and Northern Ireland (UK), Germany, the United States of America, Sweden, Romania, France, Poland, Italy, Denmark, Ireland, Finland, Estonia, Spain, Australia, Portugal, Austria, Luxembourg, Greece, Croatia, Czech Republic, Bulgaria, Malta, Norway, Belgium, Canada, Netherlands, Slovenia, Cyprus and Liechtenstein in *ICJ Allegations of Genocide under the Convention on the Prevention and Punishment of the Crime of Genocide (Ukraine v. Russian Federation: 32 States Intervening) Preliminary objections, ICJ GL 182, 2 February 2024* para 14; *Separate opinion of Judge Charlesworth, ICJ Allegations of Genocide under the Convention on the Prevention and Punishment of the Crime of Genocide (Ukraine v. Russian Federation: 32 States Intervening) Preliminary Objections, ICJ GL 182,* (2 February 2024) para 2; Juliette McIntyre, 'Less a Wave than a Tsunami: Procedural Implications for the ICJ of the Article 63 Interventions in *Ukraine v. Russia*' (*Völkerrechtsblog*), 11 October 2022.

57 *Ukraine v. Russian Federation: 32 States Intervening (n 56)* reference in paras 134, 141 and 145 among others.

58 Jacob K Cogan, 'Competition and Control in International Adjudication' (2007) 48 Va J Int'l L 411, 421.

> guage by issuing interpretive statements and agreements. In addition, States may intervene in dispute settlement proceedings. Furthermore, after the dispute has been decided, States can scrutinize arbitral awards and comment on the interpretation by tribunals.[59]

Besides making definitions in treaties more detailed, some State parties to investment treaties further stipulate strict guidelines that the ISDS proceedings must follow.[60] The guidelines and agreements by States may either be expressly stipulated as binding on the tribunal or not.

2.2.2 States Parties' Control of Interpretative Authority through Binding Subsequent Agreements

While it is acknowledged that States parties have a role in interpreting their treaties, the weight of the subsequent agreements and practice attracts different opinions. It is noted that there is a lack of clarity between the resolute view that authentic interpretation is "authoritative" and thus binding on the one hand.[61] The phrase "binding" has been construed as meaning "mandatory."[62] On the other hand, some scholars have construed the language of the VCLT's Article 31(3), which requires the "taking into account" of subsequent agreement and practice as being "persuasive" rather than obligatory or necessarily binding.[63]

Nevertheless, despite the VCLT not explicitly stating that subsequent agreements are binding, some IIAs deviate from the VCLT provisions and expressly provide for binding subsequent interpretations.[64] In this regard, Marotti notes that joint subsequent interpretations by State parties in investment treaties can be designated as binding and conclusive as opposed to the subsequent

---

59 UNCTAD, 'UNCTAD, Interpretation of International Investment Agreements (IIA), What States Can Do-Issues Note No. 3 December 2011' 6.

60 Joachim Pohl and Kathryn Gordon, 'Investment Treaties over Time-Treaty Practice and Interpretation in a Changing World' [2015] OECD Working Papers on International Investment 39; UNCTAD WG III (n 42) para 25.

61 ILC 2018 (n 13) Conclusion 3 (subsequent agreements as authentic); Mark E Villiger (n 19) 429.

62 *Pope &Talbot Inc v Government of Canada (Award of damages)* NAFTA *Ch 11 Arb Trib 31 May 2002* para 51 (Pope & Talbot 2002); Michael Ewing-Chow and Junianto James Losari, 'Which Is to Be the Master? Extra-Arbitral Interpretative Procedures for IIAs' [2015] Reshaping the Investor-State Dispute Settlement System 91, 103.

63 Crawford (n 20) 31; J R Weeramantry (n 2) 80 para 3.102.; ILC 2018 (n 13) Conclusion 3 Commentary 4; *Interpretation of the Air Transport Services Agreement between the USA and Italy, 17 July 1965* (RIAA Vol XVI) 99.

64 Catharine Titi (n 42).

agreements under Article 31(3), which are not necessarily binding.[65] This approach may be aligned with the ILC's conclusion that State parties can agree to have binding subsequent agreements.[66]

The binding subsequent agreements apply primarily where interpretive authority has been delegated to a tribunal or court. An example of State control over the adjudicating bodies' interpretation was contained in the North American Free Trade Agreement (NAFTA). The 1992 NAFTA stipulated that the NAFTA's Free Trade Commission (FTC), which consisted of representatives from the three NAFTA State parties, had the authority to interpret NAFTA provisions, with the FTC's interpretations being binding on NAFTA dispute resolution panels.[67] The NAFTA agreement is considered the first to introduce provisions that made subsequent agreements binding.[68] In this regard, the ILC has noted that arriving at a binding subsequent interpretive agreement is clearer in cases where the treaty expressly provides so.[69] Notably, State parties may issue a joint binding interpretation of treaty provisions, which may be general or specific to the dispute.[70]

Such provisions making subsequent agreements binding are currently standard in several Business Investment Treaties (BIT s) and the practice of the NAFTA governments.[71] For example, the ASEAN Comprehensive Agreement provides that "a joint decision of the Member States, declaring their interpretation of a provision of this Agreement shall be binding on a tribunal, and any decision or award issued by a tribunal must be consistent with the joint decision."[72] Article 30(3) of the 2004 US Model BIT is phrased in similar binding

65 Marotti (n 21).

66 ILC 2018 (n 13) Conclusion 3 Commentary 5.

67 Agreement between USA-Can-Mexico (now USMCA), 1 July 2020, Articles 30.1, 30.2 (e&f) formerly NAFTA; NAFTA USA-Can-Mexico, 2001, Arts 1131(2), 2(c).

68 NAFTA USA-Can-Mexico, CH 11 1992, Art 113(2) (which came into force on January 1, 1994); David Gaukrodger, 'The Legal Framework Applicable to Joint Interpretive Agreements of Investment Treaties' (OECD 2016) 5.

69 ILC 2018 (n 13) Conclusion 3 Commentary 6 citing NAFTA USA-Can-Mexico, CH 11 (1992), Art 113(2).

70 Methymaki and Tzanakopoulos (n 10) 162.

71 2004 Agreement between Canada and [...] for the Promotion and Protection of Investments (Model Canadian FIPA), Article 40(2); Dominican Republic-Central America-United States Free Trade Agreement (2004) (CAFTA-DR), Article 10.22(3); People's Republic of China (China)-Mexico BIT, 2008, Article 19(2); CETA Article 8.31.3 stipulates that interpretation by the CETA Joint Committee is binding on the Tribunal; UNCTAD WG III (n 42) para 36; See also Article X(6) of the Canada-Czech Republic BIT (2009).

72 ASEAN Comprehensive Investment Agreement (2009), Article 40(3); See similar wording in United States – Korea FTA (2019) Article 11.22(3).

terms. By expressly stipulating the binding and conclusive nature of the State parties' agreements in the treaty, any doubt regarding their interpretative force is settled, thus obligating the court or tribunal to apply the agreements. Notably, State parties can reach an agreement with a binding effect on the tribunal regarding the interpretation of treaty provisions at any time.[73] It is suggested that binding treaty interpretations contribute to establishing consistent interpretations.[74]

On the other hand, the United States–Korea Free Trade Agreement (FTA) provides for both the binding States parties' interpretation and the nonbinding option, which is only advisory.[75] Gazinni, however, notes that most States are unwilling to take advantage of their authority to seek binding joint interpretations, even where there is legal uncertainty regarding some treaty provisions.[76] Nevertheless, where the State parties adopt subsequent agreements or practice, they may use these to correct, reject, or shape the tribunals' decisions.

2.2.3 States Parties' Role in Shaping, Correcting, or Rejecting Judicial Interpretations

Significantly, and based on State parties being the masters of their treaties, it is averred that they can exercise powers over the tribunals or courts when they reach decisions that the States are uncomfortable with. One way for State parties to exercise their powers is by using their interpretive agreements to "shape, correct, or reject" the interpretations reached by the tribunals or courts.[77] In this respect, Villiger asserts that as masters of the treaty, the State parties' interpretation is the "correct one."[78] The power to correct treaty interpretations has been expressly provided for in certain investment agreements, such as the EU-Canada Comprehensive Economic and Trade Agreement (CETA), which stipulates that the member states will use the provisions "to avoid and correct any misinterpretation of the Agreement by the Tribunals."[79] Following a similar approach, States parties under the UNCTAD sought to give more control to treaty parties over treaty interpretation to address the

73 Gazzini (n 48) 328.
74 Titi (n 42).
75 Lee (n 40) Article 11.23 (2).
76 Gazzini (n 48) 338.
77 Anthea Roberts, 'State-to-State Investment Treaty Arbitration: A Hybrid Theory of Interdependent Rights and Shared Interpretive Authority' (2014) 55 Harvard International Law Journal 53.
78 Mark E Villiger (n 19) 429.
79 Article 8.31.3 of CETA.

"lack of consistency, coherence, predictability, and correctness of decisions by ISDS tribunals."[80] The State parties can exercise their interpretive mandate by correcting the divergent or inconsistent interpretations through their authoritative subsequent agreements and practice.[81]

In the same vein, the UNCTAD Working Group, in their report, echoes Article 31(3)(b) of the VCLT, providing that States can clarify treaties through subsequent agreements and practice.[82] The UNCTAD report allows the treaty parties to either unilaterally or jointly affirm or reject specific interpretations by the tribunals.[83] Through such interventions by treaty parties and publishing such interpretations, treaty parties guide future ISDS tribunals decisions.[84] For example, State parties under the NAFTA, through the NAFTA FTC, which is made up of representatives of the NAFTA State parties, decided in 2001 that interpretations made by the different adjudicating panels[85] were erroneous. The NAFTA FTC instead adopted its own different interpretation.[86] Emanating from the FTC's interpretation, other subsequent dispute panels in the *Loewen Group Inc. vs the United States*[87] and *Pope & Talbot Inc. v Canada*[88] cases adopted the FTC's interpretation as the correct one.

In *Pope & Talbot vs Canada* specifically, the parties agreed on a different interpretation after the tribunal had already made its decision, and the only aspect pending was the award of damages.[89] The NAFTA FTC interpretation overruled the tribunal's previous decisions, which had gone against the treaty parties' agreements.[90] Similarly, Argentina and Chile agreed to set aside the

---

80 UNCTAD WG III (n 42) para 6.

81 Kasikili/Sedudu (n 1) 1075–1076 paras 47–49.

82 UNCTAD WG III (n 42) para 35.

83 Ibid. para 43.

84 Ibid.

85 *Metalclad Corp. v. United Mexican States, ICSID Case No. ARB(AF)/97/I, Award of the NAFTA Chapter 11 Tribunal (30 Aug 2000); S D Myers Inc v Canada, Partial Award of the NAFTA Chapter, 11 Tribunal (13 Nov 2000); Pope & Talbot, Inc. v. Canada, Award on the Merits of Phase 2 (10 April 2001).*

86 Interpretation by NAFTA FTC through Notes of Interpretation of Certain Chapter 11 Provisions, 31 July 2001 (The FTC interpreted NAFTA article 1105 (l) provision on 'minimum standard of treatment in accordance with international law').

87 *The Loewen Group Inc and R L Loewen v USA, ICSID Case No ARB (AF/98/3), Award of the NAFTA Chapter 11 Arb Trib, 26 June 2003* paras 125–128.

88 Pope &Talbot 2002 (n 62) para 51.

89 Ibid. paras 45–49.

90 NAFTA Free Trade Commission, Notes of Interpretation of Certain Chapter 11 Provisions (July 31, 2001); Roberts, 'Power and Persuasion in Investment Treaty Interpretation' (n 41) 180; Cogan (n 58) 411, 422.

arbitral award in the *Beagle Channel* case.[91] From this perspective, State parties can override any interpretation given by a treaty organ established to interpret on the basis that State parties, as masters of their treaty acting in consensus, can determine the treaty meaning with binding force.[92]

On the other hand, it is contended that while State parties are deemed to be the masters of their treaties, the limitations imposed by international lawmaking, including the politics and the diplomacy involved, make State parties incapable of having complete control over international courts.[93] As Cogan avers, due to the constraints, "States generally lack the ability to correct interpretive errors made by courts, and because of the principle of judicial independence, States are unable to direct judges to decide cases in certain ways or otherwise control the substance of judicial decisions."[94] Nevertheless, because State parties cannot conduct most interpretations independently, they usually delegate their interpretive authority to other institutions, such as the courts or tribunals.

2.3 *States Parties Delegated Authority to Other Institutions to Interpret Their Treaties*

States can consent to delegate their interpretive powers to other bodies. On this basis, State parties may create courts, which have to interpret the law.[95] While giving priority to the State parties role in interpretation, Yuwen asserts that it is only when States agree to confer the power to interpret a treaty to a third party, such as a court, "can the court actually get to interpret treaties."[96] The emphasis is that even where State parties delegate interpretive power to another body, the adjudication is still based on State parties' consent.[97] Consequently, some scholars aver that while State parties are considered supreme in creating the law, and the tribunals interpret and apply the law, the separa-

---

91 *Dispute between Argentina and Chile concerning the Beagle Channel*, RIAA *18 February 1977, Volume XXI* 228–251.

92 Mark E Villiger, 'The Rules on Interpretation: Misgivings, Misunderstandings, Miscarriage? The 'Crucible 'Intended by the International Law Commission' in Cannizzaro Enzo (ed), *The Law of Treaties Beyond the Vienna Convention* (Oxford Scholarly Authorities on International law 2011) 105, 110.

93 Cogan (n 58) 415.

94 Ibid.

95 Robert Cryer, 'Royalism and the King: Article 21 of the Rome Statute and the Politics of Sources' (2009) 12 New Criminal Law Review: An International and Interdisciplinary Journal 392.

96 Yuwen (n 45).

97 Cogan (n 58) 418.

tion between the two roles is not distinct.[98] In other instances, however, State parties may use express treaty provisions to delegate adjudicatory powers to arbitral tribunals to interpret and apply the law.[99]

On the other hand, it is contended that the delegation of interpretive power from treaty parties to tribunals may be "implied and partial, rather than express and exclusive."[100] In this respect, Solan argues that where the legislature uses broad and ambiguous language, it would be presumed to have intended to delegate lawmaking authority.[101] Davidson also contends that in cases where States are uncertain about the issues that may arise later, they "implicitly empower the tribunal to resolve disputes and clarify conventions."[102] In the same vein and while discussing investment treaties, Roberts avers that investment treaties in the past shifted a lot of interpretive power from treaty parties to investor-state tribunals to enable the tribunals to interpret broad and ambiguous treaty provisions.[103] The implication is that treaty parties currently reserve more interpretative power for themselves, unlike in the past.

The delegation of the interpretive authority to other bodies, when the States also enjoy interpretive powers, raises the question of who retains the exclusive authority to interpret the treaty or if the authority is shared equally. In this regard, the mandate of treaty parties to have interpretive control over their treaties is said to exist "in tension" with the claim to interpretive authority by international courts and tribunals.[104] This tension is especially evident where State parties seemingly give judicial independence to the international courts but the State parties reserve some power over the court's independence.[105] In this case, the State parties subsequent agreements and practice in interpreting a particular treaty form the center between rival sources of

---

98 Roberts, 'Power and Persuasion in Investment Treaty Interpretation' (n 41) 179.

99 Methymaki and Tzanakopoulos (n 10) 176; Laurence R Helfer and Anne-Marie Slaughter, 'Why States Create International Tribunals: A Response to Professors Posner and Yoo' (2005) 93 Calif L Rev 937.

100 Roberts, 'Power and Persuasion in Investment Treaty Interpretation' (n 41) 180.

101 Tom Ginsburg, 'Bounded Discretion in International Judicial Lawmaking' (2004) 45 Va J Int'l L 631, 644; Lawrence M Solan, 'Statutory Inflation and Institutional Choice' [2003] 44 Wm & Mary L Rev. 2261.

102 Caroline Davidson, 'How to Read International Criminal Law: Strict Construction and the Rome Statute of the International Criminal Court' (2017) 91 St John's Law Review 62.

103 Anthea Roberts, 'Recalibrating Interpretive Authority' (Columbia FDI Perspectives 2014) Research Report 113.

104 Roberts, 'Subsequent Agreements and Practice' (n 11).

105 Cogan (n 58) 414.

interpretative power,[106] which are the treaty parties and the courts or tribunals adjudicating the disputes.

In Robert's view, for instance, where there is an established court or tribunal, the treaty parties' subsequent agreements and practice before the said international courts and tribunals end up being a "battle over interpretive power."[107] In such cases, the conflict over interpretive power may either result in a dialogue between the treaty parties and international courts and tribunals on the correct interpretation of the treaties or, conversely, a resultant power play between two rival entities on opposing sides.[108] For example, it is pointed out that while the State parties delegate interpretive power to the tribunals as treaty owners, they still reserve both formal and informal means of inflicting penalties on the judicial bodies when they act beyond their given authority.[109]

2.3.1 Theories of Delegating Interpretive Power by States Parties

The delegation of interpretive power by State parties and the retention of certain powers by State parties may be explained through two main theories: the principal-agent theory and the principal trustee theory.[110] The principal-agent theory provides that States, in their capacity as principals, delegate to courts and tribunals (considered as agents) the responsibilities that States are unable to carry out efficiently.[111] The agents (the tribunals and courts) are given the obligation of resolving disputes, with their legitimacy derived mainly or solely from the principals' consent and on following the principals' (treaty parties) wishes.[112] Under the said theory, the treaty parties, as the principals, will ordinarily retain powers to control the tribunals and courts as their agents through "recontracting" to avert or punish[113] agents acting independently and against the principal's wishes (agency slack).[114] The State parties may, for instance, as principals, refuse to reappoint the judges or arbitrators, reduce the court's or tribunal's jurisdiction, or even override their interpretations as a corrective measure.[115]

---

106 Roberts, 'Subsequent Agreements and Practice' (n 11).
107 Ibid.
108 Ibid.
109 Ibid.
110 Helfer and Slaughter (n 99) 932; Roberts, 'Power and Persuasion in Investment Treaty Interpretation' (n 41) 186.
111 Ginsburg (n 101) 643–644.
112 Roberts, 'Power and Persuasion in Investment Treaty Interpretation' (n 41) 186.
113 Ibid.
114 Ibid.
115 Ibid.

The second theory of power delegation to courts and tribunals is based on the principal-trustee theory. Under the theory, States (as principals) delegate authority to courts and tribunals (as trustees) to resolve disputes and additionally ensure the States' obligations are more credible and judicially enforceable.[116] Unlike the agent, the trustees are selected based on professional qualifications and are permitted substantial independent decision-making authority.[117] In this case, the legitimacy of the courts and tribunals (as trustees) is attributable to the principals' (State parties) consent and, additionally, to the trustees' "reputation and independence."[118] Under the Principal-trustee delegation, State parties retain some control and "recontracting" powers over trustees, but the control is less than that exercised on agents.[119]

From the above theories, the degree of interpretive authority the courts and tribunals have is based on whether the State parties use the principal-agent approach, which gives States more control, or the principal-trustee approach, with less control by States. Roberts nonetheless argues that based on "the explicit delegation of dispute resolution powers, and the implied and partial delegation of interpretive authority, treaty parties cannot expect to exercise complete control over tribunals" even as agents.[120]

It is, however, noted that irrespective of which model is adopted or even where a mix of the two models is adopted, the "underlying tension" between State control and judicial independence that is central to the legitimacy of international delegation remains.[121] This tension is based on the thinking that no precise balance exists since international judicial institutions are seen to have "constrained" or restricted independence.[122] In this respect, when the States exercise a lot of control over the courts or tribunals, the tribunal's independence is lost. The loss of independence would arguably defeat the purpose of setting up the tribunals or courts in the first place. In many other instances, however, several treaties fail to explicitly have provisions indicating who has the power of authoritative interpretation.[123] This omission

---

116 Cogan (n 58) 416; Helfer and Slaughter (n 99) 933.

117 Roberts, 'Power and Persuasion in Investment Treaty Interpretation' (n 41) 186; Karen J Alter, 'Agents or Trustees? International Courts in Their Political Context' (2008) 14 European Journal of International Relations 33, 38.

118 Ibid.

119 Ibid. 186–187.

120 Ibid., 198.

121 Cogan (n 58) 414.

122 Ginsburg (n 101) 632; Helfer and Slaughter (n 99) 930; Steinberg (n 38) 247, 249.

123 Roberts, 'Power and Persuasion in Investment Treaty Interpretation' (n 41) 180.

may lead to the power being shared or one institution or other claiming the primary interpretive authority.

2.4 *The Mandate of Courts and Tribunals to Interpret Treaties*

For scholars who contend that State parties are the masters of their treaties and, therefore, capable of interpreting their treaties, the question of whether the courts or tribunals created have any or some interpretive power is raised. In this regard, some scholars argue that the courts or tribunals bear the primary interpretive role once State parties have delegated the interpretive authority. Waibel and Roberts, for instance, assert that the generally accepted position is that the States create international law, but the interpretation and application mandate belongs to international courts and tribunals.[124] Ashworth similarly asserts that courts are the "authoritative agency" in interpreting statutes.[125] It has also been observed that while court judgments are considered subsidiary sources of law under the ICJ Statute,[126] many international courts are granted the jurisdiction to interpret and apply the law.[127] In the same vein, it is recognized that judicial interpretation is inevitable despite the clear drafting of legal provisions.[128] Gazzini, therefore, argues that tribunals have the right to give meaning to vague treaty terms or provisions.[129]

On his part, Waibel contends that States only retain the superior interpretive role where no authorized legal body has "compulsory" jurisdiction to interpret.[130] The implication is that where there is an authorized body to interpret, the State parties no longer have the superior mandate to interpret their treaties. De Lapradelle, a delegate in the ICJ Statute drafting, took the same approach, arguing that interpretation "must be left to the judges." [131] In

124 Ibid., 188.; M Waibel, 'Demystifying the Art of Interpretation' (2011) 22 European Journal of International Law 571, 584.

125 Andrew Ashworth and Jeremy Horder, *Principles of Criminal Law* (Oxford University Press 2013) 69.

126 Statute of the ICJ Art. 38(1)(d).

127 See European Convention on Human Rights (ECHR), Art. 32(1) gives the European Human Rights Court {ECtHR} jurisdiction to interpret and apply the ECHR; Several treaties give the ICJ the jurisdiction to interpret and apply their provisions e.g the Convention on the Prevention and Punishment of the Crime of Genocide, Art. IX December 9, 1948.

128 *C R v United Kingdom (Judgment) Application no. 20190/92)* ECHR *22 November 1995*, para 34.

129 Gazzini (n 48) 329.

130 Waibel (n 124) 571, 584.

131 League of Nations (n 30) 295.

De Lapradelle's view, "confidence must be put in the judges, and they must be allowed" to consider the different interpretive elements.[132]

Seemingly advocating for the court's conclusive role in interpretation, the PCIJ, in its judgment, held that it would be "incompatible…with its position as a Court of Justice to give a judgment which would be dependent for its validity on the subsequent approval of the parties."[133] Similarly, Yuwen points out that State parties to the ECHR commit to adhere to the court's final judgment regarding the Convention even when they are uncomfortable with the ECtHR's decisions.[134] These approaches appear to reiterate that the court's decision supersedes the State parties' subsequent agreements and practice. Nevertheless, even when the courts interpret, the States' intentions have to form a central part of the interpretation process.[135] All the above views seemingly acknowledge that both the States parties and the courts or tribunals have some authority during treaty interpretation.

2.5 *Shared General Interpretive Authority between States and Existing Tribunals or Courts*

A different view advocates for the joint responsibility of States and the courts or tribunals in treaty interpretation. However, the actual balance of power between treaty parties and tribunals regarding the authority to interpret investment treaties is unclear.[136] This sentiment is also taken to apply to established courts. In this respect, it is argued that neither the treaty parties nor the international courts and tribunals established by the parties have exclusive authority to interpret treaties in all circumstances.[137] Roberts, therefore, states that treaty parties cannot expect to have complete control over the interpretation of their treaties when they have delegated some interpretive power to international courts and tribunals.[138] On the other hand, the international courts and tribunals cannot have exclusive interpretive power over treaties when State parties retain some rights to continuously influence the

132 Ibid., 296.

133 *PCIJ, Series A/B, No. 46, Case of the Free Zones of Upper Savoy and the District of Gex (7 June 1932)* 161 para 200.

134 Yuwen (n 45); Article 46(1) of the ECHR.

135 Joseph Powderly, *Judges and the Making of International Criminal Law* (Brill Nijhoff 2020) 260.

136 Roberts, 'Power and Persuasion in Investment Treaty Interpretation' (n 41) 179.

137 Ibid., 179 para 1.

138 Roberts, 'Subsequent Agreements and Practice' (n 11) para 1; Roberts, 'Power and Persuasion in Investment Treaty Interpretation' (n 41) 179 para 1.

interpretation of those treaties mainly through their subsequent agreements and practice.[139]

Similarly, Ginsburg avers that international courts have "interdependent" interpretational power since the interpretation of international law is limited by the States preferences and that of other actors.[140] It is additionally noted that the courts or tribunal's continued existence is hinged on the State parties' approval, meaning that the courts have to create a balance between control by treaty parties on one hand and judicial independence on the other.[141]

Johnstone suggests that the mandate of authoritative interpretation is not vested in the treaty parties and tribunals individually but in the combined institution formed by both the treaty parties and tribunals.[142] The same reasoning was adopted in *Sempra Energy International v. Argentina*, where the ICSID tribunal found that "interpretation is not the exclusive task of States. It is also the duty of tribunals called upon to settle a dispute, particularly when the question is to interpret the meaning of the terms used in a treaty."[143]

The reiteration is that where an existing court or tribunal exists, the interpretative mandate is not absolute for either organ but is shared between tribunals and State parties.[144] Ishikawa further emphasizes that to achieve the stability of investment treaties, States and tribunals must recognize that they should share the power and obligations related to treaty interpretation.[145] Roberts observes that shared interpretive authority between treaty parties and tribunals enhances the legitimacy of the investment treaty interpretation as opposed to where one entity has the authority to dictate to the other.[146] In the same vein, Methymaki avers that while State parties remain the masters of

---

139 UNCTAD, 'Interpretation of International Investment Agreements (IIA), What States Can Do' Issues Note No. 3 December 2011.

140 Ginsburg (n 101) 633.

141 Roberts, 'Power and Persuasion in Investment Treaty Interpretation' (n 41) 187; Cogan (n 58) 414.

142 Ian Johnstone, 'Treaty Interpretation: The Authority of Interpretive Communities' (1990) 12 Michigan Journal of International law 380.

143 *Sempra Energy International v Argentine, No ARB/02/16 ICSID, Decision on Objections to Jurisdiction (May 11, 2005)* para 147; *In the Proceedings between Camuzzi International S A (Claimant) and The Argentine Republic (Respondent), Decision on Objection to Jurisdiction, ICSID Case No (ARB/03/2)* para 135.

144 Roberts, 'Power and Persuasion in Investment Treaty Interpretation' (n 41) 225; Gazzini (n 48) 329.

145 Tomoko Ishikawa, 'Keeping Interpretation in Investment Treaty Arbitration "on Track": The Role of State Parties' in Jean E Kalicki and Anna Joubin-Bret (ed), *Reshaping the Investor-State Dispute Settlement System* (Brill | Nijhoff 2015) 149.

146 Roberts, 'Power and Persuasion in Investment Treaty Interpretation' (n 41) 194.

their treaties, tribunals are not "their puppets," but neither can tribunals be the masters of the treaty.[147]

Roberts suggests that the sharing of interpretive power is becoming more acceptable rather than being seen as a threat to the legitimacy of judicial decisions.[148] An example of acknowledged shared interpretive authority was indicated by the UNCTAD Working Group on ISDS, noting that treaty parties and the ISDS tribunals play different roles in interpreting investment treaties, but they share interpretive authority.[149] It was proposed that treaty parties should jointly determine the principles of interpretation usable by ISDS tribunals to ensure the treaty interpretation is hinged on the State parties' intentions.[150]

Consequently, Roberts asserts that treaty parties and tribunals both enjoy a balance of interpretive power, and in practice, neither enjoys overall interpretive authority in all circumstances.[151] This position was reiterated in the *Beagle* case, where the tribunal held that; "interpretation is thus a function determined and regulated by international law and not a task left simply to the discretion or whim of the judge. He is not allowed to overstep the established limits, for then he would not be interpreting the law but revising it."[152] Impliedly, the shared and limited interpretive authority means that the tribunals do not enjoy complete independence in interpretation.

Interventions by State Parties in proceedings related to treaty interpretations could also be seen as an acknowledgment of the shared role of State parties and the courts or arbitral institutions in the interpretation of treaties. As an example, the Statute of the ICJ, as earlier mentioned, grants State parties to a Convention being considered by the ICJ, other than the parties in the case, the right to intervene in the proceedings when the construction of the Convention is in issue.[153] In this case, on the one hand, Article 63 gives State parties to Conventions under ICJ consideration, the right to be heard, and to express their preferred interpretation to the ICJ, before the Court gives its

147 Methymaki and Tzanakopoulos (n 10) 181.

148 Roberts, 'Power and Persuasion in Investment Treaty Interpretation' (n 41) 194.

149 UNCTAD WG III (n 42) para 13.

150 Submission from the Government of Thailand (A/CN.9/WG.III/WP.162); UNCTAD WG III (n 42) para 9.

151 Roberts, 'Power and Persuasion in Investment Treaty Interpretation' (n 41) 179.

152 *Dispute between Argentina and Chile concerning the Beagle Channel*, RIAA *18 February 1977, Volume XXI* 231.

153 Article 63 of the Statute of the International Court of Justice; Miron and Chinkin (n 54) 1742.

interpretation of the matter.[154] On the other hand, the construction given by the ICJ in its decision, is binding on both the State parties which make interventions, and the parties in the case, who must accept the interpretation as authoritative.[155] The interventions therefore allow for wider State party participation in the interpretation process[156] while binding them to the ICJ judgment. Miron and Chinkin suggest that Article 63 interventions were based on the notion that State parties are the "natural guardians" of their treaties or Conventions.[157]

As previously mentioned, thirty-three (33) State parties to the 1948 Genocide Convention intervened in the *Ukraine v Russia* case proceedings pursuant to Article 63.[158] It was pointed out that State parties to the Genocide Convention used Article 63 as an opportunity to offer their joint interpretation of the Genocide Convention.[159] In the same vein, Judge Charlesworth acknowledged that the State party interventions in the *Ukraine v Russia* case "enriched the Court's consideration of the Parties' arguments."[160] Article 63 is consequently seen as balancing the roles of the State parties and the ICJ as interpreters, and building "bridges" between them.[161]

To emphasize that the roles of the tribunals and State parties are interlinked, it is pointed out that how treaty parties interpret and apply the law impacts the tribunals' decisions, and on the other hand, tribunal awards in particular cases unofficially contribute to the interpretation of the law.[162] Similarly, it has been recognized that the arbitral tribunal's role is to interpret and apply investment treaties while the treaty parties clarify the treaty's meaning through their authoritative interpretation.[163]

---

154 Ton Nu Thanh Binh (n 54); Miron and Chinkin (n 54) 1773 para 73.

155 Article 63 of the ICJ Statute; Miron and Chinkin (n 54) 1743.

156 Ton Nu Thanh Binh (n 54).

157 Miron and Chinkin (n 54) 1742.

158 *Ukraine v. Russian Federation: 32 States Intervening Preliminary Objections* (n 56).

159 Kyra Wigard, Ori Pomson and Juliette McIntyre, 'Keeping Score: An Empirical Analysis of the Interventions in Ukraine v Russia' (2023) 14 Journal of International Dispute Settlement 305, 306.

160 Separate decision by J Charlesworth, *ICJ Allegations of Genocide under the Convention on the Prevention and Punishment of the Crime of Genocide (Ukraine v. Russian Federation): 32 States Intervening) Preliminary Objections*, 2 February 2024 para 2; William Schabas, 'The Damp Squib of Third Party Intervention in Ukraine v. Russia' (*EJIL: Talk!*, 5 February 2024) <https://www.ejiltalk.org/the-damp-squib-of-third-party-intervention-in-ukraine-v-russia/> accessed 13 May 2025.

161 Miron and Chinkin (n 54) 1743.

162 Roberts, 'Power and Persuasion in Investment Treaty Interpretation' (n 41) 179.

163 UNCTAD WG III (n 42) para 15.

To resolve any conflict related to interpretational authority between State parties and the tribunals, Roberts proposes that tribunals should consider more State parties subsequent agreements and practice based on Article 31 (3)(a) and (b) of the VCLT.[164] In this regard, the study argues that the requirement that the parties' agreements can only be construed as subsequent agreements where they have been reached by "all" the treaty parties[165] may counterbalance the State parties unlimited interpretational authority. This view is taken because it is uncommon and challenging to get all State parties to adopt a unanimous agreement after a treaty's conclusion.

It is therefore contended that where such exceptional agreement by all parties is achieved, the courts or tribunals should decisively apply such subsequent agreements in their decisions. As Akande points out, ASP resolutions adopted by consensus of all State parties "must" be taken into account by the ICC during the treaty interpretation.[166] The need for the courts or tribunals to obligatorily consider such agreements was arguably best expressed by the ICSID tribunal in the *ADC vs USA NAFTA* case, which found that where all the parties have spoken, there is "no more authentic and authoritative source of instruction on what the parties intended to convey in a particular provision". [167]

Another proposed way for State parties to share interpretive authority with the tribunals is for the tribunals to consult State parties on the interpretation where the tribunal is in doubt regarding the interpretation.[168] This approach would also work where courts are involved. As an acknowledgment of the State parties as treaty owners, the court can seek clarification on ambiguous provisions to ensure the parties' intent prevails.

In conclusion, it is clear that besides the State parties, the courts and tribunals also have interpretive authority. The book aligns with the approach that State parties and courts have shared interpretive authority, with none enjoying a superior monopoly. However, the shared interpretive authority and the different institutions' specific roles may be more challenging to distinguish and balance when subsequent agreements and practice are reached when there are ongoing related cases.

---

164 Roberts, 'Power and Persuasion in Investment Treaty Interpretation' (n 41) 179.

165 ILC 2018 (n 13) Conclusion 4 Commentary 4.

166 Dapo Akande and Talita De Souza Dias, 'How the UNSC and ASP Can Enhance Cooperation with the ICC, Policy Brief 124' (Institute for Security Studies (ISS) 2019).

167 *In the matter of an Arbitration under Chapter Eleven of the North American Free Trade Agreement between ADF Group Inc. and USA, ICSID Case No. Arb (AF/00/1)* para 177.

168 Submission from the Government of Costa Rica (A/CN.9/WG.III/WP.164, Annex II); UNCTAD WG III (n 42) para 10.

2.6 *Subsequent Interpretive Agreements by States Parties When There Is an Ongoing Case*

It has been previously pointed out that State parties generally enjoy the authority to interpret their treaties through subsequent agreements and practice. On the other hand, the tribunals and courts also require judicial independence during interpretation. However, the role of State parties' intervention through subsequent agreements or statements is not precise when there is an ongoing case. In this regard, Titi has observed that the application of joint interpretive statements by States when there is an ongoing dispute remains controversial.[169] It has, however, been noted that whether a common interpretation by States will bind a tribunal in a pending case depends on the specific treaty.[170]

Part of the tension between tribunals and the State parties' role in interpretation during ongoing cases may arise due to what is considered the States "dual role" in treaties.[171] On the one hand, States as treaty parties have an interest in their treaty interpretation generally, and on the other, they are actual or potential respondents in disputes trying to avoid liability.[172] The controversy may also arise on the one hand due to the tribunals' interpretive powers being partly limited by State party interpretations while on the other hand, there is concern that treaty parties may abuse their interpretive powers during ongoing disputes.[173]

Some scholars outrightly view interpretive agreements reached during an ongoing dispute as "abusive attempts" by respondents to limit their liability in existing or future claims.[174] For example, the ICSID tribunal in the *Camuzzi* case cautioned that where an investor-state treaty dispute had arisen, it was unfair to allow the State parties to interpret the treaty with the aim of avoiding liability in the ongoing claim.[175] In the same vein, Schreuer asserts that where a party to a dispute "is able to influence the outcome of judicial proceedings, by issuing official interpretation to the detriment of the other party, it is

169 Titi (n 42) 34.

170 Lee (n 40).

171 Roberts, 'Power and Persuasion in Investment Treaty Interpretation' (n 41) 180.

172 Ibid.

173 Ibid. 194 footnote 73.

174 Anthea Roberts, 'State-to-State Investment Treaty Arbitration' (n 77) 53.

175 *In the Proceedings between Camuzzi International S A (Claimant) and The Argentine Republic (Respondent), Decision on Objection to Jurisdiction, ICSID Case No (ARB/03/2)* 32; J R Weeramantry (n 2) 32 para 2.44.

incompatible with principles of a fair procedure and is hence undesirable."[176] Consequently, some scholars propose that where the joint State agreements or practice appear to interfere with the tribunal's judicial independence or the equality of parties, the tribunal should disregard such joint agreements.[177]

On the other hand, Titi suggests that to balance the role of the State parties' joint interpretations and prevent interference with the tribunal in an ongoing dispute, the tribunal or the disputing parties can seek a binding interpretation from the treaty parties.[178] An example of this approach is the agreement establishing the ASEAN–Australia–New Zealand FTA, which provides that "the tribunal shall, on its own account or at the request of a disputing party, request a joint interpretation of any provision of this Agreement that is in issue in a dispute."[179] This approach may reduce the tension between the tribunals, courts, and State parties.

In a related approach, however, the effect on the tribunal or court's independence remains unclear where the treaty specifies that the parties' joint interpretation is binding on "any" tribunal.[180] For instance, the Korea-Vietnam FTA provides that an interpretation issued by the treaty's joint committee "shall be binding on a Tribunal ... and an award ... shall be consistent with that interpretation."[181] Such provisions acknowledge the parties as masters of the treaties. However, such provisions also imply that any tribunal seized of a matter related to the relevant treaty must only apply the parties' joint agreement on interpretation with no room for judicial independence.

Nevertheless, seemingly minimizing the perceived interference with a tribunal's decision, the Dutch Model BIT of 2019 stipulates that a joint interpretative declaration adopted by the contracting parties is binding on a Tribunal but does not apply to pending cases. It states:

> A joint interpretative declaration adopted as a result of consultations by the Contracting Parties shall be binding on a Tribunal established under Section 5 of this Agreement. Such joint interpretative declaration is not applicable in cases where a claim has been submitted by an investor.[182]

---

176 Christoph Schreuer, 'Diversity and Harmonization of Treaty Interpretation in Investment Arbitration', *Treaty Interpretation and the Vienna Convention on the Law of Treaties: 30 Years on* (Brill Nijhoff 2010) 148.

177 Marotti (n 21).

178 Titi (n 42) 24.

179 Art. 27(2) of Chapter 11.

180 Titi (n 42) 20.

181 Korea-Vietnam FTA (2015) Article 9.24.

182 Article 24(2) of the Dutch Model Bilateral Investment Treaty (BIT) 22 March 2019.

Similarly, the Court of Justice of the European Union (ECJ) found that to ensure the independence of the CETA Tribunal and the Appellate Tribunal, the interpretations issued by the CETA Joint Committee can "have no effect on the handling of disputes that have been resolved or brought prior to those interpretations."[183] The ECJ, therefore, discouraged the use of joint interpretive agreements when the dispute was ongoing. In this respect, treaties can specify that interpretive agreements only have prospective or future effects in order to respect judicial independence. For instance, the Norwegian BIT provides that the "joint Committee should refrain from adopting interpretations of provisions already submitted to a Tribunal in a dispute."[184] In this case, the States joint agreements do not affect the ongoing disputes but only the future ones.

An example of the discomfort with States' joint agreements or statements during an ongoing arbitration arose when the NAFTA tribunal questioned Canada's participation in the FTC's deliberations while it was a party to an ongoing dispute.[185] The NAFTA tribunal raised the salient question of how Canada's participation in the FTC statements could be balanced alongside the international principle "that no one shall be judge in his own cause" and the rule of law principle of having an unbiased tribunal.[186] The timing of the FTC interpretation particularly concerned the tribunal since it was adopted after the tribunal reached a contrary decision on interpretation at the merits stage and before the tribunal could award the damages.[187] In the same vein, Eleni argues that when State parties issue a joint interpretation related to an ongoing case before an arbitral tribunal, it could be argued that the State, which is a party to the treaty and also to the dispute, is using the other State parties to change the rules unfairly. [188]

On the other hand, some scholars and tribunals find the issuance of binding joint State parties' interpretation when a dispute is ongoing positive. Lee, for example, argues that the binding effect of joint interpretations where States clarify the meaning of particular provisions may contribute to greater consistency and predictability in treaty interpretation.[189] In this case, the tribunals

183 Opinion 1/17 of the Court of Justice of the European Union (CJEU), 30 April 2019 paras 236–237; Titi (n 42) 22.

184 Norwegian Model BIT 2015 Article 23(4)(ii).

185 *Pope &Talbot 2002* (n 62) paras 11–16.

186 Ibid. para 13.

187 Roberts, 'Power and Persuasion in Investment Treaty Interpretation' (n 41) 180–181 footnote 7.

188 Methymaki and Tzanakopoulos (n 10) 180.

189 Lee (n 40).

would adhere to the meaning clarified by the joint interpretations, thereby creating consistency. The converse side is that the tribunal's independence and impartiality are compromised when the States common interpretation becomes binding on a tribunal in a pending case.[190]

Other scholars have instead maintained that since the tribunals are obligated to treat the joint interpretations by States parties as conclusive in the interpretative process, the tribunals must do so even where the interpretation interferes with ongoing proceedings.[191] States parties under this approach aim to "control" the interpretation process and ensure the State parties' joint agreements prevail.[192]

It is, however, notable that in certain instances, the timing of State parties' practice or agreements may determine their weight. In this respect, Roberts argues that when States adopt an interpretation before a dispute arises, they are likely to be seen as creating a legitimate balance between investors' rights and the sovereign rights of States.[193] In contrast, when treaty parties enter into an interpretive agreement when there is already a dispute, the interpretation may raise concerns that it is an attempt to influence an ongoing case where one of the State parties is a respondent.[194] This scenario has also played out when States Parties to the Rome Statute have pushed for subsequent agreements where their heads of State and government are subjects of ongoing ICC proceedings.[195]

The framework for the general role of State parties in their treaty interpretation and the ensuing challenges have been laid out. This context will help to analyze whether the States Parties to the Rome Statute have a role in its interpretation, especially with an existing permanent ICC. The following section examines this interplay between the ICC's interpretive role and that of the States Parties.

190 Ibid.; ECJU Opinion 1/17, 30 April 2019 para 236.

191 ILC 2018 (n 13) Conclusion 3 Commentary 4; Marotti (n 21).

192 Ibid.

193 Roberts, 'Power and Persuasion in Investment Treaty Interpretation' (n 41) 212.

194 Ibid.

195 *Ruto Defence Request for Mr Ruto's Excusal from Presence at Trial under Rule 134 ter, The Prosecutor v William Samoei Ruto and Joshua Arap Sang, ICC-01/09-01/11-1998 (TrC V) 03 November 2015* (Kenya sought an ASP resolution on excusal from continuous presence under Rule 134 when its then President Kenyatta and Deputy Ruto were on trial at the ICC).

3 The Rome Statute Provisions on the Entity to Interpret the Statute

Article 119 of the Statute provides guidance on which organs have the authority to interpret the Rome Statute. Article 119(1) provides: "Any dispute concerning the judicial functions of the Court shall be settled by the decision of the Court." The Statute neither defines what a dispute is nor what judicial functions entail. Clark nevertheless suggests that disputes concerning the judicial functions of the ICC may include issues of jurisdiction and interpretation of the definitions of crimes within the ICC's jurisdiction.[196]

Besides the ICC, Article 119(2) of the Statute gives the ASP jurisdiction to settle "any other dispute between two or more States Parties relating to the interpretation or application" of the Statute after three months of failed negotiations between the parties. However, Article 119(2) does not provide for a role for States Parties in the judicial interpretation. Nevertheless, the obligation to the ICC under Article 119 (1) and to the ASP under Article 119 (2) both entail interpretation, albeit in different circumstances. It can, therefore, be argued that on this basis, both the ICC and the ASP have a role in interpreting the Rome Statute.

On the other hand, other scholars posit that Article 119(1) underscores the ICC's exclusive and "inherent"[197] authority to exercise judicial functions. In the same vein, some scholars have interpreted Article 119(1) as taking precedence over Article 119(2), arguing that the dispute settlement process of Article 119(2) only applies where the ICC has no power to settle the matter under Article 119(1).[198] Pellet, for instance, finds that Article 119(1) takes precedence over Article 119(2) since any dispute between two or more States which is judicial, still has to be handled by the ICC, and the ASP only comes in when the dispute is non-judicial.[199] Pellet reiterates the ICC's role with respect to Article 119(1) and 119(2), stating that;

196 RS Clark, 'Article 119; Settlement of Disputes' in Otto Triffterer and Kai Ambos (eds), *Commentary on the Rome Statute of the International Criminal Court* (3rd edn, Beck/Hart 2016) 2276.

197 *Nuclear Tests (Australia v France), Judgment, ICJ Reports 20 December 1974* para 23; Allain Pellet, 'Settlement of Disputes' in A Cassese et al. (ed), *The Rome Statute of the ICC: A Commentary*, vol 2 (Oxford University Press 2002) 1841, 1848.

198 Timothy O'Neill, 'Dispute Settlement under the Rome Statute of the International Criminal Court: Article 119 and the Possible Role of the International Court of Justice' (2006) 5 Chinese Journal of International Law 67, 71.

199 Alain Pellet, 'Applicable Law' in A Cassese et al. (ed), *The Rome Statute of the ICC : A Commentary*, vol 2 (Oxford University Press 2002) 1054.

> However, it must be noted that the first criterion seems to have precedence over the second since paragraph 2 expressly reserves the competence of the Assembly of States Parties over any disputes other than those mentioned in paragraph 1, which means that, should two or more State Parties have a dispute concerning the judicial functions of the Court, the latter would be competent to rule on the dispute.[200]

In resolving disputes under Article 119(2), which includes interpretation, the ASP is given two avenues to pursue dispute settlement. It may seek to settle the dispute directly or recommend further means, including referral to the ICJ. This position where the ASP can adjudicate a dispute involving two or more State parties arguably shows that the distinction between the disputes relating to "judicial functions" and "other disputes" arising between two or more States Parties is unclear.[201] As an example of the blurred distinction, the African Union (AU) recommended that the dispute regarding Articles 27 and 98 of the Rome Statute be referred to the ASP for interpretation based on Article 119(2) of the Statute.[202] This recommendation was made despite the issue being the subject of an ongoing case before the Court and presumably falling under the ICC's "judicial functions."

Clark consequently argues that there will inevitably be some "hotly debated areas" in which it is not clear where the competence lies between the ICC judges and the ASP to resolve a particular dispute.[203] This lack of clarity may arise from courts being given interpretative independence yet with States Parties still retaining control in one form or another.[204] With specific reference to the ICC, the seeming conflict may also arise as a result of the dual nature of the

200 Allain Pellet 'Settlement of Disputes' (n 197) 1843.

201 Max Du Plessis and Christopher Gevers, 'The Role of the Assembly of States Parties for the ICC' in Richard H Steinberg (ed), *Contemporary Issues Facing the International Criminal Court* (Brill Nijhoff 2016) 162.

202 Recommendations of the Ministerial Meeting on the Rome Statute of the International Criminal Court, November 6, 2009, Addis Ababa Min/ICC/Legal/Rpt (11). Recommendation 5 states: 'State Parties should consider having recourse to the provisions of Article 119 of the Statute and Rule 195 of the Rules of Procedure and Evidence of the ICC to settle disputes regarding the implementation of Articles 27 and 98 of the Rome Statute.' See also African Union, 'Decision on the Report of the Second Meeting of States Parties to the Rome Statute of the International Criminal Court (ICC),' Doc. Assembly/AU/8(XIV), January 2010 (recommendations were endorsed by the AU Assembly in January 2010).

203 RS Clark (n 196) 2275 para 3.

204 Cogan (n 58) 414.

Court as both a judicial institution and an international organization.[205] As a judicial entity, the ICC needs to have judicial independence, while as an international organization, State parties expect to guide and shape the ICC,[206] including its interpretive role.

Following the same approach, Guilfoyle asserts that despite the ICC enjoying judicial independence, it remains an international organization borne out of States' consent and delegated authority. He consequently urges the ASP to reassert that the ICC's legal authority is derived from the States Parties, without whom the Court would be nonexistent.[207] The implication is that the ICC's judicial independence is constrained by the States Parties who established it. However, the ASP has attempted to delineate its role from that of the ICC through the passed procedures relating to cooperation between the ICC and States Parties to the Statute.[208] The ASP reiterated that "given the respective roles of the Court and the Assembly, any response by the Assembly to non-cooperation would be non-judicial in nature."[209] The ASP has further emphasized that the promotion of cooperation with the ICC should "not replace judicial determinations" to be reached by the ICC in ongoing proceedings.[210]

Despite the unclear demarcation and potential tension in their interpretive roles, it is noted that Articles 112 and 119 of the Rome Statute do not provide a forum to address existing or potential disputes between the ICC and the ASP.[211] However, it has been posited that to ensure the legitimacy of judicial decisions, the ICC should consider the division of interpretive powers between the ASP and the Court provided in the Statute.[212] The following section, therefore, addresses the ASP's specific role in interpreting the Statute.

---

205 'Independent Expert Review of the International Criminal Court and the Rome Statute System Final Report, 30 September 2020' para 26.

206 Ibid.

207 Douglas Guilfoyle, 'Reforming the International Criminal Court: Is It Time for the Assembly of State Parties to be the Adults in the Room?' (*EJIL: Talk!* 8 May 2019) <https://www.ejiltalk.org/reforming-the-international-criminal-court-is-it-time-for-the-assembly-of-state-parties-to-be-the-adults-in-the-room/> accessed 25 November 2022.

208 Strengthening the International Criminal Court and the Assembly of States Parties, ICC-ASP/ 10/Res.5, 21 December 2011.

209 Ibid. para 9 and annex para 6.

210 Ibid.

211 Kritika Sharma, 'The Curious Case of Rule 165 of the Rules of Procedure and Evidence: The Effect of Control Exercised by the Assembly of States Parties over the International Criminal Court' (2020) 20 (2) International Criminal Law Review 285, 316.

212 Leena Grover, *Interpreting Crimes in the Rome Statute of the International Criminal Court* (Cambridge University Press 2014) 74.

3.1 *The Role of the ASP in the Interpretation of the Rome Statute*

The ICC and the ASP structures are sometimes described as representing a separation of powers.[213] Emphasizing the States parties' role, some scholars like Tladi maintain that the primary mandate of interpreting a particular instrument "remains with the State parties collectively even when there is an institution established specifically to interpret that instrument."[214] Following the same approach, the Working Group of the Independent Oversight Mechanism (IOM) of the ICC set up in 2009[215] stated that "the interpretation of the Rome Statute is primarily the task for the States since it was the States who adopted the Rome Statute."[216]

As previously mentioned, Article 119(2) allows the ASP interpretive powers to settle disputes between two or more States Parties relating to the interpretation or application of the Rome Statute after three months of failed negotiations between the Parties. It remains debatable what body between the ICC and the ASP would handle a judicial interpretation dispute involving two or more State Parties to the Statute. However, no disputes have so far been brought to the ASP under Article 119(2).[217] Besides Article 119, Article 112(2) of the Statute, for instance, gives the ASP a broad mandate, including legislative and management administrative roles, with the probability of some ASP functions intersecting with the ICC's judicial functions.[218] The ASP, therefore, retains the "management oversight and legislative" power over the ICC.[219]

---

213 Kenneth S Gallant, 'The International Criminal Court in the System of States and International Organizations' (2003) 16 Leiden J Int Law 559–560; Dominic Raab and Hans Bevers, 'The International Criminal Court and the Separation of Powers' (2006) 3 International Organizations Law Review 93, 131.

214 Dire Tladi, 'Presence of the Accused: Right or Duty?The Art of Interpretation in a Tense Political Climate' in Bantekas Ilias Jalloh Charles C (ed), *The International Criminal Court and Africa* (Oxford University Press 2017) 178 para 1; William Schabas, *The International Criminal Court; A Commentary on the Rome Statute 2010* (2nd edn, Oxford University Press 2010) 645; Guidelines of ILC in its Guide to Practice on Reservations to Treaties 1.6.3 commentary para 2.

215 Establishment of an Independent Oversight Mechanism, ICC-ASP/8/Res.1, November 26, 2009.

216 Report of the Bureau on the Independent Oversight Mechanism, ICC-ASP/9/31, November 19, 2010 para 53.

217 IBA, 'Strengthening the International Criminal Court and the Rome Statute System: A Guide for States Parties, October 2021' 80.

218 D Donat-Cattin, 'Decision-Making in the International Criminal Court: Functions of the Assembly of States Parties and Independence of the Court's Judicial Organs' in Flavia Lattanzi and William Schabas (eds), *Essays on the Rome Statute of the International Criminal Court* (© Editrice il Sirente 1999) 73–74.

219 Article 112, Rome Statute.

The ASP additionally has an implicit role in the Rome Statute's interpretation through the ASP's subsequent agreements and practice based on Article 31(3) of the VCLT. In this respect, the ASP's legislative functions of approving amendments to the RPE and the Statute become relevant.[220] The Rome Statute provides that changes to the RPE, which may be proposed by a State Party, the Prosecutor, or a majority of judges, "enter into force upon adoption by a two-thirds majority" of the ASP members.[221] As previously discussed, the resolutions or amendments of the States Parties may be construed as subsequent agreements where they meet Article 31(3) VCLT requirements. By dint of the Statute being a treaty, it follows that Article 31(3) of the VCLT applies. Based on Article 31(3), States Parties retain the right to participate in interpreting the Rome Statute through subsequent agreements and practice even when not expressly provided for in the treaty.[222]

Grover reiterates this aspect, arguing that there are "direct mechanisms for States Parties to influence interpretation, such as amending the Rome Statute or Elements of Crimes and reacting to the Court's decisions through subsequent law, agreements, and practice."[223] It is contended that the ASP's general legislative authority arises from the Rome Statute being a treaty subject to amendment and modification by its member states under customary law.[224] Additionally, States Parties are expressly mandated to amend the Rome Statute in line with Articles 121–123 of the Statute.[225] Consequently, besides resolving disputes between States parties on interpretation, the legislative mandate of the ASP to amend the Statute,[226] the Elements of Crime, and the RPE[227] could arguably directly influence the interpretation and outcome of the ICC's decisions. The amendments may either limit or enhance the ICC's powers regarding the Rome Statute's interpretation, especially where they are construed as subsequent agreements that have to be considered in the Statute's interpretation.

---

220 Ibid. Art 121.

221 Ibid. Art 51(2).

222 Sinclair (n 17) 136; Roberts, 'Power and Persuasion in Investment Treaty Interpretation' (n 41) 208.

223 Grover (n 212) 145.

224 Du Plessis and Gevers (n 201) 160–161.

225 Grover (n 212) 146.

226 Art 121(2) of the Rome Statute (Amendments to the Statute shall enter into force upon adoption by a two-thirds Assembly of States Parties' members) Article 51(4) of the Rome Statute.

227 Article 112 of the Statute, Rule 96 of ASP rules, Article 112(7) of the Rome Statute and Article 121 of the Rome Statute.

In the same vein, some scholars contend that, due to its legislative role, the ASP may adopt rules that dictate the judicial interpretation of the Rome Statute provisions or that are inconsistent with the Statute.[228] Secondly, it is argued that the ASP consultations regarding the RPE provisions may provide a forum for individual States Parties, or the ASP as a whole, to attempt to control the judicial interpretation of the Rules.[229] It is consequently observed that the ASP's powers are interlinked with the ICC's judicial functions in that in exercising the ASP's powers to amend or adopt the laws and the RPE, there is some risk to the ICC's independence.[230] Davidson, however, argues that despite the ASP's powers to adopt and amend the legislation, the assumption that legislation by the ASP is superior to judicial decisions is doubtful.[231]

Nonetheless, reinforcing the vital role of States Parties in the Rome Statute's interpretation, it is acknowledged that the ICC as a judicial body mainly depends on the political will of States Parties in prosecuting crimes.[232] In the same regard, Guilfoyle asserts that the ASP represents the States Parties who grant the ICC its legal authority, without which the Court would not exist.[233] Similarly, the fact that States have the right to decline the ICC's jurisdiction may be a strong reminder to judges to interpret the Rome Statute while closely respecting the text.[234]

Akande adds that States Parties retain the right to challenge the ICC's interpretation after it is given, with the occasional rare effect of "relegating the interpretation of a court to the dustbin of history."[235] From Akande's view, States Parties retain the final say in whether to adhere to or disregard the ICC's interpretation. Schabas has similarly stated that the ASP can amend the rules to adjust or overrule decisions reached by the ICC.[236]Akande and Schabas' approach may be in tandem with Frowein's, who argues that all the

---

228 Hannah Woolaver and Emma Palmer, 'Challenges to the Independence of the International Criminal Court from the Assembly of States Parties' (2017) 15 JICJ 646.

229 Ibid.

230 Ibid., 643, 646.; Coalition for the International Criminal Court (CICC), 'Statement at the 14th Session of the Assembly of States Parties, Niccolo' A Figa'-Talamanca, Secretary General, No Peace without Justice', 26 November 2015.

231 Caroline Davidson (n 102) 61.

232 Grover (n 212) 80.

233 Guilfoyle (n 207).

234 Grover (n 212) 77.

235 Akande and Tzanakopoulos (n 33) 948.

236 William Schabas, The International Criminal Court, a commentary on the Rome Statute, 2010, 645.

treaty parties, by unanimous decision, can override all constraints contained in specific treaty provisions.[237]

The ASP may thus be considered able to enhance or restrict the ICC's interpretive mandate. The following section examines the specific role of the ICC in the Rome Statute's interpretation.

3.2 *The International Criminal Court as the Primary Interpretive Organ of the Rome Statute*

Proponents of the ICC being the dominant interpreter of the Rome Statute assert that Article 119 (1) of the Statute, which gives the ICC authority to resolve judicial disputes, was intended to make the Court the "master of its own house."[238] The scholars assert that Article 119(1) was designed to empower the ICC and make it independent.[239] From this perspective, based on Article 119(1), the ICC possesses the inherent power to adjudicate on any dispute, issue, or difficulty arising in exercising its judicial functions.[240] Reiterating this position, the International Federation for Human Rights (FIDH) noted that judicial independence must be upheld and interpretation of the Rome Statute lies "solely with the judges."[241] Grover further suggests that judges have greater discretion in multilateral treaties since it is difficult to amend the treaty to overrule the judges' decisions when States Parties are dissatisfied with the Court's decisions.[242]

Importantly, it is pointed out that it is only through judicial interpretation that legal ambiguities can be resolved.[243] Nevertheless, this argument needs to be tempered with the realization that the competence and powers of the ICC, as an international organization,[244] are limited to those attributed to it explicitly by States Parties through the Rome Statute and the RPE or through implied powers.[245] As previously mentioned, this view is due to States being

237 Jochen A Frowein, 'Are There Limits to the Amendment Procedures in Treaties Constituting International Organisations?', *Liber Amicorum*: Professor Ignaz Seidl-Hohenveldern in honour of his 80th birthday (1998) p 204.

238 RS Clark (n 196) 2279.

239 O'Neill (n 198) 67, 71.

240 Alain Pellet, 'Settlement of Disputes' (n 197) 1844.

241 FIDH, Position Paper, Ninth session of the ICC Assembly of States Parties (2010) at p 17

242 Grover (n 212) 79; Ginsburg (n 101) 670.

243 Leila N Sadat and Jarrod M Jolly, 'Seven Canons of ICC Treaty Interpretation: Making Sense of Article 25's Rorschach Blot' (2014) 27 LJIL 763.

244 The ICC was established under international law by a multilateral treaty and has international legal personality by virtue of Art. 4 of the Rome Statute.

245 Emma Irving, 'The Other Side of the Article 21 (3) Coin: Human Rights in the Rome Statute and the Limits of Article 21 (3)' (2019) 32 LJIL 848.

the only actors recognized by international law as having complete original personality and powers [246] with the competence and powers of other actors attributed explicitly or impliedly to States.[247] However, in advocating for the ICC's role in interpretation, it has been argued that discussions regarding Articles 112 and 119 indicate a deliberate decision by States to prevent the ASP from dealing with matters of a judicial nature.[248] Notably, Article 112 lays out the duties of the ASP, including setting up the independent oversight mechanism to oversee the ICC, but does not expressly give the ASP any judicial functions of interpretation.

Also related to the dispute resolution by the ICC and the ASP under Article 119 is Article 40(1) of the Rome Statute, which provides that "the judges shall be independent in the performance of their functions." Independence is said to "allow judges to develop legal opinions unconstrained by the preferences of other actors."[249] Additionally, the ASP, in its resolutions, has reiterated its respect for the ICC's judicial independence and its commitment to ensuring respect for and implementing its judicial decisions.[250] Significantly, judicial independence was considered a primary area of concern during the initial negotiations about the Rome Statute.[251] It is nevertheless arguable to what extent the independence of the ICC goes in interpretation when Articles 121–123 of the Statute allow the ASP to amend any law or rule without any express limitation to the timing.

Clark points out that Articles 119(1) and 119(2) make a "strong statement on the power of the Court itself to settle disputes on its judicial functions" with the ASP and the ICJ only playing a discretionary role.[252] The articles are deemed to endow the ICC with rights to protect its independence but also obligate States Parties to respect judicial independence. In further emphasis on the ICC's interpretive role, Grover asserts that in light of the express references to interpretation in Articles 9(1), 21(3), and 22(2) of the Statute, "it seems untenable to suggest that judges have not been tasked with interpreting the

246 Schermers, Blokker (n 7) para 1565.

247 *Reparation for Injuries Suffered in the Service of the United Nations, Advisory Opinion of 11 April (1949) ICJ Rep* 179–180.

248 Du Plessis and Gevers (n 201) 160.

249 Erik Voeten, 'International Judicial Independence' [2011] SSRN Electronic Journal 3.

250 ICC-ASP/10/Res.5, Strengthening the International Criminal Court and the Assembly of States Parties Adopted at the 9th plenary meeting, on 21 December 2011, by consensus; Resolution ICC-ASP/12/ RES 6 Independent Oversight Mechanism (IOM) 27 November 2013 ICC-ASP /12/20, Annex Operation Mandate of the IOM para 27.

251 Du Plessis and Gevers (n 201) 160.

252 RS Clark (n 196) 2275 para 3.

Rome Statute."[253] Article 9(1) provides that the Elements of Crimes shall assist judges in the "interpretation and application of articles 6, 7, 8 and 8 *bis*." Article 22(2) requires judges to strictly construe the definitions of crimes in the Rome Statute while prohibiting the expansion of the definitions by analogy. Additionally, Grover contends that by States referring expressly to interpretation in Articles 21 and 22 of the Statute, the role of judges as interpreters of international criminal law, which was a controversial issue, is legitimized.[254]

The definition of interpretation "as the public or external expression by judges of how the Rome Statute is to be construed" also seems to give the interpretive role to the ICC.[255] Specifically, Grover adds that the ICC Judges are mandated to interpret and apply the law, which requires considering the text in light of its ordinary or special meaning, the context, object, and purpose, together with the subsequent practice, subsequent agreements, and applicable law.[256] Grover posits that the ICC's interpretation of the Rome Statute is final, and States Parties are bound by the ICC's decisions, irrespective of their approval or opposition to it.[257] However, Grover's position is arguable since States Parties still reserve the right to reach subsequent agreements or take political measures that would enable the rejecting, accepting, or amending the ICC's interpretation. The actions of the ASP may, therefore, impact the accuracy and consistency of the Statute's interpretation.[258]

The ICC's primary role in interpretation is also supported by Benatar, who posits that it is ultimately up to the Court to determine the role and the correctness of the interpretive declarations by States by applying the relevant interpretation rules in the Statute and the VCLT.[259] This argument may generally be aligned to that of delegate De Lapradelle, who, while participating in the drafting of the ICJ Statute, argued that "a judge must, of course, judge according to law," which has to be established, "but this duty must be left to

253 Grover (n 212) 5.

254 Leena Grover, 'A Call to Arms: Fundamental Dilemmas Confronting the Interpretation of Crimes in the Rome Statute of the International Criminal Court' (2010) 21 Issue 3 EJIL 550.

255 Grover (n 212) 8.

256 Grover, A Call to Arms (n 254) 555.

257 Grover (n 212) 365 para 1.

258 Tarcisio Gazzini, 'Authentic (or Authoritative) Interpretation of Investment Treaties by the Treaty Parties' (*EJIL: Talk!*, 17 August 2020) <https://www.ejiltalk.org/authentic-or-authoritative-interpretation-of-investment-treaties-by-the-treaty-parties/> accessed 21 August 2020.

259 M Benatar, 'From Probative Value to Authentic Interpretation: The Legal Effects of Interpretative Declarations' (2011) 44 Revue Belge de Droit International 170, 194–195.

the judges."[260] De Lapredelle appeared to emphasize that judges should be given the discretion to interpret the law without interference. Sheppard further asserts that the courts generally have the primary interpretive authority while the legislature determines the courts' approach towards interpretation by including interpretation principles in the criminal code.[261]

While some scholars have found the listing of the 'applicable law' under Article 21 of the Rome Statute as restricting the ICC's discretionary powers, a different approach finds that Article 21(1) (a) opens up the Court's interpretive creativity. For example, some scholars argue that Article 21(1)(a), which requires that preference be given to the Rome Statute, the RPE, and the Elements, allows the ICC to ignore the ASP rules or resolutions inconsistent with the Statute.[262] Hochmayr suggests that the ICC can choose not to apply the RPE as agreed by the ASP, and the Court further has the right to propose amendments.[263] Similarly, other scholars consider Article 21(3) as one way of "circumventing the strict hierarchy of sources instituted by Article 21(1)."[264]

In this regard, some scholars point out that Article 21(3) gives the ICC evolutive powers to come up with remedies not expressly provided for in the Statute by States Parties besides filling existing gaps within the Statute based on human rights law.[265] In the same respect, Powderly contends that the ICC's jurisprudence confirms that neither Article 21 nor Article 22(2) on strict construction have restrained the Court's creative interpretive freedom despite the attempt to do so by the States Parties.[266] It has been additionally observed that despite the attempted constraint on the ICC's interpretive discretion and the supposed textual clarity of the treaty, the judge's primary task of interpretation remains undiminished.[267]

The ICC's mandate to interpret can be argued to be partly derived from the general mandate of courts and tribunals to interpret treaties. In this respect,

260 League of Nations (n 30) 296.

261 Daniel Sheppard, 'The International Criminal Court and "Internationally Recognized Human Rights": Understanding Article 21(3) of the Rome Statute' (2010) 10 Int CLR 62.

262 Woolaver and Palmer (n 228) 663; Article 51(4) of the Statute.

263 Gudrun Hochmayr, 'Applicable Law in Practice and Theory Interpreting Article 21 of the ICC Statute' (2014) 12 JICJ 658.

264 Powderly (n 135) 518.

265 Göran Sluiter, 'Human Rights Protection in the ICC Pre-Trial Phase' in G Sluiter and C Stahn (eds), *The Emerging Practice of the International Criminal Court* (Martinus Nijhoff 2009) 466.; Mahnoush H Arsanjani, 'The Rome Statute of the International Criminal Court' (1999) 93 AJIL 22; Powderly (n 135) 526.

266 Powderly (n 135) 539.

267 Ibid., 456.

the ICJ, while dealing with the court's operational authority, held that "such jurisdiction [...] derives from the mere existence of the court as a judicial organ established by the consent of States, and is conferred upon it in order that its basic judicial functions may be safeguarded."[268] On his part, Cryer avers that States Parties to the ICC consented to create a court and "courts, by their nature, have to interpret the law."[269] Taking the same approach, Woolaver has argued that the Rome Statute did not give the ASP the function of analyzing the ICC's interpretation, and therefore, the implementation of the Statute and the RPE should be left to the Court and not to the ASP.[270]

It is also posited that for the ICC to operate, it must be given the power to decide questions arising from exercising its judicial functions.[271] In this regard, it is contended that the *travaux* of the Rome Statute show that many States Parties intended to delegate some powers to the ICC to fill in gaps or clarify ambiguous provisions by making the provisions vague.[272] A contrary but minority view is given by Jacobs, who argues that it is not the role of international criminal judges to fill the gaps.[273]

In a further reiteration of the ICC's authority to interpret, Clark suggests that the Appeal Chamber's decisions may not be reviewed or appealed in any other forum since the Chamber's decisions are final and binding on the parties.[274] These excluded forums presumably include the ASP. In the same vein, it has been observed that while the ICC did not participate in drafting the Statute, the Court has the role of ensuring that clarity, certainty, and coherence are achieved through the interpretation.[275] This approach recognizes that the interpretive mandate of the Rome Statute belongs to the ICC. It, however, cannot be ignored that while interpreting the Rome Statute, the judges

268 *Nuclear Tests (Australia v France), Judgment, ICJ Reports 1974* 259–260; *Judgment on the Request of the Republic of Croatia for Review of the Decision of Trial Chamber II of 18 July 1997, Prosecutor vs Tihomir Blaskic, 29 Oct 1997* para 33.

269 Cryer (n 95) 392.

270 Woolaver and Palmer (n 228) 651; Art 119(2) of the Statute; FIDH Position paper 9th Session of the ICC ASP, 2010 17.

271 RS Clark (n 196) 69.

272 Caroline Davidson (n 102) 63.; Jared Wessel, 'Judicial Policy-Making at the International Criminal Court: An Institutional Guide to Analyzing International Adjudication' (2005) 44 Columbia Journal of Transnational Law 377, 386.

273 Dov Jacobs, 'International Criminal Law' in Jean D'Aspremont and Kammerhofer Jörg (eds), *International Legal Positivism in a Post-Modern World* (Cambridge University Press 2014) 473; Beth Van Schaack, 'Crimen Sine Lege: Judicial Lawmaking at the Intersection of Law and Morals' (2008) 97 Georgetown Law Journal 119, 137.

274 RS Clark (n 196) 2277.

275 Powderly (n 135) 336–337.

resolve the dispute using not just general principles of interpretation but also referring to the subsequent agreements by States Parties.[276]

Additionally, States Parties as the Statute owners have arguably limited the ICC's interpretive authority in different ways.

3.2.1 Limitations on the ICC's Interpretive Powers by the ASP through Detailed and Precise Provisions in the Rome Statute

Several scholars have argued that States Parties sought to constrain the ICC's interpretational freedom by drafting a very "precise Statute of 128 articles and very precise Rules of Procedure and Evidence comprised of 225 rules."[277] Powderly avers that by the comprehensive drafting of the Statute, States Parties took significant measures to ensure that judicial discretion in interpreting and applying the law would be minimal.[278] Reiterating this aspect, Hunt posits that the "drafting of the ICC Statute and of the Elements of Crimes illustrates clearly an intent on the part of the States Parties to the Rome Statute .... to keep a tight leash on the ability of international judges to go beyond what States have agreed to."[279] The detailed rules in Article 21 and the RPE are considered a way for States to have control over the interpretative mandate granted to the ICC.[280] The comprehensive definitions of the ICC's subject-matter jurisdiction in Articles 6, 7, and 8 of the Statute are consequently seen as a way to restrict the Court's interpretive freedom.[281]

Article 21 of the Statute hierarchically provides for the law applicable, with the Rome Statute, the Elements, and the RPE placed first, followed by applicable treaties and rules of international law in second place, among others. Bitti avers that Article 21's existence, the specificity of its content, and the hierarchy it imposes are designed to limit the ICC's creative interpretational capacity.[282]

---

276 William A Schabas, *An Introduction to the International Criminal Court 2020* (6th edn, Cambridge University Press 2020) 213.

277 Gilbert Bitti, 'Article 21 and the Hierarchy of Sources of Law before the ICC' in Carsten Stahn (ed), *The Law and Practice of the International Criminal Court* (Oxford University Press 2015) 427.

278 Powderly (n 135) 540.

279 David Hunt, 'The International Criminal Court: High Hopes, Creative Ambiguity, and an Unfortunate Mistrust in Judges' (2004) 2 JICJ 59; Cogan (n 85) 421.

280 Cryer (n 95) 391; Cogan (n 58) 421; Powderly (n 135) 489.

281 Joseph Powderly, 'The Rome Statute and the Attempted Corseting of the Interpretative Judicial Function: Reflections on Sources of Law and Interpretative Technique' in Carsten Stahn (ed), *The Law and Practice of the International Criminal Court* (Oxford University Press 2015) 444–445.

282 Gilbert Bitti, 'Article 21 Of the Statute of the International Criminal Court and the Treatment of Sources of Law in the Jurisprudence of the ICC' in Carsten Stahn (ed), *The*

Powderly adds that even the Statute's preparatory material (*travaux*), stipulating the applicable law in Article 21, shows that the object was to ensure that the ICC did not infringe on the sovereign consent of States while resolving disputes.[283]

Several other scholars have reiterated that the comprehensive drafting of the Rome Statute was aimed at curtailing the ICC's interpretative freedom.[284] This argument aligns with Helder and Slaughter's general contention that clear and precisely defined substantive rules impose limitations on tribunals and the parties using them since they restrain the creation of expansive jurisprudence.[285] The detailed drafting of the Statute is construed to represent a fundamental mistrust in the competence and independence of the judiciary tasked with its interpretation and application.[286]

Additionally, Article 22, as an interpretation rule which requires strict construction and prohibits the use of analogy by the judges, is also seen to limit the judges' interpretational freedom.[287] The legality principle in Article 22 has been described as "a constraint on lawmaking [...] relied upon by those seeking to have the crimes within the jurisdiction of the Court defined expressly in the Statute, rather than leaving the Court to interpret general international law."[288] In a general reference to the legality principle, the ICTY, in the case of *Odjanić*, held that the principle prevents "a court from creating new law or from interpreting existing law beyond the reasonable limits of acceptable clarification."[289]

With further respect to Article 22, Pellet maintains that while States needed to define the ICC's jurisdiction and describe the legality principle, "there was no need to go into such great detail, or even to set out the substantial rules

Emerging Practice of the International Criminal Court (Brill Nijhoff 2009) 286; G Hernandez, The International Court of Justice and the Judicial Function (Oxford University Press 2014) 13.

283 Powderly (n 135) 489.

284 Cogan (n 58) 455.

285 Helfer and Slaughter (n 99) 945.

286 David Hunt, 'The International Criminal Court: High Hopes, Creative Ambiguity, and an Unfortunate Mistrust in Judges' (2004) 2 JICJ 56; Antonio Cassese, 'The Statute of the International Criminal Court: Some Preliminary Reflections' (1999) 10 EJIL 144, 163.

287 Camilla Lind, 'Article 22', *Commentary on the Law of the International Criminal Cour* (Mark Klamberg (ed) FICHL 2017) 255.

288 Bruce Broomhall, 'Article 22, Nullum Crimen Sine Lege' in Otto Triffterer and Kai Ambos (eds), *Commentary on the Rome Statute of the ICC Observers' Notes, Article by Article* (Beck/Hart 2016) 950.

289 Decision on Dragoljub Ojdanic's motion challenging jurisdiction – Joint Criminal Enterprise, Ojdanić, IT-99-37-AR72, AC, ICTY, 21 May 2003, paras 37–38.

applicable."[290] Similarly, it has been further averred that while the legality principle was necessary to ensure certainty and predictability, the drafters sought to ensure that the ICC could not engage in the "judicial creativity" practiced in other jurisdictions.[291] In this respect, it is observed that, unlike the ad hoc tribunal statutes, which trusted the judges with creative interpretation, the Rome Statute set out to discourage any interpretational creativity by providing the interpretation.[292]

By discouraging the ICC from extending terms by analogy, through the detailed definitions and the strict construction principles, it is averred that States Parties wanted to ensure they retained "near total control" over the Court's ability to extend the textual interpretative boundaries and the ordinary meaning.[293] The States Parties, therefore, arguably gave the ICC only limited jurisdiction in interpretation since the Court lacks the discretion to disregard the Rome Statute's terms and must act only within the Statute's framework.[294]

Judge Herrera agreed with this approach in her dissenting opinion in the *Ruto* case, holding that:

> The Court shall exercise its functions and powers "as provided for in the Statute" and this provision "is directed against an expansion of the Court's powers beyond the Statute" ...It also strikes me as particularly difficult to rely on the implied powers doctrine in a context where the drafters of the Statute have demonstrated a deliberate intent to limit the Court's authority.[295]

Judge Herrera, therefore, seemed to agree with the States restrictive approach to the ICC's interpretation through the legality rule. In the same vein, Grover defends the State Parties against criticism of imposing the strict legality rule in

290 Pellet (n 199) 1055.

291 Powderly (n 135) 528; W A Schabas, 'Strict Construction and the Rome Statute' in S Dewulf (ed), *la* [CVDW]*: Liber Amicorum Chris Van den Wyngaert* (Maklu 2017) 429.

292 Powderly (n 135) 465.

293 Ibid., 547; Grover (n 212) 35.

294 Pellet (n 199) 1079.

295 Dissenting Opinion of Judge Herrera Carbuccia on the '*Decision on Prosecutor's Application for Witness Summonses and Resulting Request for State Party Cooperation', Ruto and Sang, Situation in the Republic of Kenya, ICC-01/09-01/11-1274-Anx, TC V(A), ICC, 29 April 2014*, para 21.

Article 22, averring that States have the right to protect their interest by insisting that judges respect the strict legality principle.[296]

On the other hand, it is asserted that legislative supremacy is only achieved through strict construction where there was no intention by States to delegate lawmaking or interpretational authority to the courts to fill identified gaps.[297] It has consequently been argued that delegated interpretation and the requirement of strict construction cannot function simultaneously.[298] The implication is that States cannot insist on a strict construction of the treaty provisions when they have given interpretational authority and discretion to the courts.

While some scholars have defended the States Parties constraint of the ICC's interpretational discretion, Woolaver differs. Woolaver argues that using the ASP's powers to influence the interpretation of the RPE and the Rome Statute goes contrary to Article 40 of the Statute, which requires judges to be independent in performing their functions.[299] Woolaver's argument, while significant, may be challenged by Cryer's view that the ICC must exercise caution in its interpretation since States are unlikely to support a Court that is a "loose interpretative cannon."[300] This approach correctly shows that while the ICC is free to interpret the Statute, the ASP can take punitive measures against the Court where it goes contrary to their expectations. Some of these measures may be political as provided for under Article 112 and other Statute provisions or as generally based on customary international law. The study takes the position that clear and precise Statute provisions are necessary to guide the Court in determining the intentions of States Parties. It is however argued that the provisions should not be so constraining that they leave no room for the ICC to exercise some interpretational discretion when circumstances call for it.

296 Grover (n 212) 188.

297 John Calvin Jeffries, 'Legality, Vagueness, and the Construction of Penal Statutes' (1985) 71 Virginia Law Review 189, 204.

298 Dan M Kahan, 'Lenity and Federal Common Law Crimes' (1994) 1994 The Supreme Court Review, University of Chicago 345, 347.

299 Woolaver and Palmer (n 228) 663.

300 Cryer (n 95) 392.; Robert Cryer, 'The International Criminal Court and Its Relationship To Non-Party States' in G Sluiter & C Stahn (ed), *The Emerging Practice of the International Criminal Court* (Brill Nijhoff 2009) 121.

3.2.2 The ASP's Political Constraints Impacting the ICC's Interpretive Decisions

When States Parties are displeased with the ICC's decisions, they have varied responses. They can decide to ignore the ICC's decisions[301] or point out their disapproval of the Court's decisions at the ASP yearly meetings.[302] The ASP's disapproval can consequently influence the ICC's future interpretation. States may also refuse to cooperate with the ICC regarding its investigations, the enforcement of sentences, and witness relocation,[303] effectively hindering the Court's work since the ICC is dependent on States for evidence, defendants, and witnesses. In this respect, Article 86 of the Rome Statute requires that States Parties cooperate with the ICC, which cooperation depends on political will.[304] The ASP may also reduce the ICC's budget or refuse to contribute to necessary funds such as the Victims Trust Fund.[305] The ASP can also reward favourable decisions aligned with the States Parties' intentions by appointing or reappointing judges.[306] These means are used to exert political constraints on the ICC,[307] to show dissatisfaction with the Court's interpretive decisions, and may, therefore, influence the ICC's ongoing or future decisions.

Consequently, determining the place of the ASP's political oversight management and the place of the ICC's judicial functions is essential.[308] On the one hand, there is the need for States to address their legitimate concerns and dissatisfaction with the ICC decisions through the ASP, including withdrawal attempts.[309] On the other hand, ensuring that the ASP carries out its functions without unduly interfering with the ICC's independence is necessary.[310] Related to this view, Woolaver and Palmer state that challenging or defying the ASP would be a "self-defeating" move by the ICC; hence, the Court has instead sought to harmonize the ASP resolutions or amendments with the Rome Statute through the Court's interpretation.[311] An example is the embrace of amended Rules 134 *bis*, *ter*, and *quarter*, where the Trial Chamber referred to the ASP Rule amendments as "subsequent agreements" that influenced the deci-

301 Ginsburg (n 101) 660.
302 Ibid., 666.
303 Grover (n 212) 80.
304 Ibid.
305 Ibid.
306 Ginsburg (n 101) 665.
307 Grover (n 212) 80.
308 Woolaver and Palmer (n 228) 661.
309 Ibid., 663.
310 Ibid., 662.
311 Ibid., 664.

sion, even when the prosecution had argued that the amendments were inconsistent with the Rome Statute.[312]

The mandate of the ASP and the ICC regarding interpretation brings to the fore the balancing of the ASP's broad mandate and the need for States Parties to have a forum to address their concerns while simultaneously protecting judicial integrity and independence.[313] Consequently, some conflict areas may arise because of the ASP and the ICC's different but sometimes seemingly overlapping roles. This overlap may be more evident when the ASP exercises its interpretive or legislative role on issues related to ongoing cases in the Court.

3.2.3 The State Parties (ASP) Role in Interpretation When There Is an Ongoing Case in Court

While the meaning arrived at by the treaty parties is construed as the correct meaning,[314] there arises the dilemma of the place of States Parties' subsequent agreements when a case is ongoing concerning the same issue. In this regard, Gardiner points out that there are challenges when States reach a subsequent interpretative agreement when a process of interpretation is already underway by a body possessing the authority to interpret the treaty.[315] The possibility of tension between the ASP's role and the ICC's role in interpretation may arise when amendments to the Statute or RPE are adopted during and aimed at specific ongoing Court cases, especially where the national interests of one or more States Parties are affected.[316]

Consequently, Trahan suggests that where a matter is ongoing in Court (*sub judice*), the ASP should have no role.[317] Similarly, the International Bar Association (IBA) report on Strengthening the ICC recommended that "States Parties should ensure that amendments to the Rules of Procedure and Evidence and the Elements of Crimes do not interfere with matters under consideration by

312 *Reasons for the Decision on Excusal from Presence at Trial under Rule 134 quater, The Prosecutor v William Samoei Ruto and Joshua Arap Sang, ICC-01/09-01/11-1186 (TC V(A)) 18 Feb 2014* para 56; Ibid., 663.

313 Ibid., 662.

314 Gardiner (n 25) 236.

315 Ibid.

316 Woolaver and Palmer (n 228) 649.

317 Jennifer Trahan, 'The International Criminal Court's Assembly of States Parties Meetings: Challenges to the Work of the Court' (*Opinio Juris*, 7 December 2015) <http://opiniojuris.org/2015/12/06/the-international-criminal-courts-assembly-of-states-parties-meetings-challenges-to-the-work-of-the-court/> accessed 22 September 2022.

the ICC (*sub judice*)."[318] In this respect, the IBA report proposed that to ensure that the ASP respects the ICC's judicial independence, it should defer discussing any proposals for amendments related to matters under consideration by the ICC until after the Court has determined the matter.[319]

The ASP also recognized the need for non-interference in the ICC's judicial decisions. While discussing cooperation procedures between States Parties and the ICC, the ASP acknowledged that the States Parties' discussions should not intrude on the "merits of the Court request or otherwise undermine the findings of the Court."[320] This approach aligns with some investment treaty provisions, which stipulate that treaty parties should issue express interpretive joint statements before or after a particular dispute, to minimize concerns about the possible misuse of interpretations by States during the tribunals' decision-making.[321] Similarly, some treaties stipulate that States parties' joint interpretation, given after the tribunal's establishment, does not apply.[322]

In the same vein, Woolaver and Palmer suggest that in some instances, the ASP has influenced the exercise of judicial functions in cases where their interests were affected in ongoing proceedings.[323] Such a question arose in the *Ruto Excusal* case where the ASP amended Rules 134 *bis*, *ter*, and *quarter* as read with Article 63(1) on the requirements for an accused to be excused from attendance while the trial on the issue was going on.[324] Some scholars have construed that as interference by the ASP, considering that Article 119(1) of the Rome Statute protects the ICC's interpretive powers.[325]

3.3 *Conclusion*

The chapter considered the role of States Parties in interpreting the Statute as juxtaposed against the ICC's role. It was noted that State parties are the initial interpreters of their treaties. However, when treaty parties establish courts and tribunals, part of the State parties' authority to interpret is transferred to the courts or tribunals. In effect, even where it is not expressly stated, State

318 IBA, 'Strengthening the International Criminal Court and the Rome Statute System: A Guide for States Parties, October 2021' Recommendation 38.

319 Ibid. Recommendation 80.

320 Strengthening the International Criminal Court and the Assembly of States Parties, ICC-ASP/10/Res.5, 21 December 2011, Annex para 12.

321 UNCTAD WG III (n 42) para 20.

322 See Article 24 (2) of The Netherlands Model BIT (2019).

323 Woolaver and Palmer (n 228) 645.

324 Amendments to the Rule 100, 68, 134 *bis* and 134 *ter* of the Rules of Procedure and Evidence, ICC-ASP/12/Res.7, 27 November 2013.

325 Woolaver and Palmer (n 228) 647.

parties share interpretive authority with established courts and tribunals. The study noted that State parties may impact the courts or tribunal's interpretation through their subsequent agreements and practice. In most cases, the tribunals and the courts have to decide whether the subsequent agreements and practice are binding or discretionary in the treaty's interpretation. In other instances, State parties, especially in investment treaties, expressly stipulate that the subsequent agreements are binding on the tribunals.

Regarding the Rome Statute, it is recognized that Article 119 gives interpretive roles to both the ICC and the ASP. However, the ICC retains the express interpretative authority related to judicial functions. Some articles nevertheless appear to constrain the broad interpretive role of the ICC. The study concluded that the interpretive roles of the ICC and the ASP may be a source of likely tension since the distinction is not clearly laid out. As analyzed, this tension may especially play out where the adoption or amendments of the legislation or rules as subsequent agreements occur during an ongoing case. This overlap may blur the line between judicial independence and the States Parties right to have their intentions adhered to.

The book consequently suggests that a balance needs to be achieved between the ASP's right to play some role in the Statute's interpretation and the ICC's role to interpret independently. From the analysis, this balance could be attained by States Parties avoiding adopting amendments or resolutions related to ongoing (*sub judice*) cases in the Court. Such amendments could instead be undertaken before any cases have been filed or after the conclusion of cases before the ICC. As noted, some investment treaties specifically stipulate the same. Such rules would prevent the seeming interference by the ASP with the ICC's judicial independence in interpreting the Rome Statute.

On the other hand, the ICC should make the deliberate decision to incorporate adopted ASP resolutions and amendments that meet the requirements of subsequent agreements or practice in the Statute's interpretation. Where these resolutions or amendments are adopted by consensus, the ICC should make it a unanimous practice to obligatorily not only take into account but incorporate such resolutions decisively into their decision outcome. It is noted that since States Parties own the Rome Statute, where they clarify the meaning of particular provisions or rules through resolutions or amendments passed by consensus, the ICC should have no reason to look for meaning elsewhere. However, where there is a lack of consensus by the ASP, the ICC has an obligation to consider the resolutions or amendments by the ASP as supplementary subsequent agreements but is not necessarily obligated to apply them in its decisions.

CHAPTER 5

The Coherence of States Parties Amendments and Resolutions versus the Court's Jurisprudence in the Statute's Interpretation

1 Introduction

The States Parties to the Rome Statute of the International Criminal Court (States Parties), through their legislative role of adopting amendments, resolutions, and declarations, when construed as subsequent agreements or practice, may appear to influence the interpretation of the Rome Statute of the International Criminal Court (Rome Statute)[1] by the International Criminal Court (ICC). In some instances, the role of States Parties in interpretation through their subsequent agreements and practice and that of the ICC appear to overlap, seemingly creating uncertainty and tension between the two entities' roles.

This chapter interrogates two specific instances when the States Parties collectively as the Assembly of States Parties (ASP), have adopted amendments to the rules and made resolutions or affirmations, in the process appearing to expressly or implicitly influence the ICC's interpretation of the Statute. The chapter also assesses whether, and if so, to what extent, the judicial mandate of the ICC has affected the role of States parties in interpreting the Rome Statute. In this regard, the chapter also analyzes whether the ICC has correctly construed or should have construed ASP resolutions or amendments as subsequent agreements or practice applicable in the Statute's interpretation.

The chapter consequently explores two specific instances. In the first instance, the chapter examines the ASP's amendment to rule 134 incorporating 134 *bis*, *ter*, and *quate*r of the Rules of Procedure and Evidence (RPE) adopted by consensus, which deal with the accused's presence in Court. The discussion first considers whether the amendment amounted to a subsequent agreement. It also examines the implications of the timing of the amendment when a related matter was ongoing in the Trial Chamber. It further considers the implication of adopting the amendment when the Appeal's Chamber had already

1 *Rome Statute* of the International Criminal Court, 2187 UNTS. 90, entered into force July 1, 2002.

 | DOI:10.1163/9789004725515_006

decided on the same issue of excusal of an accused from continuous presence at trial.

The second illustration relates to Kenya's push as an ASP member, to have the ASP reaffirm that the amendment to rule 68, which involves prior recorded evidence, did not apply retroactively. The implication of the ASP's reaffirmation when there was an ongoing case on the same issue involving Kenya's leaders is explored. The discussion also considers whether the reaffirmation fit the criteria of a subsequent agreement that the ICC should have considered in interpretation.

The book recognizes a related third instance, which involved the conduct of a section of ASP members who openly criticized and rejected the ICC's interpretation of Articles 27 and 98 of the Statute within and outside the Court regarding the arrest and surrender of then Sudan President *Omar Al Bashir* in light of his perceived immunity. On the basis that only a section of ASP members was involved and not the joint ASP, the study excludes the case from the detailed scope of the discussion. This exclusion is done because the cases do not raise the same conceptual challenges between the ASP's collective resolutions and amendments and the ICC in their interpretive roles, which is the basis of this book.

2 ASP Amendments to Rule 134 *bis*, 134 *ter*, and 134 *quater* Regarding the Accused's Presence during Trial

2.1 *General*

As discussed in earlier chapters, while the ASP is not accorded express judicial interpretive powers under the Rome Statute, the States Parties subsequent agreements and practice illustrated through its resolutions, and amendments to the Statute and the RPE, may arguably have some influence on the Statute's interpretation. As stated by Grover, States Parties can influence interpretation through amendments to the Statute or Elements of Crimes, as well as by responding to the ICC's decisions through subsequent agreements and practice.[2] The result is a seeming explicit or implicit overlap with the ICC's judicial interpretive role, which may create some tension. One of the instances where the ASP amendments raised the possibility of directly influencing the ICC's inter-

2 Leena Grover, *Interpreting Crimes in the Rome Statute of the International Criminal Court* (Cambridge University Press 2014) 145.

pretation arose regarding Rule 134 of the RPE, with the amendments titled 134 *bis*, *ter*, and *quater* adopted by the ASP in 2013.[3]

2.2 *Background to the Adoption of Rule 134* bis, ter, *and* quater *by the* ASP

The ASP amended the RPE in 2013 by consensus, adding three new provisions to rule 134 allowing for the presence of an accused "through the use of video technology" under 134 *bis*, "excusal from presence from trial" as 134 *ter*, and "excusal from presence from trial due to extraordinary public duties" under 134 *quater*.[4] In line with Articles 51, 112, and 121 of the Rome Statute, the ASP is mandated to amend the RPE and the Statute, respectively.

The clamor for the Rule 134 amendments began in 2013 when Uhuru Muigai Kenyatta (Kenyatta) and William Samoei Ruto (Ruto), both facing charges of crimes against humanity before the ICC and awaiting the beginning of their trials were elected President and Deputy-President of Kenya, respectively.[5] Kenyatta and Ruto applied to the Trial Chamber to be excused from regular attendance during the trial in light of their official responsibilities.[6] In the *Ruto* case, the Trial Chamber held that an accused's presence at trial could be waived in "exceptional circumstances" such as where "an accused person has important functions of an extraordinary dimension to perform."[7] Granting the Ruto application, the Trial Chamber consequently exempted Ruto from con-

---

3 Amendments to the Rules of Procedure and Evidence, ICC-ASP/12/Res 7, (Adopted at the Twelfth Plenary Meeting of the ASP by consensus), 27 November 2013.

4 Ibid.; Rule 134 *bis* entitled 'Presence through the Use of Video Technology'; Rule 134 *ter* entitled 'Excusal from Presence at Trial' and Rule 134 *quater* entitled 'Excusal from Presence at Trial due to Extraordinary Public Duties' pp 53–54.

5 'Kenya Election: Uhuru Kenyatta Wins Presidency' *BBC News* (8 March 2013) <https://www.bbc.com/news/world-africa-21723488> accessed 22 February 2023; *The Prosecutor v William Samoei Ruto and Joshua Arap Sang, Separate further opinion of Judge Eboe-Osuji to the 'Reasons for the Decision on Excusal from Presence at Trial under Rule 134 quater', ICC-01/09-01/11-1186-Anx, Tr Ch V(a), 18 Feb 2014* (Separate Opinion of Judge Eboe-Osuji on Ruto's excusal); *The Prosecutor v Uhuru Muigai Kenyatta, ICC-01/09-02/11*; William A Schabas, *An Introduction to the International Criminal Court, 2017* (5th edn, Cambridge University Press 2017) 286.

6 *Defence Request for Conditional Excusal from Continuous Presence at Trial, The Prosecutor v Uhuru Muigai Kenyatta, ICC-01/09-02/11(TrC V B) 23 Sep 2013; ICC Defence Request pursuant to Article 63(1) of the Rome Statute, The Prosecutor v William Samoei Ruto and Joshua Arap Sang, ICC-01/09-01/11-685 (Tr C V) 17 April 2013*; Ibid., 287.

7 *Decision on Mr Ruto's Request for Excusal from Continuous Presence at Trial, The Prosecutor v William Samoei Ruto and Joshua Arap Sang, ICC-01/09-01/11-777, 18 June 2013, Trial Chamber V (A)* para 49 (Decision on Ruto's Excusal Request).

tinuously attending the full trial except for the opening and closing statements, the presentation of the victims' views, judgment delivery, and any other attendance directed by the Chamber.[8] The Trial Chamber subsequently issued a similar decision regarding Kenyatta.[9]

Upon the Prosecutor's appeal against the Trial Chamber's decision in the *Ruto* case, the Appeal Chamber, by a majority, reversed the Trial Chamber's decision.[10] The Appeal's Chamber found that the Trial Chamber exercised its discretion "too broadly" by authorizing a "blanket excusal" to the accused and making his absence at trial the general rule rather than the exception.[11] The Appeal's Chamber gave conditions for waiving an accused's continuous presence, including that alternative measures to excusal should have been considered, the absence must be strictly necessary, the accused must have waived their right to be present, and the decision on excusal had to be taken on a case by case basis.[12]

Seemingly dissatisfied with the Appeal Chamber's judgment, States Parties under the African Union (AU), in their individual statements to the ASP, called for amendments to the Rome Statute and the RPE seeking the flexibility of Court attendance for indicted heads of State.[13] The ASP, by consensus, consequently adopted the 134 *bis, ter*, and *quater* amendments.[14] It has therefore been suggested that the catalyst for adopting the amendments to rule 134

8 *Reasons for the Decision on Excusal from Presence at Trial under Rule 134 quater, The Prosecutor v William Samoei Ruto and Joshua Arap Sang*, ICC-01/09-01/11-1186 (*TrC V[A] 18 Feb 2014* para 104(a) and (b) (Reasons for the Decision on Ruto Excusal)

9 *ICC Decision on Defence Request for Conditional Excusal from Continuous Presence at Trial, The Prosecutor v Uhuru Muigai Kenyatta*, ICC-01/09-02/11-830 (*TrC V b*) *18 October 2013* para 5(a) and (b).

10 *Judgment on the appeal of the Prosecutor against the decision of Trial Chamber V(a) of 18 June 2013 entitled 'Decision on Mr Ruto's Request for Excusal from Continuous Presence at Trial', The Prosecutor v William Samoei Ruto and Joshua Arap Sang*, ICC-01/09-01/11 OA 5 (*26 Oct 2013*) (Appeal's Chamber) para 65 (Judgment on the appeal against Ruto's Excusal decision); William A Schabas (n 5) 287.

11 Judgment on the appeal against Ruto's Excusal Decision (n 10) paras 62, 63.

12 Ibid., 3-4 paras 2, 62.

13 ASP Special segment as requested by the African Union: "Indictment of sitting Heads of State and Government and its consequences on peace and stability and reconciliation", Informal Summary by the Moderator', ICC-ASP/12/61, 27 November 2013 para 8; Abel S Knottnerus, 'The International Criminal Court on Presence at Trial: The (In)Validity of Rule 134 quarter' [2014] ICD Brief 5 p 4.

14 Amendments to the Rules of Procedure and Evidence, ICC-ASP/12/Res 7, (Adopted at the Twelfth Plenary Meeting of the ASP by consensus), 27 November 2013.

and especially 134 *quater* was to placate the AU's unease and consequently prevent the withdrawal of AU member States Parties from the Statute.[15]

Significantly, the Appeal Chamber's interpretation of Article 63(1) and the conditions given for an accused's absence were primarily replicated in the new Rule 134 *ter*,[16] which is largely considered uncontroversial. However, Rule 134 *quater*, which allows an accused "mandated to fulfill extraordinary public duties at the highest national level" to be excused from being continuously present at their trial, has appeared to raise the most controversy.[17] There have been differing views by scholars and variance in the Trial and the Appeal Chamber's decisions regarding Rule 134 *quater*.[18] Contrary to the Appeal Chamber's decision, the Rule 134 *quater* amendment allows an accused to be excused from continuous presence at trial without specific limitations.[19] It has consequently been pointed out that the ASP overruled the Appeal Chamber's decision delivered a month before the amendments, instead mainly adopting the terms for excusal earlier given by the Trial Chamber from which the appeal was lodged.[20]

Even more significantly, rules 134 *bis*, 134 *ter*, and 134 *quater* were adopted during ongoing ICC proceedings against Kenyatta, a sitting President, and Ruto, a sitting Deputy president, with 134 *quater* immediately used by Ruto

15 Dire Tladi, 'Presence of the Accused: Right or Duty?The Art of Interpretation in a Tense Political Climate' in Bantekas Ilias Jalloh Charles C (ed), *The International Criminal Court and Africa* (Oxford University Press 2017) 165; Jonathan O'Donohue, 'The ICC and the ASP' in Stahn Carsten (ed), *The Law and Practice of the International Criminal Court* (Oxford University Press 2015) 121.

16 Gilbert Bitti, 'Article 21 and the Hierarchy of Sources of Law before the ICC' in Carsten Stahn (ed), *The Law and Practice of the International Criminal Court* (Oxford University Press 2015) 417; Abel S Knottnerus (n 13) p 4; Judgment on the appeal of Ruto's Excusal Decision (n 10) para 62.

17 Amendments to the Rules of Procedure and Evidence, ICC-ASP/12/Res 7, Adopted at the Twelfth Plenary Meeting of the ASP, 27 November 2013; Rule 134 *quater* entitled 'Excusal from Presence at Trial due to Extraordinary Public Duties'; Abel S Knottnerus (n 13) p 4.

18 See *Prosecutor* v. *William Samoei Ruto and Joshua Arap Sang, 'Trial chamber V (a) Decision on Ruto's Request for Excusal from Continuous Presence at Trial' Dissenting Opinion of Judge Herrera Carbuccia, ICC-01/09-01/11-777-Anx2, June 18, 2013* paras 1-4; *Prosecutor Vs Uhuru Muigai Kenyatta, Decision on defence Request for conditional Excusal from Continuous Presence at Trial, 18th Oct 2013, ICC-01/09-02/11* at para 23; Judgment on the appeal against Ruto's Excusal Decision (n 10).; William A Schabas, *An Introduction to the International Criminal Court 2020* (6th edn, Cambridge University Press 2020) 306.

19 Abel S Knottnerus (n 13) p 4.

20 Separate Opinion of Judge Eboe-Osuji on Ruto's excusal (n 5) para 22; Schabas (n 18) 306.

to request the Court to excuse him from continuous attendance at trial.[21] Applying the new rule 134 *quater*, which the Court construed as a subsequent agreement by the ASP, the Trial Chamber V(a) excused Ruto from continuous presence at trial except for a few specified instances.[22]

Several issues, therefore, arose from the amendment. First was whether the amendment to Rule 134 amounted to a subsequent agreement. The second issue was the implication of the timing of the amendments when a related case was ongoing in Court. The third aspect is the implication of the amendment appearing to overrule the Appeal Chamber's decision on the same issue.

2.2.1 Was Amended Rule 134 *ter* and *quater* a Subsequent Agreement by the ASP?

It is essential to determine whether the ASP's amendment to rule 134 *ter* and *quater* reached by consensus could be considered a subsequent agreement. If the resolution met the requirements of a subsequent agreement based on Article 31(3)(a) of the VCLT, the ICC had the obligation to take the agreement into account in the Rome Statute's interpretation. Article 31(3)(a) of the VCLT provides that there shall be taken into account, together with the context, any subsequent agreement between the parties regarding the interpretation of the treaty or the application of its provisions. As previously discussed, subsequent agreements include adopted interpretative declarations or recommendations passed through "consensus or unanimous vote."[23]

In determining whether the Rule 134 amendments were subsequent agreements, one vital consideration is whether there was agreement by *all* the States parties as required by the International Law Commission (ILC).[24] Additionally, and as discussed earlier, while consensus is essential, it is not sufficient unless it is accompanied by agreement on the substance for it to be

21 *Defence request pursuant to Article 63(1) of the Rome Statute and Rule 134 quater of the Rules of Procedure and Evidence to excuse Mr William Samoei Ruto from attendance at trial*, ICC-01/09-01/11-1124, *16 December 2013*.

22 Reasons for the Decision on Ruto Excusal (n 8) para 79.

23 ILC, 'Guide to Practice on Reservations to Treaties, Report of the ILC on the Work of Its Sixty-Third Session, 2011, Vol II, A/66/10' 35 para 4.7.3; *ICJ Whaling in the Antarctic (Australia v Japan: New Zealand intervening): Judgment of 31 March 2014* para 46; Tarcisio Gazzini, 'Subsequent Agreements and Subsequent Practice, Interpretation of International Investment Treaties' [2016] Oxford Hart Publishing, 192 para 1.

24 ILC, 'Draft Conclusions on Subsequent Agreements and Subsequent Practice in Relation to the Interpretation of Treaties, Seventieth Session, (A/73/10) 2018' (ILC) Conclusion 4 Commentary 4 (ILC 2018)

deemed a subsequent agreement.[25] In this context, it is noted that the ASP adopted the rule 134 amendments by consensus, meaning there was an agreement by all the parties present. Additionally, no objection was raised to the substance of the amendment by any ASP member.

Further, the amendment sought to clarify the interpretation and application of Article 63(1) of the Rome Statute, which states that the accused shall be present at trial. The book, therefore, argues that the amendment also fulfilled the VCLT's Article 31(3)(a) requirement that the agreement should relate to the interpretation or application of the treaty. Based on the above, the study construes the amendment as a subsequent agreement since it fulfilled all the essential requirements of a subsequent agreement under Article 31(3)(a) of the VCLT and the ILC provisions.

The consideration of the Rule 134 amendments as subsequent agreements is also bolstered by Akande's position that a resolution adopted by consensus by a Conference of States Parties (the ASP in this case) can be regarded as a subsequent agreement or practice establishing the authentic interpretation of the Rome Statute within the meaning of the VCLT.[26] As discussed in Chapter 2, the study proceeds from the premise that the ASP falls under the Conference of States Parties.

In the same vein, the Trial Chamber construed the rule 134 *ter* and *quater* amendment as a subsequent agreement by the ASP. In granting Ruto's request for excusal from continuous presence at trial, the Trial Chamber relied on the amended rule 134 *quater*, finding that the ASP amendment constituted a subsequent agreement. The Court specifically held that

> The Chamber notes Article 31(3)(a) of the Vienna Convention on the Law of Treaties (Vienna Convention), which lays down that together with the context, an exercise of treaty interpretation must take into account "any subsequent agreement between the parties regarding the interpretation of the treaty or the application of its provisions." Rules 134 ter and 134 quater of the Rules are part of the Resolution adopted by the ASP, and as such, can be regarded as a "subsequent agreement" about the scope and application of Article 63(1) of the Statute under Article 31(3)(a) of the Vienna Convention.[27]

25 Ibid., Conclusion 11(3).

26 Dapo Akande and Antonios Tzanakopoulos, 'Treaty Law and ICC Jurisdiction over the Crime of Aggression' (2018) 29 EJIL 939.

27 Reasons for the Decision on Ruto's Excusal (n 8) para 56.

In this regard, Tladi notes the acknowledgment by the Trial Chamber of subsequent agreements as an interpretation tool in relation to Article 63(1) of the Statute.[28] As Tladi notes, however, the judges failed to explain whether the Rule 134 *quater* amendment satisfied the requirements under Article 31(3)(a) of the VCLT to warrant the conclusion that the amendments were "subsequent agreements."[29] In the same respect, the study notes that the Chamber did not determine that the agreement or consensus "must" have been reached by "all" States Parties, a prerequisite for parties' agreement to be deemed a subsequent agreement based on the ILC requirements discussed earlier.

Nevertheless, the Trial Chamber attempted to show that the amended Rule 134 *quater* was consistent with Article 63(1) of the Statute, qualifying it as related to the Rome Statute's interpretation and application.[30] In this respect, the Trial Chamber held that

> The specific rules were adopted to provide greater clarity to the Court on the scope and application of Article 63(1) of the Statute. This is especially true in relation to Rule 134 *quater* of the Rules, which was adopted specifically to cover persons who are "mandated to fulfill extraordinary public duties at the highest national level."[31]

The linking of the amendment to the interpretation and application of Article 63(1) is argued to have met the requirement under Article 31(3)(a) of the VCLT, which provides that the agreement must relate to the interpretation or application of the treaty. The Court, therefore, appeared to acknowledge that the States Parties retain authority to interpret the Rome Statute and clarify the meaning of ambiguous Statute provisions.

While the Trial Chamber did not explicitly lay out the requirements of a subsequent agreement and whether the amendment fulfilled the requisite aspects, the book agrees with the Court's overall decision that the ASP amendments on rule 134 amounted to a subsequent agreement under Article 31(3)(a) of the VCLT.

28 Tladi (n 15) 179.
29 Ibid.,
30 Ibid.,
31 Reasons for the Decision on Ruto Excusal (n 8) para 56.

2.2.2 The Legal Effect of Finding Rule 134 *ter* and *quater* Amendments to Be a Subsequent Agreement by the States Parties

Having resolved that the resolution by the ASP adopting the rule 134 amendments by consensus was a subsequent agreement, it follows that the Chamber had an obligation to take the subsequent agreement into account in the Rome Statute's interpretation based on Article 31(3) (a) of the VCLT. In this respect, Judge Eboe-Osuji, in regard to the Rule 134 amendments, stated that subsequent agreements and practice under Article 31(3) of the VCLT "must" be taken into account in the treaty interpretation.[32] As argued in previous chapters, "taking into account" has been interpreted differently, with some considering the phrase as meaning "binding" while others contend that it is not necessarily binding or conclusive. Nonetheless, the importance of subsequent agreements in interpretation cannot be underestimated.

The ILC reiterates the significance of considering subsequent agreements by construing subsequent agreements as "authentic" interpretation means which give the parties' objective meaning of the treaty. It also finds subsequent agreements and practice as means of interpretation equal to the other means under Article 31(1), which constitute the ordinary meaning, the context, and the object and purpose, with none having priority over other means.[33]

The fact that the ASP adopted the Rule 134 amendments by consensus can be deemed to have given the subsequent agreement more weight in the Rome Statute's interpretation.[34] This argument is bolstered by the ICJ decision in the *Whaling* case, which emphasized the importance of consensus. It specifically held that "these recommendations of the IWC, which take the form of resolutions, are not binding. However, when they are adopted by consensus or by a unanimous vote, they may be relevant for the interpretation of the Convention or its Schedule."[35]

Commenting on the effect of an ASP resolution passed by consensus, Akande averred that an ASP resolution adopted by consensus should be taken as "decisive" in the Rome Statute's interpretation since it represents the parties' subsequent agreement or subsequent practice within the meaning of Article 31

32 Separate Opinion of Judge Eboe-Osuji on Ruto's excusal (n 5) para 16.

33 ILC 2018 (n 24) Conclusion 2 Commentary 12.

34 D M Mcrae, 'The Legal Effect of Interpretative Declarations' [1979] British Yearbook of International Law 169.

35 Whaling in the Antarctic (Australia v. Japan: New Zealand intervening), Judgment, 31 March 2014, ICJ Reports (2014) 226; International Convention for the Regulation of Whaling 1946, 161 UNTS 72 para 46.

(3)(a) and (b) of the VCLT.[36] This approach considers the State parties subsequent agreements as authoritative and legally binding.[37] The study argues that Akande's position similarly applies to the Rule 134 *ter* and *quater* amendments, which were passed by consensus and were therefore decisive in the Rome Statute's interpretation. As Kirsch and Oosterveld also note, the ASP has the authority to make decisions which are binding on the ICC.[38] However, as discussed previously, neither Article 31(3)(a) of the VCLT nor the ILC expressly regard subsequent agreements as binding.[39] Nevertheless, Trial Chamber V seemed to rely conclusively on the Rule 134 *quater* amendment to hold that *Ruto* was not required to be continuously present for the whole trial.[40] In this case, the Trial Chamber appears to have treated the ASP amendment as a binding subsequent agreement.

The ILC, however, notes that subsequent agreement and practice may be deemed binding when the States parties intend so.[41] The book consequently argues that by adopting Rule 134 amendments by consensus and with no objections regarding substance, the States Parties expected the amendments to be treated as binding or conclusive in interpreting the relevant Rome Statute provisions. The expectation of the States Parties may have been captured by Kenya's statement to the ASP president, questioning why, despite the ASP giving "specific legislative guidance by amending Rule 134" of the RPE, the ICC had failed to recognize the amendments to Rules 134 *bis* and *quate*r in its decisions.[42] Kenya's argument appeared to be that the ICC lacked discretion and was obligated to implement the ASP amendment by consensus to Rule 134 *bis* and *quarter* in its decisions.

However, the ILC also emphasizes that objective evidence of the parties' understanding expressed through subsequent agreements possesses "considerable authority" regarding the treaty's meaning.[43] Considering the difficulty

36 Akande and Tzanakopoulos (n 26) 944.

37 Ibid., 948; *In the matter of an Arbitration under Chapter Eleven of the North American Free Trade Agreement between ADF Group Inc. and USA, ICSID Case No.Arb* (AF/00/1) para 177.

38 P Kirsch and V Oosterveld, 'The Post-Rome Conference Preparatory Commission' in A Cassese and Others (eds.), The Rome Statute of the International Criminal Court: A Commentary, vol. I (Oxford University Press 2002) 225.

39 Article 31(3)a of the VCLT; ILC 2018 (n 24) Conclusion 3 Commentary 4.

40 Reasons for the Decision on Ruto Excusal (n 8) para 79.

41 ILC 2018 (n 24) Conclusion 3 Commentary 5.

42 ICC-ASP/13/34/Rev.2, 5 December 2014 Annex 1 Note verbale from Kenya no. 561/14, dated 3 November 2014, addressed to the President of the Assembly, Ambassador Tiina Intelmann II, F para 8.

43 ILC 2018 (n 24) Conclusion 3 Commentary 9.

of achieving the unanimous agreement of over 122 States Parties, including those absent who did not object, the study contends that the Trial Chamber correctly treated the amendment as legally binding. Reinforcing this approach, Judge Oboe-Esuji held that interpretation cannot be deemed to be determining the States Parties intention when the judges can disregard the States Parties "clear, direct and unanimous communication of that intent, whatever be the method and manner and timing employed by the States Parties in registering that communication."[44] From this perspective, it is argued that the ICC would be remiss in failing to take the States Parties unanimous subsequent agreement as conclusive in its decisions.

Notably, the Chamber's reference to subsequent agreements constitutes one of the few or only instance when the ICC explicitly referred to and applied subsequent agreements as the main interpretational element in its decision. This approach seems to consider subsequent agreements not merely as confirmatory of interpretation reached under Article 31(1) of the VCLT, which prioritizes the ordinary meaning and the context during interpretation, but as a binding interpretation element.

Taking a different perspective, Woolaver and Palmers questioned the Trial Chamber's emphasis on the Rule 134 amendments in its decision, averring that by doing so, the Chamber granted States Parties a powerful tool to keep directing the ICC's interpretation of the Rome Statute and the RPE.[45] Hansen similarly faulted the Court's consideration of the amendments as decisive subsequent agreements, arguing that the Trial Chamber should have instead relied on the clear wording and intent in Article 63(1) on presence at trial and Article 27, which require all persons to be treated equally under the Statute rather than on what he terms "dubious" interpretive means.[46]

The book, as earlier stated, adopts the position that the 134 *bis*, *ter*, and *quater* amendments were subsequent agreements, a position also taken by the Trial Chamber V. The study also takes the position that with States Parties as masters of the treaty and based on their unanimous agreement on Rule 134 amendments, it would have been unjustifiable for the Trial Chamber to treat the amendment as anything other than a binding subsequent agreement.

---

44 Separate Opinion of Judge Eboe-Osuji on Ruto's excusal (n 5) para 34.

45 Hannah Woolaver and Emma Palmer, 'Challenges to the Independence of the International Criminal Court from the Assembly of States Parties' (2017) 15 JICJ 652.

46 Thomas O Hansen, 'Caressing the Big Fish? A Critique of ICC Trial Chamber V(a)'s Decision to Grant Ruto's Request for Excusal from Continuous Presence at Trial' (2013) 22, No 1 Cardozo Journal of International and Comparative Law (JICL) 33.

As earlier mentioned, the ASP's Rule 134 amendment and the subsequent Trial Chamber V's decision nevertheless appeared to override the Appeal Chamber's decision on the excusal of an accused from attendance at trial. This overriding of the Appeal Chamber's decision arguably illustrates the overlap in the interpretive roles of the ASP and the ICC, which could create some uncertainty and tension.

2.3 *Implications of the ASP 134* quater *Amendment Overriding the Appeal Chamber's Decision*

As noted earlier, the 134 *quater* amendments appeared to go against the conditions for excusal laid down in the Appeal Chamber's decision on the same issue in the *Ruto Excusal appeal* case.[47] Notably, contrary to the Appeal chamber's decision, Rule 134 *quater* does not require that excusals from trial attendance by the accused be limited to what is strictly necessary or that such decisions be taken on a case-by-case basis.[48] From this perspective, the amendments by the ASP to 134 *quater* "overrode" the Appeal Chamber's interpretation of the same issue.[49] In this vein, Tladi posits that the ASP's amendment of Rule 134 *quater* consequently gave broad discretion to the Trial Chamber in the excusal of an accused from a trial, therefore seemingly overriding the Appeal Chamber's interpretation on the same issue.[50]

Different opinions arise from this seeming overrule of the Appeal Chamber's decision. Tladi, for instance, emphasizes that regardless of whether State parties have established an institution to interpret a particular instrument, they collectively retain the primary mandate to interpret their treaty.[51] This approach implies that the ASP retains the ultimate authority to clarify or correct an erroneous judicial interpretation of Article 63(1) through its amendments. Indeed, the Trial Chamber appeared unwilling to go against the ASP's amendments, finding instead that imposing the conditions in 134 *ter* as laid down by the Appeal's Chamber into those of 134 *quater* by the ASP as requested by the prosecutor would "run counter" to the drafters' intention.[52]

47 Judgment on the appeal against Ruto's Excusal decision (n 10); Schabas (n 18) 306.

48 Abel S Knottnerus (n 13) p 4.

49 Tladi (n 15) 179; Schabas (n 18) 306 (however Schabas does not refer to the amendment as a subsequent agreement).

50 Tladi (n 15) 179.

51 Ibid., 178; See also generally *Delimitation of the Polish-Czechoslovakian Frontier* (*Question of Jaworzina*), *Advisory Opinion of 6th December 1923, PCIJ Ser. B No. 8, 37* para 80; Specific to the Rome Statute, Schabas (n 18) 645.

52 Reasons for the Decision on Ruto Excusal (n 8) para 52.

In contrast, some scholars have argued that even when changes must be made to the RPE, they should not infringe on the ICC's role under Article 119(1) of handling judicial functions.[53] On this basis, Knottnerus and Heller faulted the Rule 134 *quater* amendment for deviating from the conditions the Appeal's Chamber laid down for excusing an accused from continuous presence at trial.[54] In the same respect, the Prosecutor argued that the Rule 134 amendments and any related interpretation could not "overrule" the Appeals Chamber's interpretation.[55] Knottnerus similarly posited that the Appeal Chamber's decision was "authoritative" and that an ASP amendment to the RPE could not overrule the Appeal Chamber's interpretation of Article 63(1).[56]

In the same vein, O'Donohue questioned the ASP's approach, noting that the ASP adopted Rule 134 *quater* despite knowing that the rule deviated from the Appeals Chamber's interpretation of Article 63(1) and the conditions established for determining excusal requests.[57] Similarly, Broomhall points out that despite the ICC being the determinant of whether the ASP has respected the consistency requirement between the RPE and the Rome Statute,[58] the States Parties still amended the rules despite the Appeal Chamber's decision. This perspective impliedly construes the ASP's Rule 134 amendment as directly interfering with the ICC's interpretative independence. The study, however, identifies with the approach that the States Parties reserve the right to clarify ambiguous Statute provisions and correct what they consider an inaccurate interpretation of the Statute while considering judicial independence.

---

53 FIDH, 'FIDH Recommendations to the 14th Assembly of States Parties to the Statute of the ICC' (*International Federation for Human Rights*, 10 November 2015) <https://www.fidh.org/en/issues/international-justice/fidh-recommendations-to-the-14th-assembly-of-states-parties-to-the> accessed 23 December 2022 (FIDH Recommendations to the 14th ASP).

54 Kevin J Heller, 'Will the New RPE 134 Provisions Survive Judicial Review? (Probably Not.)' (*Opinio Juris*, 28 November 2013) <http://opiniojuris.org/2013/11/28/will-new-rpe-134-provisions-survive-judicial-review/> accessed 9 May 2020; Abel S Knottnerus, 'Emerging Voices: Extraordinary Exceptions at the ICC–What Happened with Rule 134 quater?' (*Opinio Juris*, 18 July 2014) <http://opiniojuris.org/2014/07/18/emerging-voices-extraordinary-exceptions-icc-happened-rule-134 quater/> accessed 25 April 2020.

55 *ICC, Prosecutor v Ruto and Sang, Prosecution response to Defence request pursuant to Article 63(1) and Rule 134 quater for excusal from attendance at trial for William Samoei Ruto, ICC-01/09-01/11, 8 January 2014*, para 30.

56 Abel S Knottnerus (n 13) p 4,7; Abel S Knottnerus, Emerging Voices (n 54).

57 Abel S Knottnerus, Emerging Voices (n 54); Jonathan O'Donohue (n 15) 122.

58 B Broomhall, 'Article 51 Rules of Procedure and Evidence' in O Triffterer and K Ambos (eds), *Commentary on the Rome Statute of the International Criminal Court, Observers' Notes, Article by Article* (Third Edition, C H Beck, Hart Nomos, Munich 2016) 1343 para 32.

Nevertheless, regardless of which side of the argument is taken, the timing of the amendments during related ongoing cases raises the aspect of whether the ASP intended to influence the ICC's decisions in specific cases.

2.4 *Implications of the Timing of the ASP Amendment to Rule 134* quater *When There Was a Related Ongoing Court Case*

Besides other reasons raised for the 134 *quater* rule controversy, the timing of the amendments highlighted the seeming overlap between the ICC's interpretive role and that of the ASP's interpretive function through their subsequent agreements. Several implications on the Statute's interpretation may arise. First, it may raise the question of whether the ASP's mandate to adopt amendments or resolutions when a related case is ongoing may directly or implicitly pressure the interpretational outcome by the ICC, with a possible consequence of blurring the interpretive roles. Second is whether the amendment, if it meets the requirements of a subsequent agreement, must obligatorily be taken into account and treated as binding or discretional in interpreting the ongoing case. Notably, the Rome Statute does not set any timeline for when the ASP can adopt amendments or resolutions.

As previously indicated, the amendments were adopted during ongoing proceedings against Kenyatta and Ruto, then President and Deputy President of Kenya, respectively.[59] As mentioned, Ruto's defense immediately relied on the Rule 134 *quater* amendment to apply for excusal from continuous attendance at trial in the Trial Chamber.[60] The timing arguably left the Trial Chamber with no choice but to determine how to incorporate the ASP amendment in its interpretation.

The possible blurring of roles is highlighted by Woolaver and Palmer, who assert that the ASP used its powers in amending Rule 134 *quater* to directly influence the Court's interpretation of the Rome Statute in an ongoing case, contrary to the protection given to the ICC's interpretative role by Article 119(1) of the Statute.[61] In this vein, Woolaver and Palmer observe a possible "overlap" between some ASP functions and the ICC's judicial functions, which may undermine the Court's judicial independence.[62] Woolaver and Palmer

59 *Situation in Kenya, The Prosecutor v. Uhuru Muigai Kenyatta, Case No. ICC-01/09-02/11, and The Prosecutor v. William Samoei Ruto and Joshua Arap Sang, Case No. ICC-01/09-01/11.*

60 *Defence request pursuant to Article 63(1) of the Rome Statute and Rule 134 quater of the Rules of Procedure and Evidence to excuse Mr William Samoei Ruto from attendance at trial, ICC-01/09-01/11-1124, 16 December 2013.*

61 Woolaver and Palmer (n 45) 667, 668.

62 Ibid., 641.

further point to the potential conflict between the ASP's and the ICC's role in interpretation, stating that it is problematic for amendments to be undertaken during and targeted at specific ongoing judicial processes.[63]

Ambach similarly questioned the timing of the ASP amendments and the fact that Kenya, an ASP member, spearheaded the proposal to amend Rule 134 based on ongoing Court cases against the two Kenyan leaders before the ICC.[64] Ambach, therefore, criticized the amendments not only for the timing but for being passed at the time for a "singular, specific case scenario" involving Kenya's political situation.[65] Ambach and Woolaver's position constitutes one perspective, which implies that affected States Parties sought to interfere with the ICC's interpretation through the amendments.

However, a counterargument would be that whether the rule was politically expedient or not does not detract from the fact that States Parties have the authority to clarify what they consider an ambiguous provision. Additionally, States Parties are mandated to correct what they deem an inaccurate representation of their intent by the ICC through amendments amounting to subsequent agreements. As the *Methanex v. the United States* tribunal found, "if a legislature, having enacted a statute, feels that the courts implementing it have misconstrued the legislature's intention, it is perfectly proper for the legislature to clarify its intention."[66]

Guilfoyle, on the other hand, acknowledges that the ASP has the authority to have discussions and adopt amendments where necessary, but he also posits that attempts by the ASP to influence underway cases infringe on the ICC's judicial independence.[67] From this perspective, the ICC may feel pressured into applying the ASP's resolution or amendment in its decision where it relates to an ongoing case. This presumed pressure may arguably contradict Article 40 of the Rome Statute, which provides for the judges' independence.

---

63 Ibid., 649.

64 Philipp Ambach, 'A Look towards the Future-The ICC and "Lessons Learnt"' in Carsten Stahn (ed), *The Law and Practice of the International Criminal Court* (Oxford University Press 2015) 865; Both then Kenyan President, Uhuru Kenyatta, and the Vice-President, William Ruto, had cases before the ICC, in *Situation in Kenya, the Prosecutor v. Uhuru Muigai Kenyatta, Case No. ICC-01/09-02/11, and The Prosecutor v. William Samoei Ruto and Joshua Arap Sang, Case No. ICC-01/09-01/11.*

65 Ibid.,; Amendments to the Rules of Procedure and Evidence, ICC-ASP/12/Res.7, 27 November 2013).

66 *Methanex V United States, Jurisdiction and Merits* (*NAFTA Ch 11/UNCITRAL Arb Trib 3 Aug 2005* Part IV, Chapter C para 22.

67 Douglas Guilfoyle, 'Lacking Conviction: Is the International Criminal Court Broken? An Organisational Failure Analysis' (2019) 20 Melb J Int'l L 443.

2.4.1 The Protection of the ICC's Judicial Independence by the Statute and Its Possible Undermining by the ASP's Rule 134 Amendments

Judicial independence forms a primary part of the Rome Statute's objectives.[68] The preamble of the Statute provides for "an independent" and permanent Court. Additionally, the ICC's interpretive authority and judicial independence are expressly given under Article 40(1) of the Statute. Article 40(1) provides that "the judges shall be independent in the performance of their functions." Similarly, Article 119(1) of the Rome Statute leaves any dispute concerning the ICC's judicial functions subject to the Court's decision. It is contended that these provisions protect the ICC's judicial independence and its authority to interpret the Rome Statute.

In the same vein, it is averred that Article 112, which lists the ASP's functions, expressly failed to include judicial functions among the ASP's management powers. In this respect, it is posited that the Rome Statute's preparatory documents show that several States Parties opposed the inclusion of judicial functions as part of the ASP's management oversight duties, contending that this would undermine the ICC's judicial independence.[69] The exclusion of the ASP from judicial functions, expressly bestowed upon the ICC, is considered to protect the judges' independence, which the States Parties should respect.[70]

The ASP has similarly frequently reiterated the "respect" for the ICC's judicial independence and committed to ensuring "respect for and the implementation of the Court's judicial decisions" in all its meetings and resolutions.[71] In the same vein, Judge Fernández summarized that "without independence, the Court's whole *raison d'être* is compromised," meaning that without judicial independence, the whole reason for the Court's being is compromised.[72]

Since judicial independence goes hand in hand with impartiality, it has been contended that impartiality requires that international judges must be

68 Woolaver and Palmer (n 45) 643–644.

69 Philipp Ambach and S Rama Rao, 'Article 112, Assembly of States Parties' in Otto Triffterer and Kai Ambos (eds), *Commentary on the Rome Statute of the International Criminal Court, Observers' Notes, Article by Article* (Beck/Hart 2016) 2240 para 14.

70 Woolaver and Palmer (n 45) 645.

71 For example, in Resolution ICC-ASP/17/Res.5, 12 December 2018 at p 33 and para 1; Resolution ICC-ASP/19/Res.6, 16 December 2020 at 2 and at para 1; Resolution ICC-ASP /20/Res.5, 9 December 2021 at p 2 and para 1; Resolution ICC-ASP/10/Res.5, 21 December 2011 at p 28.

72 'ICC Presents Annual Report to the ASP: Strong Cooperation, Adequate Resources and Preserving Judicial Independence Are Crucial Needs' (*International Criminal Court*, 18 November 2015) <https://www.icc-cpi.int/news/icc-presents-annual-report-asp-strong-cooperation-adequate-resources-and-preserving-judicial> accessed 1 July 2023.

free from undue influence or interference from any entity or person.[73] Additionally, where the court is established as an organ or under an international organization, the court and judges should be free from interference from other organization organs or the management bodies of the organization.[74] Impartiality and independence further require that judges are not subordinated to, among others, parties to the dispute or authorities with an interest in the decision.[75] The threats to a court's judicial independence include instructions from the executive.[76] Applying the indicated approach to the ICC would require that the Court's independence remains unaffected by any undue influence or direction from other sources, including the States Parties.

Based on the Statute and the ASP's declarations, it can be presumed that matters that are either *sub judice* (ongoing) or have been adjudicated fall under the ICC's judicial functions. The ASP's call for respecting the ICC's judicial independence and decisions would presumably call for adherence to the separation of powers in the interpretative roles of the Court and the ASP. From this perspective, discussions, resolutions, or amendments to the RPE by the ASP, as happened regarding Rule 134 amendments when a related matter was pending in Court, seemingly interfere with the ICC's protection and judicial independence.

The ICC president also illustrated this perspective in the letter to the ASP President, averring that several issues proposed by the ASP for discussion in the special session requested by Kenya concerned matters within the ICC's judicial competence protected under Article 40(1) of the Rome Statute.[77] The letter further reiterated that "it is crucial that the Assembly is not per-

73 Philippe Sands, Ruth Mackenzie and Campbell McLachlan, 'The Burgh House Principles on the Independence of the International Judiciary' (2005) 4. The Law & Practice of International Courts and Tribunals 247, para 1.1.

74 Ibid. para 1.2.

75 Pasquale Pasquino, 'Prolegomena to a Theory of Judicial Power: The Concept of Judicial Independence in Theory and History' (2003) 2 Law and Practice of International Courts and Tribunals 11, 25.

76 Guilfoyle (n 67) 442.; James Crawford and Joe McIntyre, 'The Independence and Impartiality of the "International Judiciary" in Shimon Shetreet and Christopher Forsyth (eds), *The Culture of Judicial Independence: Conceptual Foundations and Practical Challenges* (Brill Nijhoff 2012) 201.

77 ICC-ASP/13/34/Rev.2, 5 December 2014 Letter from the Principals of the Court, dated 7 November 2014, addressed to the President of the Assembly, Ambassador Tiina Intelmann, with regard to the Note verbale from Kenya no. 561/14 Annex III para 2 (Letter from the Court Principals); ICC, Letter to the President, Assembly of States Parties to the Rome Statute, 7 November 2014, at pg 2.

ceived as interfering with judicial matters which strictly belong in the courtroom."[78] The ICC president was responding to Kenya's *Note Verbale*, which sought an ASP discussion about the Court's failure to recognize "specific legislative guidance" by the ASP on Rule 134 *bis* and *quater* amendments in its decisions.[79] The ICC letter implied that the ASP discussions on Rule 134 amendments when the related case was ongoing or had been decided was an overreach into the ICC's interpretive role and outside the ASP's purview.

Woolaver and Palmer also contend that the ASP's assessment of the ICC's interpretation of the Rome Statute or the RPE interferes with the guarantee of judicial independence given by the Statute and contravenes the Statute's object and purpose of establishing an independent Court.[80] It has further been suggested that the ASP's power to debate and decide on the Rome Statute or RPE amendments can also be used to restrict the ICC's interpretation of the Statute, potentially undermining the Court's judicial independence.[81] From this perspective, it is contended that, through its authority to adopt rules or debate RPE provisions, the ASP may provide a forum for individual States Parties, or the ASP as a whole, to attempt to control the judicial interpretation of the Statute provisions.[82]

Similarly pointing out how the ASP resolutions and amendments may undermine the ICC's interpretative role, especially in ongoing or decided cases, then ICC Prosecutor Fatou Bensouda, in her statement to the ASP, asserted that

> The integrity of the Court's proceedings continues to be challenged. Matters that are either *sub judice* or have already been adjudicated must not be undermined by virtue of discussions and decisions of States Parties [...] Discussions and decisions of the States Parties must respect the separation of powers and the constitutional framework of the ICC in a manner that fully protects the Court's independent judicial process and integrity.[83]

---

78 Letter from the Court Principals (n 77) Annex III para 4.

79 Note verbale from Kenya no. 561/14, dated 3 November 2014, addressed to the President of the Assembly, Ambassador Tiina Intelmann para 8, ICC-ASP/13/34/Rev.2, 5 December 2014 Annex 1.

80 Woolaver and Palmer (n 45) 651.

81 Ibid., 646.

82 Ibid.

83 Fatou Bensouda, 'Statement by the ICC Prosecutor at the opening of the 14th Session of the Assembly of States Parties to the Rome Statute of the International Criminal Court'

However, in reaction to the former Prosecutor Bensouda's address to the ASP decrying the ASP's discussion of adjudicated or ongoing cases, Guilfoyle argues that the ASP can debate the outcome of cases and judicial interpretations of the Rome Statute without infringing judicial independence.[84] Guilfoyle and Ambos aver that criticizing particular court decisions does not in itself infringe judicial independence.[85]

Nevertheless, Judge Usacka also faulted the States Parties perceived interference with the ICC's independence, holding that:

> A distinction must be drawn between the role of the judiciary, on the one hand, and the role of States Parties, on the other hand [...] A strict separation between these two roles must be observed in order to preserve the independence of the judiciary. In the circumstances of the present case, the intervention by five interested States [...] engenders the risk of distorting the judicial process or, at a minimum, creating the appearance that States have inappropriately encroached upon the functions of the judiciary.[86]

However, these views constitute only one perspective. On the other hand, there are several arguments justifying the passing of amendments or resolutions by the ASP to the RPE, including when a related case is ongoing.

2.4.2 Justifying the ASP's Amendments to Rule 134 and the Timing

Contrary to the criticism against the ASP's adoption of amendments, it can also be argued that States Parties, as the owners of their treaty, can intervene in the Rome Statute's interpretation at any given time, including when a related case is underway. As noted previously, the Working Group of the Independent Oversight Mechanism (IOM) of the ICC[87] asserted that the Rome Statute's interpretation is primarily the task of the States Parties since they adopted

(*International Criminal Court*, 18 November 2015) <http://www.icc-cpi.int/fr/news/statement-icc-prosecutor-opening-14th-session-assembly-states-parties-rome-statute> accessed 19 October 2022.

84 Guilfoyle (n 67) 443.

85 Ibid., 442.

86 *Dissenting Opinion of Judge Anita Usacka in Decision on the Requests for Leave to Submit Observations under Rule 103 of the Rules of Procedure and Evidence, The Prosecutor v William Samoei Ruto and Joshua Arap Sang*, ICC-01/09-01/11-942 (*Appeal's Chamber*) *13 September 2013* para 4.

87 Establishment of an Independent Oversight Mechanism, ICC-ASP/8/Res.1, November 26, 2009.

the Statute.[88] Along the same lines, it was therefore noted that the ASP's adoption of Rule 134 *quater* was consistent with the "sovereignty and independence of States" based on international custom.[89] This assertion seems to give absolute interpretive authority to the ASP without limitation regarding the timing or the context. However, with an existing Court in place, the IOM's position, if implemented fully, would render the ICC's interpretive role nonexistent.

Similarly justifying the ASP's actions, Guilfoyle reiterates that States Parties are justified in using the ASP to comment on whether they consider that the Rome Statute is being correctly interpreted and applied.[90] In this respect, Guilfoyle has argued that criticizing the ASP for commenting on the ICC's judicial interpretation would suggest that the Court is "immune" to criticism, which he insists is not the meaning of judicial independence.[91] Similarly, it is noted that States Parties have the right to discuss their dissatisfaction with the ICC within the ASP, ensuring that legitimate concerns are addressed, thereby preventing the withdrawal of States from the Rome Statute.[92]

The above approaches appear to align with the view that while judges have discretionary power, the rule of law does not provide for such power to be "unlimited and uncontrolled."[93] Indeed, it is further reiterated that the principle of judicial independence cannot be used to prevent discussions on the ICC's functions, and neither can Article 119(1) be used to restrict the discussion of legal disputes by the ASP.[94] Based on this approach, the ASP's discussion of the ICC's decisions and its response to the decisions through amendments such as Rule 134 *quater* would not necessarily be seen as interference with the Court's judicial independence.

Akande, on the other hand, also acknowledges the right of States Parties to dispute the ICC's interpretation after it issues a decision, but he recognizes that it is only in rare instances that the States Parties relegate "the interpretation of a court to the dustbin of history."[95] Akande's perspective appears to recognize the ICC's primary interpretive role but with States able to overrule the decision

88 Report of the Bureau on the Independent Oversight Mechanism, ICC-ASP/9/31, November 19, 2010 para 53.
89 Separate Opinion of Judge Eboe-Osuji on Ruto's excusal (n 5) para 24.
90 Guilfoyle (n 67) 443.
91 Ibid., 401.
92 Woolaver and Palmer (n 45) 656, 663.
93 Crawford and McIntyre (n 76) 199.
94 Guilfoyle (n 67) 444.
95 Akande and Tzanakopoulos (n 26) 948.

in some instances. Using the above approach, the ASP had the right to overrule the Appeal Chamber's decision through the Rule 134 *quater* amendment if dissatisfied.

The same approach was taken by Judge Eboe-Osuji while commenting on the Rule 134 *quater* amendment. The Judge stated that, while judges may attempt to fill gaps in the Statute through reasonable interpretation, "it remains the prerogative of the legislature to fill any gaps they see a need to fill, regardless of the interpretations offered by judges. That is precisely what the ASP did by adopting r 134 quater."[96] Judge Eboe-Osuji further found that the fastest way for the ASP to "have corrected any judicial misapprehension of legislative intent underlying Article 63(1)" was by adopting Rule I34*ter* and 134 *quater*.[97] Akande has similarly argued that an ASP resolution adds weight in determining the correct interpretation to be given to the Rome Statute.[98]

To further justify the ASP's amendments, Woolaver and Palmer note that the ASP is mandated to carry out RPE amendments, a role that does not fall within judicial functions under the Rome Statute.[99] From this perspective, if the ASP is to amend the rules, it is free to discuss how the ICC has judicially applied them.[100] This approach regards the claim that the ASP's influence on the interpretation of the RPE and Statute controverts the ICC's judicial independence under Article 40 of the Statute as inapplicable in every instance.[101] Similarly, Guilfoyle adds that since amendments form a core part of the ASP's functions, it does not always follow that the ASP's amendment of rules clarifying its intent when there is an ongoing case would infringe on the ICC's judicial independence.[102] The above positions imply that the ASP has the right to correct the ICC's interpretation where it is considered contrary to the States Parties intentions or clarify ambiguous provisions, including when related cases are ongoing.

However, the varied opinions criticizing and justifying the ASP's timing of the Rule 134 amendments arguably show the lack of clear distinction and possible consequent tension between the ASP's and the ICC's interpretive roles. As Sharma states, the ambiguity and failure of the Rome Statute to give a

96 Separate Opinion of Judge Eboe-Osuji on Ruto excusal (n 5) at 9.
97 Ibid. para 23.
98 Akande and Tzanakopoulos (n 26) 949.
99 Woolaver and Palmer (n 45) 650.
100 Guilfoyle (n 67) 443.
101 Ibid.
102 Ibid.

precise boundary in the mandate and the procedure of the ASP and the ICC have resulted in an "overlap of competency."[103]

In conclusion, it is noted that the ICC, therefore, has constrained interpretive power.[104] At the same time, States Parties also have or should have some limitations in exercising their interpretive mandate through subsequent agreements and practice, having willingly established the ICC to interpret the Rome Statute. These limitations are discussed next.

2.5 *Suggested Limitations to the States Parties Interpretation of the Rome Statute*

The discussion above shows that the ASP and the ICC share interpretive authority regarding the Statute, but no clear demarcation is provided. As stated earlier, there is no express limitation or guidelines on when the ASP can adopt amendments, leaving its mandate to influence interpretation almost uncontrolled. Arguably, the existence of the ICC means that the ASP's powers may need to be limited to allow for the Court's judicial independence.

2.5.1 The *Sub Judice* Rule

One proposed way to limit the States Parties role in the Statute's interpretation would be through implementing the *sub judice* rule. The *sub judice* rule in this case, as borrowed from the United Kingdom (UK), generally prohibits members of parliament or other entities from discussing or making reference to current or pending court cases.[105] The *sub judice* rule mainly seeks to prevent the legislators from debating or discussing ongoing cases, in the process, possibly influencing the legal outcome of the cases.[106]Applied to the ICC, the States Parties could decide to respect ongoing cases and allow the Court to hear the cases to their conclusion without seeming interference or influence from the ASP. The *sub judice* rule is seen as balancing the mandate of the ASP to debate issues of concern while respecting the ICC's judicial independence by providing time and context limitations on the ASP's consideration of issues related to ongoing cases.[107] It is argued that implementing the *sub judice* prin-

103 Kritika Sharma, 'The Curious Case of Rule 165 of the Rules of Procedure and Evidence: The Effect of Control Exercised by the Assembly of States Parties over the International Criminal Court' (2020) 20 (2) International Criminal Law Review 285, 303.

104 Laurence R Helfer and Anne-Marie Slaughter, 'Why States Create International Tribunals: A Response to Professors Posner and Yoo' (2005) 93 Calif L Rev 901.

105 'Sub Judice' <https://www.parliament.uk/site-information/glossary/sub-judice/> accessed 29 July 2023.

106 Ibid.

107 Woolaver and Palmer (n 45) 662.

ciple will guide the ASP on how to exercise its role without seeming to interfere with the ICC's judicial independence.[108]

Implementing the *sub judice* rule would require that the ASP does not discuss or adopt any amendments related to ongoing cases, such as occurred with Rule 134 *quater*. Based on this approach and as Trahan suggests, where a case is proceeding in Court, the ASP should play no role in the matter.[109] In the same vein, Woolaver proposes that the ASP should adopt rules barring the discussion of ongoing cases before the ICC (*sub judice*).[110] Similarly, O'Donohue suggests that the ASP should establish general principles to guide its approach to amendments that consider the ICC's jurisprudence while clarifying potentially ambiguous provisions.[111] Notably, the ASP has also acknowledged that States Parties' discussions should not "undermine the findings of the Court."[112] Based on the *sub judice* rule, the ASP can exercise its mandate to discuss or make amendments to the RPE or Statute, but only before related cases are filed or after they have been finalized in Court. The States Parties would consequently have their say while respecting the ICC's judicial independence.

Besides the *sub judice* rule, another suggested limitation to the States Parties interpretive role could be ensuring that the ASP follows the "roadmap" it had put in place encouraging consultations with the ICC to guide the structure of rule amendments.

2.5.2 The ASP "Roadmap" for Amendments to Rules

The limitation could arguably arise from the adherence of the ASP's amendments to the recommended 2011 "roadmap," which advocates for consultations between the ASP and the ICC before any amendments are made to the RPE. The consultation process approved under the "roadmap" was aimed to reinforce the States Parties role in the amendment process while allowing the ICC to also give its views on any amendment proposals.[113] Based on discussions

---

108 Ibid.

109 Jennifer Trahan, 'The International Criminal Court's Assembly of States Parties Meetings: Challenges to the Work of the Court' (*Opinio Juris*, 7 December 2015) <http://opiniojuris.org/2015/12/06/the-international-criminal-courts-assembly-of-states-parties-meetings-challenges-to-the-work-of-the-court/> accessed 22 September 2022.

110 Woolaver and Palmer (n 45) 661–663; Fatou Bensouda (n 83); Guilfoyle (n 67) 443.

111 Jonathan O'Donohue (n 15) 126.

112 Strengthening the International Criminal Court and the Assembly of States Parties, ICC-ASP/10/Res.5, 21 December 2011, Annex para 12.

113 Philipp Ambach (n 64) 865.

between the ICC and the ASP,[114] the ASP began the "roadmap" process in 2010, which sought to create a forum allowing for "a structured and fruitful dialogue" between States Parties and the ICC.[115] The ASP then established the Study Group on Governance (SGG) to facilitate consultations with the ICC to identify areas where further action, including amendments, was required and formulate recommendations to the ASP through the Bureau.[116] The roadmap, therefore, provided a way for both the ICC and the States Parties proposals on amendments to be considered and recommendations reached.[117]

Significantly, the ASP, through the SGG, stated that without prejudice to Article 51 of the Statute on amendments, States Parties and the ICC were encouraged to engage through the "roadmap" to avoid a "disparate and unstructured approach" to amending the Rules.[118] However, despite the ASP Bureau encouraging engagement through the consultative roadmap to prevent an "unstructured" approach, it is pointed out that the ASP adopted rules 134 *bis*, *ter*, and *quater* without following the roadmap, thus avoiding consultation with the ICC.[119] Ambach concedes that no provision under Article 51(2) obligates States Parties to consult with the ICC when they need to amend the rules.[120] Ambach, however, faulted the ASP's decision to adopt Rules 134 *bis*, *ter* and *quater* without following the consultative roadmap approach, which excluded the ICC, the main appliers of the amendment.[121]

Consultations between States Parties and the ICC would provide a forum to deal with developments arising, even in ongoing cases, in a consultative manner.[122] The book argues that had the ASP followed the roadmap it had put in place regarding the Rule 134 amendments, a common and consultative posi-

114 Philipp Ambach, 'The "Lessons Learnt" Process at the International Criminal Court – a Suitable Vehicle for Procedural Improvements?' [2016] ZIS 854 <www.zis-online.com> accessed 20 October 2021.

115 Report of the Bureau on the Study Group on Governance, Eleventh session, ICC-ASP/11/31, 23 October 2012 para 1 (Report of the Bureau on SGG); Establishment of a Study Group on Governance (Fifth Plenary Meeting of the ASP) ICC-ASP/9/Res.2, 10 December 2010 para 1 (Establishment of SGG).

116 Establishment of SGG (n 115) paras 2, 3.

117 Report of the Bureau on SGG (n 115) para 16.

118 Ibid. para 15 and Annex I, Draft Roadmap on Reviewing the Criminal Procedures of the International Criminal Court.

119 Philipp Ambach (n 64) 864; Report of the Bureau on SGG (n 115) para 15.; Amendments to the Rules of Procedure and Evidence, ICC-ASP/12/Res.7, 27 November 2013.

120 Ibid.

121 Ibid. 864–865.

122 Ibid., 865.

tion would have been achieved between the ASP and the ICC. This approach would also arguably prevent the seeming overlap and tension between the ASP's interpretive role through amendments and that of the Court, even in ongoing cases.

2.5.3 The ICC's Discretion to Only "Take into Account" Subsequent Agreements and Practice

It is also suggested that another limitation on the ASP's interpretation role may arise from the power retained by the ICC to only "take into account" subsequent agreements or practice of States Parties. As discussed earlier, taking into account has been interpreted by the ILC, some scholars, and courts to mean that the court can consider the subsequent agreements but is not under obligation to apply them in the decision outcome.

It is also argued that the language used in Article 31(3) of the VCLT and the ILC provisions, which refer to subsequent agreements as nonconclusive and not legally binding,[123] gives discretion to the ICC not to automatically apply the resolutions or amendments by the ASP as subsequent agreements or practice in its decisions. When the ICC has reason not to use the States Parties agreement, the nonbinding aspect of subsequent agreements gives the ICC the leeway to refer to the subsequent agreements and practice but not incorporate them in the final decision. Therefore, the ASP's powers to use subsequent agreements to influence the interpretation may be limited in this context.

3 The Implications of the ASP's Reaffirmation of Rule 68 as Nonretroactive on the ICC's Interpretation

Another instance when the ASP passed an "affirmation" that stood a high chance of influencing the ICC's interpretation of the Rome Statute in an ongoing case, arguably as a subsequent agreement, relates to the amended Rule 68 of the RPE.[124] The amended rule deals with the ICC's admission of prior recorded evidence, while the reaffirmation by the ASP confirmed the nonretroactive application of the rule.

123 ILC 2018 (n 24) Conclusion 3 Commentary 4.

124 Resolution ICC-ASP/12/Res.7, Amendments to Rules 100, 68, 134 *bis*, 134 *ter* and 134 *quater* of the Rules of Procedure and Evidence, 27 November 2013.

3.1 *Background*

In its 12th plenary meeting, the ASP amended Rule 68 of the RPE by consensus.[125] The amendment allowed the admission of previously recorded audio or video testimony or transcripts as long as it was not prejudicial to or inconsistent with the accused's rights, among other conditions.[126] Following this amendment, Kenya requested the ASP at the 14th session to reaffirm that the amendment to Rule 68 did not apply retroactively to hearings that commenced before the amendment came into force.[127] Additionally, Kenya stated that the amended Rule 68 was being "interpreted and implemented" by the ICC in a manner inconsistent with the ASP's Resolution.[128] The ASP acceded to Kenya's request and reaffirmed that the Rule 68 amendment did not apply retroactively. The resolution read

> Following the debate on the supplementary item "Review of the Application and Implementation of Amendments to the Rules of Procedure and Evidence introduced at the 12th Assembly," the Assembly recalled its resolution ICC-ASP/12/Res.7 dated 27 November 2013, which amended rule 68 of the Rules of Procedure and Evidence, which entered into force on the above date, and consistent with the Rome Statute reaffirmed its understanding that the amended rule 68 shall not be applied retroactively.[129]

The ASP, however, included the affirmation only in the official records of the 14th ASP session but did not list it as a formal ASP Resolution.[130] Significantly, the Appeal's Chamber was considering appeals by Kenyans *Ruto and Sang* concerning the retroactive application of amended Rule 68 when Kenya sought the reaffirmation, and the ASP granted it.[131]

---

125 Ibid.

126 Ibid.

127 ICC-ASP/14/35, 27 October 2015, Request by Kenya for the inclusion of a supplementary item in the agenda of the fourteenth session of the Assembly titled 'Review of the Application and implementation of amendments to the Rules of Procedure and Evidence introduced at the 12th Assembly' Annex 11, paras 2, 7.

128 Ibid. Annex 11 para 3.

129 ASP Official Records ICC-ASP/14/20 (14th session)18-26 November 2015, Vol 1 p 12-13 para 61; ICC-ASP/12/Res.7, 27 November 2013.

130 Ibid.; ICC-ASP/12/Res.7, 27 November 2013; Woolaver and Palmer (n 45) 651.

131 *Public redacted version of the "Ruto Defence appeal against the 'Decision on Prosecution Request for Admission of Prior Recorded Testimony'", 5 October 2015, ICC-01/09-01/11-1981-Conf.*

3.2 *Was the Reaffirmation of Rule 68 by the* ASP *a Subsequent Agreement?*

Notably, *Ruto and Sang*,[132] supported by the AU[133] as *amicus curiae*, cited the "reaffirmation" in the Appeal's Chamber, arguing that the Rule 68 amendment on prior recorded evidence did not apply retroactively and, therefore, prior recorded evidence was inapplicable to their ongoing case. Specifically, *Sang*, in his submissions to the Appeal's Chamber, argued that the ASP resolution reaffirming the amended Rule 68 as nonretroactive in application was relevant to the appeal and should be considered by the ICC in its interpretation.[134] The appeal arose from the Trial Chamber's decision, which held that nothing in amended Rule 68 prevented it from being applied retroactively.[135]

Sang urged the ICC to consider the ASP's affirmation, which he referred to as a resolution, in interpreting the amended Rule 68.[136] Additionally, the AU submissions in the case explicitly stated that the "interpretive declarations" made by Kenya, Nigeria, and South Africa[137] during the ASP debate on the Rule 68 amendment being nonretroactive constituted subsequent agreements to be considered by the ICC.[138]

---

132 *ICC, Judgment on the Appeals of William Samoei Ruto and Joshua Arap Sang against the decision of Trial Chamber V(A) of 19 August 2015 entitled "Decision on Prosecution Request for Admission of Prior Recorded Testimony", ICC-01/09-01/11-2024 (Appeal's Chamber) 12 February 2016* para 24 (Judgment on the Appeals of Ruto and Sang on Prior recorded Testimony).

133 Ibid. paras 25, 26.

134 *Sang Defence Submission in addition to Appeal against the decision of Trial Chamber V (A) of 19 August 2015 entitled "Decision on Prosecution Request for Admission of Prior Recorded Testimony" (Prosecutor vs William S Ruto and Joshua A Sang) ICC-01/09-01/11 (AC) 17 December 2015* para 7.

135 *Public redacted version of 'Decision on Prosecution Request for Admission of Prior Recorded Testimony', Prosecutor v. William Samoei Ruto and Joshua Arap Sang (ICC-01/09-01/11-1938-Corr-Red2 (TrC V(a), 19 August 2015.*

136 *Decision on the appeals of William Samoei Ruto and Joshua Arap Sang against the decision of Pre-Trial Chamber II of 23 January 2012 entitled 'Decision on the Confirmation of Charges Pursuant to Article 61(7) (a) and (b) of the Rome Statute' (Appeals Chamber), ICC-01/09-01/11-414, 24 May 2012* (ICC) para 18 (Decision on Ruto and Sang's appeal on Charges confirmation).

137 Cited in *The African Union's Amicus Curiae Observations on the Rule 68 Amendments at the Twelfth Session of the Assembly of States Parties (Prosecutor vs William S Ruto and Joshua A Sang) ICC-01/09-01/11 (AC) 19 October 2015* paras 59-61 (AU's Amicus Curiae Observations Rule 68) as Transcription of audio recording of the Plenary (Formal) Session of the Working Group on Amendments, 27 November 2013.

138 AU's Amicus Curiae Observations Rule 68 (n 137) paras 62-63 citing International Law Commission, UN Doc. A/CN.4/491 and Add.1-6, Third report on reservations to treaties, by Mr. Alain Pellet, Special Rapporteur, YBIL (1998) Vol. 2, Part 1 para 330.

However, the Appeal's Chamber declined to take the "reaffirmation" by the ASP into account. The Chamber held firstly, that "contrary to Mr Sang's assertion, the document to which Mr Sang refers is not a resolution, but is part of the official records of the proceedings of the Fourteenth session of the ASP."[139] The Chamber, therefore, seemed to construe the affirmation, included only in the official records, as lacking substantive weight compared to an official resolution by the ASP. Secondly, the Chamber found that even if the ASP's reaffirmation document was considered a resolution, no amendment to the text of amended Rule 68 resulted from it.[140] Based on the two grounds, the ICC consequently found the reaffirmation to be "irrelevant for the determination" of the appeal.[141]

The ICC's decision, therefore, raises two questions. First is whether the form that an agreement by States Parties takes, determines whether a subsequent agreement exists. Secondly is whether the affirmation by the ASP should consequently have been construed as a subsequent agreement or not. Disappointingly, the ICC failed to consider whether the reaffirmation by the ASP was a subsequent agreement or not, which would then have determined whether the reaffirmation would be obligatorily considered in the interpretation of Rule 68. The ICC failed to use the words "subsequent agreement" anywhere in the decision.

The study argues that the ICC should have first expressly analyzed whether the ASP's reaffirmation on Rule 68 amounted to a subsequent agreement or not. In this regard, the book argues that the ICC should have construed the ASP's affirmation as a subsequent agreement, which ought to have been considered in the interpretation of Rule 68 based on Article 31(3) of the VCLT. The study posits that the ASP reaffirmation met the requirements of subsequent agreements under the VCLT Article 31(3)(a) and the ILC conclusions on subsequent agreements. Firstly, it is argued that the requirement that all the States Parties had to have reached the agreement[142] was met. The book takes the position that since the ASP agreed to the reaffirmation and went further to have it recorded in the ASP's official records, this amounted to a sufficient expression of the States Parties agreement regarding the application of amended Rule 68. Additionally, it is argued that the requirement under Article 31(3)(a) that an agreement has to relate to the treaty interpretation was also met,

139 Judgment on the Appeals of Ruto and Sang on Prior Recorded Testimony (n 132) para 19.

140 Ibid.

141 Decision on Ruto and Sang's appeal on Charges confirmation (n 136) para 19.

142 ILC 2018 (n 24) Conclusion 4 Commentary 12.

since the reaffirmation sought to clarify the interpretation and application of the amended Rule 68 as being nonretroactive in application.[143]

The book further contends that having construed the affirmation as an agreement by all the ASP members, it follows that the form or manner in which the agreement was reached or recorded did not affect its being construed as a subsequent agreement. The Appeal Chamber only considered the form in which the ASP agreement was reached, finding that the inclusion of the affirmation in the ASP's official records and not as a resolution held little or no relevance in interpreting amended Rule 68. This position is contestable.

The study instead observes that based on Article 31(3) of the VCLT, it is the existence of an agreement between the parties that matters, regardless of what form the agreement takes.[144] This approach is bolstered by Judge Eboe-Osuji, who, as earlier mentioned, found that determining the States Parties intention cannot be achieved when the "judges can disregard the States Parties 'clear, direct and unanimous communication of that intent, *whatever be the method and manner* and timing employed by the States Parties in registering that communication."[145]

As the ILC also provides, a decision adopted within the framework of a Conference of States Parties embodies a subsequent agreement or subsequent practice under Article 31(3) of the VCLT if it expresses agreement in substance between the parties' "*regardless of the form and the procedure* by which the decision was adopted, including adoption by consensus."[146] Similarly, the ILC cited the IMO Sub-Division for Legal Affairs, reiterating that as long as "its intention is clear .... resolutions adopted at a meeting of the Parties, or even a decision recorded in the summary records of a meeting of the parties" can be considered subsequent agreements.[147] As recognized explicitly by the ILC, an agreement in the form of summary records of a meeting, in this case the ASP records regarding Rule 68, constitute subsequent agreements as long as the parties' intention regarding the interpretation is clear. Therefore, the form or manner the agreement takes is immaterial in construing it as a subsequent agreement. The book consequently contends that the Appeal's Chamber should not have disregarded the ASP's reaffirmation only because it was indi-

143 Ibid. Conclusion 4 Commentary 13.

144 Rahim Moloo, 'When Actions Speak Louder than Words: The Relevance of Subsequent Party Conduct to Treaty Interpretation' (2013) 31 Berkeley Journal of International Law 57.; *United States – Measures Affecting the Production and Sale of Clove Cigarettes, WTO, Appellate Body Report adopted on 4 April 2012, WT/DS406/AB/R* para 267.

145 Separate Opinion of Judge Eboe-Osuji on Ruto's excusal (n 5) para 34.

146 ILC 2018 (n 24) Conclusion 11 para 3.

147 Ibid. Conclusion 11 Commentary 12.

cated in the official records and not in the formal resolutions since the ASP's intention and agreement had been expressed.

This perspective, therefore, equally means that if the ASP's affirmation had been a resolution, the ICC would not have considered it unpersuasive. It is however argued that in interpretation, the ICC should be determining the States Parties intentions, and where the States confirm their intention through an agreement in whatever form, the ICC should consider it in interpretation decisively. As Grover generally cautioned, the ICC should avoid deviating from the understandings reached by States Parties by general consensus, which fall under subsequent agreements, when seeking the parties' common intention.[148]

Besides *Sang's* submissions, the Appeal's Chamber was presented with the opportunity to determine the validity of the AU's *amicus curiae* submissions that the "interpretive declarations" by Kenya, Nigeria, and South Africa regarding Rule 68 being nonretroactive constituted "subsequent agreements."[149] The AU argued that since the other State parties remained silent during the ASP discussions, they implicitly agreed with the position that amended Rule 68 did not apply retroactively as the three countries suggested.[150] The Appeal's Chamber again avoided analyzing explicitly whether the "declarations" amounted to subsequent agreements as submitted by the AU. The Chamber instead restricted itself to rejecting the AU's argument that the statements by the three ASP members were interpretative declarations to be considered in interpretation and that the silence of the other parties constituted "implicit agreement" with the declaration.[151] The study argues that the Appeal's Chamber should have gone further to consider whether the declaration by the three countries regarding Rule 68 amounted to a subsequent agreement as argued.

Using this perspective, the Appeal's Chamber would have used the ILC provisions and other scholarly material to determine whether silence amounted to an agreement. For instance, the ILC provides that "silence on the part of one or more parties may constitute acceptance of the subsequent practice when the circumstances call for some reaction."[152] On the other hand, it has also been stated that subsequent agreement under Article 31 (3) (a) must

148 Grover (n 2) 372.

149 AU's Amicus Curiae Observations Rule 68 (n 137) paras 62-63 citing International Law Commission, UN Doc. A/CN.4/491 and Add. 1-6, Third report on reservations to treaties, by Mr. Alain Pellet, Special Rapporteur, YBIL (1998) Vol. 2, Part 1 para 330.

150 AU's Amicus Curiae Observations Rule 68 (n 137) paras 62-63.

151 Judgment on the Appeals of Ruto and Sang on Prior recorded testimony (n 132) para 42.

152 ILC 2018 (n 24) Conclusion 10(2).

be "reached," which "presupposes a deliberate common act or undertaking by the parties."[153] Applied to the current case, this provision could be read in two ways. On the one hand, the deliberate silence by other States Parties could be taken as a common act to show a lack of agreement with the three countries' submissions. On the other hand, it alternatively showed implicit agreement with the submissions by Kenya, Nigeria, and South Africa that Rule 68 did not apply retroactively.

The book concludes that the silence and lack of objection by the other State Parties to the three ASP members statements denoted agreement by all parties, which would have been construed as a subsequent agreement to be taken into account based on Article 31(3)(a) of the VCLT. In this study's perspective, while only three ASP members made the statement, the other States Parties present did not object when the opportunity called for a reaction. The book aligns with the WTO finding in the *Chicken Cuts* case that where a party has participated in a forum where a practice is discussed but fails to react to it, this can be construed as acceptance or agreement.[154]

In conclusion, the book argues that the ICC missed an opportunity to interpret the ASP's reaffirmation as a subsequent agreement to be considered in relation to amended Rule 68's interpretation.

Nevertheless, as previously averred, while the ASP had the mandate to reach the reaffirmation or resolution, its adoption when there was an ongoing related case raised the probability of interference with the ICC's judicial independence.

3.3 *Implications of the Timing of the ASP's Reaffirmation on Amended Rule 68*

As noted earlier, the reaffirmation was reached when the Appeal's Chamber was handling the *Ruto* and *Sang* case concerning the same issue of the retroactive status of amended Rule 68. This timing may attract different arguments. On the one hand, and as previously stated, it may be argued that the ASP is not bound by any particular timing. On the other hand, the timing of the reaffirmation could appear to have been aimed at pressuring the Appeal's Chamber into giving a specific interpretation, seemingly contrary to its judicial independence.

153 Ibid. Conclusion 4(10).

154 *Appellate Body Report WTO, European Communities – Customs Classification of Frozen Boneless Chicken Cuts*, WT/DS269/AB/R, WT/DS286/AB/R, WT/DS269/AB/R/Corr1, WT/DS286/AB/R/Corr1 (*adopted 12 Sept 2005*) 106 para 272.

Several authors and groups demonstrated the seeming overlap between the ASP's and the ICC's interpretive role. In this regard, Woolaver and Palmers pointed out that if the ASP, on Kenya's urging, provided an interpretation of the revised Rule 68, there was a possibility of it conflicting with the Appeal Chamber's decision pending in Court.[155] Other scholars also faulted the ASP's discussion of a matter under appeal at the time, deeming it a politicization of the judicial process and interference with the ICC's judicial independence.[156] Some States Parties and civil organizations argued that since the matter was pending before the Appeal's Chamber, the ASP should not have considered Rule 68 and the related issues during its discussions.[157]

In this regard, the Coalition for the ICC (CICC) warned against the ASP discussing Rule 68 while the case was ongoing, stating that it aimed to influence the ongoing trial of Kenya's Deputy President, which set "a dangerous precedent for the Court's independence."[158] Other organizations and scholars have also posited that a discussion of an ongoing matter by the ASP amounted to interference in the ICC's judicial proceedings.[159] The International Federation for Human Rights (FIDH) reiterated that since the Ruto case was under appeal in the Court, the judges should have addressed any questions regarding the application of Rule 68 rather than the ASP.[160]

In the same vein, Kegoro, a former director of Kenya Human Rights Commission, brought out the seeming overlap concerning the Rule 68 reaffirmation and the Rule 134 amendment, stating that "once again, the Assembly of States Parties has relented to the pressure of getting Kenya's cases before the

155 Woolaver and Palmer (n 45) 650; *Public redacted version of the "Ruto Defence appeal against the 'Decision on Prosecution Request for Admission of Prior Recorded Testimony", 5 October 2015, ICC-01/09-01/11-1981-Conf*).

156 Jennifer Easterday, 'ASP to Begin in The Hague' (*International Justice Monitor* (*a project of Open Society Justice Initiative*), 16 November 2015) <https://www.ijmonitor.org/2015/11/asp-to-begin-in-the-hague/> accessed 22 December 2022; FIDH, 'The Independence of the International Criminal Court Must Be Enhanced' (*International Federation for Human Rights*, 27 November 2015) <https://www.fidh.org/en/issues/international-justice/international-criminal-court-icc/the-independence-of-the-international-criminal-court-must-be-enhanced> accessed 28 October 2022 (FIDH, 'The Independence of the ICC); FIDH Recommendations to the 14th ASP (n 53); Guilfoyle (n 67) 443; Woolaver and Palmer (n 45) 649–652.

157 FIDH, 'The Independence of the ICC' (n 156).

158 CICC, 'ASP 14: ICC Independence under Threat at Annual Assembly' (27 November 2015) <https://ciccglobaljustice.wordpress.com/2015/11/27/asp-14-icc-independence-under-threat-at-annual-assembly/> accessed 25 April 2020 (CICC on ICC Independence).

159 FIDH Recommendations to the 14th ASP (n 53) 7; Guilfoyle (n 67) 443; Woolaver and Palmer (n 45) 649–652.

160 FIDH Recommendations to the 14th ASP (n 53).

ICC tried in the Assembly rather than in Court."[161] The Human Rights Watch similarly contended with regards to the ASP's reaffirmation of Rule 68, that efforts to prosecute judicial decisions before the ASP were incompatible with the full respect for the ICC's independence.[162] From these perspectives, the ASP was impliedly construed to have taken over the interpretative mandate of the ICC.

The ASP's action was further seen as undermining the ICC's independent mandate,[163] especially since the request by Kenya to the ASP criticized the Court's interpretation of Rule 68 in the Kenyan cases of *Ruto and Sang*.[164] From a related perspective, it has been contended that the Rome Statute does not give the ASP the function of analyzing the ICC's interpretation.[165] Under this approach, the interpretation of the Statute and RPE should be left to the ICC and not to the ASP.[166] Woolaver contends that such clear demarcation of roles would prevent the ASP from interfering with the ICC's judicial independence.[167] It was consequently argued that while the instances of ASP "interference" were infrequent, they demonstrated its ability to potentially direct the Rome Statute's judicial interpretation through adopting amendments or formal resolutions that interpret previous rules.[168]

Pace, the CICC convener, further reiterated the unclear boundary in the roles, stating that the Kenyan government had pushed for the ASP's reaffirmation of Rule 68, which pressured the judges in their decision-making, consequently affecting their independence.[169] Similarly, disapproving of the ASP's confirmation of Kenya's request on Rule 68, the FIDH Vice President stated that "we must not allow States to believe they can influence judicial proceed-

161 George Kegoro, then Executive director of the Kenya Human Rights Commission cited in CICC on ICC Independence (n 158).

162 'Recent International Criminal Court Developments on Kenya, South Africa' (*Human Rights Watch*, 27 January 2016) <https://www.hrw.org/news/2016/01/27/recent-international-criminal-court-developments-kenya-south-africa> accessed 8 April 2023.

163 FIDH Recommendations to the 14th ASP (n 53).

164 FIDH, '14th ASP: States Should Refrain from Discussing Judicial Matters during the ASP' (*International Federation for Human Rights*, 19 November 2015) <https://www.fidh.org/en/issues/international-justice/14th-asp-states-should-refrain-from-discussing-judicial-matters> accessed 23 December 2022.

165 Woolaver and Palmer (n 45) 652.

166 Ibid., 651.; Czech Republic speaking on behalf of EU States plus Moldova, Liechtenstein, Costa Rica H, Australia, Canada, 20 November 201; Art. 119(2.1) of the Statute; FIDH Position paper 9th Session of the ICC ASP, 2010 17.

167 Ibid.

168 Ibid., 652.

169 CICC on ICC Independence (n 158).

ings. The judges of the ICC must remain free of political pressure."[170] Woolaver even further cautioned against the ICC's citing of the ASP amendments and resolutions in their judicial decisions, on the basis that it gave a potentially strong impetus to States Parties keen on influencing the ICC's judicial interpretation.[171]

The above positions illustrate the tension and uncertainty that arise when the ASP reaches resolutions or affirmations when there is an ongoing related case. As previously discussed, the book acknowledges that States Parties have the authority to interpret the Rome Statute through their subsequent agreements and practice based on Article 31(3) of the VCLT. Nonetheless, the timing of the amendments, resolutions, or reaffirmations when there are ongoing related cases in Court arguably blur the separation of the interpretive roles. In such instances, it is feared that the ICC would feel pressured to apply the subsequent agreements in its decisions contrary to its judicial independence.

As previously suggested, to minimize the impression that the ASP is trying to directly influence the decisions in ongoing cases, contrary to judicial independence protections, the ASP may need to adopt the affirmations or resolutions only after the conclusion of the ICC cases. On the other hand, by incorporating the ASP's amendments and resolutions reached by consensus as subsequent agreements in its decisions, the seeming overlap and tension between the ICC and the States Parties on their interpretive roles could be eased.

3.4 *Conclusion*

The chapter considered two instances when the ASP has collectively adopted amendments or resolutions that deal with the same issues as those in ongoing ICC cases and the consequent implications. In this regard, it was concluded that the ASP amendment to Rule 134 *ter* and *quarter*, which deals with exemptions of the accused from continuous presence at trial, met the requirements of subsequent agreements under Article 31(3)(a) of the VCLT. This conclusion was reached on the basis that the amendment was adopted by consensus and clarified the interpretation of Article 63(1) of the Rome Statute. Based on this

170 Katherine Gallagher, FIDH Vice President, 'The Independence of the International Criminal Court Must Be Enhanced' (*International Federation for Human Rights*, 27 November 2015) <https://www.fidh.org/en/issues/international-justice/international-criminal-court-icc/the-independence-of-the-international-criminal-court-must-be-enhanced> accessed 22 December 2022.

171 Woolaver and Palmer (n 45) 652.

conclusion, it was noted that the Trial Chamber correctly applied the Rule 134 amendments as the decisive factor in its decision.

The study also concluded that while the Rule 134 *quater* amendment appeared to overrule the Appeal Chamber's decision, seemingly creating an overlap in the interpretive roles, the States Parties retained the authority to correct what they deemed erroneous interpretations by the ICC or clarify ambiguous provisions. However, to avoid the overlap in interpretive roles, the ASP should pass resolutions and amendments before related cases are filed or after their conclusion.

The second instance discussed the reaffirmation by the ASP of the nonretroactive application of amended Rule 68 on prior recorded evidence, which was adopted at Kenya's request. In this regard, the study concluded that the ASP's reaffirmation constituted a subsequent agreement clarifying the States Parties intention since it was the agreement and not the form of the agreement that was important. The study argues that the ICC should have expressly treated the reaffirmation as a subsequent agreement and considered it in its decision to determine that the application of Rule 68 was nonretroactive. It is concluded that the Chamber missed the chance to incorporate the ASP reaffirmation as a subsequent agreement when interpreting the Rule 68 nonretroactive status.

However, it was noted that adopting the "reaffirmation" when there was an ongoing related case could also be seen as a bid by the ASP to directly influence the ICC's interpretation with a resultant blurring of the interpretive roles. A conclusion similar to that reached regarding Rule 134 amendments was made. The conclusion was that while the ASP had the authority to reach affirmations or resolutions at any time, the ASP should avoid adopting such reaffirmations or resolutions when a related case was going on in Court, to protect the ICC's judicial independence.

CHAPTER 6

Conclusions and Recommendations

1 Introduction

This final chapter begins with a summary of the analysis' most significant findings. The findings and conclusions are based on the two main questions that the book sought to answer. The book set out firstly, to assess the role, if any, of States Parties to the Rome Statute of the International Criminal Court (States Parties), acting individually or collectively, in the interpretation of the Rome Statute of the International Criminal Court (Rome Statute) in light of an existing International Criminal Court (ICC). It secondly sought to determine the extent to which any such role might cause tension and, if so, how such tension might be eased.

Recommendations on the way forward follow.

2 Summary of Findings

This chapter gives general conclusions that run throughout the book.

2.1 *States Parties Have a Role in the Interpretation of the Rome Statute*

On the question of whether States Parties had a role in the Statute's interpretation, it emerged that there is no express recognition of the role of the States Parties in the judicial interpretation of the Rome Statute. The analysis was made in Chapters 2, 3, 4, and 5. It was noted that the ICC has been given the express role of interpretation under Article 119(1) of the Statute, where the Court makes decisions related to its judicial functions. However, to situate the States Parties role in interpretation after the treaty's conclusion, the book referred to the rules of interpretation contained in Articles 31 and 32 of the Vienna Convention on the Law of Treaties (VCLT). The study established that based on Article 31(3) of the VCLT, which provides for the taking into account of States parties subsequent agreements and practice during the treaty interpretation, States Parties have a continued role in the Rome Statute's interpretation. It was noted that such subsequent agreements and practice took the form of interpretive declarations, amendments, or resolutions, among others.

To determine the place of subsequent agreements and practice in the interpretation of treaties, the book assessed the rules of interpretation contained in

 | DOI:10.1163/9789004725515_007

Articles 31 and 32 of the VCLT and the 2018 ILC Draft Conclusions on Subsequent Agreements and Practice. Court and tribunal decisions were also evaluated. Several conclusions emerged from this discussion contained in Chapter 2. Firstly, it was established that the VCLT interpretation rules have been accepted as customary law on interpretation, applicable to all international treaties. In this context, the book concluded that since the Rome Statute is an international treaty, the VCLT interpretation rules also applied to it. Secondly, it emerged that the place or weight of subsequent agreements and practice in interpretation as highlighted by the ILC, is not uniform and still depends on the interpretation of individual courts and tribunals.

This lack of uniformity was noted to be mainly attributable to two aspects. First, it was whether Article 31(3) also falls under the general rule, similar to Article 31(1), or whether only Article 31(1) forms the general rule. It was found that some courts and scholars consider Article 31(1), which encompasses the ordinary meaning, the context, in the light of its object and purpose as the general rule. In contrast, others include Article 31(3), constituting subsequent agreements and practice as part of the general rule.

As part of the general rule, Article 31(3), just like Article 31(1), was bound to be treated as obligatory in the treaty interpretation. Based on this argument, for those who contended that subsequent agreements and practice fell under the general rule, the consideration of subsequent agreements and practice in the interpretation outcome was considered obligatory and conclusive in effect. In the same vein, it emerged that, to all intents, Article 31(1) elements undoubtedly deemed part of the general rule are considered obligatory in the decision outcome. For those who argued that subsequent agreements and practice do not fall under the general rule, it followed from this perspective that they were discretionary and not binding in interpretation. The position of subsequent agreements and practice in interpretation was found not to be uniform but varied from court to court.

The second aspect that contributed to the lack of a uniform position is the phrasing under Article 31(3) of the VCLT that the interpreter is required to "take into account" subsequent agreements and practice. The study noted that while some courts, tribunals, and scholars interpret this phrase to mean that subsequent agreements and practice are binding on the courts or tribunals, others find it nonobligatory and discretionary in the treaty interpretation. In this context, the subsequent agreements and practice can be taken into account in interpretation but not necessarily applied in the decision outcome.

Additionally, while the ILC has highlighted the role of subsequent agreements and practice, it fails to give a uniform and consistent position on the place and weight of subsequent agreements and practice in interpretation. On the one hand, the ILC states that the subsequent agreements and practice are neither conclusive nor legally binding.[1] On the other hand, the ILC considers all the Article 31 elements, including subsequent agreements and practice, as forming part of a single interpretation process, with all elements carrying equal weight.[2] The lack of a uniform position on the place of subsequent agreements and practice was also reflected by the court and tribunal decisions and scholarly literature.

The study further noted that most courts and tribunals commonly refer to Article 31(1) elements compared to the subsequent agreements and practice under Article 31(3) of the VCLT. It also emerged that even when referred to, subsequent agreements and practice are rarely found to be binding or decisive except where the treaty expressly makes them binding, such as in the case of the former NAFTA agreement and others.[3]

Having established that State parties can participate in treaty interpretation based on Article 31(3) of the VCLT, the next analysis focused on whether the VCLT interpretation rules were specifically applicable to the Rome Statute's interpretation. In this context, the book examined whether the VCLT rules applied or the Statute had its own interpretation rules that displace the VCLT rules. The study noted that the significance of the VCLT rules applying to the Rome Statute was that if the VCLT applied, then a legal basis was laid for the States Parties participation in the Rome Statute's interpretation through their subsequent agreements and subsequent practice. If the VCLT did not apply, the legal basis for the States Parties participation in the Statute's interpretation was lost. Based on the VCLT Article 31(3) and the ILC Draft Conclusions on Subsequent agreements, it was concluded that the Assembly of States Parties (ASP) amendments and resolutions were examples of the form that subsequent agreements or subsequent practice can take.

The Rome Statute does not explicitly stipulate the rules applicable to its interpretation. As a result, various views have been offered. For instance, a few scholars and ICC decisions have considered the "applicable" law under

1 ILC, 'Draft Conclusions on Subsequent Agreements and Subsequent Practice in Relation to the Interpretation of Treaties, Seventieth Session, (A/73/10) 2018' (ILC) Commentary to Draft Conclusion 3 para 4 (ILC 2018).

2 Ibid. Conclusion 2 Commentary 5 and 11.

3 Article 1131 para 2 of the North American Free Trade Agreement between the Government of the United States of America, the Government of Canada and the Government of the United Mexican States (1992).

Article 21 as interpretation principles. The applicable law includes the Statute, the Elements of crimes (Elements), and the RPE in the first hierarchy. The other applicable rules include applicable treaties and the principles and rules of international law, the general principles of law derived by the ICC from national laws of legal systems of the world, and the ICC's previous decisions. The book concludes that application and interpretation are related but distinguishable. Consequently, it was ruled out that the applicable law in Article 21, except for Article 21(3), equates to interpretation rules as suggested by a few scholars and court decisions. It was found that they only apply as sources of law.

On the same basis, Article 21(3) of the Rome Statute, which provides that the application and interpretation of the Statute provisions must be consistent with internationally recognized human rights, was also examined. It was noted that Article 21(3) has been referred to as a rule of interpretation by some ICC decisions and scholars. The analysis showed that Article 21(3) forms an internal interpretation rule under the Rome Statute. Similarly, it was concluded that Article 22 is also an internal interpretational rule under the Statute. Article 22 provides for the strict construction of words without extension by analogy, with any ambiguity being determined in favor of the accused. The study, however, noted that the Rome Statute fails to explicitly recognize the two articles as interpretation rules. This book argues that although Articles 21(3) and 22 are considered interpretation rules by several ICC decisions, the articles do not form independent substantive rules of interpretation on their own. It was concluded that they could only operate within the contours of the VCLT interpretation rules.

In effect, the study established that the VCLT remains the primary interpretive rule for the Rome Statute by virtue of the VCLT being customary law and the Statute being an international treaty, albeit with unique criminal features. Articles 21(3) and 22 require to be interpreted within the VCLT Article 31 rules. This conclusion was reinforced by several ICC decisions, which showed that even when mentioned as interpretation rules, they were primarily referred to in addition to the VCLT interpretation rules and not as stand-alone interpretation rules.

In the same regard, it was noted that the strict construction of words under the legality rule in Article 22 emphasized the textual interpretation also contained in Article 31(1) of the VCLT. The analysis showed that determining the meaning of the text and deciding that a strict construction of words has been adhered to requires reference to the Article 31(1) elements of interpretation, which include the ordinary meaning of words in their context based on their object and purpose. Similarly, as several ICC decisions showed, determining that the human rights interpretation has been consistently applied in accordance with Article 21(3) would first require an interpretation of the ordinary meaning of the words in their context based on Article 31(1) of the VCLT.

It was noted that the ICC referred to the VCLT interpretation rules, and specifically Article 31(1), in most of its decisions. These frequent and consistent references were found to confirm the VCLT as the primary rule for the Rome Statute's interpretation. This approach counters the argument by a few scholars that the Statute has its own interpretation rules and the VCLT interpretation rules do not apply. It was nevertheless noted that the ICC's reference to the States Parties subsequent agreements and subsequent practice was negligible despite their significance in interpretation.

2.1.1 The Effect of the States Parties Role on the ICC's Interpretation

With the results establishing the VCLT's application to the Rome Statute, the book proceeded from the premise that the States Parties consequently have a role in interpreting the Statute. As previously discussed, this position is based on Article 31(3) of the VCLT. It was noted that there is, therefore, a likely impact on the ICC's interpretation of the Rome Statute.

Before examining the specific role of States Parties in the Statute's interpretation, the study first examined the general role of State parties in interpreting their treaties. In this context, arguments advocating for the State parties as the primary interpreters were assessed on the one hand. On the other hand, other views sought to justify that once a court or tribunal was established, they took over the primary interpretive authority from the State parties. The third argument provided for the shared interpretative authority between State parties and the courts or tribunals.

Based on Article 31(3) of the VCLT, it can be construed that State parties generally share interpretive authority with the courts and tribunals in interpreting their treaties. It was noted that treaty parties had the initial interpretive role but delegated some of this power to established courts and tribunals. In this respect, courts have restricted independence where the States parties establish independent international courts or tribunals but use other means, such as political means or the treaty structure, to limit the courts or tribunal's interpretive freedom.[4] From this context, the judges' discretionary power is limited or controlled by State parties in different ways.

---

4 See generally Laurence R Helfer and Anne-Marie Slaughter, 'Why States Create International Tribunals: A Response to Professors Posner and Yoo' (2005) 93 Calif L Rev 901.

The book concludes that this position also applies to the Rome Statute's interpretation. In this context, it was shown that sharing interpretive authority means that neither the States Parties to the Statute nor the ICC have the exclusive authority to interpret the Statute in all circumstances.[5]

Based on the shared interpretive authority between States Parties and the ICC, the study noted that, as a result, there has occasionally appeared to be a "battle for interpretive power" between the two entities as rivals, with consequent tension.[6] In this respect, the seemingly unclear roles regarding the Rome Statute's interpretation were illustrated in two instances. In these instances, the ASP affirmations, amendments, and resolutions appeared to overlap with the ICC's interpretive role, seemingly creating tension between the two entities and also individual ASP members. These instances were discussed in Chapter 5.

The first instance analyzed the adoption of the ASP amendments to Rule 134, including 134 *bis*, *ter*, and *quarter*, which allowed for the exemption of the accused from continuous presence at trial. It was noted that the Rule 134 *quater* amendment, which permitted those with the highest responsibilities in a State to avoid being present in Court continuously with no specific limitations, was the most controversial. The resolutions were deemed controversial on account of two factors. The first significant issue was that the ASP amendment on Rule 134 was passed by consensus when a matter on the same issue was ongoing in the Trial Chamber in the *Ruto Excusal* case.[7] In this regard, the discussion considered whether the Rule 134 amendment constituted a subsequent agreement to be taken into account by the Trial Chamber.

The study found that the Rule 134 amendments met the ILC and the VCLT Article 31(3) requirements on subsequent agreements. This conclusion was reached on the basis that the amendment was passed through consensus by the ASP and secondly, because it related to clarifying the interpretation and application of Article 63 (1) of the Rome Statute on the presence of an accused in Court. Based on this finding and Article 31(3) of the VCLT, the Trial Chamber was expected to consider the subsequent agreement in interpreting

5 Based generally on Anthea Roberts, 'Power and Persuasion in Investment Treaty Interpretation: The Dual Role of States, Vol 104, Issue 2' [2010] AJIL 179 para 1.

6 Based on Anthea Roberts, 'Subsequent Agreements and Practice: The Battle Over Interpretive Power' [2013] SSRN Scholarly Paper.

7 *Ruto Defence Request for Mr Ruto's Excusal from Presence at Trial under Rule 134 ter, The Prosecutor v William Samoei Ruto and Joshua Arap Sang,* ICC-01/09-01/11-1998 (*TrC* V) *03 November 2015.*

the relevant Statute provisions. This book, therefore, agrees with the Trial Chamber's decision that the ASP amendment to Rule 134 constituted a subsequent agreement by the ASP. It also agrees with the Chamber's decision to rely on the amendment conclusively in its decision outcome granting the accused's prayers. The study considered that after the difficulty of having all ASP members agree to one common position, it would be unconscionable for the Chamber not to consider such an amendment or resolution as decisive.

The amendment was also analyzed with respect to whether there was probable interference with the ICC's judicial independence based on its timing. Significantly, the study concluded that the timing of the ASP amendments, when there was an ongoing related case, appeared designed to interfere with the ICC's interpretive independence, consequently blurring the interpretive roles of the Court and the ASP. The possible interference was also notable on the basis that the amendments were spearheaded by Kenya, an affected ASP member, whose President and Deputy were at the center of the ongoing ICC case.

The analysis showed that this was the only case to date in which the ASP amendments or resolutions were construed explicitly as a subsequent agreement, and applied as the decisive element in the ICC decisions.

The second significant issue analyzed relating to Rule 134 amendments was that the Appeal's Chamber had already given its decision on the same matter of an accused's presence in Court. It disagreed with the Trial Chamber's decision, which granted broad freedom to accused leaders not to attend trial. Both the criticisms and justifications for the ASP's action were considered with the effect on the ICC's interpretive independence in mind. The conclusion was that the ASP retained the authority to pass resolutions and amendments at any given time, aimed at either correcting what they considered an erroneous ICC decision or clarifying ambiguous Statute provisions. In effect, even if the Appeal's Chamber had reached a decision earlier, the States Parties retained the mandate to correct what they thought was an erroneous decision or one that failed to accurately capture the States Parties intentions. However, as previously noted, the timing of the ASP amendments or resolutions was significant.

The second demonstration of overlap related to the reaffirmation by the ASP that the Rule 68 amendment passed earlier regarding admitting prior recorded evidence did not apply retroactively. The ASP similarly reached the reaffirmation, spearheaded by Kenya, when there was an ongoing related case on the same issue in the Appeal's Chamber in which Kenya's Deputy President was an accused party. It was noted that the Appeal's Chamber failed to acknowledge the reaffirmation as a subsequent agreement despite submissions by the AU as *amicus curiae* that it was, and submissions by one of the accused that it should have been considered. The Chamber failed to consider the reaffirmation in the interpretation partly because the reaffirmation was not recorded as an ASP resolution but was only contained in the ASP's official records of the proceedings. The study concluded that based on the findings in Chapter 2, a subsequent agreement did not require a particular form as long as there was an agreement by the parties. Consequently, the Chamber should not have dismissed the reaffirmation as being inapplicable on this basis.

Instead, the Appeal's Chamber should have treated the reaffirmation as a subsequent agreement and considered it decisively in interpretation. This conclusion was reached on the basis that the affirmation met the requirements of a subsequent agreement under Article 31(3)(a) of the VCLT and the ILC Conclusions. These included the fact the ASP parties reached an agreement that was recorded formally, even if it was not referred to as a resolution. Secondly, the agreement, in line with Article 31(3)(a), related to the interpretation and application of the amended Rule 68 on the admission of prior evidence.

Regarding the ASP's timing, it was construed that similar to the Rule 134 amendment, the ASP affirmation when a related case was going on appeared aimed at influencing the Chamber's decision contrary to the Court's judicial independence.

2.2 *Reconciling the Interpretative Mandate Bestowed on the ICC with the Interpretative Role of States Parties to the Rome Statute*

On the basis that the roles of the States Parties and those of the ICC in interpreting the Rome Statute may result in some tension, the sub-theme considered whether there were any rules under general international law or the Statute to address any such conflict arising. The question of whether the roles of the States Parties and the ICC can be reconciled was addressed in chapters 3, 4, and 5. The conclusion was that neither the Rome Statute, the VCLT, nor other general international law has any express rules to address the likely conflict emanating from the shared interpretive roles. It emerged that the Statute does not address the issue at all.

The findings appeared to indicate that without an explicit acknowledgment of the States Parties role, the existence or potential existence of the overlap between the States Parties role with that of the ICC in the Statute's interpretation is also unacknowledged.

On the other hand, it was also concluded that while the States Parties limited the ICC's interpretive role through subsequent agreements and practice among other means, similarly, despite the States Parties being the treaty owners, their role in interpretation is not unrestricted either. In this regard, it was shown that among the probable limitations on the States Parties and the ASP is the *sub judice* principle, which protects the judicial independence of courts by prohibiting discussion on matters pending before the Court.

A further possible limitation and balancing of the ASP's amendments was the "roadmap" formally set up by the ASP, which encouraged consultations between the ASP and the ICC before any amendments to the rules were adopted. The "roadmap" was established to get views on proposed amendments by both the States Parties and the ICC to prevent unstructured and unilateral amendments. The study concluded that the roadmap acts as a probable limitation if adhered to by the ASP, although, as noted, it was not followed regarding Rule 134 amendments.

As a further possible restriction on the ASP's interpretive open mandate, the study concluded that while the legal basis for incorporating States Parties interpretation was through subsequent agreements and practice, the ICC is only under an obligation to "take into account" the subsequent agreements and practice but is not obligated to incorporate them in its decision. This conclusion was based on Article 31(3) of the VCLT and the ILC draft conclusions. This phrasing means that the ICC has some control over whether to apply the subsequent agreements and practice in the Statute's interpretation or not. The above measures were found to act as possible limitations on the ASP's uncontrolled mandate to adopt subsequent agreements and practice, which may pressure the ICC in its interpretive role contrary to its judicial independence.

In summary, this book has addressed the existing gap by recognizing that despite the existence of the established ICC, the States Parties retain an interpretative role in the Rome Statute's interpretation through their subsequent agreements and practice. These are mainly illustrated through their resolutions and amendments to the RPE and the Statute. The study has further highlighted the possible resultant tension due to the shared interpretive roles and the lack of clear boundaries in playing this role. The book consequently proposes ways to prevent or ease the tension by creating a balance that will enable both the States Parties and the ICC to play their interpretive roles effectively. This proposed balance would likely enhance the effective fulfillment of the Rome Statute's aims and objectives and further avoid threats by State Parties to withdraw from the Statute. This forms the main contribution of the book.

Recommendations on how to reconcile the States Parties and the ICC's role in the Rome Statute's interpretation with a view to prevent or ease future tension follow.

3 Recommendations

Based on the above findings, this book presents recommendations as discussed below. These are directed to the ICC, the ASP, and the States Parties to the Rome Statute, among others.

3.1 *The ICC Should Uniformly Reach Decisions Confirming That the VCLT Is the Main Interpretive Rule Guiding the Rome Statute's Interpretation*

As the findings showed, several ICC decisions consider the VCLT interpretive rules as the primary guide to the interpretation of the Statute. Some chambers, as discussed, have, however, considered Article 22 on legality and Article 21(3) on interpretation consistent with human rights as overriding the VCLT. As concluded, the two articles are not independent of the VCLT interpretation rules. This book consequently recommends that all the ICC chambers should uniformly confirm the VCLT interpretive rules as the primary interpretive rule for the Rome Statute thereby eliminating any disparity. The ICC Chambers should then make deliberate interpretation decisions that harmonize the application of the VCLT interpretation rules with the legality principle and human rights. For instance, the ICC can interpret the ordinary meaning of the words in their context while ensuring that it does not give an expansive meaning that would go against the strict construction under the legality rule.

Having recognized the application of the VCLT interpretive rules to the Rome Statute, this book further recommends that the ICC should expressly and consistently acknowledge that based on the VCLT Article 31(3), the States Parties retain a role in the Rome Statute's interpretation through their subsequent agreements and practice. On the other hand, it is essential that the ICC and the States Parties recognize and explicitly acknowledge their shared interpretive role in the Statute's interpretation. Neither the ICC nor the ASP has made this acknowledgment expressly. The study suggests that this approach will assist in giving each entity its rightful position in the Rome Statute's interpretation, rather than acting as rivals, as has occasionally happened.

3.2 *The ICC Should Adopt Policy and Practice Rules Requiring It to Incorporate More States Parties Resolutions and Amendments as Subsequent Agreements in the Rome Statute's Interpretation*

Related to the first recommendation, the ICC should explicitly and more frequently refer to and apply the ASP's subsequent agreements and practice in its interpretation where relevant. As stated in the findings, the ICC rarely considers or even refers to the States Parties subsequent agreements and practice in its decisions. To avoid possible tension and dissatisfaction where States Parties feel that the ICC ignores their views, the Court should make a deliberate effort to recognize subsequent agreements and practice of States Parties where they exist and incorporate them in its decisions. The ICC could adopt practice rules reiterating this position to ensure adherence.

The book further recommends that the ICC treat such subsequent agreements and practice as binding and conclusive in interpretation when the ASP adopts amendments or resolutions by consensus. The study proposes that since the primary purpose of the Statute's interpretation is to implement the States Parties intentions, the best and most precise way for that intention to be determined is through the States Parties unanimous reiteration of their intention through their resolutions or amendments. The study proposes that searching through the ordinary words in their context for the meaning would be self-defeating for the ICC when the parties have already clarified the meaning.

Another way to recognize both the States Parties role and that of the ICC is for the Court to provide in its decisions that the ASP should adopt rules specifying particular exceptions or clarifying ambiguous provisions in their legislative capacity. Under this approach, the ICC recognizes its role and equally that of the ASP to clarify ambiguous provisions or specify exceptions to certain provisions where necessary. Once adopted, the ICC would then consider these ASP amendments or resolutions as subsequent agreements or practice which are decisive in the Court's decisions. The study suggests that if the Chamber had used this approach in the Rule 68 reaffirmation case, the ASP would have been compelled to expressly clarify through an amendment or resolution that the Rule 68 amendment did not apply retroactively. The ICC would have been left in no doubt as to the ASP's intentions, thereby minimizing the tension with the affected ASP members.

On the other hand, it is also recommended that States Parties should recognize that even as treaty owners, some constraints arise due to the existence of the Court, which the parties endowed with interpretive powers under the Rome Statute. In this regard, it is suggested that the States Parties should, except where necessary, allow the ICC the freedom to interpret the Statute in fulfillment of its judicial functions under Article 119(1) of the Rome Statute without seeming interference.

3.4 *Consultation between the ASP and the ICC before the Adoption of Far-Reaching Amendments (Including Implementing the Roadmap)*

In recognition of the shared interpretive authority between States Parties and the ICC, as concluded earlier, it is recommended that the ASP should avoid unilateral amendments without consultation or limit them to a minimum. The book acknowledges that there is no legal requirement for the ASP to consult with the ICC before making amendments. However, the proposal could help reconcile the shared interpretive roles and minimize potential tension between States Parties and the ICC.

One of the ways for the consultations to take place is through the committed implementation of the "roadmap" suggested by the ASP and the ICC in 2013.[8] Under the roadmap, consultations between the ICC and the ASP are encouraged before any amendment of the rules or Statute is done. The consultation would be inclusive and bring on board views from the States Parties, the ICC, and the prosecution, all of whom hold a high stake in the Rome Statute's interpretation and implementation. As the Bureau of the Assembly stated in 2013, the "roadmap" should be followed to avoid a fragmented and unstructured approach to proposals amending the Statute's provisions and rules.[9]

As previously concluded, the roadmap consultation was not observed regarding some significant amendments, such as those relating to rule 134 *bis, ter*, and *quater*. It is suggested that such consultative amendments may prevent situations where the ASP appears to overrule the ICC decisions, as happened in the *Ruto* and *Sang* case discussed earlier. This approach would require both the States Parties and the ICC to acknowledge that they are equal stakeholders in the effective implementation of the Statute. A proposal for amendments by the ASP could be shared with the Presidency of the Court, who will select a team to prepare responses and share them with the ASP bureau. Such consultations should consider any current or emerging issues, especially those not addressed by the Rome Statute or those with ambiguous provisions. The process would need to be done speedily to avoid defeating the purpose of the consultations.

It is further recommended that the ICC utilize the consultations to seek clarification from the ASP on ambiguous or conflicting provisions in which the States Parties intentions are unclear.

---

8 ICC-ASP/11/31, Report of the Bureau on the Study Group on Governance, 23 October 2012 para 15 annex I, Draft roadmap for reviewing the Criminal Procedure of the ICC; Report of the Bureau on Study Group on Governance, ICC-ASP/12/37 15 October 2013; See generally Philipp Ambach, 'The "Lessons Learnt" Process at the International Criminal Court – a Suitable Vehicle for Procedural Improvements?' [2016] ZIS 867 <www.zis-online.com> accessed 20 October 2021.

9 ICC-ASP/11/31, Report of the Bureau on the Study Group on Governance, 23 October 2012 annex I; Report of the Bureau on Study Group on Governance, ICC-ASP/12/37 15 October 2013 para 10.

The ASP could then adopt the amendments agreed upon after all the consultations are completed. This book proposes that properly implementing the "roadmap" would be one sure way of reaching well-formulated and thought-out amendments to the Rules without the ASP appearing to infringe on the ICC's judicial independence. Additionally, it is suggested that this would prevent the ASP from adopting amendments based on one particular situation and make it easier for the ICC to refer to the amendments as subsequent agreements and incorporate them in interpretation.

3.5 *The States Parties Should Adopt Rules Implementing the* Sub Judice *Principle*

From the findings above, the overlap in interpretive roles and consequent tension primarily arises between the ASP and the ICC when the ASP reaches resolutions or amendments directly related to ongoing cases in the Court. As discussed, this occurred in the case of the amendments to Rule 134 *bis*, *ter*, and *quarter*, which were passed to excuse those with high state responsibilities from continuous attendance in Court. The same position arose regarding the Rule 68 reaffirmation on prior recorded evidence. The book recommends that to avoid the overlap in roles and ease tension, when a matter is ongoing in the ICC (*sub judice*), the ASP should refrain from discussing the issue.[10]

To make the *sub judice* rule effective, it is recommended that the ASP adopt rules explicitly stating that discussions on issues that are the subject of ongoing ICC proceedings are prohibited from discussion or are suspended until after the case's conclusion. In this case, any clarifications or corrections by the ASP through resolutions or amendments should be made before a case reaches the ICC or after the conclusion of the case. This rule would especially apply where the discussion would likely prejudice the case outcome or the ICC's judicial independence.

A leaf could be borrowed from the Norwegian BIT, which explicitly provides that the "joint Committee should refrain from adopting interpretations of provisions already submitted to a Tribunal in a dispute."[11] This idea has been floated before by the IBA recommendations on Strengthening the ICC, which report this book recommends should be implemented. The IBA report recommended that to ensure that the ASP respects the ICC's judicial indepen-

10 Jennifer Trahan, 'The International Criminal Court's Assembly of States Parties Meetings: Challenges to the Work of the Court' (*Opinio Juris*, 7 December 2015) <http://opiniojuris.org/2015/12/06/the-international-criminal-courts-assembly-of-states-parties-meetings-challenges-to-the-work-of-the-court/> accessed 22 September 2022.

11 Norwegian Model BIT 2015 Article 23(4)(ii).

dence, any proposals for amendments related to matters under consideration by the ICC should wait until after the Court has made its determination.[12] In this respect, it is proposed that the ASP should wait until the matter is heard and determined up to the highest appeal level. After the conclusion of the ICC cases, the States Parties can then react and comment on the interpretation to correct erroneous interpretation or clarify ambiguous issues for the future guidance of the Court.

It is proposed that in the alternative, even if the ASP engages in discussions and reaches some resolutions related to ongoing cases, they should specify that the interpretive agreements or any resolutions reached should only have a future effect, not an immediate one. If this recommendation is implemented, it would mean that even where the ASP arrives at resolutions or amendments touching on matters before the ICC, the amendment or resolution would not apply to the immediate case but only to future cases. The seeming interference with the ICC's judicial interpretation would be minimized or eliminated, leading to less overlap and tension.

As an added counterbalance to the ASP's passing of resolutions while cases are ongoing, it is suggested that the ICC could exercise its discretion to decide not to apply ASP amendments or resolutions passed in relation to ongoing cases. The ICC has the discretion not to apply the subsequent agreements and practice in its decisions based on the phrase "taking into account" under Article 31(3) of the VCLT, which has been interpreted by some scholars and the ILC as denoting discretionary language. While this action is proposed to discourage the adoption of ASP resolutions during ongoing proceedings (*sub judice*), it is also acknowledged that this may not entirely reduce the tension between States Parties and the ICC. It would, however, act as a limitation on the ASP to allow the ICC judicial independence in interpretation and discuss related matters either before a case is filed or after the Court has made its decision. Such an approach acknowledges that States Parties retain the authority to discuss issues of concern, including ICC decisions, but should not do so when Court cases are ongoing to allow the ICC to exercise its judicial independence.

3.6 *The ASP's Stipulation of Binding Provisions in the Rome Statute*

Related to the need for amendments, a different way to ensure the ICC uses the ASP amendments or resolutions decisively when relevant, would be to include express provisions in the Rome Statute or rules, stipulating that spe-

12 IBA, 'Strengthening the International Criminal Court and the Rome Statute System: A Guide for States Parties, October 2021' 80.

cific provisions are binding on the ICC. Admittedly, this approach may seem to take the independent interpretive power of the ICC away. However, it may work if applied to specific challenging or controversial provisions or where consultation is made mandatory before an amendment is adopted.

For instance, the States Parties may include provisions stating that where the ASP adopts a resolution or amendment by consensus, it will be binding on the ICC. In this regard, a leaf could be borrowed from the Korea-Vietnam FTA, which provides that joint interpretation of treaty provisions by Parties is binding on the respective tribunals.[13]

3.7 *Generation of More Relevant Subsequent Agreements and Practice by States Parties*

This book also recommends that States Parties should ensure they take an active role in interpreting the Rome Statute by generating adequate subsequent agreements and practice that the ICC could take into account when interpreting the Statute.[14] It is proposed that when States Parties wish to have a common position, more States Parties, if not all, should, among others, issue joint public statements about their understanding of particular provisions, reach common decisions domestically, have more or less similar submissions in Court among other conduct relating to the interpretation of the Rome Statute.[15] Where the conduct is consistent and widely practiced by States Parties, the ICC would find it difficult to avoid considering such conduct as subsequent agreements or practice that is binding and decisive in the Rome Statute's interpretation.

3.8 *Reference to the International Court of Justice (ICJ) in the Interpretation of Contentious International Law Matters Arising before the ICC*

The ASP and the Court can seek ICJ advisory opinions on contentious international law issues, therefore avoiding acrimony between the ICC and the State Parties. This approach would be particularly applicable in contentious cases such as the implementation of ICC arrest warrants against non-state party heads of state. As an example, in 2018, the AU Assembly resolved to seek,

---

13 Korea-Vietnam FTA (2015) Article 9.24; United Nations Commission on International Trade Law (UNCTAD) Working Group III (Investor-State Dispute Settlement Reform) Thirty-ninth session New York, 30 March–3 April 2020; Possible reform of investor-State dispute settlement (ISDS) Interpretation of investment treaties by treaty Parties, para 8.

14 Roberts (n 5) 194.

15 Ibid.

through the UN General Assembly (UNGA), an advisory opinion from the ICJ on the question of immunities of heads of State as it relates to Articles 27 and 98 and the obligations of States parties under international law.[16] This request arose after the PTC II had held in the *Jordan* case that Jordan failed to comply with its obligations by not arresting and surrendering Al Bashir to the Court while he was on Jordanian territory.[17] The request for the ICJ advisory was not followed to its conclusion, but the Court's decision led to a lot of tension between the Court and the AU, with some AU ASP members threatening to withdraw from the Statute.

As previously indicated, a similar situation has arisen in which Mongolia declined to arrest Putin in accordance with the ICC arrest warrant. Similarly, Hungary has given notice of intention to withdraw from the Rome Statute due to being required by the ICC to make submissions on why it failed to arrest Netanyahu. With Russia and Israel not being State parties to the Rome Statute, enforcing the arrests by the ICC State Parties could prove challenging while the question of head of State immunity remains unresolved conclusively. Since Russia and Israel are members of the UN but not party to the Rome Statute, this study proposes that an ICJ decision on the immunity or lack of it from arrest and prosecution of such heads of State for war crimes might be more persuasive to the parties.

The ICJ can be approached as an alternative court through the UNGA, and not as a superior court to the ICC, especially when there is tension or reluctance to implement an ICC decision based on an international law issue, such as the immunity question. The ICC could then refer to the ICJ decisions therefore maintaining a non-acrimonious working relationship between the ICC

16 AU Assembly, Decisions, Declarations and Resolution, 30th Ordinary Session, Assembly/AU/Dec.672(XXX) Jan 28–29 2018 Page 2, Para 5(i), (ii) ; AU Assembly, Decisions, Declarations, Resolution and Motions, 32nd Ordinary Session, Assembly/AU/Dec.738 (XXXII), 10-11 Feb 2019 paras 3 and 5; Note; The AU through Kenya wrote a Letter dated 9 July 2018 addressed to the Secretary-General seeking the inclusion of an item titled "Request for an advisory opinion of the ICJ on the consequences of legal obligations of States under different sources of international law with respect to immunities of Heads of State and Government and other senior officials in the provisional agenda of the seventy third session of the General Assembly under heading ' Promotion of justice and international law.'; Priya Pillai, 'The African Union, the International Criminal Court, and the International Court of Justice: At the Fault Lines of International Accountability (ASIL)' (2018) 22 Issue 10.

17 *ICC Decision under article 87(7) of the Rome Statute on the non-compliance by Jordan with the request by the Court for the arrest and surrender of Omar Al-Bashir, ICC-02/05-01/09-309 (PTC II), 11 December 2017.*

and States Parties and preventing withdrawal from the Statute by dissatisfied States.

The ICJ alternative option is becoming more plausible with the eminent adoption of the Convention on the Prevention and Punishment of Crimes Against Humanity.[18] The UN General Assembly in December 2024 adopted a resolution to conclude a legally binding draft treaty on the prevention and punishment of crimes against humanity.[19] If adopted, the Convention will provide a clear pathway for issues relating to the prosecution of war crimes and crimes against humanity, to be handled by the ICJ directly, besides the ICC.

In conclusion, ensuring the achievement of the Rome Statute's objectives requires that the States Parties and the ICC acknowledge their shared interpretive roles and find a working balance. Based on the recommendations above, it is suggested that instances where the States Parties and the ICC operate as interpretive rivals rather than as a team to fight impunity would be significantly minimized, if not eliminated.

---

18 (A/74/10) ILC Seventy-first session, 2019.

19 Official Records of the General Assembly, Seventy-ninth Session, Agenda item 80 (A/74/10). A/C.6/79/L.2/Rev.1 on 15 November 2024.

Bibliography

Journal Articles

Abel S Knottnerus, 'Emerging Voices: Extraordinary Exceptions at the ICC–What Happened with Rule 134 quater?' (*Opinio Juris*, 18 July 2014) <http://opiniojuris.org/2014/07/18/emerging-voices-extraordinary-exceptions-icc-happened-rule-134 quater/> accessed 25 April 2020.

Abel S Knottnerus, 'The International Criminal Court on Presence at Trial: The (In) Validity of Rule 134 quarter' [2014] ICD Brief 5.

Akande D and Dias TDS, 'How the UNSC and ASP Can Enhance Cooperation with the ICC, Policy Brief 124' (Institute for Security Studies (ISS) 2019).

Akande D and Tzanakopoulos A, 'Treaty Law and ICC Jurisdiction over the Crime of Aggression' (2018) 29 EJIL.

Alter K J, 'Agents or Trustees? International Courts in Their Political Context' (2008) 14 European Journal of International Relations 33.

Ambach P, 'The "Lessons Learnt" Process at the International Criminal Court – a Suitable Vehicle for Procedural Improvements?' [2016] ZIS <www.zis-online.com> accessed 20 October 2021

Arato J, 'Subsequent Practice and Evolutive Interpretation: Techniques of Treaty Interpretation over Time and Their Diverse Consequences' (2010) 9 No. 3 The Law & Practice of International Courts and Tribunals.

'Assembly of States Parties' (*International Criminal Court*) <https://www.icc-cpi.int/asp> accessed 13 February 2023.

Bailey S, 'Article 21(3) of the Rome Statute: A Plea for Clarity' (2014) 14 Int CLR.

Berman F, 'International Treaties and British Statutes' (2005) 26 Statute Law Review.

Cassese A, 'The Statute of the International Criminal Court: Some Preliminary Reflections' (1999) 10 EJIL 144.

CICC, 'ASP 14: ICC Independence under Threat at Annual Assembly' (27 November 2015) <https://ciccglobaljustice.wordpress.com/2015/11/27/asp-14-icc-independence-under-threat-at-annual-assembly/> accessed 25 April 2020

Clearwater D, 'When (and How) Will the Crime of Aggression Amendments Enter into Force? Interpreting the Rome Statute by Recognizing Participation in the Adoption of the Crime of Aggression Resolutions as "Subsequent Practice" under the VCLT' (2018) 16 JICJ.

Cogan J K, 'Competition and Control in International Adjudication' (2007) 48 Va J Int'l L 411.

Crema L, 'Subsequent Practice in Hassan v United Kingdom: When Things Seem to Go Wrong in the Life of a Living Instrument' [2015] (QIL) 3–22.

Cryer R, 'Royalism and the King: Article 21 of the Rome Statute and the Politics of Sources' (2009) 12 New Criminal Law Review: An International and Interdisciplinary Journal.

Davidson A, 'Human Rights Protection before the International Criminal Court: Assessing the Scope and Application of Article 21 (3) of the Rome Statute' (2016) 18 International Community Law Review.

Davidson C, 'How to Read International Criminal Law: Strict Construction and the Rome Statute of the International Criminal Court' (2017) 91 St. John's Law Review.

Ewing-Chow M and Losari J J, 'Which Is to Be the Master? Extra-Arbitral Interpretative Procedures for IIA s' [2015] Reshaping the Investor-State Dispute Settlement System 91.

FIDH, '14th ASP: States Should Refrain from Discussing Judicial Matters during the ASP' (*International Federation for Human Rights*, 19 November 2015) <https://www.fidh.org/en/issues/international-justice/14th-asp-states-should-refrain-from-discussing-judicial-matters> accessed 23 December 2022.

FIDH, 'The Independence of the International Criminal Court Must Be Enhanced' (*International Federation for Human Rights*, 27 November 2015) <https://www.fidh.org/en/issues/international-justice/international-criminal-court-icc/the-independence-of-the-international-criminal-court-must-be-enhanced> accessed 28 October 2022.

French D, 'Treaty Interpretation and the Incorporation of Extraneous Legal Rules' (2006) 55 ICLQ.

Gallant K S, 'The International Criminal Court in the System of States and International Organizations' (2003) 16 Leiden J Int Law.

Gaukrodger D, 'The Legal Framework Applicable to Joint Interpretive Agreements of Investment Treaties' (OECD 2016).

Gazzini T, 'Authentic (or Authoritative) Interpretation of Investment Treaties by the Treaty Parties' (*EJIL: Talk!*, 17 August 2020) <https://www.ejiltalk.org/authentic-or-authoritative-interpretation-of-investment-treaties-by-the-treaty-parties/> accessed 21 August 2020.

Ginsburg T, 'Bounded Discretion in International Judicial Lawmaking' (2004) 45 Va J Int'l L 631.

McGinley G P, 'Practice as a Guide to Treaty Interpretation' (1985) 9 Fletcher Forum.

Gourgourinis A, 'The Distinction between Interpretation and Application of Norms in International Adjudication' (2011) 2 Journal of International Dispute Settlement.

Grover L, 'Call to Arms: Fundamental Dilemmas Confronting the Interpretation of Crimes in the Rome Statute of the International Criminal Court' (2010) 21 Issue 3 EJIL.

Guilfoyle D, 'Lacking Conviction: Is the International Criminal Court Broken? An Organisational Failure Analysis' (2019) 20 Melb J Int'l L.

Guilfoyle D, 'Reforming the International Criminal Court: Is It Time for the Assembly of State Parties to Be the Adults in the Room?' (*EJIL: Talk!*, 8 May 2019) <https://www.ejiltalk.org/reforming-the-international-criminal-court-is-it-time-for-the-assembly-of-state-parties-to-be-the-adults-in-the-room/> accessed 25 November 2022

Hafner G and Binder C, 'The Interpretation of Article 21 (3) ICC Statute' (2006) 9 Austrian Review of International and European Law Online 161.

Helfer L R and Slaughter A-M, 'Why States Create International Tribunals: A Response to Professors Posner and Yoo' (2005) 93 Calif L Rev.

Heller K J, 'The Uncertain Legal Status of the Aggression Understandings' (2011) SSRN Scholarly Paper ID 1883351 <https://papers.ssrn.com/abstract=1883351> accessed 20 April 2022

Hochmayr G, 'Applicable Law in Practice and Theory Interpreting Article 21 of the ICC Statute' (2014) 12 JICJ.

Hudson M O, 'The Twenty-Sixth Year of the World Court' (1948) 42 American Journal of International Law <https://heinonline.org/HOL/P?h=hein.journals/ajil42&i=7> accessed 2 July 2021

Hunt D, 'The International Criminal Court: High Hopes, Creative Ambiguity, and an Unfortunate Mistrust in Judges' (2004) 2 JICJ.

Jacobs D, 'Positivism and International Criminal Law: The Principle of Legality as a Rule of Conflict of Theories' (2012) SSRN Scholarly Paper ID 2046311.

Jacobs D, 'Positivism and International Criminal Law: The Principle of Legality as a Rule of Conflict of Theories' [2012] SSRN Electronic Journal.

Jeffries J C, 'Legality, Vagueness, and the Construction of Penal Statutes' (1985) 71 Virginia Law Review 189.

Easterday J, 'ASP to Begin in The Hague' (*International Justice Monitor (a project of Open Society Justice Initiative*), 16 November 2015) <https://www.ijmonitor.org/2015/11/asp-to-begin-in-the-hague/> accessed 22 December 2022

Trahan J, 'The International Criminal Court's Assembly of States Parties Meetings: Challenges to the Work of the Court' (*Opinio Juris*, 7 December 2015) <http://opiniojuris.org/2015/12/06/the-international-criminal-courts-assembly-of-states-parties-meetings-challenges-to-the-work-of-the-court/> accessed 22 September 2022.

Jimenez D A A, 'The International Law Gaze: Subsequent Agreements and Subsequent Practice in the Interpretation of International Treaties'

Johnstone I, 'Treaty Interpretation: The Authority of Interpretive Communities' (1990) 12 Michigan Journal of International law.

Kadelbach S, 'International Law Commission and Role of Subsequent Practice as a Means of Interpretation under Articles 31 and 32 VCLT' (*QIL QDI*, 2018)

Kahan D M, 'Lenity and Federal Common Law Crimes' (1994) 1994 The Supreme Court Review, University of Chicago 345.

Gallagher K, FIDH Vice President, 'The Independence of the International Criminal Court Must Be Enhanced' (*International Federation for Human Rights*, 27 November 2015) <https://www.fidh.org/en/issues/international-justice/international-criminal-court-icc/the-independence-of-the-international-criminal-court-must-be-enhanced>

'Kenya Election: Uhuru Kenyatta Wins Presidency' *BBC News* (8 March 2013) <https://www.bbc.com/news/world-africa-21723488>

Kevin J Heller, 'Will the New RPE 134 Provisions Survive Judicial Review? (Probably Not.)' (*Opinio Juris*, 28 November 2013) <http://opiniojuris.org/2013/11/28/will-new-rpe-134-provisions-survive-judicial-review/>

Koskenniemi M and Leino P, 'Fragmentation of International Law? Postmodern Anxieties' (2002) 15 LJIL 553.

Kumar A, 'Is Article 21 of the Rome Statute Aiming for Legality or Hierarchy? A Dilemma' [2020] Vol 20 ISIL Year Book of International Humanitarian and Refugee Law 56.

Solan L M, 'Statutory Inflation and Institutional Choice' [2003] 44 Wm & Mary L Rev.

Lee S-W, 'States' Right to Interpret a Treaty and Whether It Should Be Binding in a Pending Case' (*Kluwer Arbitration Blog*, 3 August 2020) <http://arbitrationblog.kluwerarbitration.com/2020/08/03/states-right-to-interpret-a-treaty-and-whether-it-should-be-binding-in-a-pending-case/>

Legum B and Crevon-Tarassova A, 'VCLT Article 33: Interpretation of Treaties Authenticated in Two or More Languages' [2021] SSRN Scholarly Paper.

Verhoeven J, 'Article 21 of the Rome Statute and the Ambiguities of Applicable Law' (2002) 33 NYIL.

Marotti L, 'Masters of Their (Investment) Treaties? States Mutual Treaty Actions between the Law of Treaties and the Integrity of Arbitration' (*Kluwer Arbitration Blog*, 5 March 2022) <http://arbitrationblog.kluwerarbitration.com/2022/03/05/masters-of-their-investment-treaties-states-mutual-treaty-actions-between-the-la w-of-treaties-and-the-integrity-of-arbitration/>

McGinley G P, 'Practice as a Guide to Treaty Interpretation' (1985) 9 Fletcher Forum.

Mimoza Sadushaj and others, 'Interpretation and Application of Article 98 of the Rome Statute' (2017) Vol. 6 No. 1 (2017) Academic Journal of Interdisciplinary St udies.

Mitchell A D and Heaton D, 'The Inherent Jurisdiction of WTO Tribunals: The Select Application of Public International Law Required by the Judicial Function' (2009) 31 Mich J Int' L 1559.

Moloo R, 'When Actions Speak Louder than Words: The Relevance of Subsequent Party Conduct to Treaty Interpretation' (2013) 31 Berkeley Journal of International Law.

Morse O, 'Schools of Approach to the Interpretation of Treaties' 9 Issue 1 Catholic University Law Review 17.

Nolte G, 'First Report on Subsequent Agreements and Subsequent Practice in Relation to Treaty Interpretation ILC Sixty-Fifth Session (A/CN.4/660) 2013'

Nolte G, 'ILC Second Report on Subsequent Agreements and Subsequent Practice in Relation to the Interpretation of Treaties 66th Session (26 March 2014)'

O'Neill T, 'Dispute Settlement under the Rome Statute of the International Criminal Court: Article 119 and the Possible Role of the International Court of Justice' (2006) 5 Chinese Journal of International Law 67.

Pasquino P, 'Prolegomena to a Theory of Judicial Power: The Concept of Judicial Independence in Theory and History' (2003) 2 Law and Practice of International Courts and Tribunals 11.

Pohl J and Gordon K, 'Investment Treaties over Time - Treaty Practice and Interpretation in a Changing World' [2015] OECD Working Papers on International Investment.

Pillai P, 'The African Union, the International Criminal Court, and the International Court of Justice: At the Fault Lines of International Accountability (ASIL)' (2018) 22 Issue 10.

Raab D and Bevers H, 'The International Criminal Court and the Separation of Powers' (2006) 3 International Organizations Law Review 93.

'Recent International Criminal Court Developments on Kenya, South Africa' (*Human Rights Watch*, 27 January 2016)

Roberts A, 'Power and Persuasion in Investment Treaty Interpretation: The Dual Role of States, Vol 104, Issue 2' [2010] AJIL.

Roberts A, 'Subsequent Agreements and Practice: The Battle Over Interpretive Power' [2013] SSRN Scholarly Paper.

Roberts A, 'Recalibrating Interpretive Authority' (Columbia FDI Perspectives 2014) Research Report 113.

Roberts A, 'State-to-State Investment Treaty Arbitration: A Hybrid Theory of Interdependent Rights and Shared Interpretive Authority' (2014) 55 Harvard International Law Journal.

Sadat L N and Jolly J M, 'Seven Canons of ICC Treaty Interpretation: Making Sense of Article 25's Rorschach Blot' (2014) 27 LJIL.

Sands P, Mackenzie R and McLachlan C, 'The Burgh House Principles on the Independence of the International Judiciary' (2005) 4 The Law & Practice of International Courts and Tribunals 247.

Schabas William, 'The Damp Squib of Third Party Intervention in Ukraine v. Russia' (*EJIL: Talk!*, 5 February 2024)

Sharma K, 'The Curious Case of Rule 165 of the Rules of Procedure and Evidence: The Effect of Control Exercised by the Assembly of States Parties over the International Criminal Court' (2020) 20 (2) International Criminal Law Review 285.

Sheppard D, 'The International Criminal Court and "Internationally Recognized Human Rights": Understanding Article 21(3) of the Rome Statute' (2010) 10 Int CLR.

Steinberg R H, 'Judicial Lawmaking at the WTO: Discursive, Constitutional, and Political Constraints' (2004) 98 AJIL 247.

'Sub Judice' <https://www.parliament.uk/site-information/glossary/sub-judice/> accessed 29 July 2023

'The International Criminal Court's Assembly of States Parties Meetings: Challenges to the Work of the Court' (*Opinio Juris*, 7 December 2015) <http://opiniojuris.org/2015/12/06/the-international-criminal-courts-assembly-of-states-parties-meetings-challenges-to-the-work-of-the-court/>

Hansen T O, 'Caressing the Big Fish? A Critique of ICC Trial Chamber V(a)'s Decision to Grant Ruto's Request for Excusal from Continuous Presence at Trial' (2013) 22, No 1 Cardozo Journal of International and Comparative Law (JICL)

Titi C, 'The Timing of Treaty Party Interpretations A Treaty-Design Perspective on Webinar on Treaty Parties' Involvement and Control Mechanisms in Treaty Interpretation, UNCITRAL WG III' (4 June 2020)

Titi C, 'The Timing of Treaty Party Interpretations' (*EJIL: Talk!*, 18 August 2020) <https://www.ejiltalk.org/the-timing-of-treaty-party-interpretations/>

Tladi D 'Is the International Law Commission Elevating Subsequent Agreements and Subsequent Practice?' (*EJIL: Talk!*, 30 August 2018) <https://www.ejiltalk.org/is-the-international-law-commission-elevating-subsequent-agreements-and-subsequent-practice/>

Ton Nu Thanh Binh, 'Article 63 Intervention Before the International Court of Justice: New Developments and the Way Forward' (*Opinio Juris*, 26 July 2024)

UNCTAD, 'UNCTAD, Interpretation of International Investment Agreements (IIA), What States Can Do-Issues Note No. 3 December 2011' <https://unctad.org/en/pages/publications/Intl-Investment-Agreements---Issues-Note.aspx>

Van Schaack B, 'Crimen Sine Lege: Judicial Lawmaking at the Intersection of Law and Morals' (2008) 97 Georgetown Law Journal 119.

Voeten E, 'International Judicial Independence' [2011] SSRN Electronic Journal.

Waibel M, 'Demystifying the Art of Interpretation' (2011) 22 European Journal of International Law 571.

Weisburd A M, 'The International Court of Justice and the Concept of State Practice' (2009) 31 U Pa J Int'l L.

Wessel J, 'Judicial Policy-Making at the International Criminal Court: An Institutional Guide to Analyzing International Adjudication' (2005) 44 Columbia Journal of Transnational Law 377.

Wigard K, Pomson O and McIntyre J, 'Keeping Score: An Empirical Analysis of the Interventions in Ukraine v Russia' (2023) 14 Journal of International Dispute Settlement 305, 306.

Wong M S, 'The Activation of the International Criminal Court's Jurisdiction over the Crime of Aggression: International Institutional Law and Dispute Settlement Perspectives' (2020) 22 International Community Law Review 197.

Woolaver H and Palmer E, 'Challenges to the Independence of the International Criminal Court from the Assembly of States Parties' (2017) 15 JICJ.

Young R, 'Internationally Recognized Human Rights' before the International Criminal Court' (2011) 60 The International and Comparative Law Quarterly.

Yuwen F, 'Revisiting E CtHR Interpretation of the ECHR: Living Up to a Living Instrument' TOAEP FICHL Policy Brief Series No. 65 (2016)

Books and Book Chapters

Akande D, 'Sources of International Criminal Law' in Antonio Cassese Antonio (ed), *The Oxford Companion to International Criminal Justice* (OUP Oxford 2009)

Ambach P, 'A Look towards the Future-The ICC and "Lessons Learnt" in Carsten Stahn (ed), *The Law and Practice of the International Criminal Court* (Oxford University Press 2015)

Ambach P and Rao S R, 'Article 112, Assembly of States Parties' in Otto Triffterer and Kai Ambos (eds), *Commentary on the Rome Statute of the International Criminal Court, Observers' Notes, Article by Article* (Beck/Hart 2016)

Arsanjani M H, 'The Rome Statute of the International Criminal Court' (1999) 93 AJIL 22.

Ashworth A and Horder J, *Principles of Criminal Law* (Oxford University Press 2013)

Aust A, *Handbook of International Law* (Cambridge University Press 2010)

Berner K, *Subsequent Agreements and Subsequent Practice in Domestic Courts* (Springer 2017)

Bitti G, 'Article 21 and the Hierarchy of Sources of Law before the ICC' in Carsten Stahn (ed), *The Law and Practice of the International Criminal Court* (Oxford University Press 2015)

Bitti G, 'Article 21 of the Statute of the International Criminal Court and the Treatment of Sources of Law in the Jurisprudence of the ICC' in Carsten Stahn (ed), *The Emerging Practice of the International Criminal Court* (Brill Nijhoff 2009)

Bjorge E, *The Evolutionary Interpretation of Treaties* (Oxford University Press 2014)

Broomhall B, 'Article 51 Rules of Procedure and Evidence' in O Triffterer and K Ambos (eds), *Commentary on the Rome Statute of the International Criminal Court, Observers' Notes, Article by Article* (Third Edition, C H Beck, Hart Nomos, Munich 2016)

Broomhall B, 'Article 22, Nullum Crimen Sine Lege' in Otto Triffterer and Kai Ambos (eds), *Commentary on the Rome Statute of the ICC Observers' Notes, Article by Article* (Beck/Hart 2016)

Buga I, *Modification of Treaties by Subsequent Practice* (1st edition, OUP Oxford 2018)

Chang-fa Lo, *Treaty Interpretation Under the Vienna Convention on the Law of Treaties: A New Round of Codification* (Springer Singapore 2017)

Clark R S, 'Article 119; Settlement of Disputes' in Otto Triffterer and Kai Ambos (eds), *Commentary on the Rome Statute of the International Criminal Court* (3rd edn, Beck/Hart 2016)

Crawford J, 'A Consensualist Interpretation of Article 31 (3) of the Vienna Convention on the Law of Treaties' in Georg Nolte (ed), *Treaties and Subsequent Practice*, vol 29 (Oxford University Press 2013)

Crawford J and McIntyre J, 'The Independence and Impartiality of the "International Judiciary" in Shimon Shetreet and Christopher Forsyth (eds), *The Culture of Judicial Independence: Conceptual Foundations and Practical Challenges* (Brill Nijhoff 2012)

Crema L, 'Subsequent Agreements and Subsequent Practice within and Outside the Vienna Convention in Treaties and Subsequent Practice.' in Georg Nolte (ed) (Oxford University Press 2013)

Cryer R, 'The International Criminal Court and Its Relationship to Non-Party States' in G Sluiter & C Stahn (ed), *The Emerging Practice of the International Criminal Court* (Brill Nijhoff 2009)

Donat-Cattin D, 'Decision-Making in the International Criminal Court: Functions of the Assembly of States Parties and Independence of the Court's Judicial Organs' in Flavia Lattanzi and William Schabas (eds), *Essays on the Rome Statute of the International Criminal Court* (© Editrice il Sirente 1999)

deGuzman M M, 'Article 21, Applicable Law in Kai Ambos, Otto Triffterer (Ed)', *The Rome Statute of the International Criminal Court, A Commentary* (3rd edn, Nomos 2016)

Dörr O, 'Article 31, General Rule of Interpretation, 2018' in Oliver Dörr and Kirsten Schmalenbach (eds), *Vienna Convention on the Law of Treaties: A Commentary* (Springer 2018)

Dörr O and Schmalenbach K (eds), *Vienna Convention on the Law of Treaties: A Commentary* (Springer-Verlag 2012)

Du Plessis M and Gevers C, 'The Role of the Assembly of States Parties for the ICC' in Richard H Steinberg (ed), *Contemporary Issues Facing the International Criminal Court* (Brill Nijhoff 2016)

Gardiner R, *Treaty Interpretation 2015* (2nd edn, Oxford University Press 2015)

Gardiner R K, *Treaty Interpretation 2008* (Oxford University Press 2008)

Gazzini T, 'The Role of States in the Interpretation of Investment Treaties', *Interpretation of International Investment Treaties*, vol 14 (Bloomsbury Publishing 2016)

Grover L, *Interpreting Crimes in the Rome Statute of the International Criminal Court* (Cambridge University Press 2014)

Ishikawa T, 'Keeping Interpretation in Investment Treaty Arbitration "on Track": The Role of State Parties' in Jean E Kalicki and Anna Joubin-Bret (ed), *Reshaping the Investor-State Dispute Settlement System* (Brill Nijhoff 2015)

Jacobs D, 'International Criminal Law' in Jean D'Aspremont and Kammerhofer Jörg (eds), *International Legal Positivism in a Post-Modern World* (Cambridge University Press 2014)

Kohen M G, 'Keeping Subsequent Agreements and Practice in Their Right Limits', *Nolte G (ed) Treaties and Subsequent practice* (Oxford University Press 2013)

Kolb R, *The International Court of Justice* (Bloomsbury Publishing 2013)

Kolb R, *The Law of Treaties* (Edward Elgar Publishing 2016)

League of Nations Advisory Committee of Jurists for the Establishment of a Permanent Court of International Justice, *Procès-verbaux Des Séances Du Comité, 16 Juin-24 Juillet 1920, Avec Annexes* (The Lawbook Exchange, Ltd 2006)

Lind C, 'Article 22', *Commentary on the Law of the International Criminal Court* (Mark Klamberg (ed) FICHL 2017)

Linderfalk U, *On the Interpretation of Treaties: The Modern International Law as Expressed in the 1969 Vienna Convention on the Law of Treaties* (Springer Netherlands 2007)

Lo C-F, *Treaty Interpretation Under the Vienna Convention on the Law of Treaties: A New Round of Codification* (Springer Singapore 2017)

Lord McNair, *The Law of Treaties* (Oxford University Press 1986)

Methymaki E and Tzanakopoulos A, 'Masters of Puppets? Reassertion of Control Through Joint Investment Treaty Interpretation' in Andreas Culick (ed), *Reasserting of Control over the Investment Treaty Regime* (Cambridge University Press 2016)

Miron A and Chinkin C, 'Commentary of Article 63 of the Statute of the ICJ' in Andreas Zimmermann and others (eds), *The Statute of the International Court of Justice: A Commentary (3rd Edition)* (Oxford University Press 2019)

Heikkila M, 'Article 21' in Mark Klamberg (ed), *Commentary on the law of the International Criminal Court editor* (Torkel Opsahl Academic Publisher 2017)

Murphy S D, 'The Relevance of Subsequent Agreement and Subsequent Practice for the Interpretation of Treaties' in Georg Nolte (ed), *Treaties and Subsequent Practice*, vol 82 (Oxford University Press 2013)

Nolte G, 'Second Report, Jurisprudence under Special Regimes Relating to Subsequent Agreements and Subsequent Practice' in Nolte G (ed), *Treaties and Subsequent Practice* (Oxford University Press, 2013)

Nolte G, *Treaties and Subsequent Practice* (OUP Oxford 2013)

Nolte G, 'Treaties and Their Practice: Symptoms of Their Rise or Decline', *Treaties and their Practice* (Brill Nijhoff 2019)

Nolte G, 'Jurisprudence of the ICJ and Arbitral Tribunals of Ad Hoc Jurisdiction Relating to Subsequent Agreements and Subsequent Practice: Introductory Report for the ILC Study Group on Treaties over Time', *Treaties and Subsequent Practice* (Oxford University Press 2013)

O'Donohue J, 'The ICC and the ASP' in Stahn Carsten (ed), *The Law and Practice of the International Criminal Court* (Oxford University Press 2015)

Pellet A, 'Applicable Law' in A Cassese et al. (ed), *The Rome Statute of the ICC: A Commentary*, vol 2 (Oxford University Press 2002)

Pikis G M, *The Rome Statute for the International Criminal Court: Analysis of the Statute, the Rules of Procedure and Evidence, the Regulations of the Court and Supplementary Instruments* (Brill Nijhoff 2010)

Pound R, *The Spirit of the Common Law* (Marshall Jones Company 1921)

Powderly J, 'The Rome Statute and the Attempted Corseting of the Interpretative Judicial Function: Reflections on Sources of Law and Interpretative Technique' in Carsten Stahn (ed), *The Law and Practice of the International Criminal Court* (Oxford University Press 2015)

Powderly J, *Judges and the Making of International Criminal Law* (Brill Nijhoff 2020)

Regan D H, 'Sources of International Trade Law: Understanding What the Vienna Convention Says about Identifying and Using 'Sources for Treaty Interpretation' in S Besson and J d'Aspremont (ed), *The Oxford Handbook of the Sources of International Law* (Oxford University Press, USA 2018)

Reuter P, *Introduction to the Law of Treaties* (Routledge 1995)

Ruiz Fabri H, 'Subsequent Practice, Domestic Separation of Powers, and Concerns of Legitimacy', *Treaties and subsequent Practice* (Oxford University Press 2013)

Schabas W A, *The International Criminal Court; A Commentary on the Rome Statute 2010* (2nd edn, Oxford University Press 2010)

Schabas W A, *An Introduction to the International Criminal Court, 2017* (5th edn, Cambridge University Press 2017)

Schabas W A, *An Introduction to the International Criminal Court 2020* (6th edn, Cambridge University Press 2020)

Schabas W A, 'Strict Construction and the Rome Statute' in S Dewulf (ed), *la [CVDW]: Liber Amicorum Chris Van den Wyngaert* (Maklu 2017)

Schermers H G, Blokker N M, *International Institutional Law* (5th edn, Brill 2011)

Schreuer C, 'Diversity and Harmonization of Treaty Interpretation In Investment Arbitration', *Treaty Interpretation and the Vienna Convention on the Law of Treaties: 30 Years on* (Brill|Nijhoff 2010)

Seibert-Fohr A, 'The Effect of Subsequent Practice on the European Convention on Human Rights: Considerations from a General International Law Perspective', *The European Convention on Human Rights and General International Law* (Oxford University Press 2018)

Sinclair I M, *The Vienna Convention on the Law of Treaties* (2nd ed, Manchester University Press 1984).

Sluiter G, 'Human Rights Protection in the ICC Pre-Trial Phase' in G Sluiter and C Stahn (eds), *The Emerging Practice of the International Criminal Court* (Martinus Nijhoff 2009)

Sorel M and Boré Eveno V, 'Article 31, General Rule of Interpretation' in Olivier Corten; Pierre Klein (ed), *The Vienna Convention on the Law of Treaties: A Commentary* (Oxford University Press 2011)

Suhr V V, *Rainbow Jurisdiction at the International Criminal Court: Protection of Sexual and Gender Minorities Under the Rome Statute* (Springer Nature 2021)

Gazzini T, 'Object and Purpose', *Interpretation of International Investment Treaties* (Oxford Hart Publishing 2016)

Gazzini T, 'Ordinary Meaning of the Terms of the Treaty', *Interpretation of International Investment Treaties* (Oxford Hart Publishing 2016)

Gazzini T, 'Subsequent Agreements and Subsequent Practice', *Interpretation of International Investment Treaties* (Oxford Hart Publishing 2016)

Gazzini T, 'Supplementary Means', *Interpretation of International Investment Treaties* (Oxford Hart Publishing 2016)

Tladi D, 'Presence of the Accused: Right or Duty? The Art of Interpretation in a Tense Political Climate' in Bantekas Ilias Jalloh Charles C (ed), *The International Criminal Court and Africa* (Oxford University Press 2017)

Vagias M, *The Territorial Jurisdiction of the International Criminal Court* (Cambridge University Press 2014)

Van Harten G, *Investment Treaty Arbitration and Public Law* (Oxford University Press 2007)

Villiger M E, *Commentary on the 1969 Vienna Convention on the Law of Treaties* (Brill 2009)

Weeramantry J R, *Treaty Interpretation in Investment Arbitration* (Oxford University Press 2012)

Declarations/Resolutions of the ASP and the AU

African Union, 'Decision on the Report of the Second Meeting of States Parties to the Rome Statute of the International Criminal Court (ICC),' Doc. Assembly/AU/8 (XIV), January 2010.

Amendments to the Rule 100, 68, 134 *bis* and 134 *ter* of the Rules of Procedure and Evidence, ICC-ASP/12/Res.7, 27 November 2013.

Amendments to the Rules of Procedure and Evidence, ICC-ASP/12/Res 7, (Adopted at the Twelfth Plenary Meeting of the ASP by consensus), 27 November 2013.

ASP Official Records ICC-ASP/14/20 (14th session) 18–26 November 2015, Vol 1.

AU Assembly, Decisions, Declarations and Resolution, 30th Ordinary Session, Assembly/AU/Dec.672(XXX) Jan 28–29 2018.

AU Assembly, Decisions, Declarations, Resolution and Motions, 32nd Ordinary Session, Assembly/AU/Dec.738 (XXXII), 10–11 Feb 2019.

ICC-ASP/9/Res.2, 10 December 2010, Establishment of a Study Group on Governance (Fifth Plenary Meeting of the ASP)

Establishment of an Independent Oversight Mechanism, ICC-ASP/8/Res.1, November 26, 2009.

Kampala Amendments on the Crime of Aggression (Kampala Amendments), Resolution RC/Res. 6, 11 June 2010, available at https://asp.icc-cpi.int/iccdocs/asp_docs/Resolutions/RC-Res.6-ENG.

New York Resolution, ICC-ASP/16/Res.5, Activation of the jurisdiction of the Court over the Crime of Aggression, 14 December 2017.

RC/Res.6, Adopted at the 13th plenary meeting, on 11 June 2010, by consensus.

Resolution ICC-ASP/10/Res.5, 21 December 2011, Strengthening the International Criminal Court and the Assembly of States Parties.

Resolution ICC-ASP/17/Res.5, 12 December 2018.

Resolution ICC-ASP/19/Res.6, 16 December 2020.

Resolution ICC-ASP/20/Res.5, 9 December 2021.

Resolution ICC-ASP/12/ RES 6, Independent Oversight Mechanism (IOM) 27 November2013 ICC-ASP /12/20, Annex Operation Mandate of the IOM.

International Criminal Court/International Tribunals Reports/Relevant Documents

ASP Special segment as requested by the African Union: "Indictment of sitting Heads of State and Government and its consequences on peace and stability and reconciliation", Informal Summary by the Moderator', ICC-ASP/12/61, 27 November 2013.

'Comments from the United States on the ILC's Draft Conclusions on Subsequent Agreements and Subsequent Practice in Relation to the Interpretation of Treaties as Adopted by the Commission in 2016 on First Reading'

Fatou Bensouda, 'Statement by the ICC Prosecutor at the opening of the 14th Session of the Assembly of States Parties to the Rome Statute of the International Criminal Court' (*International Criminal Court*, 18 November 2015) <http://www.icc-cpi.int/fr/news/statement-icc-prosecutor-opening-14th-session-assembly-states-parties-rome-statute>

FIDH, Position Paper, Ninth session of the ICC Assembly of States Parties (2010)

FIDH, 'FIDH Recommendations to the 14th Assembly of States Parties to the Statute of the ICC' (*International Federation for Human Rights*, 10 November 2015) <https://

www.fidh.org/en/issues/international-justice/fidh-recommendations-to-the-14th-assembly-of-states-parties-to-the>

IBA, 'Strengthening the International Criminal Court and the Rome Statute System: A Guide for States Parties, October 2021'

'ICC Presents Annual Report to the ASP: Strong Cooperation, Adequate Resources and Preserving Judicial Independence Are Crucial Needs' (*International Criminal Court*, 18 November 2015) <https://www.icc-cpi.int/news/icc-presents-annual-report-asp-strong-cooperation-adequate-resources-and-preserving-judicial>

ICC-ASP/13/34/Rev.2, 5 December 2014 Annex 1 Note verbale from Kenya no. 561/14, dated 3 November 2014, addressed to the President of the Assembly, Ambassador Tiina Intelmann.

ICC-ASP/13/34/Rev.2, 5 December 2014 Letter from the Principals of the Court, dated 7 November 2014, addressed to the President of the Assembly, Ambassador Tiina Intelmann, with regard to the Note verbale from Kenya no. 561/14.

ICC-ASP/14/35, Fourteenth session, Request by South Africa for the inclusion of a supplementary item in the agenda of the fourteenth session of the Assembly titled 'Application and Implementation of Article 97 and Article 98 of the Rome Statute, 27 October 2015, Annex 1.

ICC-01/18-433, Transmission of Hungary's submission in response to Pre-Trial Chamber I's "Invitation to Hungary to provide submissions for the purposes of proceedings under article 87(7) of the Rome Statute", 16 April 2025, ICC-01/18-421, 23 May 2025.

ILC, 'Draft Conclusions on Subsequent Agreements and Subsequent Practice in Relation to the Interpretation of Treaties, Seventieth Session, (A/73/10) 2018'

ILC, 'Guide to Practice on Reservations to Treaties, Report of the ILC on the Work of Its Sixty-Third Session, 2011, Vol II, A/66/10'

Independent Expert Review of the International Criminal Court and the Rome Statute System Final Report, 30 September 2020.

International Law Commission, UN Doc. A/CN.4/491 and Add.1–6, Third report on reservations to treaties, by Mr. Alain Pellet, Special Rapporteur, YBIL (1998) Vol. 2, Part 1.

Nolte G, 'First Report on Subsequent Agreements and Subsequent Practice in Relation to Treaty Interpretation ILC Sixty-Fifth Session (A/CN.4/660) 2013'

Opinion 1/17 of the Court of Justice of the European Union (CJEU), 30 April 2019.

Recommendations of the Ministerial Meeting on the Rome Statute of the International Criminal Court, November 6, 2009, Addis Ababa Min/ICC/Legal/Rpt (11).

Report of the Bureau on the Independent Oversight Mechanism, ICC-ASP/9/31, November 19, 2010.

Report of the Bureau on the Study Group on Governance, Eleventh session, ICC-ASP/11/31, 23 October 2012 para 1 (Report of the Bureau on SGG)

Report of the Conference of the Parties to the Basel Convention on the Control of Transboundary Movements of Hazardous Wastes and Their Disposal on its tenth meeting (Cartagena, Colombia, 17–21 October 2011), UNEP/CHW.10/28

Standard Minimum Rules for the Treatment of Prisoners and the United Nations Body of Principles for the Protection of All Persons Under Any Form of Detention or Imprisonment.

Submission from the Government of Costa Rica (A/CN.9/WG.III/WP.164, Annex II).

Submission from the Government of Thailand (A/CN.9/WG.III/WP.162)

UNCTAD, 'UNCTAD, Interpretation of International Investment Agreements (IIA), What States Can Do-Issues Note No. 3 December 2011'

UNCTAD Working Group III (Investor-State Dispute Settlement Reform) Thirty-ninth session New York, 30 March–3 April 2020; Possible reform of investor-State dispute settlement (ISDS) Interpretation of investment treaties by treaty Parties.

Waldock, 'Third Report on the Law of Treaties', 2 ILC Yearbook (1964)

'Yearbook of the ILC 1964, Vol II, A/CN.4/SER.A/1964/ADD.1'

'Yearbook of the ILC 1966 Volume II'

'Yearbook of the ILC 1966 Volume I Part II'

'Yearbook of the ILC 1966 Volume II'

Treaties and Free Trade Agreements (FTA)

Agreement between USA-Can-Mexico (now USMCA),1 July 2020, Articles 30.1, 30.2 (e&f) formerly NAFTA.

Agreement between Canada and [...] for the Promotion and Protection of Investments (Model Canadian FIPA) (2004)ASEAN-Australia-New Zealand FTA.

ASEAN Comprehensive Investment Agreement (2009)BIT between the United Kingdom and Mexico.

Canada-Czech Republic BIT (2009)

Comprehensive Economic and Free Trade Agreement (CETA)

China-Mexico BIT, 2008.

Dominican Republic-Central America-United States FTA (2004) (CAFTA-DR)

Dutch Model Bilateral Investment Treaty (BIT) 22 March 2019.

Korea-Vietnam FTA.

NAFTA USA-Can-Mexico, CH 11 1992.

NAFTA USA-Can-Mexico, 2001.

North American FTA USA-Canada-Mexico, Dec. 17 1992, Article 1131, 2001.

Norwegian Model BIT 2015.

United States – Korea FTA, (2019)

US Model BIT (2004)

The Netherlands Model BIT (2019)
US Model BIT (2004)

Conventions and Statutes

Convention on the Prevention and Punishment of the Crime of Genocide, Art. IX Dec. 9, 1948.
European Convention on Human Rights (ECHR)
Statute of the International Court of Justice (ICJ) UNSC Res. 808 of 22 February 1993.
The Rome Statute of the International Criminal Court UN Doc. 2187 UNTS 90, entered into force July 1, 2002.
UN Vienna Convention on the Law of Treaties, 23 May 1969, UN Treaty Series, Vol 1155.

Cases and Awards

Appellate Body Report WTO, European Communities–Customs Classification of Frozen Boneless Chicken Cuts, WT/DS269/AB/R, WT/DS286/AB/R, WT/DS269/AB/R/Corr1, WT/DS286/AB/R/Corr1 (adopted 12 Sept 2005)
Appellate Body Report, WTO, United States–Countervailing Duties on Certain Corrosion-Resistant Carbon Steel Flat Products from Germany, WT/DS213/AB/R, WT/DS213/AB/R/Corr1 (adopted 19 Dec 2002)
Application of the International Convention on the Elimination of All Forms of Racial Discrimination (Qatar v United Arab Emirates), Preliminary Objections, Judgment, ICJ Reports 2021.
Arbitral Award of 31 July 1989 (Guinea-Bissau v Senegal), Judgment ICJ Rep 1991.
Asian Agricultural Products Ltd AAPL v Sri Lanka, ICSID ARB/87/3 Final Award 27 June 1990.
Assange (Appellant) v The Swedish Prosecution Authority (Respondent), Judgment, Easter Term (2012) UKSC 22 On appeal from (2011) EWHC Admin 2849 118.
Case concerning Oil Platforms (Islamic Republic of Iran versus United States of America 2003 (ICJ)
Case Concerning Sovereignty over Palau Ligitan and Palau Sipidan (Indonesia/Malaysia) Judgment of 17 December 2002 (ICJ)
Case concerning the Temple of Preah Vihear (Cambodia v Thailand), Merits, Judgment of 15 June 1962, ICJ Reports 1962.
Certain Expenses of the UN (Article 17(2) of the Charter) Advisory Opinion of 20 July 1962 (ICJ)

Chile-Price Band System and Safeguard Measures Relating to Certain Agricultural Products, WTO Panel Report WT/DS207/R, 3 May 2002.

Competence of the General Assembly for the Admission of a State to the United Nations, Advisory Opinion, ICJ Rep 1950.

Concurring and Separate Opinion of Judge Antoine Kesia-MBE Mindua, Decision Pursuant to Article 15 of the Rome Statute on the Authorisation of an Investigation into the Situation in the Islamic Republic of Afghanistan, ICC-02/17-33-Anx-Corr (PTC II) 31 May 2019.

Decision Adjourning the Hearing pursuant to Article 61(7)(C)(ii) of the Rome Statute, The Prosecutor v Jean-Pierre Bemba Gombo, ICC-01/05-01/08-388(PTC III) 3 March 2009.

Decision Establishing General Principles Governing Applications to Restrict Disclosure pursuant to Rule 81 (2) and (4) of the Rules of Procedure and Evidence, Prosecutor v Thomas Lubanga Dyilo, ICC-01/04-01/06, 19 May 2006.

Decision on Application for Leave to Appeal by the Defence of Mathieu Ngudjolo Chui against the Decision on Joinder, Prosecutor v Ngudjolo Chui, ICC-01/04-01/07-384 (PTC 1) 9 April 2008.

Decision on Confirmation of Charges, Prosecutor v Germain Katanga and Mathieu Ngudjolo, ICC-01/04–01/07–717 (PTC 1) 30 September 2008.

Decision on Defence Applications for Judgments of Acquittal, The Prosecutor v William Samoei Ruto and Joshua Arap Sang, (TrC V A), ICC-01/09-01/11, 5 April 2016.

Decision on Israel's challenge to the jurisdiction of the Court pursuant to Article 19(2) of the Rome Statute, ICC-01/18–374 (PTC 1) 21 November 2024.

Decision on Joinder of the cases against Germaine Katanga and Mathieu Ngudjolo Chui, ICC 01/04–01/07–257 (PTC 1)10 March 2008 (PTC I)

Decision on Kilolo Defence Motion for Inadmissibility of Material, Prosecutor v Bemba, Kilolo et al, ICC-01/05–01/13 (TC VIII) 16 September 2015.

Decision on Mr Ruto's Request for Excusal from Continuous Presence at Trial, The Prosecutor v William Samoei Ruto and Joshua Arap Sang, ICC-01/09–01/11–777, 18 June 2013, Trial Chamber V(A).

Decision on Prosecution's Request Relating to Three Forensic Reports, Prosecutor v Katanga and Ngudjolo Chui, ICC-01/04–01/07 (TC 11) 25 March 2009.

Decision on the admissibility of the Appeal by Thomas Lubanga Dyilo against the decision of PTC I entitled "Decison Sur La Confirmation des charges' of 29/1/2007, ICC-01/04–01/06 OA8, 13 June 2007 (ICC, Appeal's Chamber).

Decision on the appeals of William Samoei Ruto and Joshua Arap Sang against the decision of Pre-Trial Chamber II of 23 January 2012 entitled 'Decision on the Confirmation of Charges Pursuant to Article 61(7) (a) and (b) of the Rome Statute' (Appeals Chamber), ICC-01/09–01/11–414, 24 May 2012 (ICC)

Decision on the Application for the Interim release of Detained Witnesses DRC-D02 -P-0236, DRC-D02-P-0228 and DRC-D02-P-0350, Prosecutor vs Germain Katanga (TRC 11) 1 October 2013.

Decision on the Powers of the Pre-Trial Chamber to Review Proprio Motu the Pretrial Detention of Germain Katanga, ICC-01/04–01/07–330 (PTC 1)19 March 2008.

Decision on the Practices of Witness Familiarization and Witness Proofing, Prosecutor v Thomas Lubanga Dyilo, ICC-01/04–01/06 (PTC 1) 8 November 2006.

Decision on the 'Prosecution request pursuant to Article 19(3) for a ruling on the Court's territorial jurisdiction in Palestine, (PTC 1) ICC-01/18, 5 February 2021.

Decision on the Prosecution's Application for a Warrant of Arrest against Omar Hassan Ahmad Al Bashir, ICC-02/05–01/09 (PTC 1) 4 March 2009.

Decision on the Prosecutor's Application for Warrants of Arrest, Article 58 against Thomas Lubanga Dyilo and Mr Bosco Ntaganda, ICC-01/04–02/06–20-Anx2 69 (ICC PTC 1)

Decision on the Requests for Leave to Submit Observations under Rule 103 of the Rules of Procedure and Evidence, The Prosecutor v William Samoei Ruto and Joshua Arap Sang, ICC-01/09–01/11–942 (Appeal's Chamber) 13 September 2013.

Decision on the Set of Procedural Rights Attached to Procedural Status of Victim at the Pre-Trial Stage of the Case, The Prosecutor v Germain Katanga and Mathieu Ngudjolo Chui, ICC-01/04–01/07 (PTC 1)13 May 2008.

Decision Pursuant to Article 15 of the Rome Statute on the Authorization of an Investigation into the Situation in the Republic of Kenya, ICC-01/09 (PTC II), 31 March 2010.

Decision Pursuant to Article 61(7)(a) and (b) of the Rome Statute on the Charges of the Prosecutor Against Jean-Pierre Bemba Gombo, ICC-01/05–01/08 (PTC 11) 15 June 2009.

Defence Request for Conditional Excusal from Continuous Presence at Trial, The Prosecutor v Uhuru Muigai Kenyatta, ICC-01/09–02/11(TrC V B) 23 Sep 2013.

Defence request pursuant to Article 63(1) of the Rome Statute and Rule 134 quater of the Rules of Procedure and Evidence to excuse Mr William Samoei Ruto from attendance at trial, ICC-01/09–01/11–1124, 16 December 2013.

Dispute between Argentina and Chile concerning the Beagle Channel, RIAA 18 February 1977, Volume XXI.

Dispute regarding Navigational and Related rights (Costa Rica v Nicaragua), Judgment of 13 July 2009 (ICJ)

Dispute regarding Navigational and Related Rights (Costa Rica v Nicaragua), Separate Opinion of Judge Skotnikov 13th July 2009 (ICJ)

ECtHR Hassan v United Kingdom (GC) App No 29750/09, ECHR 2014-VI (2014) Application no. 29750/09.

ECJ Axel Walz C-63/09 [2010] ECR I-4239

European Communities - Customs Classification of Certain Computer Equipment WTO Appellate Body Report WT/DS62/AB/R WT/DS67/AB/R WT/DS68/AB/R, 5 June 1998.

European Communities-Customs Classification of Frozen Boneless Chicken Cuts, WTO Appellate Body Report, WT/DS269/AB/R, WT/DS286/AB/R, 12 September 2005.

Finding under Article 87(7) of the Rome Statute on the Non-compliance by Mongolia with the request by the Court to Cooperate in the Arrest and Surrender of Vladimir Vladimirovich Putin and Referral to the Assembly of States Parties, ICC-01/22–90 (Pre-Trial Chambers II) 24 October 2024 (ICC) 17.

ICC Decision on Defence Request for Conditional Excusal from Continuous Presence at Trial, The Prosecutor v Uhuru Muigai Kenyatta, ICC-01/09–02/11–830 (TrC v b) 18 October 2013.

ICC, Decision on the Non-compliance of the Republic of Chad with the Cooperation Requests Issued by the Court Regarding the Arrest and Surrender of Omar Hassan Ahmad Al-Bashir, The Prosecutor V Omar H Al Bashir, ICC-02/05–01/09–15 (PTC II), 26 March 2013.

ICC Decision under article 87(7) of the Rome Statute on the non-compliance by Jordan with the request by the Court for the arrest and surrender of Omar Al-Bashir, ICC-02/05–01/09–309 (PTC II), 11 December 2017.

ICC Defence Request pursuant to Article 63(1) of the Rome Statute, The Prosecutor v William Samoei Ruto and Joshua Arap Sang, ICC-01/09-01/11-685 (Tr C V) 17 April 2013.

ICC Final Submissions of the Prosecution following the Appeal Hearing, The Prosecutor v Omar H A A L Bashir, ICC-02/05–01/09–392 (AC) 28 September 2018.

ICC Judgment in the Jordan Referral re Al-Bashir Appeal, The Prosecutor v Omar H Ahmad Al Bashir, ICC-02/05–01/09–397 (AC) 6 May 2019.

ICC, Judgment on the Appeals of William Samoei Ruto and Joshua Arap Sang against the decision of Trial Chamber V(A) of 19 August 2015 entitled "Decision on Prosecution Request for Admission of Prior Recorded Testimony", ICC-01/09–01/11–2024 (Appeal's Chamber) 12 February 2016.

ICC-01/09–01/11–1186-Anx, Separate further Opinion of Judge Eboe-Osuji to the 'Reasons for the Decision on excusal from presence at trial under Rule 134 quater' (Prosecutor vs William S Ruto and Joshua A Sang) 19 February 2014 (TrC v (a)

In the Proceedings between Camuzzi International S A (Claimant) and The Argentine Republic (Respondent), Decision on Objection to Jurisdiction, ICSID Case No ARB/03/2)

International Arbitration under Chapter 11 of the North American Free Trade Agreement and the UNCITRAL Arbitration rules, Methanex vs USA (Merits), Award of 3rd August 2005 44 ILM.

Interpretation of the Air Transport Services Agreement between the USA and Italy, 17 July 1965 (RIAA Vol XVI)

Japan Taxes on Alcoholic Beverages, WTO Appellate Body WT/DS8/AB/R; WT/DS10/AB/R; WT/DS11/AB/R, AB-1996–2, 4 October 1996.

Judgment, Allegations of Genocide under the Convention on the Prevention and Punishment of the Crime of Genocide (Ukraine v. Russian Federation: 32 States Intervening) Preliminary objections, ICJ GL 182, 2 February 2024.

Judgment on the Prosecutor's Application for Extraordinary Review of Pre-Trial Chamber I's 31 March 2006 Decision Denying Leave to Appeal (DRC) ICC-01/04–168 (AC) 13 July 2006Judgment in the Jordan Referral re Al-Bashir Appeal, Joint Concurring Opinion of Judges Eboe-Osuji, Morrison, Hofmański and Bossa ICC-02/05–01/09–397-Anx1 (AC) 06 May 2019.

Judgment on the Appeal of Thomas Lubanga Dyilo against the Decision on the Defence Challenge to the Jurisdiction of the Court pursuant to Article 19 (2) (a) of the Statute of 3 October 2006 ICC-01/04–01/06–772(AC) 14 December 2006.

Judgment on the Appeal of Mr Germain Katanga against the Oral Decision of Trial Chamber II of 12 June 2009 on the Admissibility of the Case, Prosecutor v Germain Katanga and Ngudjolo Chui, ICC-01/04–01/07 OA 8 (AC) 25 September 2009.

Judgment on the appeal of Mr Thomas Lubanga Dyilo against the decision of Pre-Trial Chamber I entitled 'Décision sur la demande de mise en liberté provisoire de Thomas Lubanga Dyilo' ICC-01/04–01/06–824 (AC) 12 February 2007.

Judgment on the appeal of the Prosecutor against the decision of Trial Chamber V(a) of 18 June 2013 entitled 'Decision on Mr Ruto's Request for Excusal from Continuous Presence at Trial', The Prosecutor v William Samoei Ruto and Joshua Arap Sang, ICC-01/09–01/11 OA 5 (26 Oct 2013) (Appeal's Chamber)

Judgment on the appeals of Mr Lubanga Dyilo and the Prosecutor against the Decision of Trial Chamber I of 14 July 2009 entitled 'Decision giving notice to the parties and participants that the legal characterisation of the facts may be subject to change in accordance with Regulation 55(2) of the Regulations of the Court', ICC-01/04–01/06, 8 December 2009.

Judgment on the Request of the Republic of Croatia for Review of the Decision of Trial Chamber II of 18 July 1997, Prosecutor vs Tihomir Blaskic, 29 Oct 1997.

Judgment pursuant to Article 74 of the Statute, Concurring Opinion of Judge Christine Van den Wyngaert, Prosecutor v Mathieu Ngudjolo Chui ICC-01/04–02/12 (TR C II) 18 December 2012.

Judgment Pursuant to Article 74 of the Statute, Prosecutor v Thomas Lubanga Dyilo, ICC-01/04–01/06–2842 (Tr C I) 14 March 2012.

Judgment pursuant to Article 74 of the Statute, The Prosecutor v Germain Katanga, ICC-01/04–01/07–3436 (TrC II) 7 March 2014.

Kasikili/Sedudu Island (Botswana/Namibia), Judgment, ICJ Rep 1999 (ICJ)

LaGrand (Germany v United States of America) ICJ Rep, 27 June 2001.

Land, Island and Maritime Frontier Dispute (El Salvador v Honduras, Nicaragua intervening), ICJ Rep 1992.

Legal Consequences for States of the Continued Presence of South Africa in Namibia (South West Africa) notwithstanding Security Council Resolution 276 (1970) Advisory Opinion, ICJ Reports 1971.

Legality of the Use by a State of Nuclear Weapons in Armed Conflict, Advisory Opinion, ICJ Reports, 1996.

Loizidou v Turkey, 40/1993/435/514, Council of Europe: European Court of Human Rights, 23 February 1995.

Maritime Delimitation and Territorial Questions between Qatar and Bahrain, Jurisdiction and Admissibility, Judgment, ICJ Reports 1991 (ICJ)Methanex Corporation v USA, UNCITRAL Final Award, Part 11 Chapter B 2005.

Maritime Delimitation and Territorial Questions between Qatar and Bahrain, Jurisdiction and Admissibility, Judgment, ICJ Reports 1991 (ICJ)

Methanex Corporation v USA, UNCITRAL Final Award, Part 11 Chapter B 2005.

Methanex v United States, Jurisdiction and Merits (NAFTA Ch 11/UNCITRAL Arb Trib 3 Aug 2005.

Military and Paramilitary Activities in and against Nicaragua (Nicaragua vs USA) Jurisdiction and Admissibility), Judgment, ICJ Reports 1984.

Minority Opinion of Judge Christine Van den Wyngaert, The Prosecutor v Germain Katanga, ICC-01/04–01/07–3436-AnxI, (TRC 11) 10 March 2014.

Nuclear Tests (Australia v France), Judgment, ICJ Reports 20 December 1974.

Oil Platforms (Islamic Republic of Iran v USA), Preliminary Objection, Judgment, ICJ Reports 1996.

Partly Dissenting Opinion of Judge Spano, Joined by Judges Nicolaou, Bianku and Kalaydjieva Hassan v United Kingdom 29750/09, 16 September 2014 (ECtHR)

Pope &Talbot Inc v Government of Canada (Award of damages) NAFTA Ch 11 Arb Trib 31 May 2002.

Public redacted version of the "Ruto Defence appeal against the 'Decision on Prosecution Request for Admission of Prior Recorded Testimony" 5 October 2015, ICC-01/09–01/11–1981-Conf.

Pulp Mills on the River Uruguay (Argentina v Uruguay) 2010 (ICJ)

Reasons for the Decision on Excusal from Presence at Trial under Rule 134 quater, The Prosecutor v William Samoei Ruto and Joshua Arap Sang, ICC-01/09–01/11–1186 (TrC v [A] 18 Feb 2014.

Reasons for the Oral Decision on the Motion Challenging the Admissibility of the Case (Art 19 of the Statute), The Prosecutor v Germain Katanga and Mathieu Ngudjolo Chui ICC-01/04-01/07 (TC 11) 16 June 2009.

[Redacted] (ICC-RoR216–01/14), Decision concerning the 'Application to the Presidency Pursuant to Regulation 216 of the Regulations of the Registry for Judicial Review of the Registrar's Decision Notified on 7 February 2014', 28 February 2014.

Reparation for Injuries Suffered in the Service of the United Nations, Advisory Opinion of 11 April (1949) ICJ Rep.

Ruto Defence Request for Mr Ruto's Excusal from Presence at Trial under Rule 134 ter, The Prosecutor v William Samoei Ruto and Joshua Arap Sang, ICC-01/09–01/11–1998 (TrC V) 03 November 2015.

Sang Defence Submission in addition to Appeal against the decision of Trial Chamber V (A) of 19 August 2015 entitled "Decision on Prosecution Request for Admission of Prior Recorded Testimony" (Prosecutor vs William S Ruto and Joshua A Sang) ICC-01/09–01/11 (AC) 17 December 2015.

Sempra Energy International v Argentine, No ARB/02/16 ICSID, Decision on Objections to Jurisdiction (May 11, 2005)

South West Africa Cases (Ethiopia v South Africa; Liberia v South Africa), Preliminary Objections, Judgment of 21 December 1962, ICJ Rep 1962 (ICJ)

Territorial Dispute (Libya v Chad), Judgment, ICJ Reports 1994.

The African Union's Amicus Curiae Observations on the Rule 68 Amendments at the Twelfth Session of the Assembly of States Parties (Prosecutor vs William S Ruto and Joshua A Sang) ICC-01/09–01/11 (AC) 19 October 2015.

The Loewen Group Inc and R L Loewen v USA, ICSID Case No ARB (AF)/98/3, Award of the NAFTA Chapter 11 Arb Trib, 26 June 2003.

The Prosecutor v Dusko Tadic Case No ICTY-94–1-A, Appeals Chamber Judgement, 15 July 1999.

The Prosecutor v Thomas Lubanga Dyilo, Decision on the Confirmation of Charges, ICC-01/04–01/06–803 (PTC 1)29 January 2007

The Prosecutor v Uhuru Muigai Kenyatta, ICC-01/09–02/11.

The Rhine Chlorides Arbitration concerning the Auditing of Accounts (The Netherlands/France), PCA, Arbitral Award, 12 March 2004.

United States – Measures Affecting the Production and Sale of Clove Cigarettes, WTO, Appellate Body Report adopted on 4 April 2012, WT/DS406/AB/R.

United States Claims Tribunal Federal Reserve Bank of New York v The Islamic Republic of Iran Bank Markazi (Decision No DEC 130-A28-FT), Case A 28 of 2000 (Iran US Claims Tribunal (USCT))

United States – Import Prohibition of Certain Shrimp and Shrimp Products WTO Report of Appellate Board AB-1998–4, WT/DS58/AB/R, 12 October 1998.

United States-Standards for Reformulated and Conventional Gasoline, WTO Appellate Body Report, WT/DS2/AB/R (adopted 20 May 1996)

US-Final Countervailing Duty Determination with Respect to Certain Softwood Lumber from Canada IV, WTO Appellate Body Report, WT/DS25/AB/R, AB-2003–6, 19 January 2004.

Index

www.ingramcontent.com/pod-product-compliance
Lightning Source LLC
Chambersburg PA
CBHW051358240926
51852CB00001B/58
* 9 7 8 9 0 0 4 7 2 5 5 2 2 *